SCHAUM'S OUTLINE OF

THEORY AND PROBLEMS

of

PSYCHOLOGY
of
LEARNING

•

by

ARNO F. WITTIG, Ph.D.

Professor of Psychology
Ball State University

SCHAUM'S OUTLINE SERIES

McGRAW-HILL BOOK COMPANY

New York   St. Louis   San Francisco   Auckland   Bogotá   Guatemala   Hamburg   Johannesburg
Lisbon   London   Madrid   Mexico   Montreal   New Delhi   Panama   Paris
San Juan   São Paulo   Singapore   Sydney   Tokyo   Toronto

ARNO F. WITTIG is currently Professor of Psychology at Ball State University in Muncie, Indiana. He received his M.A. (1962) and Ph.D. (1964) degrees from Ohio State University and joined the Ball State faculty in 1964, after teaching at Hobart and William Smith Colleges. His publications include the first Schaum's Outline in the field of psychology, *Introduction to Psychology* (McGraw-Hill, 1977).

Schaum's Outline of Theory and Problems of
PSYCHOLOGY OF LEARNING

2 3 4 5 6 7 8 9 10 11 12 13 14 15 16 17 18 19 20 SH SH 8 6 5 4 3

Sponsoring Editor, Paul Farrell
Editing Supervisor, John F. Fitzpatrick
Production Manager, Nick Monti

Library of Congress Cataloging in Publication Data

Wittig, Arno F.
    Schaum's outline of theory and problems of
psychology of learning.

    (Schaum's outline series)
    Includes index.
    1. Learning, Psychology of.   I. Title.
BF318.W57   153.1'5   80-21345
ISBN 0-07-071192-5

Preface

The psychology of learning covers a very broad range of topics. From an experimental basis, it involves numerous studies of varied processes that affect the acquisition-storage-retrieval sequence that is at the heart of learning. From an applied viewpoint, that same sequence can be considered in terms of characteristics as diverse as development, personality, intelligence, or motor skills.

It is with these two approaches in mind that this book has been written. The reader is provided with an overview of the basic principles of the psychology of learning, while at the same time many examples and solved problems highlight ways in which these principles are applied in nonlaboratory situations. This outline should therefore benefit both the student enrolled in a psychology of learning class and the reader who simply wishes to know more about learning as it occurs in or is applied to commonly encountered situations. The outline presents the basic core of materials found in leading textbooks together with examples relevant to those outside the academic community.

Each section of this outline is organized into units which can be studied relatively independently of one another yet which form a reasonable overall sequence. Repetition of materials occurs wherever it is necessary for clarity in individual units. Thus, the reader who chooses to use the outline in one continuous sequence is free to read or bypass occasional repetitive materials that are intended for those persons only using part of the outline at a given time.

The psychology of learning is an ever-changing discipline. The materials selected for this outline are intended to give the reader a firm grasp of the basics of the field, but my hope is that each reader may choose to speculate on where we can go next.

ARNO F. WITTIG

Contents

CONTENTS

CONTENTS

CONTENTS

PART I: Definitions and History

The two chapters of this part provide the background for what follows.   In Chapter 1, a definition of learning, together with an explanation of learning as an acquisition-storage-retrieval sequence, is presented.   Learning as a concept is differentiated from the actually observable performance used as the measure of learning.   Finally, you are given the opportunity to review the data-collection methods used to obtain the performance measures.

Chapter 2 presents a brief history of the study of learning.   The highlights of some pre-psychological influences on the study of learning are followed by a look at the initial psychological investigations in the area.   Subsequent influences of systems and theories in psychology are considered briefly, and then several contemporary positions are presented.   You will be able to sense the trends in the study of the psychology of learning, particularly the tendency to study more and more restricted topics rather than very broad or general areas.

Chapter 1

Introduction

An elementary school student learns long division. A young lawyer learns to ski. A dog learns to fetch a stick. A rat learns to run through a maze. We often hear and talk about learning, but it is a difficult phenomenon to describe. Perhaps this difficulty can in part be explained by the fact that learning is not directly observable. We can interpret certain kinds of behavior as evidence that learning has taken place, but we cannot measure learning directly.

1.1 A DEFINITION OF LEARNING

Psychologists who study learning have proposed a variety of definitions for the word, but no single one seems to accurately and completely describe the phenomenon. At best these definitions are tentative, so the one that follows should be taken only as a starting place. As you think about it, you should remember that it is open to questioning, new evidence, and further refinement and clarification.

Learning can be defined as any relatively permanent change in an organism's behavioral repertoire that occurs as a result of experience.

Some of the terms in this definition are themselves in need of explanation. In the first place, psychologists generally agree that only those behavioral changes that are *relatively permanent* fall into the category of learned changes. This means that temporary fluctuations in behavior are not considered evidence of learning.

EXAMPLE 1. Suppose a ten-month-old infant, babbling and gurgling in his crib, quite distinctly uttered a sound very much like the word "Paul," his own name. While the infant's parents might at first be thrilled that their son had "learned" to say his name, they would soon discover that this was not the case. The "word" that sounded like "Paul" would not be heard again from the child for many months, until well after he began to speak. It is true that the infant's behavior changed: he produced a sound that he had never produced before. But this change was temporary; any attempt on the parents' part to make their son repeat his performance would certainly fail until he began to learn to speak. Psychologists would generally agree that this ten-month-old's exclamation was the temporary and isolated product of his random vocalizing, and not a learned behavior.

It is also important to note that our definition of learning refers to changes in an organism's *behavioral repertoire* rather than to changes in behavior. Psychologists have discovered that an organism's behavior is not necessarily an indicator of learning. They have also discovered that the absence of a particular behavior cannot always be taken as an indicator that the organism has not learned that behavior. To summarize their findings, psychologists say that *learning must be distinguished from performance.* In other words, an organism may have a behavior in its repertoire and not show it, or show it and not have it in its repertoire (see Section 1.2).

EXAMPLE 2. The infant described in Example 1 showed a certain behavior—producing the sound "Paul"—that was not part of his behavioral repertoire.

EXAMPLE 3. Suppose that several years later, when he is four, Paul accompanies his mother on a trip to a large and very crowded department store. In the course of their shopping expedition, Paul strays from his mother and is lost. As soon as he realizes that he is separated from her, he begins to cry. A store clerk, trying to calm the child and reunite him with his mother, approaches and says, "I'll help you find your mother. What's your name?" But Paul, who by this time is hysterical, just continues to cry. Although he

2

is capable of understanding the question and knows how to say his name, he does not answer the clerk.   Saying "Paul" is a part of this four-year-old's behavioral repertoire, but in this situation he does not show the behavior.

Finally, our definition of learning refers to changes that occur *as a result of experience*.   Thus psychologists generally exclude from the category of learned behaviors those changes that result from long-term processes such as physical development or aging or from short-term effects like fatigue or warm-up.

EXAMPLE 4.   Menarche, or the onset of the first menstrual flow, is the result of the maturation of an adolescent girl's uterus and ovaries.   It is *not* considered a learned change in behavior because it is the direct result of physical development, and not the result of experience.

The Phases of Learning

Research in learning has shown that several stages appear to take place.   Initially, the organism must by some means assimilate ("take in") the material to be learned.   This phase has been labelled *acquisition*.

Once acquired, the learning is put into *memory*.   This phase often is called the *storage* stage.   Evidence of learning involves a third step, that of *retrieval*, or getting the information out of storage.   Each of these phases—acquisition, storage, and retrieval—is discussed in much greater detail in subsequent chapters.   Sometimes, the terms "learning" and "memory" are used to include all three stages, but generally it seems better to separate them for easier understanding of the processes involved (see also Problem 1.2).

1.2   LEARNING vs. PERFORMANCE

The fact that the learning process cannot be directly observed puts psychologists in a difficult position: they have to depend on their observation of behavior to infer learning, but behavior is not an absolutely dependable indicator of learning.   It is necessary that an organism perform a certain behavior if learning is to be inferred, but performance, in and of itself, cannot be considered an absolute measure of learning.

Nonlearning Performance Variables

Psychologists have identified several factors in addition to learning that influence performance.   These factors, which play an important part in how an organism will behave, are called *nonlearning performance variables*.   Psychologists pay a good deal of attention to these variables because they want to be able to distinguish between those aspects of performance that can be attributed to learning and those that cannot.

Motivation.   One very important influence on performance is *motivation,* which is defined as any condition that initiates, guides, and maintains a behavior in an organism.   Without motivation, an organism may very well fail to show a behavior that it has learned.

EXAMPLE 5.   A young girl who is not hungry or thirsty may ignore a bottle of milk or bowl of food her parents set before her.   Although she has learned to drink from the bottle and eat from the bowl, she will not engage in these behaviors if she is not motivated.

In general, motivation leads to the performance of certain behaviors, and as the level of motivation increases, so will the level of performance.   One could say that motivation *facilitates* performance.   Without motivation, the child in Example 5 will not show how she has learned to eat.   With motivation, she will give ample evidence of what she has learned.   The relationship between motivation and performance is not that simple, however.   When motivation is extremely high, performance may start to deteriorate.

EXAMPLE 6.   A student who has reached the finals of a nationwide spelling bee might very well "choke up" and misspell a fairly easy word—even one that she has correctly spelled many times before.   In this case motivation, which in general facilitates performance, has inhibited it.

The curve in Fig. 1-1 illustrates the relationship beween motivation and performance: in general performance increases as motivation increases, but once motivation reaches a very high level, performance may begin to fall off.

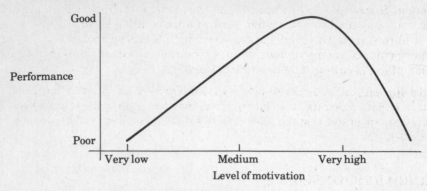

Fig. 1-1

Sensitization and habituation.   An organism may show a particular behavior (or *response*) when confronted with a particular event (or *stimulus*).   The repeated appearance of this response whenever the stimulus is present may be evidence of learning.

In some learning situations an organism's response to a stimulus will change simply as a result of having responded to that stimulus.   If the likelihood or intensity of the response is increased, this change is called *sensitization*.   If the tendency to respond or the intensity of response is reduced, the organism is said to be showing *habituation*.   In neither case, however, does the change in the organism's response necessarily indicate a learned change.

EXAMPLE 7.   Suppose a person is seated in such a fashion that the right hand is restrained and attached to electrodes through which an electric shock can be delivered.   The restraining device allows measurement of the force of muscular movement made in an attempt to withdraw from the shock.   If the shock remains the same level throughout the study but the intensity of muscular movement increases, it would appear sensitization had occurred.

EXAMPLE 8.   Imagine sitting at your desk on a warm, quiet summer day.   The window is open.   Suddenly, someone starts a power lawnmower directly below your window.   Your likely response is to startle and try to determine the source of the sound.   Once the mower has been on for a moment or two, it is likely your response will decrease.   This illustrates habituation.

Sensory adaptation.   Certain stimulus situations will have a physiological effect on an organism's sensory processes.   The adjustment of these sensory processes, which may have an effect on the organism's performance of certain tasks, is called *sensory adaptation* and is considered a nonlearning performance variable.

EXAMPLE 9.   Suppose a person has learned to successfully perform a particular task in a very brightly lit room.   This person may have some trouble continuing to perform the task if the illumination is suddenly reduced drastically.   This change in performance occurs not because the person has failed to learn the task, but because the eyes need time to adjust to the darkness.   Such a physiological adjustment, called sensory adaptation, is another nonlearning performance variable.

Physiological characteristics.   In addition to sensory adaptation, other physiological events may affect performance.   Two examples of these are *maturation,* or physical growth, and *senescence,* the physiological deterioration accompanying old age.   Again, the effects upon performance are not attributable to learning.   No matter how much training or teaching is employed, certain behaviors cannot be shown until the appropriate physiological development (maturation) has been attained.   Likewise, when there are dysfunctions of the nervous system because of degeneration (senescence), many previously learned behaviors may no longer be possible.

Fatigue. Performance is often affected by *fatigue,* another nonlearning performance variable. The inability to perform previously learned responses may occur when a person becomes excessively tired, but after a period of rest the ability to respond is recovered.

State-dependent learning. It has been found that learning which occurs in particular environmental conditions may not be shown when performance is called for in a stimulus condition that is significantly different from the conditions under which learning took place. Learning of this type, in which performance seems to depend on a stimulus situation similar to the one in which learning first took place, is called *state-dependent learning.*

EXAMPLE 10. If a student studies for an exam in a windowless room and has rock music for a background, taking that exam in a quiet classroom that has windows may be a noticeable stimulus change and affect performance. It is often suggested that the student should study in conditions as similar as possible to those that will be used for testing.

1.3 UNLEARNED RESPONSES

Psychologists studying learning have found there are a number of responses in many organisms' behavioral repertoires which appear to be unlearned. Most thoroughly studied have been reflexes and instincts.

Reflexes

A *reflex* is an unlearned, simple, immediate response to a specific stimulus. Many reflexes are not shown by an organism at birth, but develop with maturation. Others, present at birth, drop out of the behavior pattern as the nervous system develops.

EXAMPLE 11. Stroking the bottom of a human's foot produces activity of the toes. In the very young child, the toes "fan out" or extend (in what is called a Babinski reflex). Older children and adults tend to curl the toes, as maturation of the nervous system eliminates the Babinski reflex.

Instincts

An *instinct* is a complex, unlearned pattern of responses. Instincts are easily demonstrated for lower organisms such as ducks or chickens, but more debatable for humans.

EXAMPLE 12. Research on the phenomenon of *imprinting* has shown that newly hatched ducklings or chicks will follow whatever moving object is in their environment during the second half of their first day of life. Typically this is the mother, but imprinting to humans or other moving objects has also been demonstrated.

1.4 RESEARCH METHODOLOGY

Psychologists use several different methods for collecting data about learning processes. These include the experimental method (which is the most popular), naturalistic observation, causal-comparative studies, correlational studies, psychological tests and surveys, and clinical case histories.

The Experimental Method

The basis of the *experimental method* is comparison. In its simplest form, two groups, selected to be as alike as possible before the experiment begins, are given some training under differing (manipulated) conditions. Both groups are tested on some response measure. If extraneous or irrelevant variables have been controlled, any difference in performance for the two groups can be attributed to the manipulated conditions. Psychologists use the following terms to describe properly designed and executed experiments:

Independent variable: the variable under investigation which is manipulated by the experimenter is called the *independent variable.*

Dependent variable: the *dependent variable* is the measure of performance or response.

Experimental group: in most experiments, the group (or groups) tested under the conditions of interest to the experimenter is (are) called the *experimental group(s).*

Control group: the group tested under comparison ("usual") conditions is called the *control group.*

   (Note: Both the experimental and the control group are exposed to the independent variable, and both are measured on the dependent variable.)

Sampling.   When it is not possible to use the entire group to be studied (called the *population*), subjects are selected by using *sampling* procedures.   If all subjects have an equal chance of being chosen, the procedure is called *random sampling.*   *Stratified sampling* involves selecting subjects so that the sample reflects in its makeup various subgroups found in the population; in other words, if there are several subgroups in the population, they will be proportionally represented in the sample.   Sometimes experimenters believe that certain characteristics will give subjects distinct advantages or disadvantages in the experimental setting; in such cases, the experimenter may employ *matched sampling,* in which each group will receive an equal number of subjects with that particular advantage or disadvantage.

Other considerations.   The experimental method involves several other considerations.   As much as possible, the researcher should try to control *extraneous variables* (or *irrelevant variables*) that might influence the results inappropriately.   The researcher should also maintain an *objective attitude,* trying to avoid any conditions which might produce prejudice or bias in the experiment.

   The problems studied should be *meaningful* (that is, *public* or able to be discussed), *empirical* (measurable), and *replicable* (repeatable).   In addition, it is generally hoped that the research will be conducted in an *orderly* fashion, helping avoid some of the difficulties listed above.

Other Methods

   The psychology of learning is based not only on data collected in experimental research, but on information obtained from other methods as well.   Some of the most important are discussed here.

Naturalistic observation.   Psychologists sometimes make careful, unbiased recordings of events that occur in unmanipulated situations.   This is called *naturalistic observation.*

Causal-comparative studies.   Often used when experimental studies cannot be conducted, *causal-comparative* studies compare subjects showing a particular pattern of behavior with subjects who do not show such behavior in an attempt to discover possible causes for that behavior.

Correlational studies.   *Correlational studies* attempt to discover relationships between variables by using the statistical technique of correlation coefficients.   Correlation coefficients can show the degree and direction of relationships.

Psychological tests and surveys.   The amount or type of learning is sometimes evaluated by using *psychological tests and surveys* specifically designed to present stimuli to which the subjects react.   These allow rapid collection of data and the possibility of comparing one subject's responses with those of others, but there is the disadvantage that the subjects may make purposely misleading responses.

Clinical case histories.   Learning, particularly of personality patterns, may be recorded by clinical or counseling psychologists.   Such records—perhaps of problems, insights, or treatment techniques—are called *clinical case histories.*

Cause-Effect Relationships

   The only method which allows confirmation or disconfirmation of hypotheses is the experimental method.   Trying to test cause-effect relationships using any of the other methods mentioned is not possible because of the researcher's inability to properly select the sample or to control the extraneous or irrelevant variables.

EXAMPLE 13. Limitations on research procedures may require the investigator to use some method other than the experimental method. It would be inappropriate to induce aggressiveness in one group of juveniles and not in another to determine if aggressiveness is related to juvenile delinquency. However, using the causal-comparative method, a researcher could select a group of juveniles not judged delinquent to determine if they differ significantly from a group of delinquents in expressed aggressiveness. Such a study would *not* confirm or disconfirm a hypothesis linking the two variables. A relationship might be discovered, but attributing juvenile delinquency to aggression would be inappropriate because other environmental factors could be operating or the samples used might not be alike on other significant variables. Indeed, it might be that the juvenile delinquency caused the aggression rather than the reverse relationship.

Subjects other than Humans

Research in the psychology of learning often involves the use of animals as subjects. Reasons for this include reduced expense, ease of obtaining the animals, rapid reproduction rate (which allows studying many generations quickly), and the opportunity to keep the animals in the experimental setting over an extended period of time.

Additionally, a major reason for using animals rather than humans is to satisfy ethical concerns. Research in areas such as sensory deprivation, selective breeding, or experimentally induced stress is usually more appropriately done with animals than humans.

Ethics in Research

Using animals as subjects can satisfy some of the ethical concerns in research. When humans must be used in research, the investigators must be certain to protect the subjects' rights. Researchers should not allow the subjects to be placed in either psychological or physical jeopardy.

Human subjects who choose to participate in research should be thoroughly briefed on what is to happen before agreeing to take part. (This is called obtaining *informed consent*.) When the procedure would be endangered by revealing the nature of the study, the researcher should obtain clearance for conducting the study from a knowledgeable committee, then discuss the nature of the investigation with the subjects after they have completed their participation.

EXAMPLE 14. If the researcher wishes to study "learning without awareness," the procedure would be ruined by providing information to the subject beforehand. Thus, the procedure should be cleared by a committee, then explained to the subjects after the experiment is completed.

Solved Problems

1.1 Consider a hypothetical (and rather unlikely) situation. An untrained chimpanzee is placed before an electric typewriter for the first time. Psychologists observing the chimp's behavior note that the animal, in striking a few keys of the typewriter, has spelled out the word "cats." Would it make sense to say that the chimp had learned to type this word?

No. Learning is defined as a relatively permanent change in an organism's behavioral repertoire as a result of experience. The chimp *did* show a new behavior, but it would almost certainly not be possible to elicit that behavior again. The change was temporary. Furthermore, it could not be said that the behavior had become a part of the chimp's repertoire. (One occurrence of a behavior does not mean it is part of the organism's behavioral repertoire.) Finally, the chimp had never before manipulated the alphabet or a typewriter, and so would not have had previous experience with them. In all likelihood, the psychologists would describe the chimp's performance—typing out the word "cats"—as the chance product of the chimp haphazardly striking certain keys.

1.2   Psychologists studying learning often refer to three stages in the learning process: acquisition, storage, and retrieval.   Explain these terms.

    Acquisition refers to that part of the learning process during which the organism assimilates a new behavior into its repertoire through practice; it is during the acquisition phase that an association between a particular stimulus and response may be developed.   *Storage* refers to that stage in which practice has ceased but the learned response is retained as a potential behavior by the organism; this phase of learning is sometimes also referred to as the *retention stage* or as *memory.* *Retrieval,* the third stage of the learning process, refers to the phase during which the previously learned behavior, which is stored as a potentiality in the organism, is translated into overt behavior, or performance.

    It is important to note, however, that the three stages of learning do not occur completely separate from and independent of each other.   Indeed, in any given learning situation all three stages may come into play.   For example, a child learning to say "mama" may repeat the word, or approximations of it, twenty times in one hour.   This repetition of the word can be understood as part of the acquisition phase of learning, in which the child is developing an association between a stimulus (such as the presence of the mother or a verbal cue) and the response, saying "mama." It is also true, however, that each time the child repeats the phrase he is recalling it (retrieval) from memory (storage).   Thus, acquisition, storage, and retrieval overlap and interact with one another.   They are not three distinct phenomena, but aspects of a single phenomenon.

1.3   It has been said that learning is "invisible."   What does this mean?

    Learning is a concept, and not a directly observable thing.   Psychologists can see evidence of learning in an organism's performance, and learning can be used to explain or predict certain behaviors.   But learning is not in and of itself observable.   Concepts such as learning are sometimes called *hypothetical constructs.*   They are useful because they enable us to predict and explain certain behaviors, even though they are not themselves directly observable.

1.4   What is the difference between performance and learning?

    Performance is overt.   It is a form of behavior, and is therefore observable and measurable.   Learning is not directly observable or measurable.

1.5   What is the relationship between performance and learning?

    The performance of certain kinds of behaviors can be explained by the concept of learning, and it is only through the observation of performance that we can infer learning.   In a sense, learning facilitates certain kinds of performance, or makes performance possible.   A problem arises, however, because performance is not an absolutely reliable indicator of learning.   An organism may perform some behaviors it has not learned, or not perform certain behaviors it has learned.   Psychologists have identified several nonlearning performance variables—factors that are not the result of learning but that nonetheless influence performance.   In using performance as an indicator or measure of learning, psychologists must take into account the influence of these variables.

1.6   Motivation is one of the most important of the nonlearning performance variables.   What is the general finding regarding the effect of level of motivation upon performance?

    Research has indicated that the effect of motivation upon performance can be described by a somewhat lopsided and inverted U-shaped curve.   That is, performance is best when the subject experiences moderately high levels of motivation, but poorer when motivation is low or very high.   When motive conditions interfere with performance, psychologists cannot conclude that a behavior has not been learned.   Instead they must limit themselves to saying that the subject is not able to perform the response at that time.

1.7   Two additional nonlearning performance variables are sensitization and habituation. How are these alike? How do they differ?

      Both "sensitization" and "habituation" refer to a change in a subject's reactivity to stimuli not because of a learned association but simply as a result of reacting to the stimuli. They differ in that sensitization involves an increment, or increased tendency, to respond as a result of reacting to the stimuli, while habituation involves a decrement, or decreased tendency to respond.

1.8   Why is sensory adaptation also considered to be a nonlearning performance variable rather than an example of learning?

      "Sensory adaptation" refers to changes which take place for the entire sensory modality involved. Because the change in responding results from physiological adjustments rather than learned associations, sensory adaptation is labelled a nonlearning performance variable.

1.9   Older people sometimes are unable to perform previously learned responses. What nonlearning performance variable may explain this?

      Some older people become senile. Senescence is often accompanied by physiological deterioration and seeming dysfunction of the nervous system. When this happens, performance may not reflect learning acquired before the senescence developed.

1.10   It is also true that young people sometimes are unable to perform responses because of the nonlearning performance variable of maturation. What is maturation and how does it affect peformance?

      "Maturation" refers to the biological growth processes. A classic example of the effects of maturation is the development of walking in children. A child simply cannot learn to walk until the necessary muscular and nerve development (maturation) has occurred. The mere fact that a child suddenly shows a behavior does not mean that learning has just taken place. It may be that the sufficient level of maturation has finally been attained, allowing expression of the behavior.

1.11   Suppose a subject in a learning experiment agrees to perform a particular learned task for 10 hours uninterrupted. His performance of the task might deteriorate noticeably over that time span. What nonlearning performance variable might explain this deterioration?

      The most likely variable would be fatigue. While the actual retention of learning does not suffer at all, fatigue makes it impossible for the subject to actually perform the response. Once the subject has had the opportunity to rest and the fatigue has dissipated, it is likely the performance of the response would return to its previous level.

1.12   In mental hospitals, it has been found that some patients given therapy while under the influence of drugs do not retain the therapy effects when in an undrugged state. What nonlearning performance variable might explain such a result?

      The phenomenon illustrated by this example is called *stimulus change* or *state-dependent learning*. In general, this means that *if* an organism learns a response in one state (or stimulus condition) a decrease in the performance level can be expected when the stimulus situation is changed. Again, this decrease does not necessarily reflect a change in learning.

1.13   How are a reflex and an instinct different from each other? How are they similar?

      A reflex is a simple, unlearned, immediate response to some specific stimulus. Instincts are more complex, unlearned patterns of response which may be keyed by several stimuli. Reflexes and instincts differ in their complexity, but are similar in that they are both unlearned, or innate.

1.14   Attempting to study the effects of changes in room lighting on the performance of an object-sorting task, a psychologist established five different lighting conditions and measured the time for each subject's completion of the task. What type of research method is illustrated by this example? What are the principal variables of this method? Identify these variables in this example.

This is an example of the use of the experimental method. The two principal variables of the experimental method are the independent variable (the condition manipulated by the experimenter) and the dependent variable (the response measured). In this experiment the independent variable is the lighting conditions and the dependent variable is the time for completion of the object-sorting task.

1.15   Which are the experimental and control groups in the experiment described in Problem 1.14?

The control group serves as a standard of comparison against which the performance of the experimental group or groups can be evaluated. In this experiment it is likely that the control group would be the group experiencing the most "normal" or "usual" lighting conditions, with the other four groups being labelled as experimental groups. (However, statistical analyses might be made comparing the performance of subjects in any one of the groups with that of any one member or all the members of the other groups.)

1.16   Why do psychologists accept the concept that an experiment can be used to confirm or disconfirm a hypothesis but that other types of studies cannot?

The three crucial differences between experiments and other data-gathering methods are that (1) subject selection in experiments is done using a sampling technique; (2) the experimenter can manipulate the independent variable; and (3) the control of extraneous variables is possible only in experimental settings.

1.17   Suppose the subjects for the object-sorting task mentioned earlier were preschool children aged three and four. How would the psychologist use random sampling in the procedure?

All of the designated subjects (the population) would have to have an equal chance of being chosen for the experiment and for any one group in the experiment. The psychologist might take the roster comprising the population and then use a table of random numbers to select the subjects for each group. It is hoped that all groups will be as alike as possible *and* representative of the population.

1.18   What other sampling techniques are sometimes used in selecting groups for an experiment?

The other two most common sampling techniques are stratified sampling and matched sampling. When stratified sampling is used, identifiable subgroups in the population are represented according to their percentages within the composition of the population. Matched sampling is used when important characteristics of the subjects might bias the results. Subjects are selected for each experimental group and the control group so that the characteristics are balanced and no one group has an advantage or disadvantage based upon group selection. If the experimenters in Problem 1.17 wanted to create a stratified sample, they might want to make sure that the proportion of girls and boys and of three- and four-year-olds in each group would accurately reflect the proportions of the population as a whole. They would use a matched sample if they wanted to make sure each group had the same number of gifted students or slow learners—or whatever other characteristic they identified as likely to influence the outcome.

1.19   The characteristics of a worthwhile experiment are summarized by the word "mean-ingful."   What do experimenters mean when they say an experiment is meaningful?

A meaningful experiment is public, empirical, replicable, and orderly.   It is public in the sense that all data, techniques, and other information relating to the experiment are available for skeptical or critical review.   The experiment should be empirical in the sense that it employs variables that can be measured.   It is replicable if it can be repeated.   It is orderly if it is systematic, and not run in a haphazard fashion.

1.20   What data-collection techniques besides the experimental method are used for studying learning?   Why is it not possible to use these to confirm or disconfirm a hypothesis?.

Other means of gathering data include naturalistic observation, causal-comparative studies, correlational studies, psychological tests or surveys, and clinical case histories.   These studies may provide much information in the psychology of learning, but cannot be used to confirm or disconfirm hypotheses because of possibilities of bias.   Some possibilities are created by the inability to select the subjects being measured to assure representation of the population, the likelihood of extraneous or irrelevant variables influencing the results, and the lack of objective standards regarding measurements taken.

1.21   Many research studies in the psychology of learning have involved the use of animals as subjects.   What are some of the reasons for using animals rather than human subjects?

Researchers in the psychology of learning use animals for several reasons.   It is often less expensive to use animals as opposed to using humans; animals are easy to obtain as subjects; animals may be kept in experimental conditions over long periods of time; and animals reproduce more rapidly than humans, thus allowing the fairly rapid study of generational effects.   In addition, some studies conducted with animals would be unethical if done with humans—for example, selective breeding studies or investigations involving the substitution of a surrogate mother for the real mother.

1.22   Have psychologists ever attempted to study psychology of learning with subjects other than humans or high-level animals?

Research using the very simplest of one-celled animals (protozoans) has been reported, with controversial results which implied the possibility of learning having occurred.   Even more debatable, William Mikulas (1974) has reported an unpublished study supposedly involving the learning of a leaf-closing response by the plant *Mimosa pudica*. Psychologists in the future will have to decide the range of evidence that will be accepted as representing learned behavior.

1.23   Problem 1.21 mentioned ethics in research.   In addition to substituting animals for humans in some studies, what are some of the other ways psychologists show concern for ethical considerations?

Psychologists using the various research methods for gathering data from human subjects show concern for those subjects by designing their studies so that the subjects are not placed in either psychological or physiological jeopardy.   This may involve such practices as avoiding invasion of privacy, carefully controlling physical procedures such as electric shock or drug administration, or providing thorough explanations regarding the intent of the research.

1.24   What phrase has emerged as representative of the human subject's rights in a research study?

The phrase used is "informed consent."   The implication is that the subjects should not be expected to participate until they have sufficient information to have a firm understanding of the study's intent and until they have agreed (consented) to take part in the study.

1.25   Suppose the researcher fears the revelation of the study's intent will give away the purpose of the experiment and thus bias the results.   What can be done?

    When deception is necessary, the researcher can clear the study with a committee of peers and potential consumers (subjects) so that the deception can be maintained.   Once the study is completed, the researcher should inform the participants of what the actual intent was and what kinds of results were obtained.

1.26   Are there comparable concerns for the protection of animal subjects?

    Most research laboratories have very similar policies protecting the animal subjects used. Often, if the researcher has any doubt about a potential procedure, the format is submitted to a committee for review before the actual data collection is initiated.

Key Terms

Acquisition.   The phase of learning during which an organism assimilates a new behavior; the new response becomes part of the organism's behavioral repertoire.

Control group.   In a scientific experiment, those subjects whose responses are used as a standard for comparison; their responses are compared with those of the experimental group or groups.

Correlation.   The numerical representation of the relationship between two variables.

Dependent variable.   The measured response in an experiment.

Experimental group.   In a scientific experiment, those subjects who respond to the independent variable conditions of interest; their responses are compared to those of the control group.

Extraneous variables.   Conditions that might affect the result of an experiment but are irrelevant to the experiment.

Habituation.   A decrease in the tendency to respond to a certain stimulus as a result of previous response to that stimulus.

Hypothetical construct.   A concept that is not directly measurable, but that can be used to explain or predict certain observable events.

Imprinting.   The very rapid acquisition of a response during a critical period of development; particularly characteristic of birds.

Independent variable.   A condition manipulated by an experimenter in order to determine the effect of such manipulation on the dependent variable.

Informed consent.   An experimental subject's decision to participate in an experiment after having been fully familiarized with the procedures to be used.

Instinct.   An unlearned, complex response pattern made by all members of a species to particular stimulus conditions.

Learning.   A relatively permanent change in an organism's behavioral repertoire as a result of experience.

Matched sampling.   A technique for selecting subjects such that each group in an experiment has an equal number of subjects who possess some characteristic that might influence the outcome.

Motivation.   A condition that initiates, directs, and maintains responding.

Naturalistic observation.   Careful observation of events that are not manipulated.

Performance.   The responses actually shown by an organism; these may or may not reflect what has been learned.

Population.   The entire group being studied in an experiment.

Random sampling.   A technique for selecting subjects so that each potential subject has an equal chance of being chosen.

Reflex.   An unlearned, simple, and immediate response to a specific stimulus.

Retrieval.   In learning, the phase during which information is produced as a response from storage.

Sample.   A representative group selected from the population.

Sampling.   Choosing a representative group of subjects from the population.

Sensitization.   An increase in the tendency to respond to a certain stimulus as a result of previous response to that stimulus.

Sensory adaptation.   The physiological adjustment of the senses to a stimulus situation.

State-dependent learning.   The association of learned materials with the environment in which they were learned.

Storage.   In learning, the phase during which information is retained.

Stratified sampling.   A technique for selecting subjects such that any significant subgroup within the population is accurately reflected in the composition of any group (experimental or control) in the experiment.

Chapter 2

History of the Study of Learning

Interest in learning existed long before psychologists made their first formal studies of the subject. This chapter describes some of the approaches that predated the first psychological investigations and highlights subsequent developments in the field.

2.1 PREPSYCHOLOGICAL INFLUENCES ON THE STUDY OF LEARNING

As a discipline, the psychology of learning owes much to philosophy, which raised certain questions and posed many theories about learning, and to the natural sciences, which provided psychology with a method of investigation.

Philosophy

One of the subjects that has always been of interest to philosophers is the role played by the *mind* in our perception of the world. Unlike the brain, the mind cannot be directly measured or observed. The whole idea of "mind" is a hypothetical construct—we can use it to explain certain phenomena, but it is a difficult thing to describe in and of itself (see Problem 1.3).

In one sense the mind can be thought of as a kind of receptacle that receives and stores sensations. But even early philosophers were not satisfied with the idea of the mind as a passive container, and they tried to incorporate into their notion of mind those active mental processes known as *thought*. Aristotle (384–322 B.C.) proposed that certain forms of thought endowed human beings with the ability to know the truth; he believed that universal rules of *association* and the *uses of information* made it possible for humans to reason logically.

Association. Aristotle proposed three laws of association which governed thought processes. *Contiguity* meant that ideas that occurred together in time were associated. *Similarity* implied that ideas were linked because some kind of likeness or agreement existed between them. Ideas grouped because they were opposite or converse were said to exemplify the law of *contrast.*

EXAMPLE 1. Suppose several subjects are brought into a research laboratory one evening for a study. The investigator presents stimulus words and asks each subject to write down the first word that comes to mind. When the stimulus "black" is given, Lem responds "night," Marnie writes "Negro," and Ned puts down "white." These three responses represent Aristotle's three laws of association: Lem's response results from the very recent contiguity of darkness and nighttime, Marnie's shows similarity, and Ned gives a contrasting response.

Use of information. Aristotle believed that one could arrive at truths by using information, either by combining available evidence to reach some summary statement (called *induction*) or by using some already-existing proposition and appropriate rules of reasoning to reach some conclusion (called *deduction*).

EXAMPLE 2. Suppose a psychologist observes a learning sequence in several different species of organisms and then concludes that these examples represent evidence for a general principle. The psychologist's conclusion is based on inductive reasoning. A psychologist who employs a general principle to predict that a particular event will occur is using deductive reasoning.

The Sciences

The psychology of learning, like all other branches of psychology, approaches the study of behavior in a scientific way. This means that psychological conclusions must be based on observations made with the greatest possible precision and objectivity.   Perhaps the most important contribution of the natural sciences to psychology is the experimental method of conducting inquiries.

EXAMPLE 3.   Physical scientists emphasize a need for control of extraneous or irrelevant variables so that the phenomenon under investigation is not "contaminated" in some way.   Psychologists initiated study of learning principles by utilizing the same outlook, controlling outside influences (as much as possible) so that the performances observed could be interpreted in terms of learning principles.

2.2   INITIAL INVESTIGATIONS OF LEARNING—EBBINGHAUS

Very early in the development of the psychology of learning, one man conducted a series of research studies that established many principles still held today.   Hermann Ebbinghaus (1850–1909) undertook the first systematic investigations of memory.   Ebbinghaus was concerned with the effects of a number of different variables upon performance in learning situations.   His work focused on those variables that seemed to influence the rate at which an organism, having learned something, forgets it.   Using himself as a subject, Ebbinghaus isolated several important variables that influenced how well an organism retained a learned behavior.   Among the key variables he identified were: the amount of time between learning and attempted retrieval, the type of material memorized, the amount of material memorized, and the influence of one learning experience on subsequent learning experiences.

EXAMPLE 4.   At one point in his studies, Ebbinghaus was especially concerned that prior experience with the materials to be learned could bias the results observed.   In an attempt to overcome this, he devised the *nonsense syllable* (a consonant-vowel-consonant sequence, such as YOF, that does not make a word).   Ebbinghaus, who used himself as his own subject, hoped that, having had no prior experience with these syllables, he would have no associations with them.   The curve of forgetting first plotted by Ebbinghaus when using these materials has not been substantially altered in the years following his initial conclusions (see Fig. 2-1).

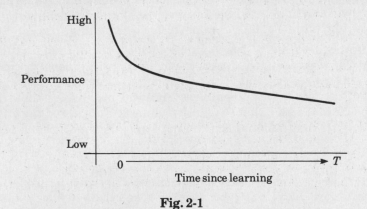

Fig. 2-1

2.3   INITIAL INVESTIGATIONS OF LEARNING—SYSTEMS

As psychology developed as a science, there were several attempts at comprehensive explanations of behavior.   These were called *systems* of psychology (while the people involved formed the various *schools* of psychology).   Systems were attempts to explain all behavior, therefore including and influencing the study of learning.

Systems vs. Theories

It is important to recognize that systems basically were attempts to explain *all* behavior, while *theories* that developed later only tried to explain a part of behavior.   Thus, theories of learning (see Section 2.4) were exclusively concerned with learning rather than the total range of behaviors within all of psychology.   Moreover, as specialization has increased in psychology, investigators have narrowed their fields of study even more, confining themselves to research on psychological models and laws.

Structuralism

The initial system of psychology was called *structuralism*.   The founder, Wilhelm Wundt (1832–1920), and his most famous student and follower, Edward Titchener (1867–1927) tried to determine the *structure* of the mind—thus the name for the system.   Structuralists collected data by using the introspective reports of normal adult human subjects.   They did this in a laboratory setting and emphasized the scientific method.   Introspection relied upon the subjective reports of the subjects, who reported the sensations, images, and feelings they experienced.   Partly as a response to structuralism, several other systematic positions developed.   Some proponents of these other systems were unwilling to limit their studies to normal adult humans; others were not satisfied with introspection as a data-collection method.

Functionalism

The proponents of one alternative viewpoint were especially interested in the purposes or functions of behavior, and their system came to be known as *functionalism*.   Adaptation to the environment was a key aspect of functionalism, which studied not only adult, normal humans, but also children, animals, and people showing abnormal personality patterns.   The functionalists helped extend psychology by studying a variety of subjects in a variety of circumstances, including the classroom, the factory, and natural settings as well as the laboratory.

Associationism

The primary concern of *associationism* was to try to understand how a stimulus-response bond is established.   As a leading proponent of associationism, Edward Thorndike (1874–1949) emphasized the importance of reinforcement by putting forward what came to be known as the law of effect.

The *law of effect* stated that responses which led to satisfaction were more likely to recur when similar stimulus situations existed.   Those responses which did not lead to satisfaction were likely to drop out.   Thorndike's research led him to conclude that punishment (discomfort) did not work in an exactly equal and opposite manner to satisfaction (reinforcement).   Rather, he advanced the idea that punishment may serve to suppress a response and, at the same time, make the organism try some other response to the stimulus. (*Note:* Thorndike also discussed the *law of exercise,* or *law of frequency of occurrence,* but believed this did not strengthen a stimulus-response as much as reinforcement did.)

EXAMPLE 5.   One of Thorndike's experiments nicely illustrates the above principles of reinforcement and punishment.   Thorndike gave chicks in an experimental setting a choice of three pathways in a maze.   His results showed that the tendency to return to the preceding choice increased if that choice had led to a reward of food, but did not decrease appreciably if the preceding choice led to a punishment of confinement in a solitary compartment.

Behaviorism

One radical position which developed as a reaction to structuralism came to be called *behaviorism*.   John B. Watson (1878–1958) championed this approach, which, in his formulation, made the organism a "black box" upon which stimuli acted and from which responses were made.   Watson believed the only responses psychologists should study were observable muscular movements or glandular secretions, and not mental activity, which is unobservable.

Watson's position represents *radical behaviorism,* the unwillingness to accept thought processes or the concept of mind at all.   It is distinguished from *moderate behaviorism,* which suggests that there is a mind which does have thought processes, but that these cannot be observed directly and must be inferred from observable responses.   Radical behaviorism stands for strict *physical determinism,* that is, responses are the direct result of environmental conditions.

Other Systems

Two other systematic positions had some influence upon the psychology of learning.   *Gestalt psychology* studied the area of perceptual learning, pointing out that some stimuli had to be treated as wholes and could not be divided into parts (elements) without losing their meaning.   Gestaltists also put forward the concept of *insight,* that is, sudden solution to a problem rather than a gradual resolution.

Psychoanalytic psychology really began because of Freud's interest in therapy rather than in systematization.   Of major interest to the psychoanalysts was the study of the *unconscious* (mental activity of which a person is unaware).   This prompted consideration of topics such as unconscious motivation and learning without awareness.

2.4 THEORIES OF LEARNING

As the importance of systems of psychology declined, theories began to be developed.   In the psychology of learning, several of these were labelled *neobehavioristic,* meaning that they followed (somewhat) the guidelines created by Watson.   Usually, the theories of learning are identified by the name of a leading proponent of the position rather than a descriptive label.

Edwin Guthrie

Edwin Guthrie (1886–1959) exemplified a single-principle theorist.   He believed that contiguity alone accounted for learning.   In a single trial the stimulus and response occurring together in time served as both the necessary and sufficient conditions for learning.   Reinforcement was important for Guthrie's theory only in that he proposed that reinforcers served to change the stimulus environment, thus keeping any other response from becoming attached to the stimulus.

Clark Hull

The learning theory proposed by Clark Hull (1884–1952) came to be known as a mathematico-deductive theory.   This meant that Hull advanced formal postulates and corollaries, deduced theorems from these, and attempted to mathematically specify results to be expected in empirical investigations.   In a simplified form, Hull's resultant explanation of a tendency to respond can be expressed as:

$$_SE_R = {}_SH_R \times V \times D \times K - (I_R + {}_SI_R)$$

where $_SE_R$ = reaction potential (the tendency to respond)
$_SH_R$ = habit strength
V = intensity of the stimulus
D = drive (motivation)
K = reinforcement value
I_R = reactive inhibition (temporary inhibitory potential)
$_SI_R$ = conditioned inhibition (learned inhibitory potential)

EXAMPLE 6.   To illustrate the detail of Hull's formulation, consider the formula for habit strength:

$$_SH_R = 1 - 10^{-a\mathbf{N}}$$

N represents the number of reinforced trials, and a is a constant with a value established by Hull as approximately 0.0306.   Based primarily upon information available to him at the time, Hull presented such designations intending for them to be tested and either accepted or modified as necessary.   (See Problem 2.19 for further discussion.)

Edward Tolman

Edward Tolman (1886–1959) accepted many of the stimulus-response propositions put forward by his contemporaries, but did not feel these encompassed all aspects of learning. He particularly emphasized the idea of stimulus-stimulus associations; that is, Tolman paid special attention to the way in which organisms developed an understanding of which environmental event would lead to the next. Such a relationship might involve reinforcement, but it could develop in nonreinforcement situations as well.

B. F. Skinner

B. F. Skinner (b. 1904) has devoted his career to attempting to determine how behavior can be manipulated by managing reinforcement conditions. He is not concerned with trying to determine internal (physiological or cognitive) explanations for the observed responses. Rather, Skinner's hope is to be able to describe operant behavior and the conditions influencing such behavior. (See Chapter 4 for a thorough discussion of operant conditioning.)

Other Learning Theories

In addition to neobehaviorism, several other approaches were developed sufficiently to be treated as theories of learning. These included physiological theories, cognitive theories, and developmental theories.

The work of Donald Hebb (b. 1904) illustrates an attempt to create a *physiological* learning theory. Hebb proposed that learning was accompanied by a very slight electrochemical change in one or more *synapses,* which are the gaps between the axon of one nerve cell and the dendrite of the next. According to Hebb, such a change in the central nervous system made it easier or more likely that the signal sequence across that particular synapse would occur again.

EXAMPLE 7. A very simplified version of Hebb's neuronal-synaptic position would be represented by your listening to the sound track of a movie (perhaps a science fiction movie) while looking at the robot featured in that movie. The theory would say that a later exposure to that sound track should conjure up visual images of that robot for you because passage of that message across the same series of synapses had been facilitated by the previous experience.

A theory such as Hebb's is only one of a variety of physiological theories. Others suggest that learning may result from the storage of messages in particular molecules, such as the protein produced by the RNA (ribonucleic acid) found in the nucleus of nerve cells.

Cognitive learning theories stress the importance of higher mental processes, such as attitudes, beliefs, and perceptions. Cognitive theorists are also especially interested in intellectual processes, and they investigate the ways subjects develop and use rules of logic, problem-solving, and language. Obviously, the subjects of their studies are almost exclusively human beings.

Developmental learning theories emphasize the interaction between physical maturation and intellectual growth. Such a theory is exemplified by the work of Jean Piaget (b. 1896), who has created a four-stage theory of development showing how each stage relates to the others, both in terms of necessary physical development and cognitive preparation.

EXAMPLE 8. A very young child, according to Piaget, may learn about gravity by repeatedly lifting and dropping an object and observing it falling. This learning cannot begin, however, until the child has matured sufficiently to perform the necessary motor tasks, such as sitting and grasping, in order to complete the sequence.

2.5 CONTEMPORARY POSITIONS

In Section 2.3 it was pointed out that psychologists have tended to reduce the scope of their investigations as the science has progressed. Much contemporary research is conducted at a *model* level, that is, the study of part of a theoretical position.

Two of the models, which reflect in their differences of approach the differences between behaviorism and cognitive theories, are the *associationistic* and the *cognitive* models. Associationistic models are based upon the study of S-R bonds, while cognitive models study the effects of experience on "higher" mental processes.

Ethology

A third type of approach which has held contemporary popularity is called the *ethological* approach. Ethologists concentrate upon observing organisms in their natural setting and attempting to determine the characteristic behavior which may be species-specific. Biological structure is seen as an important determinant of the responses studied by ethologists.

Verbal Learning

One area which does not seem to fit into any one of the above categories is that of verbal learning and language behavior. Approached in several manners (see Chapters 6 and 18), verbal learning and language-behavior studies treat topics from both associationistic and cognitive viewpoints.

EXAMPLE 9. Research on the effect of level of meaning of stimuli and responses on paired-associate learning (S-R pairs) would illustrate the associationistic approach. However, other psychologists have pointed out that some S-R pairs appear to be generated spontaneously by the subject being observed. In such cases, associationistic theories do not seem to account for the behavior, and cognitive models are called upon.

Solved Problems

2.1   Annette responds to the verbal stimulus "canine" by saying "dog." Using the principles of association attributed to Aristotle, explain her response.

Aristotle proposed three laws of association: Ideas were associated by contiguity, similarity, or contrast. In this case, Annette's response is probably the result of either association by contiguity (she has heard the words "canine" and "dog" occur together often) or, more likely, similarity (she has learned that these two words are synonyms).

2.2   What response would Annette give if her association is based on the law of contrast?

With a stimulus of "canine," Annette would probably be most likely to respond "feline." (The contrast of "dog-cat" is carried over to this response.)

2.3   Many famous detectives have built their reputations by showing how they could "piece together" bits of evidence to determine who committed a crime. Is this process representative of induction or deduction? What would a detective have to do to illustrate the opposite process?

Arriving at a conclusion by combining various pieces of evidence represents induction. To show deduction, a detective would have to take some premise (theory) and, by using reasoning, apply the theory to the particular crime to reach some conclusion.

2.4   In what ways did the natural sciences influence the development of the psychology of learning?

Sciences such as chemistry, physics, and biology influenced many fields of psychology by providing them with their basic investigative technique—the experimental method (described in Chapter 1). The natural sciences, and in particular biology, helped psychologists distinguish between behaviors that are learned and those that are inherited. Additionally, concepts such as Darwin's theory of evolution served as the basis for comparative studies of the ways various species learn certain behaviors.

2.5   Perhaps the first person to stress the idea that memory could be studied scientifically was Hermann Ebbinghaus. What were Ebbinghaus's major areas of study?

For the most part Ebbinghaus studied the effects of different variables on the rate at which an organism would forget what it had learned. His experiments, for which he himself was often the subject, resulted in the conclusion summarized in Fig. 2-1—that as the time between memorizing (learning) and recall increased, the subject's performance in recalling the learned material decreased.

2.6   What variables, besides the length of time between learning and recall, did Ebbinghaus identify as important influences on performance in a memory task?

According to Ebbinghaus, other variables that affected the rate of forgetting were: the type of materials memorized, the quantity of materials memorized, the number of repetitions involved in the memorizing procedure, and the influence of one learning task on the subsequent learning tasks. (*Note:* this last variable is sometimes called *transfer of learning* or *transfer of training*.)

2.7   The most general trend in the psychology of learning has involved the scope of study. What direction has this trend taken? What terminology describes this trend?

In general the tendency has been to study more specific (or particular) aspects of learning rather than broad concerns. Early proposals were called systems of behavior. Later propositions were described as theories of learning. Most recently, theories of learning have given way to the study of models. These are a subclass of theories, usually intended to serve as specific guidelines for empirical research.

2.8   As mentioned in the previous problem, the progress of psychology has generally been away from broad and all-inclusive systems to narrower theories and even narrower models. This move from the comprehensive to the limited has especially influenced the psychology of learning. Why?

Psychologists have not been able to establish conclusively that all types of learning are merely different expressions of a single underlying process. Thus far, no single system, theory, or model seems to suffice as an explanation of all learning processes. It may be that organisms learn in several ways, using different aspects of the nervous system in different ways, depending on what is being learned. Or it may be that future research will lead to some unifying theory that can be used to explain all types of learning. In either case, for the time being, the wide variety of limited and specific models of learning will have to suffice.

2.9   Structuralism attempted to reduce analyses of learning (and all behavior) to the most basic elements possible. What elements did the structuralists select? What were the characteristics and properties of these elements?

The structuralists selected three elements: sensations, images, and feelings. Sensations were the components of perception, images the elements of ideas, and feelings made up emotions. (Later in his career, Titchener eliminated feelings, claiming they could be attributed to sensations and images.) According to the structuralists, each element had four properties: quality (the difference in kind), attensity (clearness), intensity (strength), and protensity (duration).

2.10   What major contributions did the structuralists make to the psychology of learning?

Three contributions are usually attributed to the structuralists. First, and perhaps most important in the long run, they brought the study of learning into the laboratory and stressed the importance of scientific investigation.   In addition, the structuralists thoroughly tested the method of introspection, which was shown to be inadequate for studying behavior.   And third, they provided a target for the proponents of other systems and theories, who could use their criticisms of the structuralists as a starting place for their own explanations of behavior.

2.11   Functionalist psychologists expanded the study of learning into new areas.   What were some of these?   What were the major attitudes of functionalists?

In reaction to the structuralists, who studied the responses of only normal adult human subjects, the functionalists expanded their investigations to include children, abnormal adults, and animals as subjects.   In addition, the functionalists were involved in mental testing and the application of their psychological principles to many areas, such as education, religion, and sex.   In general, the functionalists stressed the purposes of behavior, particularly how the organism adapts to the environment.   They were also concerned with how motivation influences behavior.

2.12   A pigeon in a Skinner box often shows many diverse responses early in training, while later it is likely to appear "settled" upon the correct response (for example, pecking a disc).   Interpret such behavior according to Thorndike's law of effect.

Thorndike's law of effect proposes that a correct learned response develops because it is rewarded and that incorrect responses are gradually eliminated because they are not rewarded.   In this case, the pigeon makes the disc-pecking response because it leads to some reward (perhaps food or water).   Other responses are not learned because the reward is not forthcoming when they are made.

2.13   According to Thorndike, how does punishment affect responding?

After extensive research, Thorndike proposed that punishment serves to suppress a response and make the organism try some other response in that particular stimulus situation.

2.14   Distinguish between radical behaviorism and moderate behaviorism.

The difference between radical and moderate behaviorism is one of degree.   While both accept the position that psychologists can only know about behavior from the measurement of observable stimuli and responses, the radical behaviorist totally eliminates the concepts of mind and thought, reducing such aspects of the organism's activity to the physiological functionings of the brain.   A moderate behaviorist may accept the concepts of mind and thought, but maintain that they are not directly observable or measurable.

2.15   John B. Watson once claimed that if he were allowed to take a dozen healthy infants and specify the way they were brought up, he would guarantee that he could train any one of them to be any type of specialist.   Such a statement represents what kind of position?

Watson's statement represents a strict cause-and-effect determinism.   According to Watson, responses are the direct result of the specific environment in which the person was reared or currently inhabits.

2.16   How did the view the gestaltists took toward learning differ from the views held by the structuralists and the behaviorists?

The gestaltists held that human mental activity could not be profitably studied when it was broken down into its constituent parts.   (The structuralists divided mental activity into sensations, images, and feelings.   The behaviorists, if they accepted the notion of mind at all, accounted for it as the establishment of bonds between various stimuli and responses.)   Moreover, the gestaltists believed that *insight*—a very sudden and creative resolution of a mental problem or learning task—could be explained only if one accepted the fact that there existed in the mind certain patterns or configurations that corresponded to similar patterns or configurations in the environment.   Neither the behaviorists nor the structuralists were concerned with insight.

2.17 How did Freud's proposal of the unconscious influence the psychology of learning?

Freud proposed the existence of the unconscious, which he believed resulted in behavioral influences that were not readily detected, either by the respondent or some outside observer. This led to explorations of areas such as the effect of unconscious motives upon performance or the possibility of learning without awareness.

2.18 Why would Guthrie be considered more Aristotelian than Thorndikian?

The predominant factor in learning according to Guthrie was that of contiguity—that is, the occurrence at the same time of a stimulus and a response. Contiguity was one of Aristotle's (and subsequently many others') three laws of association. On the other hand, Thorndike emphasized the importance of reward (reinforcement) in his law of effect. Guthrie recognized the existence of reinforcers, but thought they served only to change the environment so that no other response could be attached to the particular stimulus.

2.19 Clark Hull's theory of learning proposes that the tendency to respond (called the *reaction potential* or $_SE_R$) is dependent on the interaction of two basic types of variables: those related to the stimulus environment and those related to the organism. Give a brief description of Hull's formula for calculating reaction potential.

According to Hull, reaction potential can be calculated by multiplying the values of habit strength ($_SH_R$), drive (D), stimulus intensity (V), and reinforcement (K) and subtracting from this product the temporary and permanent inhibitory potentials (I_R and $_SI_R$).

2.20 In some cases organisms make responses even under partial-reinforcement conditions (when reinforcement occurs on only some of the trials). What problems would this create for someone who subscribed to Hull's formula for calculating reaction potential?

Hull's formula involves the multiplication of habit strength, drive, the value of reinforcement, and stimulus intensity. The reaction potential would thus have to be zero or a negative value whenever any one of these four variables equals zero. In partial reinforcement, the reinforcement value (K) would be zero on the nonreinforced trials, yet responding was seen to occur. The Hullian proposal cannot account for this. (*Note:* Kenneth Spence [1907–1967], a student of Hull's modified the formula so that these four variables had the following relationship: $_SH_R \times V \times (D + K)$. Spence's explanation was that the organism could have positive reaction potential as long as there is *either* sufficient drive or sufficient reinforcement.)

2.21 Tolman's approach to behavior differed in one very important way from those of Guthrie and Hull. What was this difference? What effect would reinforcement have in Tolman's proposed theory?

Tolman suggested there were several different types of learning. While Guthrie and Hull both emphasized stimulus-response (S-R) relationships, Tolman emphasized stimulus-stimulus (S-S) learning. Essentially, learning S-S relationships meant the subject learned what leads to what. Reinforcement, according to Tolman, was not essential for such learning, but could help to accentuate the relationship between stimuli.

2.22 What does it mean to say that Skinner's approach does not include "physiologizing?" What is Skinner's attitude toward the study of learning? .

Skinner would not accept proposals regarding "interior activity" of the organism. His emphasis is on response-reinforcement relationships and the ways in which they regulate observable behaviors. Skinner's work has been especially concentrated on the effect schedules of reinforcement have upon response rate (see Chapter 4).

2.23   Most psychologists classify Guthrie, Hull, Tolman, and Skinner as neobehaviorists. What does that mean? What are some of the other kinds of theories of learning which have been developed?

A neobehaviorist is someone whose approach is a modification or extension of John Watson's behaviorism. Emphasis is placed upon observables—that is, measurable stimuli and measurable responses. There is little or no use of internal (organismic) explanations without tying them to observable events, and there is little or no reliance on unobservable concepts such as "mental activity" or "mind."

Other kinds of theories of learning which have been proposed include: *physiological,* where learning occurs when physiological changes within the nervous system take place (see Chapter 20); *cognitive,* where higher mental processes rather than simple S-R relationships are used to explain behavior; and *developmental,* where learning is described as a function of physiological and cognitive maturation.

2.24   Contemporary psychologists seem to place less emphasis on the attempts to explain all learning. Rather, there is a greater tendency to present theories or models for parts of learning. What approaches have been most popular recently?

Current studies in learning can be broadly classified in terms of three approaches. That with the longest tradition is called *associationistic,* continuing to voice the importance of S-R associations and the effects of reinforcement and punishment. A second general approach is the *cognitive* outlook, which stresses complex mental processes. *Biological* influences on behavior and the interaction of experience and biological structure are the focus for the third general contemporary approach. Much of the emphasis of this third approach arose from the work of ethologists, who studied organisms in their natural settings and evaluated innate aspects of behavior.

2.25   How do studies in verbal learning and language behavior seem to fit into these contemporary approaches?

Verbal learning and language behavior are important parts of both associationistic and cognitive studies. Some investigations are focused upon S-R bonds in paired-associate or serial-learning circumstances (see Chapter 6). Other studies approach topics such as *generative* behavior—that is, the generation of responses from past experience and the use of certain rules—as evidence for cognitive processes which go beyond the bonds described by associationistic theories (see Chapter 18).

2.26   What kinds of evidence support an ethological viewpoint toward learning?

Research on topics such as imprinting (see Chapter 1) and fixed-action patterns (FAPs) has shown that particular learned responses are affected by innate mechanisms. Thus the ducklings will learn a following response if exposed to a moving stimulus during the critical period, but which stimulus object is followed will depend upon environmental opportunity.

Fixed-action patterns are not instincts, but rather stereotyped sequences of movement found in all members of a species. FAPs are dependent upon both hereditary and environmental factors. In such cases, many different stimuli may provoke the same sequence of responses—for example, the chasing response illustrated by starlings trying to feed upon flying insects.

Key Terms

Associationism.   A system of psychology that studied the formation of S-R bonds.

Attensity.   The "clearness" of mental elements, according to the structuralist position.

Behaviorism.   A system of psychology that studied observable stimuli and responses *only,* denying the concept of mind.

Contiguity.   The occurrence of ideas or events together in time.

Deduction.   The use of an existing proposition and the rules of reasoning to develop a conclusion; reasoning from the general to the particular.

Determinism.   The concept that responses result directly from the environmental conditions which provoke them.

Ethology.   The scientific study of animal behavior, especially emphasizing biological structure as a behavioral determinant.

Fixed-action patterns (**FAPs**).   Stereotyped sequences of movement found in all members of a species, dependent upon both environmental and hereditary factors.

Functionalism.   A system of psychology that studied the purposes of behavior and the adaptation of the organism to the environment.

Gestalt psychology.   A system of psychology that concentrated upon a holistic approach to the study of behavior.

Induction.   The combining of several units of information to reach a summary statement; reasoning from the particular to the general.

Introspection.   A method of psychological investigation in which subjects report their own responses to stimuli.

Law of effect.   An explanation of S-R bonds: Those S-R patterns leading to satisfaction were likely to occur again, while S-R patterns that did not lead to satisfaction were unlikely to be repeated.

Law of exercise.   An explanation of S-R bonds: The more frequently an S-R pattern occurred, the more likely it would be learned.

Model.   A subclass of a theory, used to study a precise area of investigation.

Neobehaviorism.   A position, attributed to several theorists, believed to follow the basic tenets established by John Watson.

Nonsense syllable.   A consonant-vowel-consonant sequence that does not form a word; often abbreviated CVC.

Protensity.   The duration of mental elements, according to the structuralist position.

School of psychology.   The people who support a particular systematic interpretation of psychology.

Structuralism.   A system of psychology that studied the normal adult human mind using the method of introspection.

System of psychology.   A body of knowledge in psychology used to organize or interpret *all* behavior.

Theory of psychology.   A general principle or group of principles, based upon evidence or observation, which proposes an explanation for phenomena.

Verbal learning.   The study of the acquisition, storage, and use of words and symbols.

PART II: Acquisition Principles

Each of the four chapters in this part is concerned with a particular mode of acquisition. While there is considerable overlap among the four, they are presented separately because research investigations typically have dealt with each individually. The order of the chapters reflects historical precedence rather than any implied hierarchy of worth.

Chapter 3 explores the classical conditioning paradigm. Much of the early work in the psychology of learning was based upon this format, and several psychologists believed the ultimate explanation of all learning might be found here. Instrumental conditioning is considered in Chapter 4. Of special importance are the effect of reinforcement, schedules of reinforcement, shaping of an instrumental response, and applications of this form of acquisition. Chapter 5 looks at modeling or observation learning. This chapter emphasizes the social aspects of learning. In Chapter 6, verbal learning is considered. Most of the material presented is oriented around experimental investigations of the acquisition of verbal materials. Unlike the other three chapters in this part, Chapter 6 is almost exclusively concerned with *human* behavior.

Chapter 3

Principles of Classical Conditioning

The first investigations of learning to receive widespread public attention and acceptance were performed around the turn of the century by the Russian physiologist Ivan Pavlov (1849–1936). In his earliest experiments Pavlov was concerned with the digestive processes of dogs, and *not* with learning or any other nonmaterial mental process. As his studies progressed, however, Pavlov came to accept the idea of what he called "psychic" responses, and out of his findings grew a model, or *paradigm,* of learning that has since been called *classical conditioning.*

Very roughly speaking, what Pavlov demonstrated in his laboratory was that a dog would begin to salivate at the mere sounding of a tone if that tone had previously been paired with the presentation of food to the dog. In other words, after conditioning the dog would salivate in response to a stimulus (the tone) that under normal circumstances did not result in salivation. Pavlov's early studies were limited to dogs, but subsequent investigations have shown that the principles of classical conditioning can be successfully applied to a wide variety of organisms and a wide variety of behaviors.

3.1 THE CLASSICAL CONDITIONING PARADIGM

The basic format for classical conditioning consists of pairing a stimulus which is originally neutral (does not elicit the response under investigation) with a response-producing stimulus. After one or more pairings, the previously neutral stimulus produces the response being studied. When this occurs, classical conditioning is said to have taken place.

EXAMPLE 1. For most people, the administration of an electric shock to the fingertips will produce (among other responses) a rapid withdrawal of the hand. Usually withdrawal is not a reponse elicited by the ticking of a metronome. But if the metronome sound is presented slightly before the electric shock, it is very possible the subjects will begin withdrawal responses immediately upon hearing the sound. That is, when the withdrawal response begins to be made to the ticking sound alone, it has been classically conditioned.

Classical Conditioning Terminology

Each of the components of the classical conditioning paradigm has been designated by a particular label. The stimulus that was originally neutral but comes to be response-producing is called the *conditioned stimulus* (abbreviated as CS). The stimulus which elicits the response upon first presentation is the *unconditioned stimulus* (UCS).

The response elicited by the UCS is called the *unconditioned response* (UCR). When the response under investigation is elicited by the CS, it is called the *conditioned response* (CR). A representation of the classical conditioning design is given in Fig. 3-1.

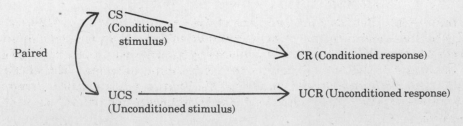

Fig. 3-1

EXAMPLE 2.   The components of classical conditioning in the situation described in Example 1 would be designated as follows: the conditioned stimulus (CS) is the ticking of the metronome; the unconditioned stimulus (UCS) is the electric shock; the unconditioned response (UCR) is the withdrawal elicited by the electric shock; and the conditioned response (CR) is the withdrawal movement at the sound of the metronome.

It should be noted that the CR and UCR are not necessarily exactly the same.   Although early researchers proposed that the CR produced by the CS was identical to the UCR elicited by the UCS, subsequent studies have shown that the CR usually differs from the UCR.   Frequently the CR is a component of the UCR, while in other cases the CR appears to be an anticipatory response made to the UCS.   In addition, it should be recognized that the stimulus used as the CS may elicit responses not under investigation.   These are called *orienting responses* (OR) and drop out after a few trials.

EXAMPLE 3.   In the metronome-shock experiment described in Examples 1 and 2, it is very possible a subject might not be familiar with the sound of a metronome.   When the initial presentation of the CS is made, it is likely that the subject may turn to try to identify the sound.   This orienting response would be likely to drop out after several trials.

Nonconditioning Variables

Researchers have identified a number of variables that affect the classical conditioning situation or produce results similar to classical conditioning.   Some of these are discussed here.

Alpha response.   When the subject makes an orienting response to the CS which happens to be in the same response category as the CR to be investigated, this response is called an *alpha response*.   It is important to distinguish between the alpha response and the CR in order to be certain the effects can be attributed accurately to the conditioning procedure rather than to this nonconditioning variable.

EXAMPLE 4.   Consider again the metronome-shock experiment.   Suppose that for some reason the sound of the metronome came on suddenly with a high intensity.   It is possible the surprise might produce a startle response, including a withdrawal of the hand.   Such a withdrawal would be an alpha response rather than a CR.

Habituation.   One means of overcoming the effects of the alpha response is to present the CS alone for a number of trials before beginning the conditioning procedure.   With repeated presentations, the alpha response eventually dissipates.   This is called *habituation*.

Sensitization.   *Sensitization* refers to an effect produced by a presentation of the CS-UCS pairing following habituation.   This sometimes augments the production of an alpha response, making it necessary to carefully identify the components of the response given, separating alpha response effects from aspects of the CR.

Pseudo-conditioning.   Repeated presentations of the UCS alone before any CS-UCS pairing may create an effect called *pseudo-conditioning*.   In such situations, a single presentation of the CS may elicit a response comparable to the CR.   Such a response is referred to as a pseudo-conditioned response because no procedure has been used to establish an association between the CS and UCS or between the CS and CR.

Latent inhibition.   Repeated presentations of the CS alone before any CS-UCS pairing is called habituation (see above), but may produce an additional effect called *latent inhibition*. Latent inhibition refers to the inhibitory condition produced by habituation.   Generally, the greater the amount of habituation, the more difficult later conditioning becomes.   The effects of latent inhibition are stronger with a greater number of habituation trials and/or a greater stimulus intensity during such trials.   Such effects tend to be stimulus-specific and will last over relatively long time periods.

EXAMPLE 5. If the researcher in the metronome-shock experiment identified the alpha response (see Example 4) and decided to use habituation to reduce or eliminate its effects, latent inhibition might result. This would mean that subsequent classical conditioning of the withdrawal response to the metronome click (CS) would take longer than if the habituation procedure had not been used. However, such a carry-over probably would not be demonstrated if some other sound were substituted for the metronome click during the habituation procedure.

Sensory preconditioning.   Occasionally, two potential conditioned stimuli are paired together before any classical conditioning takes place. Then one of these stimuli is paired with a UCS a sufficient number of times to reliably elicit a CR. Following such a pairing, the other (unpaired with the UCS) stimulus is presented by itself. If it elicits the CR, *sensory preconditioning* is said to have been demonstrated. Figure 3-2 illustrates the three steps in this procedure.

$$CS_1 - CS_2 \qquad\qquad CS_1 - UCS \qquad\qquad CS_2 \text{ presented}$$
$$\text{paired} \qquad\qquad\qquad \text{paired} \qquad\qquad\qquad \text{alone}$$
$$[CS_1 \rightarrow CR] \qquad\qquad\qquad [CS_2 \rightarrow CR]$$
$$\text{Step one} \qquad\qquad\qquad \text{Step two} \qquad\qquad\qquad \text{Step three}$$

Fig. 3-2

Strength of Stimuli

Within limits, increasing the strength of either the CS or the UCS will lead to greater conditioning. However, such a result will not be found when the intensity is great enough to produce an escape response from seemingly harmful or unpleasant effects.

3.2   EXTINCTION AND SPONTANEOUS RECOVERY

The process of reducing the strength of a CR to its preconditioning level is called *extinction*. Following acquisition of the response, repeated presentation of the CS alone (without the UCS) will eventually lead to extinction of the response. The term "extinction" is used to describe both the procedure employed and the result obtained from that procedure. (*Note:* Both extinction and habituation involve repeated presentations of the CS alone. They differ in that extinction follows acquisition of the CR, while habituation precedes acquisition.)

Spontaneous recovery of the CR can occur when the CS, after extinction and a period of rest, is reintroduced. In other words, if the subject has had no contact with the conditioning situation after extinction has taken place, and then is exposed to the CS only, the CR may recover spontaneously. Usually, the strength of the demonstrated CR in spontaneous recovery is less than what it was during peak acquisition (often around 50 percent of the previous maximum).

EXAMPLE 6.   Consider again the metronome-shock experiment. Extinction would be accomplished by repeatedly presenting the sound of the metronome without any electric shock following. The withdrawal CR would dissipate, returning to its pretraining level. If after a period of time away from the experimental setting the subject is again presented with only the sound of the metronome, the CR of withdrawal may reappear, although perhaps in a diminished or less vigorous form. This would demonstrate spontaneous recovery of the CR.

Extinction and spontaneous recovery, and the variables which affect both, are more thoroughly discussed in Chapter 9.

3.3   STIMULUS GENERALIZATION AND DIFFERENTIATION

When a subject is presented a stimulus which differs from the original (training or acquisition) CS, three possibilities for responding exist. The subject may (1) make a CR that is as vigorous as the CR to the original stimulus, (2) make a CR diminished in strength from that given to the original CS, or (3) not make a CR at all.   The first two results represent stimulus generalization, and the third illustrates differentiation.

Primary stimulus generalization. *Primary stimulus generalization* is shown when an organism responds not only to the original CS, but also to other stimuli that have physical properties similar to those of the original CS.

EXAMPLE 7.   Suppose a subject has been conditioned to make the withdrawal movement in response to the clicking metronome, as described in the previous examples. If the subject makes the same response to a similar but not identical sound—such as the amplified ticking of a clock, for example—primary stimulus generalization has been shown.

Secondary stimulus generalization. Primary stimulus generalization is based on the physical equivalence of two stimuli—for example, the similarity between the amplified sound of a ticking clock and the sound of a metronome (Example 7). *Secondary stimulus generalization* is based on a learned similarity between one stimulus and another.   When this learned equivalence of two stimuli is based on knowledge of language, the secondary stimulus generalization shown is called *semantic generalization*.

EXAMPLE 8.   Suppose the subject in Example 7 is conditioned to make the withdrawal response not to the ticking of a metronome but to the command "Start," given by the experimenter. If in one trial the experimenter substitutes the command "Begin" and if the subject responds, semantic generalization would be shown.

Differentiation

Distinguishing between the original CS and some other stimulus so that the CR is given only to the original CS and not to the other represents *differentiation* (often called *discrimination*).

Response Generalization

When the subject gives several comparable or equivalent responses to the same stimulus, *response generalization* is said to have occurred.

EXAMPLE 9.   On occasion, presentation of an especially fancy dessert is accompanied by a statement such as "OK, how does this look?" This single stimulus may produce many different but equivalent responses: cries of delight, physical gestures such as rubbing the stomach or licking the lips, or verbal responses such as "Great," "Terrific," or "Beautiful." All these responses accomplish the same purpose, that of expressing acceptance and admiration, and all are thus demonstrations of response generalization.

Generalization and differentiation are discussed more thoroughly in Chapter 10.

3.4   MEASUREMENT OF THE CONDITIONED RESPONSE (CR)

Several general properties of responses are frequently used to evaluate the strength of a CR or to distinguish a CR from some other response (such as an alpha response).   The most common are discussed in this section.

Amplitude of Response

The difference between the preconditioning base level of a response and the measured CR is called the *amplitude* of the response.   The same definition holds for *magnitude* of the CR, with the exception that amplitude is measured for all trials regardless of the presence or absence of the CR, while magnitude is referred to only when there is a measurable difference between it and the baseline measure of response.

Frequency of Response

The presence or absence of the CR following each presentation of the CS determines the *frequency* of the CR. Frequency is reported either as a number of observable CRs or as the percentage of trials in which a CR appears.

Latency of Response

Latency of response is measured as the time between the onset of the CS and the beginning of the CR. The assumption is that shorter latencies indicate stronger conditioning, but there are physiological limits to how short the latencies can become.

Resistance to Extinction

The number of trials necessary to complete extinction is used as a measure of CR strength and is called *resistance to extinction*. The assumption is that the greater the number of trials required to complete extinction, the stronger the CR.

3.5   INTERSTIMULUS INTERVAL

Interstimulus interval (ISI) is defined as the time between the onset of the CS and the onset of the UCS. Four arrangements of ISI have been tested extensively in classical conditioning situations—delay, trace, simultaneous, and backward conditioning procedures.

Delay Conditioning

In *delay conditioning,* the CS comes on before the UCS and stays on until after the onset of the UCS. Often the CS and UCS terminate at the same time.

EXAMPLE 10.   Consider another variation of the metronome-shock experiment described earlier. Delay conditioning would be illustrated if the metronome's click sound came on and continued until after the shock was presented.

Trace Conditioning

Trace conditioning involves the presentation and termination of the CS before the onset of the UCS. It is assumed that some remembrance (trace) of the CS persists after its termination and links it with the UCS. (*Note:* Trace and delay conditioning procedures often are called *forward conditioning procedures.*)

EXAMPLE 11.   If the metronome click starts and finishes before the electric shock is presented, the procedure is called trace conditioning.

Simultaneous Conditioning

Presentation of the CS and UCS at exactly the same time is called *simultaneous conditioning.* Usually both stimuli are also terminated at the same time. In his initial investigations, Pavlov treated forward conditioning procedures with relatively short ISIs as if they were simultaneous. Later investigations showed that this could lead to inaccurate conclusions because conditioning with very short intervals may produce results quite different from those obtained with true simultaneity.

Backward Conditioning

When the onset of the UCS occurs before the onset of the CS, the procedure is called *backward conditioning.* In general, backward conditioning is not very effective and does not produce very strong CRs.

EXAMPLE 12. If the shock is presented before the metronome click, backward conditioning might take place. However, the electric shock might be such a dominant stimulus that the subject's attention to the click could be minimal and a later test for a CR might prove fruitless.

Temporal Conditioning

A fifth conditioning procedure involving presentation of a UCS only is called *temporal conditioning.* In temporal conditioning, the UCS is presented repeatedly at consistent intervals. The subject appears to treat this rhythmical period as if it were a CS and eventually makes CRs in keeping with the regular time periods.

Inhibition of Delay

A principle related to interstimulus interval is that of *inhibition of delay,* which is the withholding of a CR until just before the onset of the UCS. When a consistent CS-UCS interval is used and it is longer than the typical latency of the CR, inhibition of delay is illustrated if the latency of the CR increases until the CR seems to just anticipate the onset of the UCS.

The most effective conditioning procedures often involve ISIs shorter than the latency of the CR; thus inhibition of delay could not be demonstrated. For CRs such as eyeblink responses, ISIs between 0.4 and 1.25 seconds appear to be best, although there has been great variation demonstrated for varying ISIs and CRs.

3.6 HIGHER-ORDER CONDITIONING

Higher-order conditioning occurs when a new, previously unpresented CS is paired with the CS from a well-established CS-UCS arrangement. Thus, the first CS serves the role of UCS in the new pairing. When the new CS elicits the CR, higher-order conditioning has been demonstrated.

EXAMPLE 13. Once the withdrawal CR is very well established in the metronome-shock classical conditioning procedure, the experimenter might want to try higher-order conditioning by pairing the flashing of a light with the metronome click. Demonstration of the withdrawal CR to the flashing light would illustrate higher-order conditioning.

3.7 THE PARTIAL-REINFORCEMENT EFFECT

In classical conditioning, *partial reinforcement* is defined as an acquisition procedure in which the CS is presented on every trial, but the UCS is paired with the CS on only some of the trials. Usually, partial reinforcement is reported as a percentage, giving the ratio of CS-UCS pairings to the total number of acquisition trials. (CS-UCS pairings on every trial of acquisition are called *continuous reinforcement* or *100-percent reinforcement.*)

The result of acquiring a CR under partial-reinforcement conditions is called the *partial-reinforcement effect* (PRE). Generally, CRs acquired under partial-reinforcement conditions are more resistant to extinction than those acquired in continuous-reinforcement conditions. (The PRE is discussed more thoroughly in Chapter 4.)

EXAMPLE 14. The PRE could be tested in the metronome-shock experiment by having one group of subjects under a continuous-reinforcement arrangement—click and shock paired on every trial—while another group heard the click on every trial but received the shock on only some trials. One would expect that the CR of the group experiencing partial reinforcement would take longer to extinguish than that of the continuous-reinforcement group.

3.8 COMPOUND CONDITIONING

In the early investigations of classical conditioning, Pavlov studied what he called the *stimulus aggregate*. Later researchers have renamed this *compound conditioning,* the presentation of more than one conditioned stimulus in the same pairing with a UCS.

Two forms of compound conditioning have been studied. *Simultaneous compound conditioning* involves presentation of the conditioned stimuli at exactly the same time. *Serial compound conditioning* refers to procedures where one CS precedes the other (usually with both preceding onset of the UCS).

Tests for evidence of the CR are accomplished by presenting one of the conditioned stimuli by itself. In general, such tests have revealed that the strength of the CR to either stimulus is determined by the relative effectiveness of each CS. This will be affected by the number of previous CS-UCS pairings, the amount of attention devoted to each stimulus, ISI spacing for each of the stimuli, and other similar factors.

EXAMPLE 15. A serial compound-conditioning situation could be represented by the lines shown in Fig. 3-3. For example, the two conditioned stimuli could be the flashing of a light followed by a spoken word, both preceding presentation of some UCS. The relative strength of the CR to each stimulus could be determined by presenting the color or the word independently and measuring response strength.

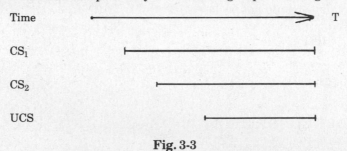

Fig. 3-3

Some research using compound-conditioning procedures has shown a phenomenon called *configuring*. In such situations, the CR strength stays high for the compound, but the individual components *lose* conditioning strength. Apparently, through training, the components develop a perceptual *gestalt* (whole) which operates as a unit, while the individual elements lose strength.

Solved Problems

3.1   Initial investigations of classical conditioning were conducted by Ivan Pavlov. What was his original intent? Why did his results seem related to Darwin's theory of evolution?

Pavlov started his research in an attempt to understand digestive processes. As a physiologist, he at first believed that study of a nonmaterial phenomenon like the mind was outside the scope of scientific investigation. Later, he viewed the "psychic" salivary secretions of the dogs he studied as evidence that the dogs had adapted to their environment—that is, made behavioral changes in response to changes in their environment as evolutionary theory might lead one to expect.

3.2   Pavlov studied the salivary responses of dogs. What was the basic design of his research?

Pavlov performed minor operations which allowed the saliva from the dogs' salivary glands to be drawn off through a tube and accurately measured. At first, commonly occurring stimuli (such as food smells or the sound of the experimenter's footsteps) were identified as the neutral stimuli which became response-producing. Later, Pavlov paired specifically selected stimuli (such as a ringing bell) with the presentation of meat powder. With repeated pairings, the dogs showed the salivary responses to the sound of the bell.

3.3   Identify the components of the classical conditioning paradigm in Pavlov's research.

The neutral stimulus that eventually comes to be response-producing is called the conditioned stimulus (CS). In this case, the CS is the sound of the bell. The meat powder or food, which even before conditioning elicited the response under investigation, is called the unconditioned stimulus (UCS). When the dog salivates to the presence of the meat powder, the response is called an unconditioned response (UCR). Salivation to the sound of the bell is called a conditioned response (CR).

3.4   In Pavlov's experiment, how might the dog show an orienting response (OR)?

When the dog has just been introduced to the research setting, the first presentations of the bell may produce turning or looking (searching) responses from the dog. Such responses are called orienting responses and usually last for a few trials, until the animal is acclimated to the testing arrangement.

3.5   Is the classical conditioning model of learning widely accepted by psychologists? Do psychologists generally agree on why classical conditioning procedures work?

The classical conditioning paradigm may be one of the most widely accepted models of learning. Psychologists have successfully used classical conditioning procedures with a wide variety of subjects and behaviors—from Pavlov's conditioning of physiological response (salivation) in dogs to later experiments in which verbal responses have been classically conditioned in human subjects. However, explanations of why classical conditioning takes place vary. For example, most psychologists believe that reinforcement is necessary for the establishment of an S-R bond, but Edward Tolman (see Chapter 2) did not. Tolman proposed instead that learning involved the establishment of S-S bonds, and he played down the importance of reinforcements.

3.6   Is the CR a substitute response for the UCR?

Early explanations of classical conditioning viewed the CR as a direct substitute for the UCR. However, subsequent research showed this was an inaccurate interpretation. The generally accepted concepts now are that the CR represents a component of the UCR or an anticipatory response made before the onset of the UCS. It is probably best to describe the CR as the same type of response as the UCR, rather than the same as the UCR.

3.7   What is an alpha response? If such a response occurred in the procedure used by Pavlov (described in the problems above), what research method could be used to distinguish between the alpha response and the conditioned response?

An alpha response is an orienting response made to the conditioned stimulus which happens to be in the same response system as the response being studied. In order to dissipate the effects of the alpha response and permit observation of the conditioned response, the researcher will repeatedly present the conditioned stimulus alone before beginning the CS-UCS pairings, until the alpha response is reduced considerably or no longer occurs. This is called habituation of the response.

3.8   What is sensitization?

In some cases, even if the alpha response has been subjected to the habituation procedure, a single presentation of the CS-UCS pairing may be sufficient to reinstate the alpha response. Such augmentation of the alpha response is called sensitization.

In a more general sense, sensitization refers to the increase in the tendency of the organism to reinstate the alpha response once a CS-UCS pairing has occurred. Careful differentiation between alpha responses and CRs is necessary to determine whether or not classical conditioning actually has taken place. This is accomplished by measuring the latency, magnitude, amplitude, or other characteristics of the responses and distinguishing between the two kinds.

3.9   What is pseudo-conditioning?   Why is a pseudo-conditioned response considered different from an alpha response?

When the researcher presents the UCS alone for a number of trials, then introduces the CS alone and observes a response which is similar to the CR, the procedure is called pseudo-conditioning.   There has been no pairing of the CS and UCS, yet the CS elicits a response comparable to the CR.

The pseudo-conditioned response differs from an alpha response in its properties.   The latency, magnitude, and amplitude of a pseudo-conditioned response often are indistinguishable from those same properties for a CR, while such properties for the alpha response usually differ noticeably.

3.10   It has been suggested that the habituation procedure used to account for the alpha response may produce latent inhibition.   What is latent inhibition?   What variables appear to affect latent inhibition?

Latent inhibition refers to the establishment of an inhibitory state which interferes with subsequent conditioning.   This state is produced by the repeated preexposure of the subject to the stimulus which will be used as the CS.

The extent of latent inhibition is influenced by the number of preexposure trials and by the strength of the stimulus during those trials.   The phenomenon appears to be relatively stimulus-specific and does not seem to be influenced appreciably by the time between the preexposure trials and actual conditioning.

3.11   How might a researcher demonstrate sensory preconditioning in the Pavlov design described above?

Sensory preconditioning refers to the transfer of assocations between two CSs before actual conditioning takes place.   In the procedure described above, the researcher would repeatedly pair two stimuli (the bell and a light, for example) before pairing one of them with the UCS.   Once the CR is well established, the experimenter can test to see if sensory preconditioning has taken place: If the second CS, which was never paired with the UCS, elicits the CR, sensory preconditioning has been demonstrated.

3.12   Suppose the experimenter is conditioning human subjects, using a light as the CS, electric shock as the UCS, and the galvanic skin response (or GSR, a measurable change in the electrical resistance of the skin) as the response.   What effect would change in intensity of the CS or UCS have upon the effectiveness of the conditioning procedure?

Within limits, an increase in the intensity of the CS or the UCS (or both) can be expected to increase the effectiveness of the conditioning procedure.   Limits seem to be reached when the intensity of the stimulation is so great as to create attempts by the subject to escape from the conditioning situation rather than attend to the stimuli.   (*Note:* There is evidence to indicate that contrast is the "key" to intensity, i.e., that the difference between the stimulus and its background determines the stimulus effectiveness.   Thus, the interruption of a continuous tone could be just as effective a CS as the onset of a tone.)

3.13   In the Pavlovian experiments described above, what procedure would be used to illustrate extinction?

Extinction is the term used to describe both a process and the result of that process.   In the Pavlovian experiments, the procedure would be to present the CS alone repeatedly.   The expected result would be that the CR would diminish, returning to its original (preconditioning) level.

3.14   What would occur if the dogs in Pavlov's experiment show spontaneous recovery of the CR?

Following extinction and a period of rest (that is, no exposure to any aspect of the conditioning situation), the CS is introduced again.   If the dogs show the salivary response (CR), spontaneous recovery of the response is said to have occurred.   (Note that this takes place without any further presentation of the UCS once extinction has begun.)

3.15   How would a test for stimulus generalization be conducted using the Pavlovian procedure?

Stimulus generalization is the term used to describe the circumstances in which the subject responds not only to the original stimulus but to other, similar stimuli.   In this situation, the dogs would hear a bell of a different tone.   If they show the CR, stimulus generalization has been shown.

3.16   Why would the stimulus generalization shown by the dogs almost *have* to be primary stimulus generalization rather than secondary stimulus generalization?

Secondary stimulus generalization is demonstrated when a subject responds not only to the original stimulus but also to other similar stimuli because the stimuli are alike in learned meaning.   Thus, secondary stimulus generalization usually depends upon knowledge of language, a uniquely human characteristic.   (Although there is some evidence for language learning in lower organisms, it is very limited and very unlikely to be a part of this generalization situation.)

Primary stimulus generalization involves responding not only to the original stimulus but also to other similar stimuli because of the similarity of physical properties of the stimuli.   Such is the case here, with the dogs responding to the similar tones of the bells.

3.17   What is response generalization?   Give an example to illustrate the phenomenon.

Response generalization occurs when a subject gives not only the originally conditioned response to a stimulus but other similar or equivalent responses as well.   For example, a person may be conditioned to respond to the greeting "Hello" by saying "Hello" in return.   Response generalization can then be shown if the same person responds to the stimulus "Hello" with equivalent but not identical greetings—such as saying "Hi" or "How are you?" or by waving and smiling.

3.18   What term would be used to label the situation if the dogs in Pavlov's experiment do *not* respond to a similar-sounding bell?

Assuming the dogs' responses have not been extinguished, it can be presumed they are able to tell the difference between the original stimulus (CS) and the new stimulus.   This is called differentiation (or discrimination)—that is, responding to the original stimulus, but not to similar stimuli.

3.19   Describe the most frequently used general measures of the conditioned response.

While many different responses may be used as CRs in classical conditioning experiments, there are several properties of these responses which are most frequently measured.   These include amplitude, magnitude, frequency, latency, and resistance to extinction.   The amplitude of a response is the differential between a baseline (or resting-state) measure of the response and the measured value of the CR.   *Magnitude* also describes the size of the response.   Amplitude and magnitude differ only in that amplitude includes the values from all test trials regardless of the presence or absence of the CR, while magnitude is measured only when the CR is present.   The *frequency* is simply a count of the number (or percentage) of CS presentations followed by a measurable CR.   The *latency* of the CR is the time between the onset of the CS and the start of the CR.   (It is assumed that shorter latencies reveal greater strength of conditioning.)   *Resistance to extinction* is measured by determining the number of extinction trials necessary for the CR to diminish or disappear.   It is presumed that the greater the number of extinction trials, the stronger the original conditioning.

3.20   For the experimental design presented in Problem 3.12, what would be the "best" spacing between onset of the CS and onset of the UCS to produce maximum conditioning?   What is this spacing called?

The spacing between the onset of the CS and onset of the UCS is called the interstimulus interval (ISI).   For GSR conditioning, an ISI of 0.4 to 1.25 seconds seems to produce maximum conditioning.

3.21   Suppose the electric shock is followed by the light.   How likely is it that conditioning will take place?   What would this be called?

Following the UCS with the CS is called backward conditioning.   In general, backward conditioning does not produce strong conditioning.   In other words, the later test for a CR to the light would result in little or no responding.

3.22   What are the two forms of forward conditioning?   How do these differ from simultaneous conditioning?

Forward conditioning exists when the onset of the CS precedes the onset of the UCS.   When the CS comes on and goes off before the onset of the UCS, the procedure is called trace conditioning.   If the CS comes on and stays on until after the onset of the UCS, the procedure is called delay conditioning.   In delay conditioning, the termination of the CS and of the UCS often occur at the same time.

Both trace and delay conditioning procedures differ from simultaneous conditioning in that the CS onset precedes the onset of the UCS, while in simultaneous conditioning both stimuli come on at the same moment.

3.23   What is the CS in a temporal conditioning situation?

Temporal conditioning occurs when there is a consistent periodic presentation of a UCS only. The subject apparently comes to recognize the cyclicity or periodicity of these presentations and treats this regular interval of time as a CS, often producing CRs just before the onset of the UCS.

3.24   How is the phenomenon of inhibition of delay somewhat comparable to temporal conditioning?

Inhibition of delay is illustrated when the subject is conditioned using a fairly long ISI.   As the conditioning becomes stronger, the subject seems to suppress (that is, delay or increase the latency of) the CR, usually making the CR just before the onset of the UCS.   This is comparable to temporal conditioning in that the subject appears to learn the appropriate interval for responding.   It differs from temporal conditioning in that there is a CS present in inhibition of delay, whereas time alone serves as the CS for temporal conditioning.   (*Note:* Many researchers believe that the subjects probably experience some sort of collateral behavior, or mediator, which serves as the cue for the time period involved in temporal conditioning.)

3.25   Describe higher-order conditioning.   Why is this procedure seemingly ineffective?

Higher-order conditioning involves the pairing of a previously neutral stimulus with the CS from a well-established classical conditioning CS-UCS pairing.   In effect, this is a CS_2-CS_1 pairing where CS_1 was paired previously with a UCS.

This procedure does not seem to work very well.   The CRs elicited by CS_2 are generally weak and can be extinguished easily.   The explanation for this may be that each CS_2-CS_1 pairing, which serves as a conditioning trial for the CS_2-CR arrangement, is also an extinction trial for CS_1-CR.

3.26   How is the partial-reinforcement effect (PRE) studied using classical conditioning procedures?   What are the general findings in such investigations?

Study of the partial-reinforcement effect (PRE) is accomplished by presenting the CS alone on some of the acquisition trials for one group, then comparing the pattern of extinction results for such a group to that obtained for a group which acquired the CR in a continuous-reinforcement situation (CS-UCS paired on all acquisition trials).   The findings for such studies have been mixed, although the majority of studies do seem to support the PRE; that is, acquisition of response under partial-reinforcement conditions leads to greater resistance to extinction than acquisition in a continuous-reinforcement condition.

3.27   Expand the design first presented in Problem 3.12 to test either simultaneous or serial compound conditioning.

To test compound conditioning, two CSs must be paired with the UCS.   Simultaneous compound conditioning means that both CSs have an identical onset.   Serial compound conditioning means that one of the two CSs has an onset which precedes that of the other, with both coming on before the onset of the UCS.   For the design mentioned, a tone might be introduced in addition to the light, either at the same time (simultaneous) or before or after (serial).   Both stimuli would precede the onset of the electric-shock UCS.

3.28   Would the light or tone be more effective as a CS in the compound-conditioning designs mentioned in the previous problem?

Either the light or the tone might be most effective (that is, show the strongest production of a CR) depending upon the stimulus salience.   In general, the stimulus which is most salient will be one to which the subject attends most, the one placed at the best ISI to produce maximal conditioning, or the one that has had the greatest previous pairing (CS-UCS) exposure.

3.29   What is configuring?   To which early system of psychology does configuring seem most related?

In compound-conditioning situations there are two (or more) conditioned stimuli, CS_1 and CS_2, that have been paired with the UCS.   In some cases the strength of the CR made to CS_1 or to CS_2 individually decreases, while the CR strength increases when both CSs are present.   Such a phenomenon is called configuring, and it seems to confirm the gestaltist idea that an organism may respond with increasing strength to a whole even as its responses to each part of the whole are decreasing in strength.

Key Terms

Alpha response.   An orienting response which is in the same response category as the CR being investigated.

Amplitude of response.   The difference between the preconditioning, baseline value of a response and the measured CR; the value is measured for all trials.   (See also *magnitude of response.*)

Backward conditioning.   In classical conditioning, any trial in which the onset of the UCS precedes the onset of the CS.

Classical conditioning.   An acquisition procedure in which a previously neutral stimulus is paired with a response-producing stimulus until the neutral stimulus elicits the same type of response; also called *respondent conditioning* and *Pavlovian conditioning.*

Compound conditioning.   In classical conditioning, the presentation of more than one CS in the same pairing with the UCS.

Conditioned response (CR). In classical conditioning, the response elicited by the CS; usually similar to the UCR.

Conditioned stimulus (CS). In classical conditioning, the originally neutral stimulus that comes to be response-producing.

Configuring. Maintenance of a high response strength to a compound stimulus, but dissipation of CR value when either CS is presented alone.

Delay conditioning. In classical conditioning, a trial in which the onset of the CS precedes the onset of the UCS, with the CS staying on at least until the occurrence of the UCS.

Differentiation. In classical conditioning, the tendency to respond to the original CS but *not* to similar stimuli.

Discrimination. Another name for *differentiation*.

Extinction. In classical conditioning, the procedure of repeatedly presenting the CS alone (without the UCS) after conditioning; also the result of this procedure, in which the CR returns to its preconditioning value.

Forward conditioning. In classical conditioning, any procedure in which the onset of the CS precedes the onset of the UCS.

Galvanic skin response (GSR). A change in the measured electrical resistance of the skin.

Habituation. The reduction of the tendency to respond to a particular stimulus brought about by repeated presentations of the stimulus.

Higher-order conditioning. In classical conditioning, a procedure in which a new CS is paired with a well-established CS from a previous instance of classical conditioning; the new CS comes to elicit the same type of CR.

Inhibition of delay. The apparent withholding of a CR during the ISI until just before the expected onset of the UCS.

Interstimulus interval (ISI). In classical conditioning, the time between the onset of the CS and the onset of the UCS.

Latency of response. In classical conditioning, the time between the onset of the CS and the beginning of the CR.

Latent inhibition. The increased difficulty in establishing classical conditioning produced by previous habituation using the CS.

Magnitude of response. The difference between the preconditioning, baseline value of a response and the measured CR; the value is measured only for trials where a difference exists.

Orienting response (OR). In classical conditioning, adjustment or reaction responses made to the initial presentations of the CS.

Partial reinforcement. In classical conditioning, occurrence of the UCS on only some of the trials when the CS is presented on all trials during acquisition.

Partial-reinforcement effect (PRE). The finding that responses acquired under partial-reinforcement conditions are more resistant to extinction than responses acquired in continuous-reinforcement conditions.

Primary stimulus generalization. Stimulus generalization based upon the physical similarities between the stimuli.

Pseudo-conditioning. Repeated presentations of the UCS alone before introduction of the CS; this may produce a CR-like response immediately after the initial presentation of the CS.

Response generalization. Responding to the original stimulus not only with the original response, but with other, similar responses.

Secondary stimulus generalization. Stimulus generalization based upon the subject's knowledge of language or some other symbol system.

Sensitization.   The increase of the tendency to respond to a particular stimulus brought about by repeated presentations of the stimulus.

Sensory preconditioning.   Repeated pairings of two potential CSs before one is used in classical conditioning; if afterwards the other stimulus also produces the CR, sensory preconditioning has taken place.

Simultaneous conditioning.   In classical conditioning, a trial in which the onset of the CS and the onset of the UCS occur at the same time; that is, the interstimulus interval equals zero.

Spontaneous recovery.   The recurrence of the CR when the CS alone is presented after a period of rest following extinction.

Stimulus generalization.   In classical conditioning, responding not only to the original CS but to other, similar stimuli as well.

Temporal conditioning.   In classical conditioning, treatment of the time intervals themselves as the CS when the UCS occurs at regular intervals.

Trace conditioning.   In classical conditioning, a trial in which the onset and termination of the CS precede the onset of the UCS.

Unconditioned response (UCR).   In classical conditioning, the response elicited by the UCS.

Unconditioned stimulus (UCS).   In classical conditioning, the stimulus that elicits the desired response on the first and every other trial.

Chapter 4

Instrumental Conditioning

Instrumental conditioning is a learning process that involves manipulating the consequences of a response in such a way as to increase or decrease the probability of that response. Instrumental-conditioning procedures can be used to increase the chances that *instrumental responses* (or goal-oriented responses) will occur. At the same time, the procedure can be used to decrease the likelihood of irrelevant or otherwise undesirable responses.

The manipulation of consequences in an instrumental-conditioning procedure involves the use of reinforcement, which for the moment you may think of as any kind of satisfying condition. Basically, the introduction or continued presence of reinforcement depends on—or is contingent upon—the subject's performance of the desired response. (The terms *reinforcement* and *contingency* are discussed in more detail in Section 4.2.)

Instrumental conditioning is sometimes called *operant conditioning* because the responses involved can be viewed as the subject's operation on the environment in order to secure reinforcement. In addition, instrumental conditioning is also called *Skinnerian conditioning* in recognition of the contributions of the American psychologist B. F. Skinner, who has devoted much of his career to the study of this type of learning.

4.1 BACKGROUND OF INSTRUMENTAL CONDITIONING

In the late 1800s and early 1900s (about the same time Ivan Pavlov was conducting the initial investigations of the classical conditioning paradigm), Edward Thorndike, an American biologist, conducted a series of experiments in which animals learned to escape from a puzzle-box apparatus in order to obtain a food reward placed outside the box. He found that early attempts were marked by much *trial-and-error* behavior—that is, a variety of responses which eventually included a correct response. With repeated trials, however, Thorndike noted that the irrelevant responses tended to drop out, while the successful responses became more and more probable. Although Thorndike did not use the terminology of instrumental conditioning, his experiments were among the first to systematically demonstrate that organisms apparently could learn to associate reinforcement with the performance of a correct response.

At about the same time, the English psychologist W. S. Small built a miniature replica of the garden maze at Hampton Court, England, and measured the time it took white rats to go from the entrance to a reward of food in the middle of the maze. These apparently were the first studies in psychology that used maze-running as an experimental task and the white rat as an experimental subject.

4.2 CHARACTERISTICS OF INSTRUMENTAL CONDITIONING

Reinforcement

As previously indicated, instrumental conditioning occurs when reinforcement is contingent on the performance of a particular response.

Positive reinforcement. A positive-reinforcement situation exists when the presence of a particular stimulus serves to increase or maintain the strength of a response. Positive reinforcers are often called *rewards*.

Negative reinforcement.   A negative-reinforcement situation exists when the removal or absence of a particular stimulus serves to increase or maintain the strength of a response.   (*Note:* The unpleasant or noxious stimulus is *not* the reinforcer; it is called the *aversive stimulus*.   It is the removal or absence of the aversive stimulus which is reinforcing.)   Some psychologists express the parallelism of positive and negative reinforcement by suggesting that the former represents the obtaining of a reward and the latter the securing of relief.

EXAMPLE 1.   In research, probably the most commonly used aversive stimulus is electric shock.   A typical experiment may require a rat to spin a wheel that opens a door and allows the rat to run from the electrified chamber to a "safe," uncharged chamber.   The reinforcement is the relief provided by the escape—a negative reinforcement which strengthens the wheel-spinning and running sequence of responses.

Contingency

Instrumental conditioning requires that an organism make an appropriate response before the reinforcement is delivered.   Such dependence of reinforcement upon the making of a response is called a *contingency* relationship.

EXAMPLE 2.   Recently, the United States government offered physical fitness medals as incentives for participation in various sporting activities.   To receive one of the medals, a person had to perform some response (such as running or swimming) a sufficient number of times to qualify for the medal.   That is, receiving the medal was contingent upon making the appropriate response.

Measures of Response Strength

The most commonly used measure of response strength in instrumental-conditioning situations is *probability of response,* the number of responses per unit of time.   Other measures used frequently are *latency of response* (the time needed for a response to begin) and *total time* of a response (how long it takes to complete a response).

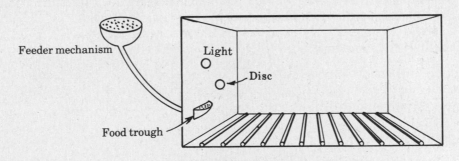

Fig. 4-1

EXAMPLE 3.   Figure 4-1 illustrates an operant-conditioning chamber (popularly known as a Skinner box).   The chamber illustrated here is set up for a pigeon that has been deprived of food and then trained to peck the disc in order to get a food reward.   The strength of the pigeon's disc-pecking response can be measured by a *cumulative recorder,* a device which keeps a continuous entry of the number of responses made per unit of time.   Figure 4-2 illustrates a typical cumulative record.

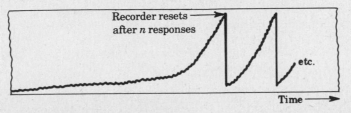

Fig. 4-2

EXAMPLE 4.   A cumulative record of performance for humans might be typified by the common measure of success in learning to type, the number of words typed correctly per minute.   Such a measure allows comparison from one instance to the next, with the assumption being that a greater rate illustrates greater strength of response.

Discriminative Tasks

Any task which requires the organism to make a choice between two or more stimuli in order to obtain reinforcement is called a *discriminative task*.   A stimulus that indicates that the response will lead to reinforcement is labeled S^D.   If the stimulus indicates that the response will not be reinforced, the label S^Δ (S-delta) is used.

When no choice between stimuli is involved in order to obtain reinforcement, the task is labeled nondiscriminative.

EXAMPLE 5.   Refer again to Example 3 and Fig. 4-1.   If the pigeon is rewarded for pecking the disc whether or not the light is on, the task is nondiscriminative.   By using the light in the conditioning chamber, the experimenter can also train the pigeon to perform a discriminative task.   If the disc-pecking response is reinforced with a reward of food only when the light is illuminated, the light serves as S^D.   If the response is reinforced only when the light is off, the illuminated light serves as S^Δ.

EXAMPLE 6.   A traffic light provides a good example of a discriminative task.   Each person must learn that red means stop, that green means go, and that reinforcements will follow responses which reflect this learning.   It can also be pointed out that the red light serves as S^D for stopping behavior but is S^Δ for going responses, while the opposite is true for the green light.

4.3   COMPARISON OF INSTRUMENTAL AND CLASSICAL CONDITIONING

There are two major differences between instrumental and classical conditioning—the production of the response and the identification of the stimuli involved.

Emitted vs. Elicited Responses

In instrumental conditioning there is no UCS which elicits a particular response.   Thus, the responses studied in instrumental conditioning are said to be *emitted* voluntarily by the subjects rather than *elicited* involuntarily from the subjects, as in classical conditioning.

Stimulus Identification

Although some instrumental-conditioning situations involve a discriminative stimulus that signals when responding is appropriate, other instances of instrumental conditioning have no such stimulus.   Regardless of the presence or absence of a discriminative stimulus, psychologists do not interpret the instrumental-conditioning situation as having a clear-cut CS which elicits a response.   In other words, the key relationship in instrumental conditioning is that between response and reinforcement—not the CS-UCS or the CS-CR relationships.

EXAMPLE 7.   Early in his marriage, Alfred discovers that performing small chores such as emptying the garbage or cleaning the car's interior seem to make life run more smoothly, while failing to do so sometimes leads to heated discussions with his wife, Pam.   Such "tidying-up" responses represent voluntarily emitted behavior not attached to any particular stimulus, but rather made in anticipation of reinforcement conditions.

4.4   CONSTRAINTS ON CONDITIONING

There are limitations upon conditioning procedures created by the organism itself.   Almost every organism appears to have innate mechanisms for responding which constrain the range of behavior possible.   These are often species-specific.

EXAMPLE 8. A number of years ago, psychologists attempted to teach a chicken to "play baseball." At first, training went very well. The chicken pulled a chain (bat) and then ran for first base, where feeding took place. The study broke down when a real ball was introduced, however. Once hit, the ball rolled through the apparatus and the chicken chased it, pecking vigorously at the ball in a food-gathering type of response. The chicken's inborn food-getting behavior made completion of the training impossible.

Preparedness

One term suggested to describe the constraints upon conditioning is *preparedness,* or the receptivity of the organism to a particular type of learning. Three different possibilities have been proposed—being *prepared* for a specific learning, being *unprepared* for learning, or being *contraprepared* for learning. The last implies that the organism is in some way prepared *not* to learn the specific task.

4.5 SHAPING

While many instrumental responses are learned in a trial-and-error fashion, others develop as a result of some external guidance. Such guidance is usually summarized by the term *shaping,* which is the reinforcing of closer and closer approximations of the behavior wanted. Shaping is used commonly in experimental situations and, perhaps without direct recognition, in many nonlaboratory settings.

EXAMPLE 9. Many businesses such as animal obedience schools rely heavily upon the principle of shaping. Interestingly, both the owner and the animal are often shaped to perform responses which are appropriate to the success of the training. The owner learns how and when to give commands and reinforcements, while the animal learns the expected behaviors, such as sitting, following, or fetching. In both cases, it can be expected that the performance will improve with appropriate guidance and reinforcement.

4.6 SCHEDULES OF REINFORCEMENT

Partial-reinforcement conditions in instrumental-conditioning circumstances usually are described by various *schedules of reinforcement.* Treated in more depth in Chapters 7 and 8, the basic schedules are presented here.

Schedules of reinforcement may be *fixed* (unchanging) on *variable* (changing from trial to trial). They are also described as *ratio* schedules (with reinforcement based upon the number of responses made) or *interval* schedules (with reinforcement delivered for a correct response made at the end of some amount of time). The various combinations of these four terms produce the names for the following four basic schedules of reinforcement:

Fixed-ratio (FR). Reinforcement is delivered after each completion of a fixed number of responses.

Variable-ratio (VR). Reinforcement is delivered after so many responses are made, but the number required changes from trial to trial, usually averaging some preestablished number over a series of trials.

Fixed-interval (FI). Reinforcement is delivered when the appropriate (instrumental) response is made at the end of a specified period of time. This period of time remains the same for each trial.

Variable-interval (VI). Reinforcement is delivered when the appropriate response is made at the end of a period of time, but that period of time changes from trial to trial. In laboratory studies the time will usually average a preselected interval when several trials are grouped.

EXAMPLE 10. A rat in an operant-conditioning chamber that requires a lever to be pressed for food to be delivered might demonstrate the four basic reinforcement schedules as follows:

FR: The rat must make 10 lever presses before a food pellet will be delivered to the trough. The speed or pattern of responding does not matter, as long as 10 responses are made.

VR: The rat is reinforced after 3, 13, 7, 10, 7, 15, 17, 10, and 5 responses.   While this pattern averages 10 required responses per reinforcement, sometimes fewer are needed, while at other times many more must be made before the reinforcement will be given.

FI: The rat must make one correct response at the end of a 30-second interval.   Responding is not required at any other time during the interval, and the interval never changes.

VI: The rat is reinforced when a correct response is made at the end of 15-, 27-, 45-, 30-, 33-, 10-, 30-, and 50-second intervals.   Although the average time is 30 seconds, the interval may be either shorter or much longer.

Partial-Reinforcement Effect

Just as with classical conditioning, instrumental responses learned under partial-reinforcement conditions prove to be more resistant to extinction than responses acquired in continuous (100-percent) reinforcement conditions.   This is called the *partial-reinforcement effect* (PRE).

EXAMPLE 11.   Autograph collectors often experience VR reinforcement, knowing that the greater the number of attempts to collect an autograph the greater the possibility of succeeding, but never knowing just which attempt will succeed.   As a result, a serious collector will try as often as possible to get autographs, realizing there may be many rebuffs, but continuing because there are the occasional reinforcements.

4.7 EXTINCTION AND SPONTANEOUS RECOVERY

Termination of the response-reinforcement contingency creates *extinction conditions* in an instrumental-conditioning situation.   Eventually it can be expected that the response strength will return to its original, preconditioning level.   In some cases, returning the subject to the conditioning circumstances will be sufficient for *spontaneous recovery* of the response, even when there is no additional reinforcement.

EXAMPLE 12.   When young Darlene was learning to speak, her parents realized very quickly that she was saying "There's four fingers" or "There's two feet."   Darlene's parents were especially careful not to reinforce such comments and encouraged her to use the grammatically correct "There are . . ." form.   About the time Darlene seemed to have mastered her numbers, she also appeared to have learned the correct form for matching singular or plural subjects and predicates.   The parents' training illustrates extinction of the incorrect response.

4.8 GENERALIZATION AND DIFFERENTIATION

In discriminative instrumental-conditioning tasks, the subject may be tested to determine whether or not the response will be made to some different, but similar, discriminative cue.   If the subject does respond, *stimulus generalization* has been demonstrated.   If no response is shown, *differentiation* is said to have occurred.

EXAMPLE 13.   Out for a walk one day, Darlene (Example 12) and her parents see a huge flock of birds overhead.   Darlene's parents ask her how many birds she sees.   Her response of "There's so many, I can't count them" illustrates both spontaneous recovery and stimulus generalization.

4.9 OTHER CONSIDERATIONS
IN INSTRUMENTAL CONDITIONING

Researchers have been concerned with several other areas relating to instrumental conditioning.   Some of the most important are presented here.

Superstitious Behavior

In certain circumstances, reinforcement will follow a particular response even though there is no contingency relationship between the response and the reinforcement.   Called a *noncontingent reinforcement,* this sequence may result in the establishment of *superstitious behavior.* Apparently the subject comes to believe that making the particular response is necessary for (or contributory to) the delivery of the reinforcement. Although such a relationship does not really exist, occasional occurrences of the reinforcement following the response may create partial-reinforcement conditions, making the superstitious behavior very resistant to extinction.

EXAMPLE 14. Driving to the dock to begin a fishing trip, Clarence follows a particular route. That day, fishing is extraordinarily good and Clarence is overjoyed. He associates his route with the fishing success and therefore is very careful to follow exactly the same route at the start of subsequent trips. While the route has no effect upon the fishing, Clarence's belief results in superstitious behavior.

Learned Helplessness

If an organism has been exposed to an uncontrollable aversive stimulus, later performance in circumstances where control could be exercised sometimes shows the organism's inability to learn or perform the controlling response. This inability has come to be called *learned helplessness.*

EXAMPLE 15. Statements such as "My vote doesn't count" probably represent a form of learned helplessness. When previous situations have led to apparently inescapable aversive conditions, such as the continuation of tax increases, the person may simply give up any hope of controlling the incidents and stop responding.

Biofeedback

It is possible to use monitoring devices to reveal the status of internal bodily reactions which would otherwise remain unobserved. Such procedures are referred to by the general term *biofeedback.*

Subjects can be taught to interpret the information provided by the monitoring equipment. Once having learned this, they can then attempt to control the internal reactions and will receive reinforcement in the form of observed changes as revealed by the monitoring equipment. This procedure is analogous to other instrumental-conditioning situations in that a contingency develops between the controlling responses and the information provided as biofeedback.

EXAMPLE 16. Biofeedback has practical applications, such as helping people with chronic headaches overcome their difficulties. Wired to appropriate sensing devices, such sufferers can learn to observe and interpret characteristics such as muscle tension or blood flow, then practice responses which will help alleviate these problems, thus reducing the headache symptoms.

Solved Problems

4.1 Thorndike's experiments using animals in puzzle-box situations illustrate trial-and-error behavior. What are such responses? Are they representative of instrumental conditioning?

Trial-and-error behavior consists of seeking a successful response, eliminating those that do not work, and refining those that do. In Thorndike's studies, the animals had to find ways to open a door to gain access to a visible food reward. At first, many different responses were tried, but later trials were characterized by repetition of those responses which had proved successful. Thus trial-and-error learning is representative of instrumental conditioning, which by definition exists in situations where obtaining reinforcement is contingent upon the organism's behavior.

4.2 What is the meaning of reinforcement?

In instrumental conditioning, reinforcement is any event which increases or maintains the strength of response.

4.3   In Problem 4.1, it was stated that reinforcement was contingent upon behavior. What does this mean? What measure of response is used to determine whether or not a contingency relationship has been established?

Contingency means that the reinforcement is not available to the organism unless and until an appropriate response (or sequence of responses) is made. In the puzzle-box situation described above, the animal might find many different ways for depressing the lever or pulling the chain to open the door, but the reinforcement (food) would not be accessible until one of the responses was made.

In instrumental-conditioning situations the measure of response strength most frequently used is probability of response, measured as the rate of responding per unit of time. Greater probability implies a stronger contingency relationship. (The latency of response or the total time for a response to be completed are used in some studies, however.)

4.4   Suppose the subject (a white rat) is learning to press a lever in order to turn off an electric shock. What type of contingency relationship is being established in such a situation? Is it comparable to that illustrated by the Thorndike puzzle-box studies?

The reinforcement in this situation is called a negative reinforcement; that is, the *removal* of the aversive stimulus (electric shock) is the event which strengthens or maintains the strength of the lever-pressing response. This is comparable to the contingency relationship illustrated in the Thorndike puzzle-box experiments except that the reinforcement used is a negative reinforcement rather than a positive reinforcement. (The delivery of food is a stimulus which when present increases or maintains the strength of the response.)

4.5   Is it possible for instrumental responses to be contingent upon stimuli that are not, in and of themselves, reinforcing?

Instrumental responses can be contingent on nonreinforcing stimuli. For example, the animals in the puzzle-box experiments could be presented with a cue stimulus (such as the onset of a light) which would indicate that pressing the lever or pulling the chain would result in a reward. Such situations are described as discriminative tasks. The stimulus indicates the occasion for making a successful response.

4.6   Does the cue stimulus such as the one described in Problem 4.5 serve the same function as an unconditioned stimulus in a classical conditioning situation?

The cue stimulus in discriminative instrumental conditioning does not serve the same purpose as the unconditioned stimulus in classical conditioning. While the cue stimulus indicates an appropriate time for a response to be made it does not elicit (that is, force) a response. In classical conditioning the UCS elicits a response, and thus the sequence of events is independent of the subject's behavior; in instrumental conditioning the reinforcement is dependent (contingent) on the subject's behavior.

4.7   Would the cue stimulus described in Problem 4.5 be labeled S^D or S^Δ?

The cue stimulus would be labeled S^D because the presence of the stimulus (the light) indicates that making the appropriate response will result in the delivery of reinforcement.

4.8   In addition to that described in Problem 4.6, is there any other characteristic which distinguishes instrumental conditioning from classical conditioning?

When comparing classical conditioning with nondiscriminative instrumental conditioning, a second distinction can be found. The clear-cut conditioned stimulus (CS) of classical conditioning is readily identified as response-eliciting once acquisition has occurred. No such CS can be recognized in the nondiscriminative instrumental-conditioning situation, yet the appropriate response frequently will be learned and produced without apparent cue or prompting. (Even in discriminative tasks, the S^D is not thought to force or elicit a response.)

4.9   In a study attempting to train raccoons to deposit two tokens in an apparatus in order to get fed, the experimenters found that instead of performing the desired response, the raccoons would dip and rub the tokens as if preparing to eat.   This behavior illustrates what aspect of response acquisition?

        Raccoons' feeding behavior is always accompanied by "washing" responses before the food is actually consumed. In this experiment, the tokens were treated as if they were food, creating a response pattern incompatible with the desired acquisition. Such a situation demonstrates that there may be innate constraints upon a conditioning situation, restricting the patterns of responses which may be learned. In this case, the species-specific food-obtaining responses make response acquisition impossible. Other circumstances may produce constraints on utilizing cues or consuming rewards.

4.10   A principle somewhat comparable to constraints upon conditioning is that of preparedness. What is this? What varieties appear to exist?

        Preparedness refers to an organism's tendency to be able to react to stimulus situations or produce given responses based upon that organism's evolutionary history. It has been suggested that any one organism may be (1) prepared to receive stimuli or respond, (2) unprepared to do so, or in some cases (3) actually contraprepared (that is, predisposed *not* to react or respond). Success of a conditioning procedure may therefore be a function of the preparedness level of the organism.

4.11   Describe how a parent might shape a child's good manners (for example, saying "please").

        Shaping is the process of reinforcing closer and closer approximations of a desired response. In this situation, the parent might combine modeling (see Chapter 5) and reward training to condition the "please" response. First approximations might include prompting ("Say please") along with acceptance of anything somewhat like the desired response (e.g., "peas"). Later reward would be given only in unprompted situations where the word was used correctly. The word "please" serves the instrumental purpose of leading to reward.

4.12   It is likely that once the "please" response has been learned the child will experience any number of occasions where "please" will be said but no reinforcement will be immediately forthcoming. At other times the good manners will "work," in terms of reinforcement being delivered. What term describes this situation? What effect can be expected?

        Being reinforced for some but not all the responses being made illustrates partial reinforcement. The expected result is that the "please" response will become more resistant to extinction than if it had been continuously reinforced. This is called the partial-reinforcement effect (PRE). (*Note:* It is unlikely that such a response would ever be subjected to complete extinction, therefore making it equally unlikely that the PRE would actually be evident with such a response.)

4.13   Because it is probable that the reinforcing conditions described in the previous two problems would be irregular, one of the basic schedules of reinforcement best labels the conditions. Which one is it?

        Such reinforcement conditions are most likely to be representative of a variable interval (VI) schedule. The parents probably reinforce the child for assorted responses without fixing either the number of responses made or a specific (regular) time interval between responses.

4.14   Describe the basic schedules of reinforcement other than variable-interval.

        There are three other basic schedules of reinforcement in addition to variable-interval (VI). They are fixed-ratio (FR), fixed-interval (FI) and variable-ratio (VR) schedules.

        Fixed-ratio schedules require a constant number of responses be made for delivery of each reinforcement. Reinforcement depends upon the making of a correct response at the end of a specified, regular time period in fixed-interval schedules. Reinforcement in a variable-ratio schedule depends upon the number of responses made, but the number required changes from one instance to the next.

4.15   What conditions are necessary to test extinction in instrumental-conditioning situations?

An instrumental response is defined as one which leads to reinforcement. A permanent break of this relationship creates extinction conditions, in which the response no longer ever leads to the reinforcement.

4.16   If an instrumental response has been extinguished, will spontaneous recovery of the response be demonstrated?

Assuming the subject conditioned has had some period of rest following extinction and is then reintroduced into the conditioning situation, spontaneous recovery may occur. Just as in classical conditioning, however, it is likely that the response will not be as strong as it was when first conditioned.

4.17   How can stimulus generalization be demonstrated in an instrumental-conditioning situation?

To demonstrate stimulus generalization in instrumental conditioning, it is necessary to establish a response made in the presence of a discriminative cue. The test for generalization is then made by determining the probability of response in the presence of a different, but similar, discriminative stimulus. (*Note:* In nondiscriminative instrumental-conditioning situations, where there are no readily identifiable stimuli which cue or elicit the response, tests for stimulus generalization would be meaningless.)

4.18   Having lived for several years in an apartment building which had a buzzer system for entry (ring the bell, wait for a return buzz, then push the door in order to enter), three-year-old Gardner and his family have moved into a private house. At first, Gardner is quite upset when he finds that ringing the doorbell does not lead to an answering buzz, nor can he simply push the door to enter. Using the terminology of instrumental conditioning, describe the conditions which have led to Gardner's distress.

While living in the apartment building, Gardner learned an instrumental response sequence which allowed him access into his home. This sequence included being able to differentiate between buzz and no-buzz conditions and making the pushing response to the appropriate discriminative cue. Now Gardner is confronted with a new set of conditions. The old response will have to be extinguished, the discriminative cue will no longer be present, and he will have to learn to turn a doorknob before trying to open the door.

4.19   In a recent youth golf tournament, the winner was described as the best player, but the worst dressed, because he insisted upon wearing a dirty, torn visor and an old glove full of holes. When asked why, his response was "I wore these when I won the high school championship. I guess I'll just keep wearing them until I lose." Explain what principle of instrumental conditioning is shown by such behavior.

This golfer's actions illustrate superstitious behavior. The reinforcement of winning has followed the response of dressing in a particular manner. Although there is no contingency between the pattern of dress and the performance, the player believes there is and thus continues to make the same response sequence. Because such superstitious responses are occasionally followed by reinforcements, the partial-reinforcement effect may occur and the responses may become very resistant to extinction.

4.20   How does the principle of learned helplessness explain the behavior of prisoners of war who become lethargic and apathetic rather than resisting or attempting to escape?

  Learned helplessness suggests that once an organism has experienced what is interpreted as an inescapable aversive stimulus, it will be less able to perform appropriate responses even when an obvious opportunity presents itself. In the prisoner of war situation, those who continue to resist apparently do not see the circumstances as uncontrollable, while those who give up believe that control is impossible.

4.21   How does biofeedback represent an instrumental-conditioning situation?

  Biofeedback is a procedure using monitoring devices to reveal to the subject internal processes that would not otherwise be readily observed. With biofeedback, the observed changes of the internal processes may serve as reinforcers, and the subject performs a self-shaping procedure, learning responses which give greater and greater control over the monitored internal process.

Key Terms

Aversive stimulus.   Any stimulus an organism judges to be noxious or unpleasant.

Biofeedback.   The use of a monitoring device to tell a subject the status of certain of his or her physiological processes not otherwise easily observed.

Contingency.   In instrumental conditioning, the requirement that certain responses be made before reinforcement can occur.

Cumulative recorder.   The device used to tally the number of acceptable responses made in a given unit of time.

Fixed schedules of reinforcement.   Partial-reinforcement schedules that remain unchanged.

Instrumental conditioning.   An acquisition procedure that involves manipulating the consequences of a response in order to alter the probability of that response; also called *operant conditioning* and *Skinnerian conditioning.*

Instrumental response.   A goal-oriented response.

Interval schedules of reinforcement.   Partial-reinforcement schedules in which reinforcement is contingent upon a response being made at the end of a given time period.

Learned helplessness.   The acceptance of what are interpreted as unalterable consequences of a situation, even when a countering response is possible.

Negative reinforcement.   A type of event in which the removal or termination of some stimulus serves as a reinforcer.

Noncontingent reinforcement.   Reinforcement that follows a response but is not contingent upon that response.

Operant-conditioning chamber.   An apparatus used for experimental investigations of instrumental conditioning; often called a *Skinner box.*

Partial reinforcement.   In instrumental conditioning, the delivery of reinforcement following some, but not all, instrumental responses.

Partial-reinforcement effect (PRE).   The finding that responses acquired under partial-reinforcement conditions are more resistant to extinction than responses acquired under continuous-reinforcement conditions.

Positive reinforcement.   A type of event in which the presence of some stimulus serves as a reinforcer.

Preparedness.   The receptivity of an organism to a particular acquisition procedure; an inherited tendency to respond or an inherited constraint against responding.

Ratio schedules of reinforcement. Partial-reinforcement schedules in which reinforcement is contingent upon the number of responses made.

Reinforcer. Any event which increases or maintains the strength of a response.

Schedules of reinforcement. Ways of arranging partial reinforcement in instrumental-conditioning situations.

Shaping. Reinforcing closer and closer approximations of a desired behavior.

Superstitious behavior. Performance of specific responses in the expectation of reinforcement when in fact there is no contingency.

Variable schedules of reinforcement. Partial-reinforcement schedules that can change, usually around some average value.

Chapter 5

Modeling

Learning by modeling involves the observation of some pattern for behaving, which is followed later by performance of that or some similar behavior. The *model* being observed may be either another person or any representation of a pattern for response. This includes humans, animals, and symbolic representations using verbal stimuli, television, movies, or other media.

EXAMPLE 1. Because of their command of language, humans are able to model behaviors without actually observing someone else making the response. For example, one person can successfully negotiate a complicated trip by using verbal directions given by another, even without seeing that other person make the trip. Told to take "Jackson Pike until you cross over the Interstate, then turn left on County Road 10 and go about half a mile to the farm," one can follow the directions easily and find the farm selling fresh strawberries.

5.1 LABELS FOR MODELING

Because psychologists have emphasized different aspects of the process of learning by modeling, the phenomenon has come to be labeled in a number of different ways. Some of the most frequently used are presented here.

Imitation Learning

Learning by modeling is called *imitation learning* when stress is placed on the copying aspects of the behavior. In some instances, responses may be copied exactly, but without understanding. Such modeling is referred to as *pure imitation*.

EXAMPLE 2. Pure imitation is often shown by amateur athletes. For example, beginning golfers often try to line up putts, even when they do not know what they should be looking for—how to compensate for the "roll" of the green. Likewise, children playing baseball may tap the flat soles of their sneakers with the bat just before stepping up to the plate. In such cases the children may be imitating the actions of professional players, who often use the bat to knock dirt from their cleated shoes before they step up to hit. In both cases the responses are copies of those postures and gestures that the successful professional athlete has shown.

Observational Learning

When learning by modeling is called *observational learning,* the emphasis is on attention to the stimulus environment. Factors which affect perception are studied to determine influences on attention to (and therefore observation of) the model.

Social Learning

Social learning theory (sometimes abbreviated SLT) accentuates the role played by interpersonal relations on learning by modeling. Explanations centering around social learning theory are used quite frequently in discussions of the development of personality characteristics.

Vicarious Learning

When the observer is able to determine not only the model's pattern of action but also the consequences of the actions, the term *vicarious learning* is used. The consequences of the action pattern help determine whether or not the behavior will be modeled.

EXAMPLE 3. Modeling of shoplifting may be initiated by vicarious learning. One person observes a peer sneak some piece of merchandise from a store without paying and then enjoy that product. This appears to be reinforcing, and the observer may believe that he or she will enjoy comparable reinforcements by imitating the behavior.   Of course if the observer sees the shoplifter get caught, subsequent modeling will be much less likely.

5.2   COMPARISON WITH OTHER FORMS OF LEARNING

Learning by modeling does not involve forcing (eliciting) a response, nor is the response being learned attached to any particular stimulus (CS).   Thus, learning by modeling is significantly different from classical conditioning.

Some psychologists have interpreted the modeled response as an instrumental response (an operant), suggesting that the observation is a necessary condition for learning by modeling, but not sufficient by itself; they stress the necessity of reinforcement.   This point is controversial, however; other psychologists analyze the effect of reinforcement as motivating and therefore contributory to (but not necessary for) learning by modeling.   Whether or not one interprets modeling as a kind of instrumental conditioning, however, research has shown that reinforced modeled responses are more likely to become part of the behavioral repertoire than those which are not reinforced.

Reinforcements Associated with Modeling

There are several forms of reinforcement which appear to be quite common in learning by modeling.   One of the most frequent is *reinforcement by the model;* that is, the model observes the imitative responses made by the observer and reinforces these.

EXAMPLE 4.   Parents frequently provide reinforcement by the model.   For instance, the father who sees his son trying to imitate snow-shoveling responses may pause and praise the child by saying, "That's the way, just like Daddy.   That's very good!"

Self-reinforcement often may also serve as a reinforcer in learning by modeling.   The observer succeeds in copying a response and experiences an "internal" sense of reward.   And in other situations the observer may recognize and perhaps identify with the reinforcement experienced by the model.   This type of situation is called *vicarious reinforcement.*   Research indicates that vicarious reinforcement may play an important part in helping establish a new, previously untrained response, but probably will not be enough without additional reinforcement to maintain that response over a long period of time.

There is also some evidence to indicate that being modeled is reinforcing.   In other words, the model experiences reinforcement by seeing the observer imitating a response.   This may serve to increase the probability of the response for the model.

EXAMPLE 5.   The conductor of a symphony orchestra introduces an unusual and rather dramatic gesture into her pattern of conducting.   While serving as a judge at a music fair, the conductor notices that some of the student conductors mimic the response.   She finds this quite reinforcing and, as a result, becomes even more likely to use the pattern in subsequent concerts.

5.3   TYPES OF MODELING

Learning by modeling can be divided into two general categories—direct sensory experiences (images) and verbal representations (ideas).

Sensory Modeling

If the exposure to the modeling stimuli seems to lead to the association of sequences of sensory experiences, *sensory modeling* is said to have occurred.   The contiguity of stimulus sequences is integrated into the behavior as direct sensory-sensory conditioning.

Verbal Modeling

When words (or in some cases other symbols) are used to stand for the actual sensory experiences, *verbal modeling* has taken place. Such verbal cues may be provided by the model or created by the observer.

EXAMPLE 6. In Example 1, the instructions for finding the strawberry farm represent externally provided verbal modeling. If the person involved finds a shortcut and decides upon a different route, a subsequent thought such as "I'll take the Westbrook Road shortcut" would be an internally created verbal model.

Live vs. Symbolic Modeling

Modeling may also be classified in terms of the presence or absence of the model. *Live modeling* means that the model is actually present in the observer's environment. *Symbolic modeling* refers to any situation where the model is not actually present in the observer's environment. Symbolic modeling may include such examples as television, movies, books, or any other symbolic source of patterns for response which may be copied.

5.4 EFFECTS OF MODELING

The effects of modeling are generally divided into four categories: the modeling effect, inhibition effects, disinhibition effects, and the eliciting effect.

Modeling Effect

When the observer acquires a response that is clearly new or novel and the result of observing some model, the *modeling effect* is said to have occurred.

EXAMPLE 7. Parents of college students have often been known to remark about the behavior of their children with comments such as "Well, she *never* smoked before she went to live in the dormitory with all those other girls!" The acquisition of the smoking behavior is new and, as far as the parents are concerned, the result of their daughter having modeled her behavior after that of others in the dormitory. The parents see this new behavior, smoking, as evidence of the modeling effect.

Inhibition and Disinhibition Effects

Observation of a model's responses and the resultant reinforcement or punishment may produce a change in the frequency of a response for the observer. If the response becomes less likely to be made, *inhibition* has taken place. *Disinhibition* refers to situations where observing the results of the model's response makes the observer's response more likely to occur. These two effects differ from the modeling effect in that novel responses are not necessarily involved.

EXAMPLE 8. The young woman from a conservative midwestern community finds that her new job is going to mean she must move to Italy. She is fortunate to move to a Mediterranean seaside community and looks forward to many days at the beach. Her first few visits to the beach are marked by some discomfort, however. She realizes she is the object of many stares and comments because she is wearing a one-piece swimsuit, and notices that *all* the women regardless of age or figure wear very skimpy bikinis. Although wearing such a suit would be unthinkable "at home," the disinhibition effect occurs and soon she is wearing a bikini and feeling very comfortable about doing so.

Eliciting Effect

Learning by modeling may produce results from observation which have come to be known as the *eliciting effect*. This happens when observation of the model's behavior serves as the stimulus to produce responses which are not novel, but belong to the same class of behaviors.

EXAMPLE 9. The eliciting effect is sometimes shown by the several children in one family. For example, if an older sister has gained some fame and recognition because she has excelled in dramatics, a younger sister may try to gain comparable excellence in musical performance or sports.   This represents the eliciting effect because the response of the younger sister is not new; it does not copy her sister's behavior exactly, but is imitatively related to what the older sister has done.

5.5   MODEL CHARACTERISTICS

The characteristics of the model appear to significantly influence how effective learning by modeling will be.   The two characteristics of the similarity and the status of the model seem to be most important.

Model Similarity

Research evidence indicates that the more similar the model's characteristics are to those of the observer, the more likely it is that learning by modeling will occur.   Attributes such as sex, age, regional background, and the like can be used to determine similarity.

Model Status

Studies also have indicated that models with higher status are more likely to be imitated by the observer than models lacking in status.   *Status* refers to the qualities of value or worth credited to the model.   In general, the more favorable the judgment of the model's values or qualities, the more likely the observer is to model responses.   Status may result from the position or role of the model.   *Position* refers to the job or function or title the model may have.   *Role* describes the actual behavior of the model in his or her position.   Position and role may intertwine, but this is not necessarily the case.

EXAMPLE 10.   Workers in a small business firm may recognize that Mr. Ravina has the title of vice-president, but that his assistant, Ms. Flume, actually functions as the leader of the division.   In such a situation, it would be likely that the workers would choose Ms. Flume as a model in preference to Mr. Ravina, basing their choice on role rather than position.

Model Standards

If the model being observed is respected, the observer may incorporate not only the type of response being shown but also the standards for performance shown by the model.   Such modeling may include standards of self-reinforcement or moral standards.

5.6   LIMITATIONS AND CONCERNS OF LEARNING BY MODELING

There are a number of other factors which may influence the success of learning by modeling.   Some of the most important are discussed in this section.

Species Limitation

Learning by modeling may be limited by the response sequences possible for certain species.   In some cases, skills either are available only to certain species or are not readily translated from the behavior of one species to another.

EXAMPLE 11.   Studies attempting to train chimpanzees to speak have generally met with failure.   Although the chimpanzees are seemingly attentive to the model, their response capability is limited by species membership and simply does not allow for vocal speech.   On the other hand, chimpanzees *have* shown an ability to learn to converse with American Sign Language, a gestural rather than vocal language.

Response Complexity

In general, investigations have shown that learning by modeling is more difficult or requires more time or practice when sophisticated or complex response sequences are being learned than when the response is relatively simple.   This finding is comparable to research results using other learning forms.

Motivation

The effect of motivation upon learning by modeling is the same as that for other forms of learning: performance can be expected to follow the inverted-U curve when related to level of motivation (see Section 1.2).

One interesting aspect of learning by modeling is that modeled responses may serve as internal sources of motivation.   The term *self-arousal* is used to describe this effect.   (See also the discussion of *functional autonomy* in Chapter 17.)

Lack of Interest in Modeling

Traditionally, the psychology of learning has concentrated upon stimulus-response (S-R) formats for explaining the acquisition of responses.   Early investigations of classical conditioning and instrumental-conditioning phenomena appeared to account for much behavior acquisition, and the vigorous positions adopted by the leading psychologists of the day helped establish the importance of both viewpoints.   Only since the 1960s has research into learning by modeling expanded the interest of the psychology of learning to include this learning form.   (Return to Chapter 2 and you will notice that the history of the psychology of learning emphasized S-R positions of people like Watson, Hull, and Skinner.)   Starting in the late 1950s, research by Albert Bandura and others initiated expanded interest into learning by modeling.

Solved Problems

5.1   What is the basic premise of learning by modeling?   Why are there so many different labels for this phenomenon?

The basis of learning by modeling is that a subject observing some pattern for behaving may later perform the same or a similar action or sequence of actions.   Learning of this type has been given several different names because of the differing emphases stressed by psychologists when trying to explain the phenomenon.

5.2   What are the most common labels used to describe learning by modeling?   Indicate the emphasis of each.

Other than learning by modeling, which stresses the presence of a model to be copied, the other terms most often used are imitation learning, observational learning, social learning, and vicarious learning.   "Imitation" emphasizes the copying aspect of this learning, while "observation" stresses the attention-perception component.   "Social learning" points out the importance of the observer's relation to the model in determining which behaviors will be learned and exhibited.   "Vicarious learning" involves not only observing some other's response, but also observing the consequences of that behavior; the emphasis is on the observation of the effects of a response rather than the response itself.

5.3   How does learning by modeling compare with classical conditioning?

Because it involves neither eliciting of the response nor any specific stimulus attached to the response being learned, learning by modeling is considered totally different from classical conditioning.

5.4   How does learning by modeling compare with instrumental conditioning?

Many psychologists interpret the response in learning by modeling as being operant in nature; that is, the learning of the response results from observation of a model but depends upon some sort of contingency between the response and a reinforcement. Others believe that reinforcement serves only as a motivating condition and that the imitated response gets into the behavior pattern simply because it is observed, *not* because it is reinforced. This is a debate which has yet to be resolved, although a reinforced imitated response is more likely to stay in the behavior pattern than one that is not reinforced.

5.5   Suppose Elmer is teaching his daughter Emily how to throw a ball. Elmer is very careful to explain the appropriate motions and goes through the throwing motion a number of times so that Emily can observe what is expected. Emily then actually throws a ball, hitting a target her father has set up. What types of reinforcement is she likely to experience?

Elmer will probably reinforce Emily, perhaps with praise and a pat on the back. In other words, Emily is reinforced directly by the model. It is probably also true that Emily will experience some reinforcement from the actual consequences of the behavior; that is, she will feel reinforced by seeing the ball hit the target.

5.6   How do the reinforcements Emily experiences in Problem 5.5 differ from vicarious reinforcement?

Emily's reinforcements are actually experienced by her. Vicarious reinforcement occurs when the observer notes the reinforcement experienced by the model. In a sense, vicarious reinforcement is a kind of second-hand reinforcement.

5.7   What does research indicate about reinforcement conditions and the behavior of the model being imitated?

There is some evidence to indicate that being imitated serves as a reinforcement. Therefore, the model may be more likely to perform the modeled response again in the future. The increase in probability of the modeled response represents instrumental conditioning with imitation serving as the reinforcer.

5.8   There is a tendency to think of models as people. What is a more general definition of model?

It is really most appropriate to define a model as any representation of a pattern for behaving. Thus, while humans often do serve as models, it is possible that animals, books, instructions, directions, television, movies, and many other sources may serve as models.

5.9   In a most general sense, learning by modeling can be said to involve "images" or "ideas." Explain the difference between these two concepts.

Modeling may occur either through contiguity of stimuli, where sequences of sensory experiences become integrated into behavior, or through verbal descriptions, where labels describe responses rather than recall sensory sequences. The former represents "image" learning, while the latter denotes "idea" learning. (*Note:* Verbal labels may be externally provided or internally created.)

5.10   Trying to explain what it was like to visit Uncle Mark's farm, young Elizabeth remarks about all the new and different noises she heard. She tries to squeal like the pigs, but finds she cannot imitate the sound. What principle does Elizabeth's difficulty seem to illustrate?

        Learning by modeling is to some extent limited by species membership. Some behaviors may be truly species-specific, while others may be more easily performed by certain species. In this case, Elizabeth is not capable of squealing. A very noticible species limitation is illustrated by language development. Humans can model using abstract verbal concepts, but other species cannot.

5.11   In Problem 5.5, Elmer both tells and shows Emily how to throw the ball. Distinguish between the two aspects of Elmer's behavior.

        The verbal representation of the throwing behavior can be called symbolic modeling, while the actual demonstration of throwing would be labeled live modeling.

5.12   Give an example of the kind of imitative responding Emily might have to show to illustrate pure imitation.

        Suppose Emily watches her father throw and miss the target. Upon missing, Elmer might shout an expletive. Although Emily does not understand the meaning of the word, she might later show pure imitation by using the same expletive in a similar circumstance.

5.13   During the worst winter weather, June's neighbor uses the plow on his four-wheel-drive vehicle to clear her driveway, those of several other people on the street, and much of the street itself. June feels this is so generous that she in turn bakes a big batch of cookies and takes them to the neighbor. June's generous response represents which effect of modeling?

        June's behavior demonstrates the eliciting effect. The model (her neighbor) is responsible for her response which is neither novel nor exactly imitative, but is related to the model's response.

5.14   Therapists frequently use models when trying to help patients overcome particular fears. If a claustrophobic patient is shown films (or actual live modeling) of a person behaving normally in an enclosed space, what effect of modeling is being sought?

        Such a procedure aims for a disinhibition effect. It is hoped that the claustrophobic patient will copy the successful performance of the model, thus coping with the fear.

5.15   Why have conditions such as plea-bargaining, probation, and suspended sentences reduced the inhibition effect expected from criminal trials?

        A premise of criminal law has been that the punished person serves as a model for inhibition of the behavior being punished. However, when the punishment does not seem adequate for the crime, the "crime does pay" reaction can develop. (*Note:* A second contributory factor in this situation could be what psychologists call *compartmentalization,* the separating of aspects of one's life. Thus, a person may read about others being arrested, tried and convicted, but react with an "it can't happen to me" feeling.)

5.16   A famous series of studies exposed young children to models making novel aggressive responses toward an inflated doll. Later, the children were tested for evidence of these aggressive responses. Which effect of modeling was being studied?

        Acquisition of novel responses in this manner is called the modeling effect. This occurs when the responses being learned are clearly novel (that is, new for the subject) and the result of observation. In these studies the children who were exposed to the aggressive models became almost twice as aggressive toward the doll afterward.

5.17   In an attempt to encourage good nutritional habits, the counselors in a school decide to make some videotapes which can be used to provide models for appropriate eating habits.   If the students to be exposed to these tapes are in the primary grades, what should the stimulus properties of the model be?

The models used should have the characteristic of similarity (such as age or similar speech patterns) and/or that of status.   In this situation if a child of primary-school age with status (such as a child television star) could be found, both factors could be combined.

5.18   How does status differ from role or position?

"Position" is the formal or informal title designated for a person's particular function or job.   "Role" is the term used to describe the person's behavior in his or her position.   These two aspects often overlap, though not in all situations.   "Status" implies the worth or value attributed to a person's role and position.   Status may be a function of position—a doctor has high status in the United States—or of role—the leader of a group may have status.   In general, people judged to have high status are more likely to serve as models than those not so judged.

5.19   In a modeling situation, the observer sees the model experience a high level of self-reward.   What behaviors is the observer likely to adopt?

The observer will not only model the observed responses but may also adopt a similar set of self-reward standards.   Such adoption of standards has been demonstrated for moral standards as well.   However, it should be realized that the observer may adopt low standards when the model has high status but shows low standards.

5.20   What effect does complexity of response appear to have upon learning by modeling?

When the skills being observed are quite complex, observers generally show poorer levels of imitation than when simpler skills are modeled.   In other words, just as in other forms of learning, mastery of a complex response requires greater exposure or practice in modeling.

5.21   In Problem 5.17, the counselors would certainly be concerned about how much retention of the "message" the children show.   In addition to careful selection of the model, what other major factor might the counselors concentrate upon?

The counselors would try to be certain the children are highly motivated to learn.   This might be accomplished in many different manners, including anticipated examinations, reward systems, or peer encouragement.   In general, learning by modeling is more successful with increased motivation—up to some relatively high level (the inverted-U curve—see Section 1.2).

5.22   Assume that one of the children in the previous problem begins to model eating responses which represent good nutritional habits.   Indeed, when given a choice between "junk" and "non-junk" foods, the child chooses the latter.   This behavior becomes so important that the child truly feels motivated to act this way.   What term describes this reaction?

The term "self-arousal" describes the child's behavior.   The images or verbal responses that the child has learned serve as motivating stimuli for additional responding, perhaps including new or novel responses.

5.23   Why, historically, has the study of learning by modeling seemed to lag behind study of other forms of learning?

The neglect of modeling by psychologists appears to have resulted from the popularity of classical conditioning and instrumental conditioning paradigms and the forcefulness of their leading proponents.   So much seemed to be explained by these positions that psychologists concentrated upon expanding their understanding of these phenomena (and the S-R viewpoint toward learning in general) while ignoring learning by modeling. Research beginning in the late 1950s has helped to popularize learning by modeling.

Key Terms

Disinhibition effect. In modeling, an increased likelihood that observation of the model's response and the consequences of that response will lead the observer to make a comparable response.

Eliciting effect. In modeling, the tendency for observation of the model's response to stimulate the observer to make responses from the same class of behaviors, although these responses are not new or novel.

Inhibition effect. In modeling, a decreased likelihood that the observer will make a comparable response following observation of the model's response and the consequences of that response.

Live modeling. One organism observing and copying a behavior of another organism that is physically present.

Modeling. The observation and subsequent incorporation and display of a response or response sequence; other names for modeling are "imitation learning," "observational learning," "social learning," and "vicarious learning."

Modeling effect. Acquisition of a new or novel response as the result of observing some model.

Position. In modeling, the designation or title of the model's job or function.

Pure imitation. The exact modeling of a response without understanding.

Role. In modeling, the actual behavior patterns of the model.

Self-arousal. In modeling, motivation that arises from the observation and retention of the behavior of others.

Sensory modeling. Direct recognition and imitation of sensory experiences; modeling based upon images.

Social learning theory (SLT). A theory of learning that accentuates interpersonal relationships between observer and model.

Status. In modeling, qualities of value or worth credited to the model.

Symbolic modeling. Copying the behavior of a model that is not actually present and observed.

Verbal modeling. Use of word cues to suggest the responses to be made; modeling based upon understanding of ideas.

Vicarious learning. The experience of observing and understanding another's response and the consequences of that response.

Vicarious reinforcement. The experience of observing, understanding, and possibly identifying with the reinforcement following the model's response.

Chapter 6

Verbal Learning

Some kinds of verbal behavior can be predicted or explained by the three basic models of learning discussed in Chapters 3, 4, and 5. It would be possible, for example, to classically condition a human subject to respond to a particular word or meaning. (See the "semantic generalization" experiment described in Example 8, Chapter 3.) Similarly, the techniques of instrumental conditioning can be used to reinforce, correct, or extinguish incorrect verbal responses. (See Examples 12 and 13, Chapter 4.) Likewise, language plays a crucial role in certain types of learning-by-modeling situations. (See Example 1, Chapter 5.) The principles of classical conditioning, instrumental conditioning, and modeling do not adequately account for all forms of verbal learning, however, and as a result some psychologists have developed special theories and experimental techniques in order to predict and explain the ways in which we learn and use language.

Some theorists distinguish between *verbal learning* (the acquisition of new verbal responses in a laboratory setting) and *verbal behavior* (the performance of already-learned verbal responses either within or without the laboratory). This Outline includes both types of verbal responses under the general heading "verbal learning," although the present chapter is primarily concerned with acquisition. Additonally, this chapter is basically confined to *human* verbal learning. Although recent attempts at teaching sign language to chimpanzees have generally been regarded as successful, human subjects provide psychologists with the greatest variety and complexity of verbal responses and are probably the best subjects to consider in introducing this topic. (The use of chimpanzees as subjects in verbal learning experiments is discussed in Chapter 18.)

6.1 BACKGROUND OF VERBAL LEARNING

As mentioned in Chapter 2, Aristotle proposed three laws of association—contiguity, similarity, and contrast—that influenced thought processes and enabled human beings to order their perceptions of the world. Implicit in Aristotle's theory is the idea that the human mind possesses a kind of "organizing agent" that acts on information it receives through the sense organs and gives human beings the ability to store this information in an orderly (and retrievable) way.

One early psychologist in particular, Herman Ebbinghaus, was especially interested in how humans store information—how they remember. Ebbinghaus's experiments with nonsense syllables (described in Section 2.2) were designed in such a way as to reveal the processes of remembering and forgetting in their "purest" possible form: By using nonsense syllables, Ebbinghaus tried to observe acquisition, storage, and retrieval of units of information that did not carry with them any personal meaning or association. In this way, Ebbinghaus hoped to neutralize the effects of previous learning and of any emotional or intellectual associations with the items to be remembered. (All "nonsense" syllables are not equally nonsensical; the problem of meaningfulness and certain related problems are discussed in Section 6.5).

EXAMPLE 1. Suppose a team of experimenters is concerned with the effect of exposure rate on acquisition processes, as measured by the performance of groups of students in a single verbal learning task. The students are divided into groups, then asked to look at a series of slides presented at differing rates. After exposure to all the slides, they try to recall all the items they can, in any order they please. The experimenters would study the results to determine which items were learned most rapidly.

If the slides present a series of highly meaningful words—for example, Hamlet, Macbeth, Othello, Coriolanus, Lear, Cymbeline—the results obtained might be a function of student familiarity with the Shakespeare plays rather than rate of presentation. Rate would become unimportant because the overriding category of Shakespeare's plays would cue all the possibilities.

60

In order to determine how great an effect rate of presentation might have on recall, the experimenters would do better to employ a list of unrelated nonsense syllables—for example, MEJ, WUG, ZAT, GIC, QEF, XID. Associations between items or with a general category name would be very low, and the effect of presentation rate might be looked at in a less confounded manner.

Ebbinghaus's conclusions can be roughly summarized by the curve of forgetting (Fig. 2-1), which he developed; his general theory of the rate of forgetting has not been disproved or substantially altered since it was first proposed.   Perhaps even more significant, however, are the techniques for studying learning that followed Ebbinghaus. In each of the types of verbal learning discussed in this chapter, the importance of Ebbinghaus's basic experimental design will become obvious.

6.2   SERIAL LEARNING

In a *serial-learning* task a subject is presented with a series of stimuli and then required to repeat them in the order in which they were presented.   Two methods of conducting serial-learning studies (anticipation and serial recall) are used frequently, a third (complete presentation) is seldom used, and a fourth (free recall) incorporates serial presentation but does not require ordered response.

Anticipation Method

The *anticipation method* entails presentation of the ordered list one item at a time. Afterwards the subject attempts to repeat the list, responding to the appearance of each item by trying to correctly anticipate the next item.   (The very next item in the list is presented whether or not the subject anticipates it correctly.)   The successful completion of a single serial-learning task is usually defined as one or more trials in which all components are anticipated correctly.

EXAMPLE 2.   In the laboratory, serial tasks are often presented with a slide projector or a *memory drum* (Fig.   6-1). If the anticipation method is being used in the serial task, the list starts with an asterisk (*), indicating that the first item is forthcoming.   The subject then attempts to make the correct response before the drum turns, confirming or disconfirming each response as the list advances one item.

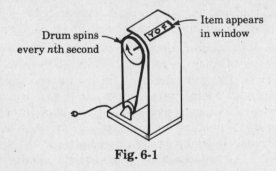

Item appears
in window

Drum spins
every *n*th second

Fig. 6-1

Serial Recall

In *serial recall* the list items are presented individually and in a particular order—just as they are in the anticipation method.   However, the subject does *not* respond during presentation. Only after the completed presentation does the subject attempt to report the entire list in order.

EXAMPLE 3.   Serial recall occurs when a performer is asked to remember and then produce an entire set of lyrics for a song.   There are no external cues available as there are in the anticipation method.   (This assumes, of course, that the performer is not receiving some form of prompting.)

Complete Presentation

A much less frequently used method of serial learning is called *complete presentation,* in which all of the items are presented simultaneously to the subject. Although instructions encouraging the subject to spend an equal amount of time concentrating upon each item may be made, there is no guarantee that subjects will not give disproportionate emphasis to certain items. The test of acquisition is similar to that for serial recall—after a given amount of time for list study, the subject is asked to report the entire list in order.

Free Recall

In the *free-recall* method, the items are presented in a serial order, but the recall need not be ordered. Instructions for recall usually ask for report of the items "in any order that you please."

EXAMPLE 4. Having returned from a tour of South America, Pearl is asked by a friend to "tell me which countries you visited." Although Pearl visited the countries in a serial order, the request does not ask that the order be repeated, and thus this is a free-recall task. On the other hand, if the questioner asks, "Where did you go first? Then where?" Pearl would be faced with a serial-recall task.

Types of Associations

One way of analyzing serial learning is to determine whether or not *associations* (bonds or connections) have been formed between items. Such analyses suggest that each item in a list may serve a *double function:* It not only represents a response to be given but also operates as a stimulus cue to prompt other responses. Three types of associations have been investigated.

Immediate forward associations. In a list composed of items A–B–C–D–E–F, *immediate forward associations* would occur between adjacent items in the order A → B, B → C, etc.

Immediate backward associations. With items A–B–C–D–E–F, *immediate backward associations* would occur between adjacent items in the order B → A, C → B, etc.

Remote associations. Using list A–B–C–D–E–F, *remote associations* could develop between nonadjacent items in either a forward or backward manner, for example, B → E or D → A.

EXAMPLE 5. Students in physiology often are asked to memorize the names of the twelve cranial nerves. Because these have been numbered, a serial order is typically imposed and used: olfactory, optic, oculomotor, trochlear, trigeminal, abducens, facial, stato-acoustic, glossopharyngeal, vagus, accessory, hypoglossal. It is possible that any of the three types of associations may develop. For example, learning "optic" may cue "olfactory" as well as "oculomotor" (immediate backward and immediate forward). "Glosso-pharyngeal" may cue "hypoglossal" (remote).

Method of Derived Lists

One means of testing for evidence of remote associations is the *method of derived lists.* Having learned an original list (e.g., A–B–C–D–E–F), subjects are tested for speed of learning a modified list (e.g., A–C–E–B–D–F) which has a certain degree of remoteness. First tested by Ebbinghaus, the evidence indicates that remote associations are stronger for shorter spans (e.g., A → C as opposed to A → E, but there appears to be some small amount of carry-over from the original list even to lists with high degrees of remoteness built in.

6.3   THE SERIAL-POSITION CURVE

When the subject is asked to produce responses in a serial order, it is likely that items at the beginning of the list will be learned most rapidly, those at the end of the list next most rapidly, and the items in the *middle* of the list will be learned with greatest difficulty. Plotted graphically, these results produce the *serial-position curve,* which represents what is referred to as the *serial-position effect.* Figure 6-2 illustrates an idealized serial-position curve. Some researchers have referred to the ease of learning the first items of a serial list as the *primacy effect* and the ease of learning the last items as the *recency effect.*

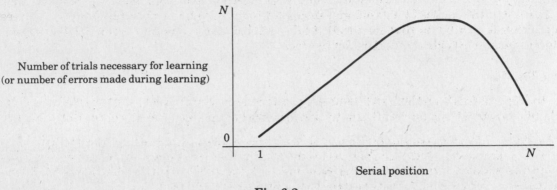

Fig. 6-2

If the subject is instructed to use free recall of the serially presented items, the serial-position curve obtained after several practice trials differs somewhat from that of serial responding. Figure 6-3 shows the differences in the two curves.

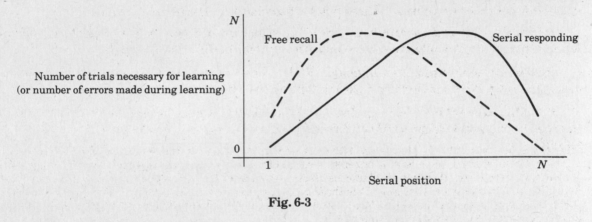

Fig. 6-3

Evidence indicates that subjects given the opportunity to use free recall will at first produce a serial-position curve comparable to that of serial responding. However, with repeated practice the emphasis shifts, with last-experienced items reported first and best, then first-experienced items, and finally the middle-list items.

Modification of the Serial-Position Curve

While in general the curves described above can be expected in many research studies, it is possible to significantly alter the shape of the obtained curve. Two ways of accomplishing this are manipulation by instruction and manipulation of the materials to be learned.

Manipulation by instruction. The serial-position curve can be significantly altered simply by instructing the subject to concentrate upon particular portions of the list. Such emphasis modifies the results obtained according to which parts of the list are stressed.

EXAMPLE 6. When instructed to concentrate upon the middle of a serially presented list, subjects will produce results which differ markedly from the usual serial position curve. Figure 6-4 illustrates a result which might be obtained.

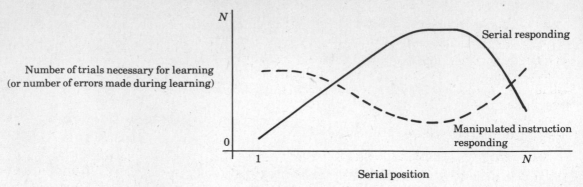

Number of trials necessary for learning
(or number of errors made during learning)

Fig. 6-4

Manipulation of materials. It is also possible to alter the shape of the serial-position curve by manipulating the materials to be learned. This is particularly the case when items within the list form units or clusters. Responses affected are said to show *clustering*.

EXAMPLE 7. One research study using a 36-item list which was effectively three 12-item lists produced results similar to the curve shown in Fig. 6-5. It can be seen that the manipulation of materials "creates" three miniature serial-position curves within the one overall list. Similar results have been obtained using groups or clusters of materials of different lengths. Additionally, clustering can be expected to alter the results obtained when using free recall.

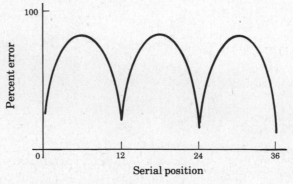

Fig. 6-5

A special example of manipulation of materials is called the *von Restorff effect* (named for the researcher who first studied it). Introduction of an unusual item into the list, regardless of its position within the list, will lead to very rapid learning of that item, although the overall shape of the curve will not be altered significantly.

EXAMPLE 8. Asked to learn the following list, subjects could be expected to produce a result similar to that shown in Fig. 6-6.

(1)	(2)	(3)	(4)	(5)	(6)	(7)	(8)
FOH,	ZOD,	XED,	KAH,	CAT,	MUQ,	VOR,	QUY

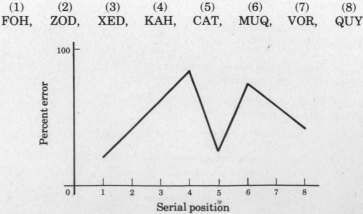

Fig. 6-6

Previously Existing Serial Order

Research has shown that acquisition of some lists may be affected by a previously learned serial order. Such orders are based on the subject's previous experience and may influence performance even if the experimenter specifically instructs the subject to disregard what he or she has learned in the past. (One such list would read as follows: January, February, April, March, May, June, August, July, etc.)

The Chaining Hypothesis

One attempt to explain the performance obtained in serial tasks has come to be called the *chaining hypothesis*. This hypothesis suggests that serial behavior be viewed as a chain in which each response serves as a link. It also allows for both immediate and remote links and tries to explain the serial position effect according to the number of links which would have to be inhibited to produce a particular item in its correct position. Figure 6-7 illustrates this proposal. (See also Problem 6.12.)

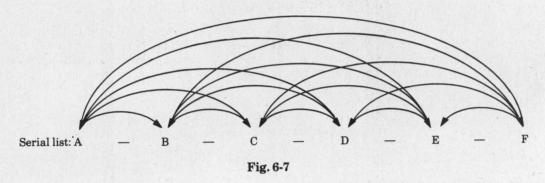

Serial list: A — B — C — D — E — F

Fig. 6-7

6.4 PAIRED-ASSOCIATE LEARNING

A task is designated as *paired-associate learning* when the list is composed of stimulus-response pairs in which each component serves either as a stimulus or a response (but not as both, as might be proposed for items in serial-learning tasks). Usually, the order of presentation of the pairs is varied for each practice trial. Several methods of studying paired-associate learning have been used.

Anticipation Method

The *anticipation method* of paired-associate learning involves presenting both the stimulus and response components on every trial. Study trials often require the subject to repeat the response (and sometimes the stimulus also) after it has appeared. Test trials require the response to be given *before* it appears, thus the name "anticipation method."

EXAMPLE 9. The anticipation method can be achieved by using a memory drum. The components are written on the tape so that at first only the stimulus appears, then both stimulus and response. The rotation speed of the memory drum can be timed so that each line appears for, say, two seconds, meaning that on test trials the subject would have two seconds to respond before both S and R appear. Figure 6-8 shows a typical memory-drum tape for paired-associate learning.

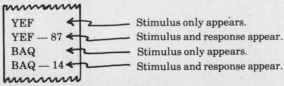

YEF ← Stimulus only appears.
YEF — 87 ← Stimulus and response appear.
BAQ ← Stimulus only appears.
BAQ — 14 ← Stimulus and response appear.

Fig. 6-8

Recall Method

Study trials for the *recall method* of paired-associate learning usually are similar to those of the anticipation method. Test trials differ, however, in that only the stimuli are presented.

Verbal Discrimination

A somewhat different version of paired-associate learning, called *verbal discrimination,* requires the subject to identify the correct response from a set of stimuli presented. This represents a recognition measure of retention rather than recall (see Chapter 13).

EXAMPLE 10. The tape on a memory drum for a verbal discrimination task could look like that shown in Fig. 6-9. Test trials would require the subject to recognize the "correct" stimulus from the three found in each stimulus group. The "correct" responses (shaded) are seen only in study trials and not in test trials.

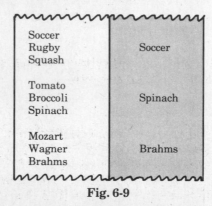

Fig. 6-9

Explanations of Paired-Associate Learning

Attempts to explain how paired-associate learning takes place have been called the two-stage model and the three-stage model. Both have similar components. (See also Problem 6.19.)

Two-stage model. *Two-stage models* of paired-associate learning propose a first phase of response learning, followed by a second phase of S-R connection or "hookup."

Three-stage model. A stimulus-encoding phase preceding the response-learning (second) and the linking (third) phase provides the first stage of *three-stage models.* Because encoding creates a representation of the stimulus, the explanation of the linking phase proposes that the "hookup" is between the encoded stimulus representation and the response learned in the second phase.

The spew hypothesis. An attempt to explain the response-learning phase has been called the *spew hypothesis.* This hypothesis proposes that availability of verbal units is a function of frequency of experience. Therefore, response learning would be more rapid when the subject's frequency of experience with the verbal units is high than when it is low.

6.5 CHARACTERISTICS OF THE MATERIALS USED

Many aspects of the materials to be learned affect the ease of acquisition. A number of these will be fully explored in Chapters 11 and 12, but because some are unique to verbal learning they are also presented here.

Meaningfulness

The most commonly reported characteristic of verbal materials is *meaningfulness,* measured by the average number of associations a verbal unit elicits. It should be noted that meaningfulness is *not* the same as meaning, which refers to the information that defines the verbal unit.

EXAMPLE 11. One of the nonsense syllables used in Example 9 was BAQ. Although BAQ has no meaning in the English language, it may elicit some associations (e.g., back, British Army Quarters) and therefore would have some level of meaningfulness.

Association Value

Another measure which is similar to meaningfulness is *association value,* defined as the percentage of respondents who report having *any* association generated by the particular verbal unit.

Familiarity

When subjects are asked to rate their "acquaintance" with a verbal unit, the resulting measure is called *familiarity.* Such ratings usually are made on a one-to-seven scale from no acquaintance at all to very familiar.

Pronounceability

Rating of ease of pronouncing a verbal unit determines its *pronounceability* value. A one-to-seven scale usually is used to denote this value as well.

Imagery

The ease with which a verbal unit generates some sort of mental picture represents its *imagery value.* (The subjects themselves are asked to rate the verbal units in this case.) One proposal based upon imagery has come to be called the *conceptual-peg hypothesis.* Research evidence has shown that as the imagery value of a stimulus increases in a paired-associate task, acquisition is facilitated. The conceptual-peg hypothesis proposes that this occurs because there is an image upon which the response can be "hung."

EXAMPLE 12. The conceptual-peg hypothesis would predict that learning the pair "basis"-"office" would be more difficult than acquisition of the pair "dinner"-"office." This would occur because of the ease of creating images for the stimulus "dinner" when compared to the relative difficulty of creating images for "basis."

Sequential Dependencies

The principle of *sequential dependencies* is based upon the knowledge that certain word, letter, and phoneme sequences occur more frequently than others. In general, a statistical prediction would be that the greater the level of sequential dependency, the easier the acquisition of the verbal unit. However, in many instances encoding of verbal information seems to occur in other than a statistically predictable manner.

EXAMPLE 13. In the English language, one letter sequence is almost exclusive in its occurence. If the letter Q appears, the expectation of U as the next letter is almost 100 percent. While other sequential dependencies are not as high, some are extremely frequent and affect acquisition accordingly.

Associative Symmetry

One principle which has been proposed but not convincingly supported by research findings is that of *associative symmetry,* suggests that when an S→R pair is learned, R→S learning is equally strong. The response-learning concept (see Section 6.4) supports S → R sequences as being stronger than R → S sequences because response learning has not occurred for the stimulus items and they are not as readily available as the original responses.

6.6   OTHER VARIABLES IN VERBAL LEARNING

A number of other factors may affect verbal learning. Those which appear to be particularly important for acquisition of verbal units are discussed here, while those influencing storage and retrieval will appear later.

All-or-None vs. Incremental Controversy

One debate regarding the acquisition of verbal units has centered around the concept of gradual (incremental) as opposed to total (all-or-none) learning. Some theorists, using techniques such as the *drop-out method,* in which any verbal unit not learned is replaced with a new one, have attempted to show that the course of learning in such a task progresses at a rate comparable to that of repeated trials with the same verbal units. This would imply that what appears to be incremental learning is actually representative of a series of one-trial learning experiences. Figure 6-10 indicates the two ways the same results could be represented. While this controversy has not been completely resolved, the weight of evidence appears to support an incremental position (see Problem 6.26).

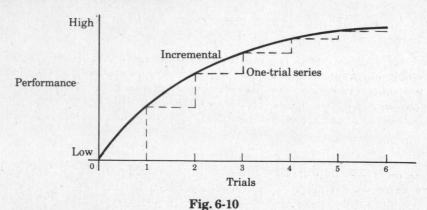

Fig. 6-10

Immediate-Memory Span

Another concern in verbal learning is with the amount of material that can be held in immediate memory at any given time—the *immediate-memory span.* Research has supported the finding that 7 ± 2 (seven plus or minus two) units of information can be held in immediate memory at one time. These units may contain more or less absolute information, depending upon the particular subject's mode of performance. The total amount can be increased by *chunking* (blocking items together) or *encoding* (developing an image, a label, or some mnenonic device to represent the information.)

Mediation

In some cases, acquisition of a verbal unit is facilitated when two things are associated together because they share something else in common. Such association is termed *mediation.* Mediation typically takes one of the three forms shown in Fig. 6-11. Often, some cue is needed to generate the mediating response in the subject (see Problem 6.29).

Steps involved	S equivalence	R equivalence	Chaining
First learning	A—B	B—A	A—B
Second learning	C—B	B—C	B—C
Test for	A—C	A—C	A—C

Fig. 6-11

The Search Hypothesis

A nonassociative explanation for verbal learning has been called the *search hypothesis,* which proposes that the learner is not necessarily forming associations but rather acquiring information. The learner's success in the verbal task will depend on the ease with which the information can be acquired or used. The emphasis of this approach is on actively seeking and organizing information rather than passively receiving it.

Evidence for the search hypothesis has been provided by tests of transfer of information from one task to another. When there is comparability of cues between the two tasks and when there is sufficient opportunity to use the previously acquired knowledge, greater knowledge seems to result in better performance. Position information, knowledge of adjacent items, temporal and spatial cues, and other information that is essentially nonassociative in the traditional S-R sense may be utilized (see Problem 6.30).

Solved Problems

6.1   Do the principles of verbal learning contradict the principles of classical conditioning, instrumental conditioning, and learning by modeling?

Not exactly. Most verbal learning theorists would agree that classical conditioning, instrumental conditioning, and learning by modeling can be employed to predict and explain many types of verbal behavior. At the same time, however, they would most likely maintain that verbal learning is not adequately accounted for by any one or even all three of these other learning models. They see verbal learning as a special case that requires additional principles and novel methods of investigation.

6.2   Ebbinghaus is best known for his research in the field of memory. He also developed a very valuable experimental tool that researchers in the field of learning use to this day. What is this tool and why is it especially important in the study of verbal behavior?

In his attempt to create what he thought would be association-free materials to be learned, Ebbinghaus developed the nonsense syllable (a consonant-vowel-consonant [CVC] sequence which does not form a word). Although his interpretation of the materials has been questioned by research indicating differences in the meaningfulness of the nonsense syllables, Ebbinghaus did initiate the use of materials which have come to be widely used in subsequent verbal learning research. Other researchers expanded upon Ebbinghaus's idea by using trigrams (CCC as well as CVC sequences), number combinations (NNN) or longer combinations (e.g., a CVCVC combination such as XUVAR).

6.3   Training for a new job, Burt is required to learn, in order, the eight components which make up the overall task. The eight parts are presented to Burt one at a time, but when tested to determine if he is ready to undertake the job, he is asked to recall all eight components in order. This training-testing program represents which form of serial learning?

Burt's training-testing sequence illustrates the method of serial recall. He has been presented with the entire task, one component at a time, and is then asked for recall of the entire task in serial order.

6.4   How could the training-testing program described in Problem 6.3 be revised in order to illustrate the method of serial anticipation?

Presentation of the components would occur in a similar manner—that is, one at a time—but tests for retention occur at each component stage of the task. This means that Burt would be asked to describe component 1, then given feedback as to whether or not his response was correct by having component 1 presented to him. Upon presentation of component 1, Burt would then try to anticipate component 2, and so on throughout the eight parts of the task.

6.5   Why are both the method of serial anticipation and the method of serial recall considered quite different from the method of complete presentation?

The method of complete presentation involves presentation of *all* components of a serial task to the subject at the same time. While instructions may request that equal study time be devoted to each component, there is no guarantee the actual presentation time will be equal. In both serial-anticipation and serial-recall methods, on the other hand, the presentation time is controlled to assure a predetermined exposure for each component of the serial task.

6.6   Regardless of the method used, many psychologists believe that each component of a serial task (with the possible exception of the last component) serves a double function. Explain what this means.

The concept of double function implies that each component of a serial task may serve as both a response and a stimulus. The component is a response because it must be retained and then produced as a part of the serial order. It serves as a stimulus in the sense that it may "key off" other components in the serial order.

6.7   Explain why the concept of immediate backward association would allow the final component of a serial task to be presumed to have double function.

Imagine that the serial list has components 1-2-3-4-5. The concept of immediate backward association would suggest that the subject may learn 1 as a *response* when 2 is the stimulus, and so on throughout the list. This would mean that item 5 could serve as the stimulus for response 4, thus assuming a double function.

6.8   Tests in serial tasks usually involve asking for the forward order of the list, although backward associations may be asked for, or they may become apparent even when they are not asked for. What third type of association may affect the way in which a subject learns a serial task?

Subjects may make, or be asked to make, remote associations within a serial task. The remote association may be based on serial position alone (as when a subject associates the odd-numbered items in a series, for example) or may be based on some other characteristic that serves to link one item in the series to another (see Example 5).

6.9   How did Ebbinghaus's method of derived lists help support the concept of remote associations?

Ebbinghaus determined the differing effects of remote associations by testing relearning of derived lists. For example, original list 1-2-3-4-5-6-7-8 relearned is 1-3-5-7-2-4-6-8, where all but the 7-2 transition represent one degree of remote association. Ebbinghaus's findings supported the idea that learning the original list to some extent aided the subject in learning the second (derived) list. This carry-over from one learning task to another decreases, however, as the second task is formed from more remote connections.

6.10   How does the serial-position curve obtained from a serial-anticipation study differ from that found when the subjects are allowed free recall of the items?

Both serial-position curves show primacy and recency effects, with the greatest number of errors being made near the center of the list. They differ in that the curve for serial anticipation shows fewest errors at the start of the list, while the curve for free recall (after several trials of free recall) shows fewest errors for the items at the end of the list.

6.11   What was the chaining hypothesis? How was it used to try to explain the serial-position curve?

The chaining hypothesis was an attempt to explain serial learning by suggesting that serial behavior was a chain in which each response served as a link. The chaining hypothesis allowed not only for contiguous links (which would create immediate forward and backward associations) but also for links to responses at some distance (remote associations). The hypothesis thus would propose that the greatest number of links spanned the middle items of a serial list, with the least number (0) at the ends.   With fewer incorrect links to be inhibited, items at the end of a list would be learned most quickly, while items in the middle would require greatest inhibition of incorrect links and thus be most difficult.

Two other explanations for serial learning have received some attention. The *cognitive-landmark view* proposes that the first, last, or some special item in a serial list may provide an anchor point from which acquisition takes place.   Theories of this nature are explored more thoroughly in Chapter 11.   The *dual-memory view* suggests that acquired items are processed from short-term memory to long-term memory.   Often, the transition from short-term memory to long-term memory occurs when items are hooked to an anchor point.   Dual-memory theory is dealt with in Chapter 13.

6.12   Is there evidence which weakens the chaining hypothesis?

Several studies have provided data which do not appear to support the chaining hypothesis.   For example, subjects who learned a 1-2-3-4-5 serial list were tested later for speed of acquisition of pairs such as 1-2, 2-3, 3-4, 4-5.   They learned the pairs no faster than subjects who had learned an irrelevant list before learning the pairs.

6.13   What are other important variables which appear to affect the serial-position curve?

There are at least three more variables which seem to affect the serial-position curve—the von Restorff effect, clustering, and manipulation by instruction.

The von Restorff effect indicates that an unusual item, regardless of its position in the serial task, will be learned more rapidly than other items.   This effect does not seem to significantly modify the remainder of the serial-position curve.

Clustering occurs when the subject recalls several parts of the serial task because they have some mutual bond.   This may alter the serial-position curve obtained, as when one of the items of the cluster falls in the middle of the task.

Finally instructions may be used to manipulate the serial-position curve obtained; for example, if the subjects are asked to concentrate upon remembering the middle of the list, the curve will be altered.

6.14   In a paired-associate learning task a subject learns to respond with the word "adult," "child," "adolescent," or "infant" to each item in a group of first names.   Later the subject is tested on how well she can identify each name (stimulus) with the correct age group (response).   What pattern of the errors would one predict in this case?

It is likely that the subject would establish a hierarchy of responses, and that this hierarchy would be ordered in terms of age.   Thus the words might well be arranged as: infant, child, adolescent, adult.   Assuming this arrangement rather than the reverse, the least number of errors should be made pairing names with "infant," then would come "adult," with the greatest number of errors made with the responses "child" and "adolescent."   In other words, the serial-position effect can be expected, with the previously existing category of age serving to order the items and influence the way in which they are learned.

6.15   Although the tasks are not those of verbal learning, is there evidence for serial learning in animals?

Several research studies have found the serial-position effect in investigations using animal subjects.   For example, in a maze-learning task using several component parts hooked together, the rats used as subjects made the fewest number of wrong turns in the first and last components, while making more errors in the middle portions.

6.16   Mrs. Fermoile is using flash cards to teach her third graders the multiplication tables. She selects eight cards for each practice session. First she shows the students the "problem" side of the card for about five seconds, then she turns the card and shows the "solution" side for a comparable amount of time. After having done this for all eight cards, Mrs. Fermoile shuffles the cards and asks the students to take paper and pencil and try to write the correct answers when she shows the "problem" side again. Which form of paired-associate learning is Mrs. Fermoile using?

Mrs. Fermoile's method represents the recall method of paired-associate learning. Both stimuli and responses are presented on the acquisition trial, but only the stimuli are presented on the test trial.

6.17   What change would Mrs. Fermoile have to make to use the anticipation method of paired-associate learning?

To use the anticipation method of paired-associate learning, Mrs. Fermoile would have to present the "solution" side of each card to the students immediately after they had written each answer. Such a procedure is somewhat unwieldy for classroom testing, but does give the students immediate feedback (knowledge of results) after each test response is made.

6.18   Why is the testing part of the verbal-discrimination method of paired-associate learning described as a recognition measure?

In a verbal-discrimination paired-associate learning task, the subject is asked to pick one of the alternatives (the "correct" one) from a display of two or more. Acquisition trials use all the words as the stimulus and the correct one as the response. Test trials present all the words again, but require the subject to select the correct response. Thus, the correct answer is present and must only be identified rather than recalled.

6.19   Suppose that one of the pairs in a paired-associate learning task consists of the stimulus GIP and the response 21. Learning this pair, Jay reverses the letters of the nonsense syllable, coding them as PIG, while Ray, a Notre Dame football fan, adds a letter to code the nonsense syllable as GIPP, the name of a famous Notre Dame player. Explain why the techniques of both Jay and Ray seem to support a three-stage model of paired-associate learning rather than a two-stage model.

Two-stage models of paired-associate learning propose a response-learning phase and a "hookup," or S-R linking stage. Three-stage models suggest that these two stages are preceded by a stimulus encoding stage, where a representation of the stimulus is developed, then used in the third stage to facilitate the linking of S and R. In this situation Jay may eventually recall the S-R pair by remembering a "pig which weighed 21 pounds," while Ray may think of "George Gipp wearing number 21."

6.20   The spew hypothesis puts particular emphasis on one characteristic of the materials to be learned. What is this? Which stage of the models described in the previous problem (6.19) is explained by the spew hypothesis?

The spew hypothesis proposes that the order of availability of verbal units is a direct function of the frequency of experience with each unit. This hypothesis has been used to try to explain the response-learning stage of paired-associate learning models. Thus, the more frequently a verbal unit has been experienced, the more rapidly it may become a response in a new paired-associate connection.

6.21   Distinguish between meaningfulness and association value. What other characteristics of verbal materials may influence how well they are learned?

Meaningfulness is defined as the average number of associations a verbal unit elicits. Association value is defined as the percentage of subjects who report having *any* associations generated by the verbal item.   Two other characteristics of verbal materials are familiarity (rated acquaintance with a verbal unit) and pronounceability (rated ease of pronouncing an item).

6.22   What is meant by the term "imagery value" as it is used in verbal learning?   How does the influence of imagery upon paired-associate learning compare with the effect of meaningfulness?

Imagery value refers to the rated ease with which a verbal unit generates some sort of "mental picture." In general, stimulus imagery is a more important factor in the rate of paired-associate learning than response imagery is.   This finding is opposite to the effect of meaningfulness, which indicates that in general response meaningfulness is more important to paired-associate learning than stimulus meaningfulness is.

6.23   One concept which has been proposed to explain paired-associate learning is that of the "conceptual peg."   Would imagery or meaningfulness be more likely to be used in describing a conceptual peg?

Because the conceptual-peg hypothesis proposes that the stimulus serves as a "peg" onto which the response may be hung, imagery is seen as being the key factor.   It should be noted, however, that regardless of whether imagery or meaningfulness is being discussed, if *both* stimulus and response values are high, the rate of paired-associate acquisition will be more rapid than when only one of the two is high.

6.24   If one group of subjects is presented with the pair "mother-child" while a second group learns "market-child," the first group should learn its pair more rapidly than the second group.   Why?

Probably the best explanation of this is the principle of sequential dependencies, essentially the frequency with which words (or letters or phonemes) occur together.   While the response-learning factor would be equal for both pairs and the stimulus values are quite comparable in terms of meaningfulness or imagery, the value of sequential dependency would be much higher for the first pair than for the second pair.

6.25   How have tests of associative symmetry tended to support the concept of the importance of response learning in paired-associate tasks?

Associative symmetry proposes that the strength of an R-S association should be equal to that of an S-R association; that is, the forward and backward associations should be equal.   In almost every case, research has failed to support the concept of associative symmetry and thus has shown the greater importance of response learning.   An R-S pair is not recalled as well until the previous stimulus is subjected to the response-learning stage.

6.26   Evidence indicates that the terminal lists in a dropout paired-associate learning procedure are easier to memorize than the initial lists.   How does this decrease the support for an all-or-none learning position?

Researchers attempting to test the concept of all-or-none learning (vs. an incremental explanation) presented an identical initial list to two groups of subjects.   One group continued to practice the same list until all pairs were learned.   For the other group, each pair that was not learned was replaced with some other pair on the next trial.   Both groups learned their lists in approximately the same number of trials.   Seemingly, the second (dropout) group learned each pair in an all-or-none fashion.   However, further investigation into this procedure produced evidence that the final composition of the list learned by the dropout subjects was easier than that of the initial list.   Thus, the claim that such a procedure, and the result obtained, supported an all-or-none explanation was considerably weakened.

6.27   When referring to immediate-memory span, reference to 7 ± 2 has become quite well known.   Why?

   Research testing the limits of immediate-memory span has revealed that a typical subject can retain 7 ± 2 units of information in immediate memory.   A unit of information may contain one or more elements of information, but it is treated as a single component when testing immediate-memory span.

6.28   If Roger has been picked as a subject in an immediate-memory span study and knows the nature of the task ahead of time, what types of techniques might he practice to increase the absolute amount he is able to include in his immediate-memory span?

   Two of the most popular techniques for increasing immediate-memory span are chunking and encoding.   Chunking means "blocking" items together and is especially effective when learning strings of digits—for example, remembering "twenty-three, sixty-two, etc." when presented with the single digits 2, 3, 6, 2, and so forth.
   Encoding is developing some sort of label, image, or mnemonic device which allows encompassing a greater amount of material.   For example, with a serial list which starts with the words "coffee" and "nothing," these could be encoded as an image of an empty coffee cup.

6.29   Coming from a party for political candidates, two of the candidates are talking about the people who were there.   One tells the other that he was amazed that she was able to remember that an important supporter liked to fish.   She responds by saying, "Oh, Mickey the fisherman?   I just remembered 'fin'."   Her response illustrates what principle of verbal learning?

   The principle illustrated in this problem is that of mediation.   This politician has used a link (in this case "fin" or "finn") to connect "Mickey" with "fish."   Thus, the mediation creates an "easy" association, Mickey Finn, and aids the politician in her attempts to appear knowledgeable and friendly to the supporter.

6.30   The search hypothesis has been proposed as a nonassociative alternative explanation for verbal learning situations.   What does this mean?

   The search hypothesis suggests that the formation of associations may not be the central feature of verbal learning tasks.   As an alternative, the search hypothesis proposes that the learner is simply acquiring information.   The ease with which the information can be acquired or the use to which the information can later be put will determine the success of the learner with the task.

Key Terms

Anticipation method.   In verbal learning, the situation in which the subject must attempt to make a response before that response is revealed.

Association value.   In verbal learning, the percentage of subjects who report having any association generated by a particular verbal unit.

Associations.   In verbal learning, connections or bonds formed between items.

Associative symmetry.   The proposal that the backward association R-S is equal in strength to the S-R connection being learned.

Backward associations.   Associations formed such that a later-presented item prompts retrieval of an earlier-presented item.

Chaining hypothesis.   The explanation of serial learning that holds that each item within a list serves as a link to each other item.

Chunking.   In verbal learning, the blocking together or grouping of items subjectively to aid memorization.

Clustering.   Organization of items in a presented list by category to form smaller units or groups.

Complete presentation.   In verbal learning, simultaneous exposure to the subject of all items to be learned.

Conceptual-peg hypothesis.   The proposal that S-R learning occurs because the stimulus provides an image to which the response can be attached.

Encoding.   In verbal learning, developing some label or image that represents several units of information.

Familiarity.   In verbal learning, the average rating of acquaintance with a verbal unit as determined from subjects' reports.

Forward associations.   Associations formed such that an earlier presented item prompts retrieval of a later presented item.

Free recall.   In verbal learning, when the subject attempts to report all responses, but may do so in any order desired.

Imagery.   In verbal learning, the "mental picture" generated by a particular verbal unit; rated by subjects as *imagery value*.

Immediate associations.   Associations formed between adjacent serial items.

Immediate memory span.   The amount of material that can be held in immediate memory at one time; believed to equal 7 ± 2 units of information.

Meaningfulness.   The average number of associations a verbal unit elicits.

Mediation.   In verbal learning, association of two items because they share some other thing in common.

Memory drum.   In verbal learning, a piece of equipment used to present stimuli at preset, timed rates.

Nonsense syllable.   A consonant-vowel-consonant sequence that does not make a word.

Paired-associate learning.   In verbal learning, tasks which link particular stimuli to specific responses.

Primacy effect.   In learning, the finding that items presented first will be acquired and retained well.

Pronounceability.   In verbal learning, the average rating of ease of pronouncing a verbal unit, as determined from subjects' reports.

Recency effect.   In learning, the finding that items presented last will be acquired and retained well.

Remote associations.   Associations formed between nonadjacent serial items.

Search hypothesis.   In verbal learning, a nonassociative explanation of acquisition that proposes success as a function of the ease with which items can be obtained and organized.

Sequential dependencies.   The statistical frequency with which words or letters or phonemes occur together.

Serial learning.   Learning in which materials are presented in a particular order or sequence that must be followed.

Serial-position effect.   The finding that retention of items presented in a serial order will be better for those items at the beginning and end of the list than for those in the middle of the order.

Serial recall.   In verbal learning, attempts by the subjects to report all responses in the correct order; there is no prompting during the recall.

Spew hypothesis.   The proposal that the availability of verbal units is a direct function of the frequency of experience with those units.

Verbal discrimination.   In verbal learning, the requirement that the subject select the correct response from a set of stimuli presented.

Verbal learning.   In the psychology of learning, those studies which emphasize the use of words or symbols, often specifying particular techniques and/or special types of equipment.

von Restorff effect.   Rapid learning of one exceedingly distinctive stimulus within a list, regardless of its position.

PART III: Influences on Acquisition

The five chapters of this part are concerned with variables or procedures that primarily influence the acquisition of a learned response. Chapter 7 concentrates on reinforcement effects, while Chapter 8 is concerned with the various outcomes produced by aversive stimuli. The principles of extinction and spontaneous recovery (Chapter 9) and generalization and differentiation (Chapter 10) expand the discussion to include what happens when the acquisition environment is changed. Chapter 11 closes this part by summarizing other variables that are related to acquisition, but are not covered in the previous four chapters.

Chapter 7

Principles of Reinforcement

A major aspect of the psychology of learning has been the study of reinforcement—any event that increases or maintains the strength of a response. This chapter will present the general characteristics of reinforcement rather than particular theories of reinforcement.

7.1 TYPES OF REINFORCEMENT

The types of reinforcement were introduced in Chapter 4; in this section they will be reviewed and discussed in greater detail.

Positive Reinforcement

A *positive reinforcement* is any stimulus or event which *when present* increases or maintains the strength of a response.

Negative Reinforcement

A *negative reinforcement* is any stimulus or event which *when terminated or removed* increases or maintains the strength of a response. Quite typically, negative reinforcement occurs when an *aversive stimulus* is terminated or removed. An *aversive stimulus* is any stimulus or event the organism finds unpleasant or noxious.

EXAMPLE 1. Coaches for athletic teams sometimes use "laps" as an aversive stimulus. If the players are able to complete practice assignments as prescribed, the laps are reduced or terminated entirely. Thus, correct responding leads to negative reinforcement.

Primary vs. Secondary Reinforcement

A *primary reinforcement* is any stimulus or event which increases or maintains the strength of a response automatically. That is, no learning need occur for the stimulus to be reinforcing. *Secondary reinforcers* are stimuli or events which increase or maintain the strength of a response only after their reinforcing properties have been learned.

Secondary reinforcers appear to gain their reinforcing properties in a manner very similar to classical conditioning. A neutral stimulus somehow is paired with a reinforcing event (either a primary reinforcement or some other secondary reinforcer). After one or more pairings, the stimulus which was neutral takes on reinforcing characteristics. In general, secondary reinforcers established under partial-reinforcement conditions are more resistent to extinction than those established under continuous reinforcement. (This is another instance of the partial-reinforcement effect.)

EXAMPLE 2. We may often hear secondary reinforcers such as "Good job," "Well done," "Nice work." All of these phrases, since they are part of an arbitrary symbol system called the English language, are originally neutral, but come to take on reinforcing properties. It should be noted that if phrases such as "Poor job," "That's bad," or "Lousy work" were paired only with reinforcing events, they would take on reinforcing properties.

Reinforcement in Classical Conditioning

In classical conditioning the event which originally elicits the response—the unconditioned stimulus (UCS)—is considered the reinforcement. This differs from instrumental conditioning or modeling, where the event accompanying or following the response is the reinforcer.

The Premack Principle

In some circumstances, the opportunity to perform a more desirable response may serve to reinforce the performance of a less-desired response. This relationship has come to be called the Premack principle after the psychologist who studied it extensively. (It has also been called "Grandma's rule" because this is supposedly how grandmothers get their grandchildren to make certain less desirable responses.)

EXAMPLE 3. Armed forces inspections often have this "if-then" quality about them. Fairly often the conditions are that *if* the barracks pass inspection perfectly, *then* all the troops will have a 48-hour pass. The less-desirable response (cleaning and straightening the barracks) is performed in order that the more desirable behavior (getting the weekend pass) may be allowed.

7.2 SECONDARY REINFORCEMENT

Secondary reinforcers, or learned reinforcement, play a crucial role in our interactions with one another.

Secondary Reinforcement as Information Transmission

One major consideration with secondary reinforcers is that they may serve as sources of information spanning a time period between completion of a response and delivery of some other reinforcer. Essentially, the secondary reinforcer serves to indicate that some other reinforcer is on the way. (While secondary reinforcement is fairly typical of human beings because of their ability to use language, appropriate training can produce similar results for animals as well.)

EXAMPLE 4. A foreman might use information in a way that provides secondary reinforcers in order to keep up morale and therefore good production. Statements such as "Good work" or "Keep that up and we're sure to get a bonus" serve as intermediary reinforcers and as the promise of reinforcers yet to be delivered.

Applied Secondary Reinforcement

Example 4 presents just one of many possible applications of secondary reinforcement. The child's expectation of additional reinforcers such as good grades or a trip to the movies is used by teachers and parents quite frequently. Secondary reinforcers are also used in clinical and training settings, such as when a *token economy* is established—tokens are given as rewards for appropriate behaviors and may later be exchanged for other reinforcers.

7.3 ASSESSMENT OF REINFORCEMENT

Three techniques are most commonly used to assess whether or not a stimulus or event is reinforcing. These techniques can be phrased as questions: (1) Does the stimulus or event maintain responding? (2) Does the stimulus or event prolong extinction? (3) Will the stimulus or event act as a reinforcer for some other response? The last technique allows establishing a *generalized reinforcer* (one which works in more than one situation) and is usually considered the strongest of the three techniques.

7.4 DELAY OF REINFORCEMENT

The period of time between the completion of a response and the delivery of the reinforcement is an important variable to consider in a learning situation. Studies of this variable—which is called *delay of reinforcement*—have generally shown that as a delay period grows longer, performance decreases.

Reduced Effects of Delay of Reinforcement

As pointed out in Section 7.2, the effects of delay of reinforcement can be reduced by using secondary reinforcers to "fill" the time period. How much the performance decrement can be reduced depends upon the effectiveness or power of the secondary reinforcer. (See Section 7.5 for a discussion of the characteristics of reinforcers.)

Learned Taste Aversions

A number of research studies have shown that animals will develop *learned taste aversions* to certain substances even when there is a long period of time between ingestion and some subsequent illness—which may or may not be caused by the substance. In other words, an organism may develop a learned taste aversion to a stimulus that is not at first aversive. However, it has been found that learned aversions are established most readily when the stimuli involved are relatively novel or salient.

EXAMPLE 5. Sitting down to dinner at an Italian restaurant, Rudy is good-naturedly persuaded by his friends to try the squid salad, a food he has never eaten before. Rudy eats half of the salad, then pushes it aside to move on to his favorite Italian dish, sausages and peppers. What Rudy doesn't know is that the sausage is tainted with salmonella. Late that evening he becomes quite ill and vows that he will never again eat squid. Rudy may well develop a learned aversion to this novel food even though it was not the squid that made him ill.

7.5 REINFORCEMENT PROPERTIES

Three factors appear to be important in determining the effectiveness of stimuli as reinforcers. These are the *quantity* of the reinforcer, the *quality* of the reinforcer, and the *amount of effort* the subject must exert in order to consume or otherwise use the reinforcer. In general (and within broad limits), the higher the value of any one of these three factors, the greater the effectiveness of the reinforcer. (It can also be expected that these variables will often operate simultaneously and interact with one another.)

Reinforcement Contrast

The way changes in the quantity (or level) of reinforcement affect performance of learned responses has been investigated in experiments on *reinforcement contrast*. In such an experiment, two comparable groups might be trained to asymptotic levels of performance in identical tasks but with differing levels of reinforcement. If the reinforcement levels are then switched for the two groups, the levels of their performance will reverse. (However, before the changed response levels stabilize at the "new" asymptotic value, each group can be expected to "overshoot" the final value.) If the change in performance is from the original asymptotic level to a higher one, *positive contrast* has been achieved; if the new performance level is lower, *negative contrast* is said to have occurred; in either case the "overshoot" phenomenon will be observed (see Problem 7.16).

Description of Reinforcement

Primary reinforcers such as food or drink are usually quite easily described in terms of quantity (e.g., how many ounces), quality (how sweet), or in some cases the amount of effort for consumption (e.g., how many sips to consume a certain amount of liquid). Secondary reinforcers are often more difficult to describe in a quantifiable way. For example, it is not easy to say which of the three verbal reinforcers in Example 2 would be the strongest. This means that it is often very difficult to designate a secondary reinforcer with a particular value or level.

Moreover, there are certain kinds of circumstances that are reinforcing but do not satisfy the criteria of either primary or secondary reinforcers; examples include mere activity (as opposed to passivity), which often is reinforcing, and certain kinds of electrical brain stimulation.

7.6 SCHEDULES OF REINFORCEMENT

The controlled establishment of partial-reinforcement conditions is frequently called *scheduling*. The resultant sequence of reinforced and nonreinforced trials constitutes the *schedule of reinforcement*. And as mentioned before, it can be expected that any schedule of reinforcement will produce the *partial-reinforcement effect* (PRE); that is, the response acquired under partial-reinforcement conditions will be more resistant to extinction than that same response acquired under conditions of continuous reinforcement.

Basic (Simple) Schedules of Reinforcement

There are two types of *basic (simple) schedules of reinforcement: ratio* schedules, in which delivery of reinforcement is based upon the number of responses made, and *interval* schedules, in which reinforcement of a response is made at the end of a certain time period. Each of these schedules, ratio and interval, may be either *fixed* or *variable*. (The four basic schedules are described below and illustrated with examples of scheduling in nonexperimental settings; for an illustration of scheduling in the laboratory see Example 10 in Chapter 4.)

Fixed ratio (FR). A *fixed-ratio* schedule of reinforcement means the reinforcer will be delivered after every nth response. The value of n does not change from trial to trial.

EXAMPLE 6. Anyone who does piecework in a factory or on a farm is on a fixed-ratio schedule of reinforcement. Fruit pickers may be paid, for example, for each basket they have filled. (This would be called an FR-1 schedule; if payment were based on every five baskets filled, the schedule could be designated as FR-5.)

Fixed interval (FI). The number of responses is not the crucial factor in a *fixed-interval* schedule of reinforcement. The key requirement is instead that the subject make one correct response at the end of the interval. For each trial, the time period of the interval remains the same, and reinforcement is delivered only at the end of that interval.

EXAMPLE 7. Aspiring professional golfers illustrate the fixed-interval schedule of reinforcement. To become a "touring professional," the candidate must exhibit excellent play at one of the association-sponsored tournaments held twice each year. Excellence in play at other tournaments may be rewarding in other manners, but the particular reinforcement of obtaining a touring professional's identification card can be obtained only at the end of the specified interval—one or the other of the qualifying tournaments. (*Note:* Preparation for an association tournament frequently follows the pattern of responding typical of FI schedules described below.)

Variable ratio (VR). Reinforcement is given following a certain number of responses, but that number may change from trial to trial when *variable-ratio* schedules of reinforcement are employed.

EXAMPLE 8. People who take jobs as telephone solicitors accept the conditions of a variable-ratio schedule of reinforcement. Basically, the more often they make calls, the more likely the reinforcement. However, no set number of calls guarantees a reinforcement, and thus the number made before delivery of the next reinforcement is likely to vary.

Variable interval (VI). A response made at the end of some time period will be reinforced, but the length of the time period may change from trial to trial when a *variable-interval* schedule of reinforcement is used.

EXAMPLE 9. Parents sometimes use variable-interval reinforcement scheduling to encourage certain types of responding from their children. Keeping a room clean on a steady basis may be prompted by producing reinforcers on an irregular basis. The children never know when the next reinforcer might be delivered but they come to realize that consistent performance will yield occasional reinforcements.

Patterns of Performance for the Basic Schedules

Each of the basic schedules of reinforcement typically produces a particular pattern of performance.   Illustrated in Fig. 7-1, the usual findings are as follows:

FR: Bursts of responses approximately equalling the number of responses required by the schedule.   Pauses (for consumption) between the bursts.

FI: A "scalloping" pattern of responding, with slow responding at the beginning of the interval increasing markedly at the end of the interval.

VR: A consistently high rate of responding.

VI: A steady, but relatively slow, rate of responding.

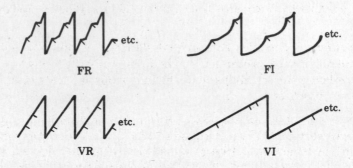

Fig. 7-1

Advanced (Complicated) Schedules of Reinforcement

Advanced (complicated) schedules of reinforcement are built from the basic schedules, using two or more basic schedule components.   The level of performance created by a particular advanced schedule can usually be predicted by analyzing the basic schedule components that make up the advanced one (see Example 10).   The three basic types of advanced schedules are labeled *multiple, compound,* and *concurrent.*

Multiple schedules.   When two or more independent schedules are presented successively to the organism, the reinforcement is being delivered according to a multiple schedule.

EXAMPLE 10.   A multiple FI-FR (FI of 90 seconds, FR of 10 responses) could produce a pattern of responding such as that illustrated in Fig. 7-2.   Note that the recognizable features of each schedule can still be identified.   There is the possibility of interaction—for example, a burst of 10 responses may be found during the rapid responding of the terminal phase of the FI.

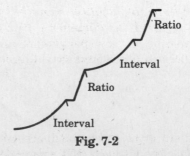

Fig. 7-2

Compound schedules.   A *compound schedule* involves a single response reinforced according to two or more simultaneously operating schedules of reinforcement.   Many compound schedules of reinforcement can be generated because the delivery of reinforcement may be dependent upon satisfying *all* aspects of the compound schedule, any *one* of the aspects, or some *combination* of the aspects.

When all aspects must be satisfied, the compound schedule is called a *conjunctive* schedule of reinforcement. Other labels include *alternative* schedules, for situations in which only one component needs to be satisfied, and *interlocking* schedules, in which some combination of the component schedules needs to be satisfied (see Problem 7.26).

An additional type of compound schedule is produced when a "reset" provision is incorporated. In such a setup reinforcement is not delivered *and* the interval starts over again if the appropriate pattern has *not* occurred during the specified time period. Labels for such schedules are *d r l* (differential reinforcement of low rates of responding) and *d r h* (differential reinforcement of high rates of responding).

EXAMPLE 11. When a teacher tells the kindergarten class that they will be allowed to have recess once they have been quiet for five consecutive minutes, a *d r l* schedule is being employed. Noise during the period would reset the schedule and keep the reinforcement (which in this case is based upon the Premack principle) from being delivered.

Concurrent schedules. Schedules that involve delivery of reinforcement for two or more different responses according to two or more schedules are called *concurrent schedules* of reinforcement. Theoretically the schedules would be independent. However, research frequently shows that interactions may occur.

EXAMPLE 12. Suppose a student has quizzes scheduled every two weeks in one course (FI—2 weeks), while in another course there are surprise exams given at no set time (VI). The student's study pattern probably would reveal this concurrent arrangement, with steady preparation for the "pop quiz" course interspersed in the time periods between the high-rate (scalloping) pattern of preparation for the biweekly quizzes.

7.7   OTHER CONSIDERATIONS FOR REINFORCEMENT SCHEDULING

Certain special cases of reinforcement scheduling as well as practical applications of scheduling have been investigated in recent years. Some of the findings from these investigations are described in this section.

Autoshaping

Autoshaping refers to a special case of scheduling in which reinforcement is delivered when a particular stimulus occurs—no response need be made. In such situations, the organism frequently responds although it is not necessary (see Problem 7.31).

Automaintenance

A second phenomenon, called *automaintenance,* supposedly occurs in situations where responding continues even though it *prevents* reinforcement from being delivered. Investigations of automaintenance have shown that the response persistence results from the cue stimulus offset serving as a reinforcer. When such reinforcement is eliminated, the automaintenance effect disappears (see Problem 7.32).

Practical Applications

The applications of reinforcement principles to business, education, family life, and clinical situations are considerable. *Knowledge of results* (KR) principles (Chapter 23) have been used to develop teaching machines and programmed learning. *Feedback* (Chapters 16 and 22) as reinforcement is the basis of sensitivity training groups. And *biofeedback* procedures (Chapter 22) make use of mechanical representations of physiological processes as reinforcement for modifying internal responding. All of these theories and techniques are based on the principles of reinforcement scheduling.

7.8   THEORIES OF REINFORCEMENT

It is beyond the scope of this book to deal with the theories of reinforcement in depth.   A brief mention here shows the variety of explanations that have been proposed.   (*Note:* It should be recognized that many psychologists simply are satisfied to know that an event *is* reinforcing and do not care why; that is, they are not theory-oriented.)

Drive-Reduction Theory

A widely accepted explanation of reinforcement is that the event reduces or lessens some need or aversive condition.   This proposal is a *drive-reduction theory*.

Optimum-Arousal Theory

A second proposal suggests that each organism has an optimum level of arousal.   Reinforcement consists of any event that helps the organism maintain that optimum level or adjust behavior in order to achieve it.   Such a proposal has been called an *optimum-arousal theory*.

Stimulus-Change Theory

Stimulus-change theory proposes that the reinforcing event simply alters the stimulus situation, thus preventing some other response from becoming attached to that stimulus.

Solved Problems

7.1   Attending a meeting of an executive-training program, Mr. Burris realizes the speaker, a psychologist, repeatedly refers to *reinforcement circumstances* rather than *rewards*.   When the period for questions begins, he asks the speaker why she prefers the term *reinforcement*.   What response is the psychologist likely to give?

Reinforcement is the more general term, referring to *any event which increases or maintains the strength of a response*.   Rewards are reinforcements, but only one of several types.

7.2   Confused, Mr. Burris pursues this by asking what else, other than reward, might be a reinforcer.   What answer might the speaker give?

Using the definition of reinforcement previously stated, the speaker points out that a response may be strengthened or maintained because some event (such as food or praise) is presented or because some event (such as electric shock or verbal abuse) is removed or terminated.   The former case, when presentation of the event or stimulus is reinforcing, is called positive reinforcement.   The latter situation, involving the removal or termination of an aversive condition, is called negative reinforcement.

7.3   One last question pins down an additional distinction for Mr. Burris.   He asks, "Well, food and praise certainly aren't the same thing.   Why do you call them both positive reinforcers?"   How would the speaker answer this?

Food and praise both operate in the same manner—that is, their presence serves to increase or maintain the strength of a response.   Therefore, both are called positive reinforcers.   The difference between food and praise as reinforcers is described by another label, however.   Food, which increases or maintains the strength of a response without the need for past learning or experience, is called a primary reinforcement.   Praise, a verbal stimulus, is a learned or secondary reinforcement.

7.4   Which conditioning principle is used to account for the development of secondary reinforcers?

    Classical conditioning principles seem to explain the establishment of secondary reinforcers.   A stimulus which is originally neutral is paired with a reinforcing event (either a primary reinforcement or some other secondary reinforcement) and comes to have reinforcing properties.

7.5   Does the definition of reinforcement given in Problem 7.1 apply equally well to classical conditioning, instrumental conditioning, and learning by modeling?

    In general, the definition of reinforcement is appropriate for all forms of learning.   However, it should be recognized that in classical conditioning the UCS which elicits the response is considered the reinforcer, whereas the event accompanying or following the response is the reinforcer in both instrumental conditioning and modeling.

7.6   What is the Premack principle (Grandma's rule)?

    The Premack principle states that performing a response may itself be considered to be reinforcing and that a lower probability response can be "prompted" by the promise of allowing a higher probability response to be made.   (Grandmothers supposedly say things like, "You can go play ball as soon as your room is cleaned.")

7.7   Secondary reinforcers have been described as information providers or carriers of information.   Why?   How does this fit with the definition of reinforcement given earlier?

    There is evidence that indicates that many secondary reinforcers help "bridge" delays between completion of a response and delivery of a reinforcement.   In such situations, the secondary reinforcer is an event or stimulus that indicates that waiting is reasonable because another reinforcement (presumably more powerful or desirable than the secondary reinforcer in question) is on the way.   This "message" acquires reinforcing properties by being paired with another reinforcer and, at the same time, serves as a carrier of the information that this other reinforcer is forthcoming.

7.8   Give examples of nonexperimental instances of secondary reinforcement.

    In clinical settings and hospitals, *token reward systems* (or *token economies*) have been established in attempts to train or modify behaviors.   In such systems, symbolic rewards such as poker chips are given for appropriate responding.   The chips can be accumulated, then traded in for other reinforcements.   *Verbal mediation* is another instance of the applied use of secondary reinforcers. Reassurance or anticipation statements can be used to span some time period preceding delivery of some other reinforcer.   Parents, teachers, and coaches use such reinforcers quite frequently.   Finally, *money* is at least in some senses a secondary reinforcer—it is a stimulus that serves as a reinforcer only after one has *learned* its value as a tool for securing other reinforcers.   (Many other secondary reinforcers could be identified; the three mentioned here are meant only to suggest the variety of secondary reinforcers.)

7.9   What three questions can be asked to assess whether or not a stimulus or event is a reinforcer?

    The three questions that best assess the reinforcing properties of an event or stimulus are: (1) Will it maintain responding? (2) Will it prolong extinction? and (3) Will it serve as a reinforcer for acquisition of some other response?   The third question is usually considered the most crucial, in that the answer to it tells us whether or not a given event or stimulus is a *generalized reinforcer*—one that can be used in a variety of situations.

7.10   It takes a person quite a long time to complete the studies necessary to qualify to be a lawyer.   The research studying the effects of delay of reinforcement on the performance of animals indicates that delay of reinforcement reduces performance.   Is this equally true for humans?   What enables humans to perform differently from animals and to perform in delayed-reinforcement situations like law school?

The principle of delay of reinforcement, when studied using animals as subjects, indicates that as the delay period grows longer, performance decreases.   With the many years involved in legal study, performance could be expected to be very poor if the same principle applied.   However, humans pursue long-term goals by creating interim reinforcers—perhaps something as "large" as attaining a bachelor's degree or as "small" as saying, "There, I got that paper done!"   The ability to use language and other symbols as secondary reinforcers makes it possible for humans to perform well under very long delays of reinforcement.

7.11   Is it possible to create situations where delay of reinforcement *can* be spanned for animals?

Secondary reinforcers can span delays of reinforcement for animals, although not to the extent they can be spanned for humans.   For animals, this delay usually involves establishing an association between the secondary reinforcement and the reinforcement that is delayed.   Quite frequently this is accomplished using classical conditioning principles (see Problem 7.4).

7.12   How do studies of learned taste aversions appear to contradict the findings regarding the effects of delay of reinforcement?

Research on learned taste aversions has shown that animals can establish a link between ingestion of a substance and later symptoms of illness even when the delay period between ingestion and illness reaches a length of three or more hours.   Such studies have shown that sensory modality is important; that is, the stimuli associated with the ingestion, such as taste and smell, and the stimuli associated with the later illness need to be in the same sensory modalities for learned aversions to develop.   Electric shock presented three hours after ingestion would *not* create a learned aversion; stomach cramps or nausea would.

7.13   Rats frequently show what has been called "bait-shyness."   What is this?   How does it relate to delay of reinforcement and learned taste aversions?

"Bait-shyness" is the term used to describe the fact that rats are extremely cautious about ingesting novel foods—that is, foods with which they do not have previous experience.   Research has shown that learned taste aversions are most readily established when the foods used are novel.   The uniqueness, or salience, of the stimuli appears to be an important aspect of spanning the delay of reinforcement period.   It also appears that rats are unwilling to ingest novel foods because of the possibility of subsequent aversive effects.

7.14   Given the following grid (Fig. 7-3), place an *x* in the square where performance would be expected to be poorest and a *y* where best performance would be expected.   Explain your choices.

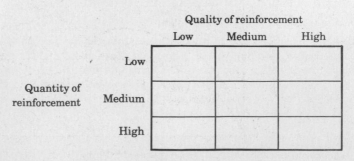

Fig. 7-3

The *x* should be placed in the upper left corner (Low-Low), while the *y* should be placed in the lower right corner (High-High). Performance is seen to be a function (within limits) of both quantity and quality of reinforcement. When both factors are manipulated simultaneously, an interaction can be expected with maximum performance achieved when both factors are highest.

7.15 Suppose the manager of a theater is quite satisfied with the performance of the orchestra, but feels the costume makers have not been doing well enough. In an attempt to prompt better performance from the costume people, the manager promises them a considerable bonus if they improve to his satisfaction. Unfortunately, because the theater is on a very tight budget the manager must cancel promised raises for the orchestra in order to meet the bonus payments. According to the principle of reinforcement contrast, what performance can be expected from the orchestra and the costume makers?

Reinforcement contrast proposes that changes (perceived or actual) in reinforcement will yield comparable changes in performance. Thus, the promised bonuses may provoke improved costume design and construction from the costume makers, and the cancelled raises may lead to decreased quality of performance from the orchestra. (It should be noted that the change in reinforcement must be *recognized* for the effect of reinforcement contrast to be observed.)

7.16 In contrast to the hypothetical situation given in Problem 7.15, study of reinforcement contrast with animals can be conducted in a carefully controlled manner. Assume that the performance represented in Fig. 7-4 has reached asymptote; then sketch the performance which would be expected following the switching of reinforcement conditions. Explain your answer.

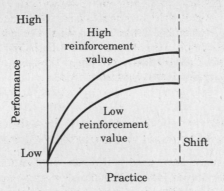

Fig. 7-4

See Fig. 7-5. The dotted lines indicate how performance would continue if the switch of reinforcement did not occur. The performance of the control groups would follow these asymptotic curves, while the performance of the switched groups would follow the solid-line curves. Both the group in which performance improved and the group in which it deteriorated can be expected to "overshoot" the new level of performance before gradually settling at the asymptotic value.

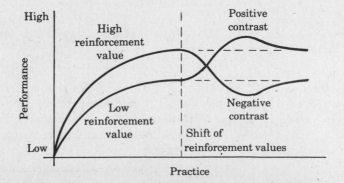

Fig. 7-5

7.17   Properties of reinforcement are sometimes difficult to describe.   Give examples of such difficulties, indicating the problems involved.

The effort for consumption (or use) of a reinforcement has been described as a property influencing the effect of the reinforcement.   However, determining effort is often difficult or impossible.   (How much effort, for example, is involved in kissing?)   In addition, it is very difficult to assess how the interaction between effort and quantity or between effort and quality might influence the effectiveness of a reinforcer.   (A pigeon may prefer the taste of smaller food pellets, but at the same time have to make more pecks to consume them.)

Other reinforcers are fairly easy to describe but difficult to explain.   For example, both activity and brain stimulation have been identified as reinforcers, but the processes involved which make these things reinforcing are not easily identified.

7.18   What is the partial-reinforcement effect (PRE)?   How would this be tested using classical conditioning?   Using instrumental conditioning?

The partial-reinforcement effect (PRE) indicates that responses learned under partial-reinforcement conditions are more resistant to extinction than those learned under continuous reinforcement.   In classical conditioning, partial reinforcement means presenting the CS on all acquisition trials but the UCS on only some of the trials.   In instrumental conditioning, the appropriate response produces the contingent reinforcement on only some of the trials.   PRE is tested by comparing the extinction performance of the partially reinforced group with that of comparable groups trained with continuous reinforcement (see Sections 3.7 and 4.6).

7.19   Distinguish between basic and complicated schedules of reinforcement.

Basic (or simple) schedules of reinforcement can be classified as one of two types: either ratio or interval schedules.   These, in turn, may be either fixed or variable, thus yielding four basic schedules: fixed-ratio (FR), fixed-interval (FI), variable-ratio (VR) and variable-interval (VI).   Complicated (or advanced) schedules are built out of the basic schedules, combining two or more aspects.   The results obtained when using complicated schedules can usually be predicted by analyzing the basic schedules of which they are composed.

7.20   Many parents allow their children to eat only at specified mealtimes regardless of requests such as "May I *please* have something to eat?"   In instances such as this, which basic schedule of reinforcement is being illustrated?

The children are being reinforced on a fixed-interval (FI) schedule of reinforcement.   The number of responses made is unimportant; it must be dinnertime before a response is reinforced.

7.21   Neil's goal as a golfer is to score at par or below.   For years he was unable to attain that goal, but recently he has begun to have an occasional par round.   His family notices that he now plays more frequently than ever.   Which schedule of reinforcement best accounts for Neil's behavior?

Neil is operating under a variable-ratio (VR) schedule of reinforcement.   He now knows he is *able* to score at par or below and realizes that the more often he plays, the greater will be his opportunity to get reinforced once again.

7.22   As manager of a fast-food restaurant, Tracy knows that a company representative may visit at any time, posing as a customer, and evaluate the quality of food and service.   As a result, she makes certain a steady maintenance and cleaning program is adhered to each day.   Which basic schedule of reinforcement describes the company's method of ensuring adequate performance?

The sporadic arrivals of the company representative represent a variable interval (VI) schedule of reinforcement.   Tracy and the restaurant crew are not reinforced for the number of responses made, but rather for being ready at any given time.   The steady maintenance program is typical of the type of response pattern expected in VI situations.

7.23   Joella's family lives on a heavily wooded lot.   She has been told that she will earn one dollar each time she rakes and removes five garbage bags full of leaves.   Such a payoff schedule represents which basic schedule of reinforcement?

Because Joella is paid each time she removes five bags of leaves, the schedule is a fixed-ratio (FR) pattern.

7.24   Joella's parents notice that the leaf accumulation is building at a rate considerably faster than her raking and removal.   They decide to modify the payoff schedule and tell her she will be paid only if she rakes and removes five bags of leaves within a two-day period.   Explain how the new conditions represent a change from a basic to a complicated schedule of reinforcement.

To get her one-dollar reward, Joella is required not only to satisfy the FR-5 schedule but to do so within a time limit; that is, a second criterion must be satisfied.   Such a schedule is called a *d r h* (differential reinforcement of high rates of responding) and represents a complicated schedule of reinforcement.

7.25   Why is a *d r h* schedule of reinforcement not considered to be a fixed-ratio–fixed-interval (FR-FI) conjunctive schedule of reinforcement?

Both the *d r h* and the FR-FI schedules require a certain number of responses to be made and involve a particular time interval.   They differ in that the *d r h* schedule demands the number of responses be made *before* the time interval has elapsed, while the FR-FI schedule requires the specific number of responses to be made *after* the time interval has passed.

7.26   Awards given for outstanding attendance during a school year represent which schedule of reinforcement?

The awards (or reinforcements) are given if *fewer* than an indicated number of absences have occurred within the specified time period.   Such a system limits the number of responses and therefore represents a *d r l* schedule of reinforcement (differential reinforcement of low rates of responding).

7.27   Distinguish between multiple schedules of reinforcement and compound schedules of reinforcement.

A multiple schedule of reinforcement includes two or more independent schedules presented *successively* to the organism.   Compound schedules reinforce a single response according to two or more schedules of reinforcement operating *simultaneously*.

7.28   Earl is a salesman whose wages are based upon two factors.   To earn each weekly base salary, he must make a minimum of 30 house calls.   In addition, Earl earns a bonus each time he actually makes three sales.   What type of reinforcement schedule is this?

Earl is being paid on a concurrent schedule of reinforcement.   Concurrent scheduling establishes reinforcement for two or more responses according to two or more schedules at the same time.   In Earl's situation, the base salary is based upon a *d r h* schedule, while the bonuses are paid out according to a FR schedule.   Note that there is interaction involved in this situation, although not all concurrent scheduling would create such interactions.   Earl will get paid for the 30-house-call schedule whether or not he makes any sales.   However, the FR-3 payoff is more likely to occur if he works harder (makes more house calls).   In other words, by their very nature the house calls made and the actual sales booked are linked.   (However, not all concurrent schedules work like this.)

7.29   What effect does partial reinforcement have upon the strength (or effectiveness) of secondary reinforcers?

In general, secondary reinforcers established under partial-reinforcement conditions are more durable (stronger or more effective over a period of time) than those established under continuous-reinforcement conditions.   This finding is parallel to the partial-reinforcement effect (PRE).

7.30   Describe autoshaping.   How is it similar to classical conditioning?

Autoshaping is a variation of reinforcement scheduling in which reinforcement is given regardless of whether a response is made.   For example, a Skinner box might be set up so that food is presented each time a warning light goes on, regardless of whether the pigeon pecks the key or not.   In such circumstances, it has been found that pigeons *will* respond even though it is not necessary for them to do this to secure reinforcement.   Can this be explained by classical conditioning?   If the light is interpreted as a CS and the food as a UCS, then the pecking for food represents the UCR and the subsequent key-pecking is the CR.   This must remain a tenuous explanation, however, unless the food-pecking response can be considered elicited rather than emitted.

7.31   What is automaintenance supposed to be?   What explanation has been provided for this effect?

In an experimental situation similar to that described in the previous problem (7.30), a pigeon was *not* reinforced with food for pecking in response to the light.   Despite this, key-pecking followed by light termination persisted although such responses did not produce food reinforcement.   Such responding was called automaintenance.   Subsequent investigations showed that when the light termination was eliminated, the automaintenance effect disappeared.   The key-pecking was being reinforced by the termination of illumination.

7.32   Very briefly present some of the theories explaining *why* a reinforcer is reinforcing.

Several theories of reinforcement are most often presented.   The drive-reduction theory explains reinforcement as the lessening of some need or unpleasant situation.   Optimum-arousal theories propose that either reduction *or* increase in arousal can be reinforcing if the change helps maintain the organism's preferred level of arousal.   Some stimulus-change theories are very similar, suggesting instead an optimal level of *stimulation*.   Others (based upon the work of Guthrie and Estes) propose that the presentation of the reinforcer simply changes the existing situation, thus "protecting" the learning that has previously taken place.

It must also be added that a number of psychologists believe it is unimportant to ask why a reinforcer is reinforcing.   They suggest that it is enough to know the reinforcer works.

Key Terms

Alternative schedule of reinforcement.   A compound schedule in which only one of the component schedules needs to be satisfied for reinforcement to be delivered.

Automaintenance.   The continuance of a response in a stimulus-reinforcement pairing even though the response prevents delivery of the nominal reinforcement.

Autoshaping.   Continued responding to a stimulus-reinforcement pairing even though the reinforcement is in no way contingent upon the response.

Aversive stimulus.   Any stimulus an organism judges to be noxious or unpleasant.

Bait-shyness.   The aversion shown by animals to novel types of food.

Compound schedule of reinforcement.   A partial-reinforcement schedule in which a single response is reinforced according to the requirements of two or more schedules that operate simultaneously.

Concurrent schedules of reinforcement.   Partial-reinforcement schedules in which two or more responses are made to satisfy two or more schedules at the same time.

Conjunctive schedule of reinforcement.   A compound schedule in which all aspects of its component schedules must be satisfied in order for reinforcement to be delivered.

d r h.   Differential reinforcement of high rates of responding; a compound schedule which delivers reinforcement if a sufficient number of responses are made during a given time period, but starts the time period again if an insufficient number are made.

d r l.   Differential reinforcement of low rates of responding; a compound schedule which delivers reinforcement when responses are withheld during a given time period, but starts the time period again if inappropriate responding occurs.

Delay of reinforcement.   A period of time between completion of a response and delivery of reinforcement.

Drive reduction.   In reinforcement, the apparent reduction by a reinforcer of some need or aversive condition.

Fixed schedules of reinforcement.   Partial-reinforcement schedules that remain unchanged.

Generalized reinforcer.   Any stimulus which is found to be reinforcing in more than one set of circumstances.

Interlocking schedule of reinforcement.   A compound schedule requiring some combination of its component schedules to be satisfied for reinforcement to be delivered.

Interval schedules of reinforcement.   Partial-reinforcement schedules in which a reinforcement is contingent upon a response being made at the end of a given time period.

Learned taste aversion.   A situation in which a previously neutral stimulus (typically food or drink) comes to take on aversive properties as a result of being associated with some aversive conditions.

Multiple schedules of reinforcement.   Partial-reinforcement schedules that require the subject to satisfy two or more independent cued schedules that are presented successively.

Negative reinforcement.   The termination or removal of some aversive stimulus; the termination or removal itself serves as the reinforcer.

Optimum arousal.   In reinforcement, the "best" level of motivation for an organism, which it will attempt to maintain.

Partial-reinforcement effect (PRE).   The finding that responses acquired under partial-reinforcement conditions are more resistant to extinction than responses acquired under continuous-reinforcement conditions.

Positive reinforcement.   The occurrence or presentation of a stimulus that serves as a reinforcer.

Premack principle.   The tendency for the granting or withholding of opportunities to perform desired responses to reinforce the performance of less-desired responses; also called Grandma's rule.

Primary reinforcer.   Any stimulus that "automatically" serves as a reinforcer; the organism does not have to learn that such a stimulus is reinforcing.

Ratio schedules of reinforcement.   Partial-reinforcement schedules in which reinforcement is contingent upon some number of responses made.

Reinforcement.   Any event which increases or maintains the strength of a response.

Reinforcement contrast.   The change in response strength associated with a change in some value of a reinforcer; may be either positive or negative.

Reward.   Another term for *positive reinforcement.*

Schedules of reinforcement.   Ways of arranging partial reinforcement in instrumental-conditioning situations.

Secondary reinforcer.   Any stimulus that serves as a reinforcer as a result of learning.

Token reward.   In therapy settings especially, the use of some symbol, such as a poker chip, as a secondary reinforcer that may later be traded for other reinforcers.

Variable schedules of reinforcement.   Partial reinforcement schedules that can change, usually around some average value.

Chapter 8

Escape, Avoidance, and Punishment

This chapter is concerned with the results of using aversive stimulation. To review, an *aversive stimulus* is any stimulus or event the organism judges to be unpleasant or noxious. Removal of an aversive stimulus may produce *negative reinforcement*. That is, when termination or removal of an aversive stimulus increases or maintains the strength of a response, negative reinforcement is said to have occurred.

The three major conditions produced by aversive stimuli are escape behavior, avoidance behavior, and punishment. *Escape* behavior occurs when an aversive stimulus is present and some response enables the organism to get away from that aversive stimulus. In *avoidance,* some particular response prevents the onset of an anticipated aversive stimulus. In *punishment,* the delivery of an aversive stimulus is contingent upon the organism's making some particular response.

EXAMPLE 1. Something as simple as loud noise may produce escape, avoidance, or punishment. A person confronted with exceedingly loud noises (such as in a factory or a disco) may show escape behavior by simply leaving the building or room in order to get away from the unpleasantly high sound level. Another person could show an avoidance behavior by wearing earmuffs or earplugs when entering a factory where aversive loud noises can be anticipated. The use of loud noise as a punishment can be illustrated by a parent's shouting at a child who has made some kind of undesirable response. (In many such cases, what is said is not nearly as important as the tone of voice used and the recognition that the shout is contingent upon the response just made.)

8.1 ESCAPE BEHAVIOR

Escape responses are thought to represent discriminative behavior (differentiation), with the aversive stimulus representing the discriminative cue. Research has shown that with repeated trials subjects learn to make escape responses when appropriate (that is, in the presence of the aversive condition), but do not continue to make the escape responses when inappropriate (for example, when other associated stimuli are present, but the aversive condition is not).

EXAMPLE 2. Little children sometimes show inappropriate escape behavior when they try to shovel large, wet snowflakes that melt upon contact with the driveway pavement. Adults usually illustrate discriminative shoveling behavior by doing this only when snow has actually accumulated on the driveway. (*Note:* In such circumstances, shoveling can only be escape behavior, happening after the aversive condition of snow accumulation has developed. Avoidance of the aversive condition would be accomplished by traveling to a warm climate.)

Variables Affecting Escape Behavior

Escape responses produce negative reinforcement—the removal or termination of the aversive condition contingent upon the appropriate response. Negative reinforcers can be manipulated in ways similar to those described in Chapter 7 for positive reinforcers. Moreover, the performance of escape responses will follow typical patterns according to the various schedules of reinforcement used.

Intensity of aversive stimulus. In general, just as with positive reinforcers, the greater the intensity of an aversive stimulus (and, therefore, the value of negative reinforcement), the higher the performance level expected. One interesting research result seems to partially contradict the above statement, however. It has been found that once escape responding has been established using some fairly strong aversive condition, less-intense stimuli that previously would not have been judged aversive will, when removed, serve to create conditions of negative reinforcement.

EXAMPLE 3. In a research study investigating the classical conditioning of the galvanic skin response (GSR), the CS of a tone and UCS of an electric shock were used. The shock level used was judged to be mild at its strongest. Despite this, one subject asked to be dismissed. When asked why, the subject explained that he was a television repairman and had recently received a very strong shock while on the job. He said that before the accident he would not have considered the low-voltage shock used in the experiment to be aversive; since the accident, however, he did consider it aversive. Thus, the termination of the experiment, and therefore the shock, was reinforcing.

Extinction of Escape Behavior

There are two possible procedures for extinguishing escape responses. In one, the aversive condition continues even though the escape response is made. In the other, the aversive condition is never presented.

Both procedures have potential flaws: The former seems to create punishment possibilities, while the latter terminates the most important discriminative cue in addition to the reinforcement. Extinction with the the first procedure tends to be irregular; with the second it tends to be much smoother.

EXAMPLE 4. Snow-shoveling can in some instances illustrate extinction. Suppose a heavy snowfall is accompanied by high winds. It is very likely that the escape response (shoveling) will produce little or no relief from the aversive condition (snow-covered walkways and driveways). The wind as a discriminative cue could lead to extinction of the shoveling behavior when the wind was present, while shoveling as an escape response would continue when no wind was present.

8.2　AVOIDANCE BEHAVIOR

Most avoidance behaviors may also be interpreted as instances of discriminative responding. Some cue indicates the possibility of impending aversive conditions, and the organism makes previously learned responses in order to keep from experiencing those aversive conditions.

Explanations of Avoidance Behavior

Early research on conditioned emotional responses (CERs) by John B. Watson led to attempts to explain avoidance responding as the result of *conditioned fear* and later fear reduction. Some discriminative cue, acting as a CS, elicits the avoidance response, and this in turn reduces the fear associated with the impending aversive conditions. (Notice that this explanation makes use of both classical and instrumental conditioning principles.)

CS offset. Several investigators were dissatisfied with the reduction-of-fear proposal stated above, mostly because fear reduction was a poorly specified concept. In an attempt to better identify the reinforcing event, *CS offset* was proposed as the moment of fear reduction. A number of studies seemed to show support for this position, illustrating for example that delaying the CS offset generated much poorer performance of the avoidance response.

CS as a discriminative cue. Subsequent research challenged the CS offset theory. Investigators reasoned that if the CS was indeed fear-producing, subjects would find CS prevention to be reinforcing. Such was not the case. Subjects in many different experiments did not prevent CS onset, but rather allowed it and then made the appropriate escape response. Such findings led to an explanation of avoidance behavior proposing that the *CS serves as a discriminative cue.* CS offset serves as information that the correct response was made.

The summary conclusion of this sequence of research studies is that the ability to avoid is the key to explaining avoidance behavior. Fear reduction and CS offset do contribute to avoidance learning, but they are not of primary importance.

Inherent responses. One alternative proposal developed in recent years suggests that every organism has an innate hierarchy of defense reactions that will be activated in avoidance circumstances.   These reactions have been called *species-specific defense reactions* (SSDRs).   The proposal suggests that the most likely response of the hierarchy will be tried first.   If unsuccessful, the next most likely is tried, and so on, until either a successful response is found or the hierarchy is exhausted.   In the latter case, some instrumental response would have to be learned or no avoidance would be possible.   SSDRs are provoked by *danger signals* (stimuli indicating impending aversive conditions) and continue until *safety signals* indicate the end of potential danger.

EXAMPLE 5.   Research with rats has supported the concept of SSDRs by showing that running responses will be acquired much more rapidly in avoidance training than lever-pressing responses.   Running apparently is much higher in the rat's hierarchy of SSDRs than lever-pressing is.

Variables Affecting Avoidance Behavior

Just as with escape behavior (and punishment, as will be seen later), performance in avoidance situations will vary when certain variables are manipulated.

Aversive stimulus intensity.   In general, as the intensity of the aversive stimulus is increased, the acquisition of and level of performance of the avoidance response will increase (or be facilitated).

CS-UCS interval.   Research regarding the manipulation of CS-UCS intervals has shown that longer time periods generally produce better performance levels.   This will vary somewhat for different species and up to some limit, with performance deteriorating at very long intervals, probably because contiguity is not established between the CS and UCS.

Interestingly, varying the CS-UCS interval around some average value produces better performance than does a consistent interval.   The likeliest explanation is that the variations of interval elicit greater attention from the subject because the moment of UCS onset is no longer so easily predictable.

Intertrial interval (ITI).   Avoidance performance varies in an inverted-U curve according to intertrial interval, with responding improving as the trial spacing increases up to some point, then deteriorating as ITI values increase further.

Retention interval.   The retention interval required seems to have little effect upon the response level in avoidance learning.   Many studies have shown that avoidance responses are retained for very long periods of time.

Extinction of Avoidance Behavior

As with escape behavior, there are two procedures for attempting extinction of avoidance behavior.   One confronts the subject with the CS (the discriminative cue), but does not allow the aversive stimulus (UCS) to occur at all.   In the other procedure the subject is confronted with the CS, and the aversive stimulus is presented regardless of whether the avoidance response is made.   The selection of one technique or the other will depend upon the kind of response situation involved.

EXAMPLE 6.   In a sense, social withdrawal responses may be considered avoidance behavior.   For example, a person who does not go to the beach because he is afraid of being seen in a bathing suit and being ridiculed would fit this description.   To extinguish the "not going" (or avoidance) response, the first of the above mentioned procedures would be used.   The person would be coaxed into going to the beach, but ridicule would not be allowed to occur.   (Indeed, positive reinforcers for beach-going behavior probably would also be used.) Extinction of the avoidance should result.

8.3   PUNISHMENT

The question of just how effectively punishment suppresses responding is not clearly settled. Does punishment work?   The best answer seems to be yes—if certain variables are manipulated appropriately.   The most important of these variables are presented here.

Contingency of Response and Punisher

It seems that if punishment is to be effective, the organism must recognize the contingency between the response being punished and the subsequent *punisher* (aversive stimulus). In other words, the fact that the punishment is being delivered *because* the response was made must be perceived by the learner. Correspondingly, *delay of punishment* can be expected to reduce its effectiveness. This appears to be comparable to results obtained when studying delay of reinforcement.

EXAMPLE 7. If Webster has been drawing on his bedroom walls and his parents wish to suppress this behavior, punishment may be needed. Extinction may be difficult because the response itself is reinforcing. One procedure that should be *avoided* is the "Wait until your daddy gets home" routine. It is very possible that Webster may greet his father at the door, forgetting entirely about the wall-drawing activity earlier in the day, and believe that the subsequent aversive condition is punishment for the greeting response rather than for drawing on the walls. In this case, greeting responses would be suppressed (the apparent contingency), while wall-drawing might continue or increase.

Intensity of the Aversive Condition

In general, the greater the intensity of the punishment, the stronger the suppression of response. In experiments in which aversive intensity is being manipulated, the strength of the punishment should *not* be increased gradually. Research has shown that in such circumstances the organism tends to adapt to each successive level and that the adaptation can be sufficient to blunt the effect of the punishment—even when it reaches what otherwise would have been an effective level.

EXAMPLE 8. Parents may unwittingly do their children a disservice by trying to use mild punishment. In an attempt to suppress an incorrect response, the parents may administer a mild punishment only to find it ineffective. A slightly more severe punishment is then tried, but at each level the child adapts. Eventually the punishment is strong but the adaptation continues to keep it from being effective. Initial strong punishment might have been sufficient to suppress the response and prevent the spiraling adaptation effect.

One other finding is that punishment of a somewhat longer duration tends to be more effective than punishment of a shorter duration. Interaction among intensity, duration, and onset can be expected.

Behavioral contrast. Specificity of punishment is sometimes illustrated by what has been called *behavioral contrast.* The suppression of response strength appears to be restricted to the given stimulus situation. When that situation no longer exists, the response may reappear at a greater strength or with greater frequency than before punishment (see Problem 8.21).

Time out. A punishment procedure comparable to the Premack principle of reinforcement has been called the *time-out* procedure. The punishment of a response is to *not* allow some response to occur for a specified period of time. This reduces the opportunities the subject would otherwise have to experience reinforcement.

EXAMPLE 9. The time-out procedure is employed when a parent tells a child, "You tracked mud into the house. You will not be allowed to go out and play for the rest of the afternoon." (*Note*: If the child does not want to go out, this procedure will be ineffective.) Teachers sometimes act in a corresponding manner when they make statements such as, "Recess will be shortened five minutes for each extra minute it takes you to settle down."

Punishment as a Facilitator

In a few instances, punishment appears to facilitate some particular response. Generally, this occurs when a response is reinforced and punished simultaneously—as in a difficult discrimination task. The punisher seems to help the subject discriminate.

Self-Punitive Behavior

When punishment is administered to a response that has been motivated by anxiety or fear, it is possible the punishment may increase the fear level and therefore enhance or sustain the response rather than suppress it.   Such a sequence of events appears to be self-punitive.

EXAMPLE 10.   Enuresis (bed-wetting) may provoke such a cycle.   The anxiety, fear, and guilt produced by severe punishment may actually increase the bed-wetting response and thus increase the following level of punishment delivered to the bed wetter.

Punishment and Neurosis

Self-punitive responses are sometimes referred to as *neurotic*.   Instances of neurotic responding are more likely to develop in some situations than others.   For example, in cases where the final instrumental response in a learned sequence is punished, neurotic responses may follow. Likewise, neurotic responding can be expected when incorrect discrimination responses in very difficult differentiation tasks are punished.   It appears that punishment relationships such as these, where conflict or stress is produced, may generate neurotic responding.

Punishment and Alternative Responses

Perhaps the single most important aspect of using punishment to suppress a response is to suggest some alternative response that can be used in the situation.   If no alternative is available, the respondent may return to the original response for want of anything else to do.

EXAMPLE 11.   In Example 7, Webster's inappropriate response was to draw on the wall.   Webster's parents might be well advised to buy a roll of shelf paper and tack up large sheets of the paper on the wall, while suggesting to Webster that an acceptable alternative to drawing on the wall would be drawing on the shelf paper.   The combination of suppression of the incorrect response and reinforcement for the correct response should prove satisfying to both Webster and his parents.

8.4   LEARNED HELPLESSNESS

An organism that is first subjected to inescapable aversive stimuli and then given the opportunity to escape or avoid those stimuli sometimes fails to make the escape or avoidance response. Such nonresponding, when responding would be reinforcing, has been called *learned helplessness*.

EXAMPLE 12.   Learned helplessness is sometimes illustrated by children who have been bullied.   Perhaps in the past the bully had sufficient strength or control to manipulate others, but eventually most of the other children "catch up" to him.   Despite this development, the bully may continue to dominate because of the others' learned helplessness.

8.5   COGNITIVE INTERPRETATION
OF AVERSIVE CONDITIONS

While not yet widely researched, cognitive interpretations of aversive situations have been supported by a growing number of studies.   Basically these approaches stress the anticipation or prediction of aversive conditions.   Because such responses are essentially "internal," they are difficult to study, but hypotheses based upon cognitive positions have been used to try to explain all the behaviors described in this chapter.

Solved Problems

8.1 Distinguish between an aversive stimulus and negative reinforcement. How do these terms relate to escape, avoidance, and punishment behaviors?

An aversive stimulus is any event that when removed increases the probability of the response that removed it. It is the presence of the event that is considered the aversive stimulus, while the removal or termination is called negative reinforcement.

Escape behavior occurs when an aversive stimulus already is present and a response is made allowing the organism to get away from that aversive stimulus, that is, experience negative reinforcement. Avoidance behavior occurs when there is the anticipation of an aversive event and a response is made preventing that experience. Punishment occurs when experiencing the aversive event is contingent upon making some response; that is, the aversive stimulus is delivered *because* that response is made.

8.2 Explain why maintaining a good diet may sometimes be considered escape behavior while at other times it would be called avoidance behavior.

The presumption of this problem is that a bad diet may lead to problems such as overweight. If such a condition already exists, the maintenance of a good diet would be an escape behavior, hopefully leading to weight reduction (removal of the aversive condition). Maintaining a good diet when at a normal weight would represent avoidance behavior, preventing the aversive condition from occurring.

8.3 Why is the aversive stimulus in an escape situation also considered to be a discriminative stimulus?

An escape response being acquired is often produced both when the aversive condition is present and when it is absent, apparently because other stimuli present at the time serve to provoke the response. However, after repeated presentations of the aversive stimulus, most organisms appear to distinguish the appropriate times (when the aversive stimulus is present) for making the escape response. The aversive stimulus thus serves as a discriminative cue for the occurrence of the escape response; the other stimuli no longer provoke the response.

8.4 What effects can schedules of reinforcement or intensity of the aversive stimulus be expected to have upon escape behavior?

If the removal of the aversive stimulus (that is, negative reinforcement) is manipulated according to some schedule of reinforcement, the pattern of responding can be expected to be very similar to those described previously for positive reinforcement (see Chapter 7). Similarly, the greater the intensity of the aversive event, the greater the expected rate of responding.

8.5 Karen is relieved that her father no longer shouts at her, and she has begun to respond to his more quiet requests that she mow the lawn, wash the car, give up smoking cigarettes, and so forth. Why does Karen respond to a low-level aversive stimulus, such as a quiet request or polite order, when a much higher-level aversive stimulus was required before?

Karen's change in responsiveness illustrates an intriguing finding regarding the intensity of an aversive stimulus in escape behavior: Once established, an escape response may continue to be made in the presence of stimuli at levels that would not have been considered aversive when acquisition first took place. In other words, stimuli that would have been too weak to be judged aversive when acquisition began are now treated as aversive, and termination creates negative reinforcement for the response involved.

8.6   Explain why it is difficult to describe a "pure" procedure for extinguishing escape responses.   What techniques are used?

By definition, extinction is the process of eliminating or removing the reinforcement following a response and the resultant return of the response to its preacquisition strength.   It has been difficult, however, to design an extinction procedure which satisfies this definition without being confounded by some other variable.

One extinction procedure is simply not to terminate the aversive stimulus after the appropriate response has been made.   While this satisfies the no-reinforcement aspect of extinction, it also creates the possibility of a seeming punishment contingency.   The response may return to preacquisition strength, but it may not be possible to know whether to attribute this to extinction or the effects of punishment.

The second common extinction procedure is to terminate the aversive stimulus completely.   This does eliminate the possibility of reinforcement, but at the same time also removes the most important discriminative cue (see Problem 8.3).   Such a situation probably changes the motivation value of the circumstances considerably, thus confounding any results.   Again, it may be difficult to determine whether the decrease in response strength should be attributed to extinction or to a decrease in motivation.

In general, the latter procedure—terminating the aversive stimulus—produces a much smoother and more rapid decrease in response strength than does the first.

8.7   The earliest explanations of avoidance behavior were based upon classical conditioning, including the concepts of conditioned fear and subsequent fear reduction.   Explain these concepts.

Avoidance was thought to be the result of classical conditioning.   Some previously neutral stimulus was paired with an aversive stimulus and came to take on aversive or fear-producing qualities.   Later presentations of the CS elicited conditioned responses that produced fear-reduction and avoidance of the aversive conditions.

8.8   Why was CS offset thought to be important to the explanation given in the previous problem?

It was posited that if CS onset generated the conditioned fear and therefore elicited the avoidance response, that CS offset, in turn, would signal the termination of the potential aversive conditions and be treated as a reinforcement.

8.9   Describe the information-providing explanation of avoidance learning which has been presented as an alternative to the classical conditioning conceptions.

When subjects were able to prevent onset not only of the aversive stimulus but also of the CS, they *did* prevent the aversive stimulus onset but *did not* prevent CS onset.   This contradicts the conception of CS onset as fear-producing and CS offset as reinforcing.

The alternative explanation is that CS onset and CS offset are information-providing: In effect, the CS onset serves as a discriminative cue indicating the appropriateness of the avoidance response, while the CS offset signals successful completion of that appropriate avoidance response.

8.10   What then is the logical conclusion of the findings described in Problems 8.7, 8.8, and 8.9?

The conclusion reached by most psychologists is that the fundamental contingency producing avoidance responding is simply the opportunity to avoid, rather than terminate, the CS or the aversive stimulus.   The opportunity to avoid appears to supersede fear-reduction, modification of the situation by conditioned stimuli or improvement of performance produced by informative (instrumental) stimuli.

8.11   Some avoidance responses appear to be more easily learned than others.   What additional theory has been proposed to account for this?

A theory based upon the notion of species-specific defense reactions (SSDRs) has been proposed.   The theory says that for every organism there is a hierarchy of innate defense reactions; when confronted with an opportunity to escape or avoid, the organism tries the most likely response first.   If a response is unsuccessful, the next most likely response is tried, and so on.   This theory is related to the concept of preparedness (Chapter 4).   A response low in the hierarchy will be more difficult to acquire than one high in the hierarchy.   Many psychologists, while admitting the importance of both classical and instrumental factors, believe this theory helps to explain why it is difficult to train certain types of avoidance responses; in addition, they believe the theory broadens the scope of our understanding of avoidance learning.

8.12   Although seemingly a biological or innate-response theory of avoidance, the proposal described in Problem 8.11 has also been treated as a cognitive theory.   Explain this latter interpretation.

It has been suggested that species-specific defense reactions result from an organism's recognition of certain stimuli as *danger signals*.   Likewise, stimuli that predict the end of unpleasant conditions are treated as *safety signals*.   Understanding of both of these conditions and the ability to act accordingly appear to depend upon the organism's capacity to predict or anticipate correctly—essentially a cognitive activity.

8.13   Why do greater levels of intensity of the aversive stimulus not necessarily produce faster or better avoidance performance?

High levels of aversive stimulus intensity often produce responses that compete with the potential avoidance response (for example, "freezing" when running is required).   Such competing responses have to be reduced or eliminated before the avoidance response can be learned.   This can be achieved in at least two ways—changing the procedure so that only the avoidance response is available, or starting the procedure with relatively weak levels of the aversive stimulus which are then increased once the avoidance response has been at least partially acquired.

8.14   What results have been obtained regarding the effects of CS-UCS interval and intertrial interval (ITI) on avoidance conditioning?

The solution to this problem may be best described by the word "mixed." In general, relatively longer CS-UCS intervals seem to produce greater conditioning, although this varies considerably for different species.   Intertrial interval variations appear to produce an inverted-U function, with moderate-length ITIs creating maximum avoidance response conditioning, while performance is poorer with both shorter and longer ITIs.   ITIs in these studies ranged from 30 seconds to 30 minutes, with best performance when trials were spaced about 5 minutes apart.

8.15   Is there any limit to the retention span of learned avoidance responses?

Research supports the finding that avoidance responses can be retained over exceedingly long periods of times.   Variables such as age when the response was learned, competition with other subsequently learned responses, or species may affect the specific results.   (See Chapter 13 for a more thorough discussion of retention.)

8.16   A phobia, such as fear of riding in elevators, is often difficult to extinguish.   Why?

The typical phobic reaction is one of avoidance; the person who has a phobia of elevators may climb stairs rather than ride up or down.   To extinguish such an avoidance response, the person must be brought into the stimulus situation and made to see that the aversive condition does not occur.   This could be accomplished in this case by having the individual take a few uneventful elevator rides.   If the person will not confront the situation, however, the avoidance response cannot be extinguished, and therefore the phobia remains.

8.17   In Problem 8.6, two procedures for extinguishing escape responses were suggested.   Are there two comparable extinction procedures for avoidance responses?

Yes.   One is described in Problem 8.16, in which the subject is confronted by the stimulus situation in question but the aversive condition does not result.   The second extinction procedure would involve presenting the aversive stimulus even though the avoidance response was made. While such a procedure would not be employed for extinguishing a response such as the phobia described in the previous problem, it might be used to try to elicit some different avoidance response (essentially a counterconditioning situation).

8.18   Explain what is meant by this statement: "Recent research on contingency has shown that Thorndike's *original* proposition of the law of effect may be correct."   (See Chapter 2 to review the law of effect, if necessary.)

Thorndike's original proposal for the law of effect stated that responses followed by satisfaction would be more likely to recur when a similar stimulus situation exists, while responses followed by dissatisfaction (or aversive conditions) would become less likely to occur.   This original proposal was modified later to indicate that punishment might suppress response strength for some time, but not necessarily work in a manner directly opposite to that of reinforcement.

Recent research has led to new support for the original proposal.   Punishment, when made contingent upon the response being studied, can be a highly effective modifier of behavior.   The key to this effect apparently is the recognition of the contingency between response and punishment.

8.19   If the aim is to maximize the effects of a punishment, what values should be assigned for the intensity, duration, and delay of the punishing stimulus?

In general and up to some limit, increasing the intensity of the stimulus and its duration will increase the effectiveness of the punishment, as will minimizing the delay between the response and the delivery of the punishment.   Reduction of intensity, reduction of duration, or introduction of a delay period between response and delivery of punishment will reduce its effectiveness.

8.20   Beginning joggers who "jump in" vigorously often quit quickly, while those who work into their programs gradually are more likely to stay with jogging.   Explain this finding in terms of punishment research.

While jogging is good for your health, there usually is some pain involved.   The results described in the problem mirror the gradual vs. sudden onset effect found when using punishment. When punishment intensities are built up gradually, high levels eventually can be tolerated and responding may continue.   However, sudden onset of a comparable high-level punisher will suppress the response, often completely.   Thus, the gradual buildup of a jogging program probably is wise when the long term effects are considered.   (*Note:* Parents might want to consider this finding also.   Gradually greater levels of punishment may be ineffective because of the child's ability to develop tolerance.)

8.21   Why might a behavior that a child's parents punish at home become *more* frequent while the child is at school?

The effect produced here is comparable to behavioral contrast.   The suppression produced by punishing a behavior under one set of conditions may be restricted to those conditions only, and the behavior actually is facilitated when those conditions no longer prevail.   For example, when the parent is no longer present to punish teasing behavior, the frequency of teasing may actually increase.   In such circumstances, the punishment effect apparently does not generalize.

8.22   Explain the circumstances under which punishment may serve as a facilitator for acquisition of a response.

In difficult discrimination learning situations, punishing the correct response may actually help
establish response learning.   When the punishment is also accompanied by some reinforcement, the
punishing stimulus apparently helps increase the differentiation of the choices available, especially
when other cues are less salient.

8.23   Self-punitive or "vicious-circle" studies have shown, for example, that dogs taught an
avoidance response will continue to make that response (and often more vigorously than
before) even when it is punished.   Suggest a comparable sort of behavior that a human
might show.

The behavior shown by the dogs may be a result of the fear produced by the punishment.   A
comparable effect for a human might be created when inappropriate responding motivated by
extreme anxiety is punished.   The punishment may increase the anxiety and therefore actually
increase the inappropriate responding rather than help eliminate it.

8.24   Vicious-circle behavior such as that described in Problem 8.23 is sometimes judged neurotic.   What is another example of the relationship of punishment to neurotic behavior?

Punishment of consummatory responses (for example, eating) may produce not only suppression
of the response but also a variety of neurotic behaviors such as aggressiveness, passivity, tremors, or
nausea.

8.25   Parents often ask about the effectiveness of punishment.   Assuming that a vicious-circle
situation is avoided, what general advice summarizes the principles of punishment?

The general advice to parents is that if punishment is to be used (an initial decision of great
importance), it should be immediate so that a contingency is established between the inappropriate
response and the punishment.   If this contingency is sufficiently strong and if it is followed by the
suggestion and subsequent reinforcement of an appropriate response, the complete termination of
inappropriate responding will be more likely.

8.26   What sequence of events produces learned helplessness?   Are there everyday examples of
this?

The phenomenon of learned helplessness occurs when an inescapable aversive condition persists
for some period of time before an escape or avoidance response can be effective.   If the organism is
exposed to conditions that are at first uncontrollable, responses that later could control the circumstances are not learned, apparently because the organism "believes" they will not work.

An example of everyday learned helplessness is the behavior of some prisoners of war.   Held at
first in uncontrollable and inescapable conditions, prisoners often refuse to attempt controlling or
escape responses even when they obviously would be successful.

8.27   Why does the phenomenon of learned helplessness seem to support a cognitive interpretation of the effects of aversive stimulation similar to that presented in Problem 8.12?

A cognitive interpretation is based upon the anticipation or prediction the organism develops in
a given situation.   The anticipations described in Problem 8.12 were correct or successful, while
those of learned helplessness are essentially unsuccessful.

Key Terms

Aversive stimulus.   Any stimulus the organism judges to be noxious or unpleasant.

Avoidance.   A response that allows an organism to keep from experiencing an anticipated aversive stimulus.

Behavioral contrast.   Extinction of a response suppressed by an aversive stimulus only in a given situation; the response increases in other situations; the effect of the aversive stimulus does not generalize.

Conditioned emotional responses (CERs).   Following pairing of a previously neutral stimulus with an emotion-producing stimulus, the former serves to elicit a comparable emotional reaction.

Danger signals.   Stimuli thought to elicit defense reactions.

Escape.   Some response that allows an organism to get away from an already-present aversive stimulus.

Learned helplessness.   The acceptance of the consequences of a situation as uncontrollable (or inescapable) even when an alternative response is possible.

Negative reinforcement.   The situation in which the removal or termination of some stimulus serves as a reinforcer.

Phobia.   An intense, compelling, and often irrational fear.

Punishment.   Conditions in which delivery of some aversive stimulus is contingent upon the organism making some response.

Safety signals.   Stimuli thought to indicate relief from aversive conditions.

Self-punitive behavior.   Responding that leads to increased aversive stimulation; possibly attributable to increased levels of anxiety or fear produced by the initial aversive circumstances.

Species-specific defense reactions (SSDRs).   Proposed innate protective responses.

Time out.   A punishment procedure that withholds the opportunity for positive reinforcement for a given period of time.

Chapter 9

Extinction and Spontaneous Recovery

Extinction and spontaneous recovery are often treated as mere aspects of larger topics in the psychology of learning (such as classical conditioning, instrumental conditioning, or schedules of reinforcement). The phenomena of extinction and spontaneous recovery can be studied in their own right, however, and this chapter summarizes some of the basic findings about them.

9.1 DEFINITION OF EXTINCTION

The word *extinction* is used two ways: to describe a procedure and the result of that procedure. The extinction procedure involves terminating the presentation of reinforcement. This can also be considered the end of the acquisition period. The expected result is that the response strength eventually will return to its pretraining level.

EXAMPLE 1. Parents might employ an extinction procedure to get their child to stop whining. Consistent failure to reinforce the whining should eventually lead to termination of such responses. It is important that occasional reinforcements *not* be allowed to occur because this would create partial-reinforcement conditions and produce the partial-reinforcement effect—great resistance to extinction.

Resistance to Extinction

One of the measures used to determine the effectiveness of a training procedure or the strength of learning is the amount of time or number of trials needed to extinguish a response. In general, the greater this value, the greater the *resistance to extinction*, or strength of the response.

EXAMPLE 2. Teachers are often amazed at the persistence of incorrect language patterns. The teachers repeatedly attempt to extinguish the incorrect responses by not reinforcing them and, at the same time, try to suggest alternative responses. What the teachers may fail to recognize is that the students are probably still receiving partial reinforcement from family or friends. If at home or among friends the students say "How's come?" (instead of "Why?") and are given an immediate answer, the incorrect pattern is reinforced and will persist.

Beginning of Extinction

One interesting finding is that before it starts to diminish, response strength often increases slightly just after the beginning of an extinction procedure.

EXAMPLE 3. "Young love," or rather the end of a relationship, sometimes produces this effect. If, for example, the girl says, "That's all. I don't ever want to see you again," and sticks to this resolve, the boy's initial reaction may be to telephone *more* often, send *more* notes, and buy *more* presents. Continued failure of the responses to produce reinforcement will ultimately lead to extinction of the responses.

Omission Training

One procedure that can be used to enhance the extinction process is *omission training*. Not only is the subject not reinforced for responding, but reinforcement is given when the response is *not* made for some period of time. In other words, the absence of response produces reinforcement.

EXAMPLE 4. When parents say, "You may have ice cream for dessert tonight if you don't bother your little brother today," they are employing omission training. Not responding (no bothering) is reinforced; bothering is not reinforced (extinction procedure).

9.2   VARIABLES AFFECTING EXTINCTION

This section discusses the major acquisition or extinction variables that affect the extinction process.

Number of Reinforcements during Acquisition

The relationship between number of reinforcements during acquisition and resistance to extinction is seen in Fig. 9-1.   The dashed portion of the curve represents speculation on the part of some researchers that resistance to extinction may actually decrease once the number of reinforcements during acquisition reaches some exceptionally high value.

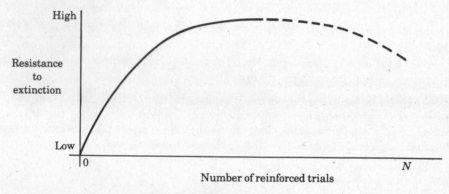

Fig. 9-1

Note that the usual finding is that the maximum value of resistance to extinction is reached after relatively few reinforced acquisition trials.   (There is also a leveling off of the curve as it approaches its maximum value.)

Amount of Reinforcement during Acquisition

There may be an interaction between the number of reinforcements and the size or amount of each reinforcement.   Assigning a value or amount to a reinforcer is not always easy (for example, when verbal praise is used as the reinforcer).   However, the general finding is that the greater the value or amount of continuous reinforcement, the smaller the value of resistance to extinction. This finding generally is attributed to the contrast between the acquisition and extinction procedures.

Secondary Reinforcement

Secondary, or learned, reinforcements may prolong resistance to extinction when some other reinforcement has been permanently terminated.   However, if the strength of the secondary reinforcement is dependent upon the occasional presentation of the terminated reinforcement, the secondary reinforcement will finally lose its reinforcing properties through extinction.   (This is comparable to extinction in classical conditioning.)

EXAMPLE 5.   Statements such as "We'll do it again.   Just bear with me," have a way of serving as secondary reinforcers.   When "again" never seems to arrive, the "bearing with" responses finally give out.   This represents the power of such statements as secondary reinforcers for humans, but also the eventual extinction that can be expected in such circumstances.

Delay of Reinforcement

If delay of reinforcement occurs during the acquisition period, the usual effect is an increase in resistance to extinction of the response being learned. This is found especially when the length of delay varies and includes some immediate reinforcement trials. It is also found that longer average delay seems to promote greater resistance to extinction.

Effort of Response

In general, the greater the effort necessary to make a response during extinction, the lower the value of resistance to extinction.

EXAMPLE 6. Extinction of a "snacking" habit can be accomplished more rapidly if the snacks are made very inaccessible. A dormitory resident might accomplish this by placing all coins in a piggy bank that cannot be opened without breaking it. This would prevent easy operation of vending machines and therefore make snacking more difficult, thus decreasing the resistance to extinction of the snacking behavior and fulfilling the dietary goals.

Intertrial Interval (ITI)

Despite many research efforts, there has been no general, conclusive finding regarding the relationship of intertrial interval (ITI) and resistance to extinction. Some results suggest that short intervals decrease resistance to extinction, while others show just the opposite. The intertrial interval does not seem to be a potent variable or one that can be manipulated to create a generally predictable effect. Instead, the effect of manipulating it needs to be tested in each unique circumstance.

Schedules of Reinforcement

Responses acquired under partial-reinforcement conditions (in which all correct responses are *not* reinforced) will be more resistant to extinction than responses acquired in continuous (100-percent)-reinforcement conditions. As mentioned in Chapters 4, 7, and 8, this general rule is known as the *partial-reinforcement effect* (PRE).

9.3 SPECIAL CASES OF EXTINCTION

Neither the model of extinction proposed in Section 9.1 nor the assorted relevant variables detailed in Section 9.2 can account for all the effects of extinction that have been observed. In this section some of the "special cases" of extinction are described.

Spontaneous Recovery

If the extinction process is rigidly employed for a sufficient period of time, at some point the response strength will return to its original, preacquisition level. At that time, it would be possible to terminate the process and claim extinction to be completed. It is known, however, that once a period of rest following extinction has taken place, *spontaneous recovery* of a response may occur—that is, when the stimulus situation is presented once again with no accompanying reinforcement, the response may reappear. The strength of the response in spontaneous recovery, which usually is less than what it was at acquisition, can be used as one measure of the effectiveness of an extinction process.

Silent Extinction

In *silent-extinction* procedures the organism is permitted to respond at acquisition levels, but no reinforcement is delivered. The absence of reinforcement serves to gradually reduce the value of the responses, which are considered extinguished when they reach some preacquisition level. Extinction trials are then continued after this point, and the general finding is that the longer they are continued the lower will be the value of any response that will be shown if spontaneous recovery is allowed to occur.

Latent Extinction

The procedure for *latent extinction* is similar to that for silent extinction in that no reinforcement is delivered during the extinction trials; it differs, however, in that the organism is *not* permitted to perform the complete learned response: only partial responding is allowed, and gradually the now unreinforced learned response will be extinguished.

EXAMPLE 7.   Suppose a rat learns to run through a T maze in order to reach a goal box where there is a food reward.   Silent extinction trials would involve removing the reward and letting the rat run the maze.   Latent extinction trials would involve placing the rat in the empty goal box—without a food reward.

Extinction without Responding

A third special case of extinction occurs when the subject is placed in the stimulus situation but not allowed to make the previously acquired response.   In some cases this involves physical restraint or the use of drugs to prevent responding.   Again, when such a group is compared with a "regular" extinction group for resistance to extinction, the "regular" group shows greater resistance.

Extinction of Escape and Avoidance

Both escape and avoidance situations may employ two different extinction procedures. The first involves the continuation of the aversive stimulus even though the previously correct response is made.   In the second there is complete removal of the aversive stimulus (see Chapter 8).

One explanation for the results obtained using these procedures has been called *expectancy*.   Essentially this explanation proposes that the subject develops an expectancy that making the response will terminate or avoid the aversive stimulus, while not responding will not.   As long as this expectancy is confirmed, the responding will continue to occur.   Repeated disconfirmation, as in the extinction procedures described above, should lead to termination of responding.

EXAMPLE 8.   Expectancy theory forms the basis for a type of psychotherapy called implosive therapy.   In one type of implosive therapy, the subject is told to imagine all the most anxiety-producing stimuli possible, but shown they do *not* produce the accompanying (expected) bad results.   Such a procedure is meant to "disconfirm" the anxiety reaction and lead to extinction of the responses.

9.4   THEORIES OF EXTINCTION

The results of extinction have been explained in several different manners.   The expectancy theory was discussed in the previous section.   Three more theories proposed as possible explanations of extinction are the *response-produced-inhibition theory,* the *competition theory,* and the *frustration-competition theory*.

Response-Produced-Inhibition Theory

Two components of inhibition are proposed in the response-produced-inhibition theory.   One, called *reactive inhibition,* is a temporary component that is comparable to fatigue and will dissipate with the passage of time.   The other, *conditioned inhibition,* is considered to be a permanent component.   These two aspects are thought to summate, preventing responding when their combined value is greater than the strength of the response.   This theory was originated by Clark Hull (see Chapter 2).

Competition Theory

Based originally on the work of Edwin Guthrie (see Chapter 2), the competition theory suggests that a new (different) response becomes attached to the stimulus; that is, extinction is essentially the process of replacing the original response with some other (competing) response. This theory is also sometimes called an *interference theory*.

EXAMPLE 9.   In a very simple form, people who substitute gum-chewing for smoking are using the competition theory of extinction.   The smoking response becomes extinguished as a substitute response replaces it.

Frustration-Competition Theory

The basic premise of the frustration-competition theory is that nonreinforcement produces frustration, which in turn energizes competing responses.   The competing responses grow in strength because they are reinforced by reducing the level of frustration.

9.5   INTERPRETATIONS OF SPONTANEOUS RECOVERY

When a response reappears upon presentation of a stimulus following extinction and a subsequent period of rest, spontaneous recovery of the response is said to have occurred.   Several theories have been proposed to explain this phenomenon.   One theory that fits many spontaneous-recovery situations very nicely is the response-produced-inhibition theory.   It proposes that the period of rest following extinction allows for the dissipation of the reactive inhibition, and response strength will once again be greater than the inhibition value.

A second interpretation proposes that spontaneous recovery represents the reappearance of a response when certain discriminative cues for responding reappear.   The typical explanation is that cues associated with the start of the response situation are not extinguished; thus, when they follow the period of rest, the response recurs.

EXAMPLE 10.   Suppose a young swimmer in training wants to perform a forward, two-and-one-half-somersault dive.   During practice, each of the swimmer's attempts is unsuccessful, and she finally gives up and says, "I'm just too tired to try any more today!"   The reactive-inhibition interpretation would suggest that the rest following that practice would allow temporary inhibition to dissipate.   The discriminative-cue interpretation suggests that returning to practice the next time would generate cues that had not been associated with the previous extinction.   In either case at the next practice, with the fatigue gone, the swimmer would make additional attempts.   If these and all attempts in succeeding practices are unsuccessful, the attempts will eventually extinguish entirely—the practice cue becoming associated with a "don't try" understanding.

Solved Problems

9.1   Explain why the term "extinction" has two meanings.

Psychologists use "extinction" to describe the procedure involved—stopping the reinforcement of a previously reinforced response.   They also use the word to specify the result obtained using that procedure—the return of the response in question to its original (preconditioning) strength.

9.2   Because of remodeling, one of the most frequently used doors in a dormitory was locked permanently.   Describe the pattern of responding that could be expected from the residents once this happened.

Locking the door permanently creates an extinction procedure, and the response pattern should be typical of extinction.   It could thus be expected that at first the residents would actually increase both the number and vigor of their responses (shaking the handle, trying to turn it with both hands, even kicking the door).   Continued lack of success would eventually produce a drop in response frequency until it would finally **approach zero**.

9.3   Using the situation described in Problem 9.2, create circumstances to illustrate the concept of resistance to extinction.

There are many possible solutions to this problem.   One possibility is to imagine that a similar dormitory's governing board had decided to lock the corresponding door on a trial basis and did so for a period of time that was both preceded and followed by periods when the door was unlocked.   Such an arrangement constitutes a partial-reinforcement condition.   It would be expected that if the final decision was to permanently lock the door, residents of the "on-again, off-again" dormitory would take longer to extinguish the door-opening attempts than residents of the one-change-only dormitory.   This illustrates a difference in resistance to extinction.

9.4   How is extinction in classical conditioning different from extinction in instrumental conditioning?

Termination of the unconditioned stimulus (UCS) and later presentation of the conditioned stimulus (CS) alone is the extinction procedure for classically conditioned responses.   In instrumental conditioning because there is no clear-cut CS or any response-provoking UCS, extinction is different, consisting simply of the complete termination of the response-reinforcement contingency.   Note, however, that although one procedure involves stopping a response-eliciting stimulus while the other terminates a response-following reinforcer, the basic result is the same in each case—reduction of the strength of the response being studied.

9.5   Explain why omission training can be interpreted as an extension of the extinction procedure.

Extinction has been defined as the procedure of terminating reinforcement and the subsequent result of the response returning to its previous, preacquisition strength.   Omission training simply "adds to" this by reinforcing the *failure* to respond; that is, if the response is *not* made for a certain period of time, the organism will be reinforced.

9.6   Training their dog, the McHills decide they will reward every correct response for quite a while and that the reward will be a big one (biscuits, a steak bone, etc.).   Once the McHills stop reinforcing every response, how resistant to extinction are the dog's responses likely to be?

Two variables are operating in this situation—the number of reinforcements given and the amount of reinforcement.   Findings regarding number of reinforcements during acquisition indicate that resistance to extinction increases in a negatively accelerated pattern up to some asymptotic value and that the asymptote is reached fairly quickly.   (There is some controversial evidence indicating that continuous reinforcement that persists well past asymptote achievement may actually produce a deterioration in resistance to extinction.)

Research on amount of reinforcement given in continuous-reinforcement conditions shows that the greater the amount given on each trial, the *more rapid* will be the extinction of the response. While this might at first seem to be opposite to the expected finding, the contrast between the reinforcement and nonreinforcement conditions apparently contributes to this result.

Thus, the solution to this problem probably is that the McHill's dog would be fairly resistant to extinction, although not as much as if smaller amounts of reward had been used or, especially, if partial reinforcement had been used.

9.7   Suppose an experiment uses three groups of rats, all to be trained to run a T maze such as the one shown in Fig. 9-2.   Before any trials in the T maze, one group of rats is fed in a neutral (gray) compartment, one in a white compartment, and one in a black compartment.   Although no food is used during training, it is always true that one of the goal boxes is white and the other black.   With this information, predict the response pattern for each group of rats.

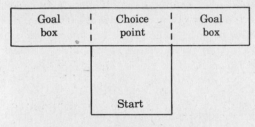

Fig. 9-2

The assumption is that the color of the feeding compartment has become a secondary reinforcer. Therefore, it may be expected that the second group will turn toward the white and the third group toward the black.   However, as the trials continue, the latter two groups should become more and more likely to show random responding.   This happens because the association between the color and food is undergoing extinction—that is, the strength of a secondary reinforcer will diminish in the same manner as a CR if extinction conditions exist.

9.8   If a delay-of-reinforcement procedure is used during acquisition of a response, what effect upon resistance to extinction can be expected?

Although not all research results support this finding, the general conclusion is that a delay-of-reinforcement procedure used during acquisition will produce greater resistance to extinction than no-delay (immediate) reinforcement.   This result is found most often when the acquisition trials have varied delay, including some 0-delay trials, and when the average delay is fairly long.

9.9   Cigarette smokers sometimes attempt to "cut down" by imposing greater and greater requirements upon themselves before a cigarette can be smoked.   Based upon the research on effort of responding during extinction, what pattern of responding can be expected?

In general, the greater the effort required to respond during the extinction period, the less resistant to extinction the response will be.   Thus, if the smokers place greater restrictions upon their responding, the frequency of smoking should decrease (for example, if the cigarettes are kept in the attic area over the garage and can only be reached by going outside and moving the car in order to pull down the attic stairs).

9.10   Just as with acquisition trials, the period of time between one extinction trial and the next is referred to as the intertrial interval (ITI).   What results have been obtained by manipulating ITI and measuring resistance to extinction?

There are no consistent findings.   Lengthening the ITI, for example, does not necessarily increase resistance to extinction.   Whether massed extinction trials or spaced extinction trials result in greater resistance to extinction appears to depend on the particular circumstances of the procedures employed.

9.11   What is partial reinforcement? What is the partial-reinforcement effect? How does this variable affect the resistance to extinction of a learned response?

Partial reinforcement is *any* response-acquisition situation in which not all correct responses are reinforced.   (Virtually all responses outside the laboratory are learned under partial-reinforcement conditions, since no responses are likely to be reinforced 100 percent of the time.)   As stated in previous chapters, the partial-reinforcement effect (PRE) shows that partial reinforcement leads to greater resistance to extinction than does continuous reinforcement.   It also is generally found that the greater the number of responses required for a single reinforcement during acquisition, the greater will be the resistance to extinction.   For example, if the training is set up in such a way that 200 correct responses must be made before 1 reinforcement is delivered, the response will be more resistant to extinction than it would have been if it were trained with a 50-to-1 ratio.

9.12   Suppose a phobia is acquired when a previously neutral stimulus, such as an elevator, is paired with a fear-producing stimulus, such as a sudden, unexpected plunge of the elevator. Subsequent extinction of the fear response may be accomplished by repeated exposures to the elevator with no accompanying fear circumstances.   Once the fear response apparently is no longer elicited by the CS, what advantage may be obtained by continuing the extinction trials?

Continuing the extinction trials beyond apparent termination of the fear response may produce an effect known as silent extinction.   Additional trials will discourage spontaneous recovery, thus reducing the likelihood of a new fear response after extinction training has been terminated.

9.13   Distinguish silent extinction, latent extinction, and extinction without responding from one another.

In silent extinction, the complete response is possible during all the extinction trials, although late in the procedure it is no longer made.   In latent extinction, the complete response is allowed only after there has been a period of partial response (usually placement in the goal box) accompanied by nonreinforcement conditions.   The number of complete responses made is considerably reduced in comparison to the responses of a group of subjects placed in some "neutral" circumstance an equal number of times.

Extinction without responding is a form of the latent-extinction procedure involving no response other than observation of the nonreinforcing stimulus.   For example, drugs may be used to temporarily paralyze the organism so that no motor responding is possible while it is being exposed to the stimuli.   Results are comparable to those obtained with latent extinction.

9.14   Two different extinction procedures for escape and avoidance were described in Chapter 8.   Explain how the concept of expectancy can be used to resolve the differing results obtained when the two different extinction procedures are used.

The key concept in these interpretations is confirmation (or disconfirmation) of expectancy. When the aversive stimulus is terminated completely, the subject will probably continue to make the avoidance response, thus confirming a "make the response = no aversive stimulus" expectancy.   There is no opportunity to confirm a "don't make the response = no aversive stimulus" expectancy, and responding continues for many trials.

When the subject's response is blocked, the situation forces disconfirmation of the "don't make a response = aversive stimulus" expectancy.   Likewise the continuation of the aversive stimulus following the (supposed) avoidance response disconfirms the "make the response = no aversive stimulus" expectancy.   Once these disconfirmations are strong enough, extinction will occur.

9.15   How does "flooding" (or implosive therapy) fit the cognitive interpretation expressed in Problem 9.14?

Flooding, which serves as the basis for implosive therapy, involves forcing a subject to remain in the presence of fear cues without eventual presentation of the aversive stimulus. (This is sometimes referred to as "reality testing.") Through a cognitive process, the subject disconfirms the expectancy that the cues indicate an aversive stimulus on the way.

9.16   Explain the response-produced-inhibition interpretation of extinction. How do phenomena such as silent extinction and latent extinction seem to contradict this interpretation?

Interpretations of extinction as a product of response-produced inhibition usually involve two inhibition components. One, reactive inhibition, is a temporary component essentially comparable to fatigue; it dissipates after a period of rest. The second component, conditioned inhibition, is thought to be a permanent effect brought about by the reinforcement of not responding (i.e., by removal of the aversive condition of reactive inhibition).

Phenomena such as silent extinction and latent extinction seem to contradict the response-produced-inhibition explanation of extinction because extinction is seemingly facilitated when responding is prevented. No inhibition can develop, yet extinction is facilitated.

9.17   Systematic desensitization is a therapy procedure involving gradual replacement of anxiety responses with coping responses. How does systematic desensitization support the competition theory of extinction?

The competition theory of extinction suggests that an initial response is extinguished when it is replaced by some competing response. Systematic desensitization is based upon this principle—replacing anxiety with relaxation. This is accomplished in gradual steps. First, the patient is exposed to mild forms of the anxiety-producing stimulus and taught to relax rather than feel anxious. In each subsequent step, a slightly stronger form of the anxiety-producing stimulus is used, with anxiety being extinguished and relaxation serving as the competing response.

9.18   Why would a frustration-competition theory not seem to explain extinction of a classically conditioned CR such as withdrawal in the metronome-click–electric-shock experiment described in Example 6 of Chapter 3?

To answer this, one needs to ask a simple question: "Where is the frustration in having electric shock terminated?" The inability to answer such a question (at least for most subjects) negates the possibility of frustration in this extinction process. Thus, while frustration-competition theory may seem to account for other types of extinction, it appears that there is no one theory to explain all extinction processes and that several interpretations may be needed.

9.19   Define spontaneous recovery, then explain how the response-produced-inhibition theory seemed to account for the phenomenon.

Spontaneous recovery is the reappearance of a previously extinguished response when the stimulus is reintroduced following a period of rest after extinction. Generally, the strength of response is less than the maximum value attained during acquisition.

The two components of response-produced inhibition provide one convincing explanation of spontaneous recovery. When both reactive and conditioned inhibition combine to reach a sufficient level, responding stops (extinguishes). But with the passage of time, reactive inhibition dissipates. Reintroduction of the stimulus situation provokes responding once again, but conditioned inhibition (which is permanent) keeps the value from being as great as was previously reached.

9.20   Suppose a child has had disruptive behavior extinguished during the spring term of the school year.   In the autumn, when school begins again, there is apparent spontaneous recovery of the disruptive responding.   Interpret this using a discriminative-cue explanation.

Some psychologists suggest that the response may be attached to at least two different sets of stimuli—those occuring *during* the extinction procedure and those signalling the *start* of the stimulus situation.   In this instance, it is possible that extinction was associated with the "during" cues, but not the "start" cues.   Therefore, when the "start" cues reappear at the beginning of the next school year, the responses appear to spontaneously recover, although this interpretation would suggest they were never extinguished.

Key Terms

Conditioned inhibition.   A permanent component of response-produced inhibition.

Expectancy.   Anticipation of a particular event.

Extinction.   Any procedure that terminates a response-reinforcement contingency; also the result of that procedure—the return of the conditioned response to its preconditioning value.

Extinction without responding.   A procedure whereby the subject is exposed to the stimulus situation without reinforcement while being kept from responding at all; generally produces reduced resistance to extinction.

Flooding.   In implosive therapy, creating conditions that produce maximum anxiety for the subject.

Implosive therapy.   A procedure whereby the subject is exposed to maximum anxiety conditions and thus enabled to recognize that aversive conditions will not necessarily ensue.

Latent extinction.   A procedure whereby only partial responses or parts of a response sequence are permitted and paired with nonreinforcement conditions; usually produces reduced resistance to extinction when the complete response or sequence is allowed.

Omission training.   The combination of extinction of a response and reinforcement when designated periods of nonresponding are completed.

Reactive inhibition.   A temporary component of response-produced inhibition; often attributed to fatigue.

Response-produced inhibition.   The belief that making a response repeatedly produces a tendency not to make the response.

Silent extinction.   The continuation of extinction trials after the preconditioning value of the conditioned response has been reached; usually reduces the chances of spontaneous recovery.

Spontaneous recovery.   A phenomenon in which, after a period of rest following extinction, the conditioned response reappears when the stimulus alone is presented.

Systematic desensitization.   A therapy based upon competing-responses extinction; generally anxiety responses are replaced with relaxation.

Chapter 10

Generalization and Discrimination

The terms *stimulus generalization* and *discrimination* are used to describe the extent to which a learned response, once linked to a particular stimulus, will also be made to other stimuli of varying degrees of similarity. The wider the variety of stimuli that key off the response, the greater the *stimulus generalization*. The more the response is restricted to stimuli identical or similar to the original stimulus, the greater the *discrimination* (or *differentiation*) shown.

There are two types of stimulus generalization. In *primary stimulus generalization,* the organism responds not only to the original stimulus, but to other stimuli with similar physical properties; thus a rat trained to respond to the sound of a ticking metronome may respond as well to the tapping of a stick on a block of wood. In *secondary stimulus generalization* an organism responds to a stimulus because of some learned equivalence between the two; thus a subject trained to respond to the word "halt" may respond as well to the word "stop."

10.1 GENERAL FACTORS AFFECTING GENERALIZATION

There are several general factors that affect generalization (and, as a result, discrimination). Some of the most important are presented here.

Attention

In the most general sense, whether or not an organism responds to a particular stimulus depends on whether or not it pays *attention* to the stimulus. Research shows that attention may be restricted to only part of a stimulus complex. This is called *selective attention.*

EXAMPLE 1. Pedestrians waiting at a busy city intersection are well advised to attend to a whole stimulus complex before they cross the street. Among the things they should attend to are visual cues (any oncoming traffic they see), audio cues (the sound of approaching vehicles), and symbolic cues (the "walk"/"don't walk" sign in front of them). Often, however, pedestrians show selective attention, crossing as soon as the light or sign is in their favor and disregarding other important cues.

Innate vs. Learned Factors

Some forms of attention appear to result from innate or inherited characteristics. Others are quite obviously learned. It is often found that innate attentional mechanisms are species-specific, while learned attention determinants may be taught to more than one species.

EXAMPLE 2. Both human beings and cats can be trained to link their responses to certain color cues, such as the appearance of a red spot of light in a line of color spots projected on a screen. (The appearance of the red spot indicates the availability of reinforcement and keys off an instrumental response.) Suppose then that with both sets of subjects giving full attention to the line of lights and awaiting the appearance of the red spot, one of the other spots begins to move off toward the edge of the screen. The cats will most likely give almost total attention to the moving spot, even to the point where they will miss the appearance of the red spot and fail to respond. The humans, on the other hand, will divert some of their attention to the moving spot, but will not disregard the appearance of the red spot. Cats apparently are born with an innate tendency to attend more to movement cues than color cues.

Stimulus Control

Stimulus control is the term used to describe the way in which a particular stimulus determines (or results in) the appearance of the correct response. A stimulus that sets the occasion for.

or cues, a particular response is called a *discriminative stimulus*. (*Note:* A discriminative stimulus differs from a UCS in that the discriminative stimulus is not thought to *elicit* or *force* the response in the manner of the UCS.)

Labels have been developed for stimuli that indicate the availability of reinforcement for responding correctly in instrumental (operant) discriminative situations. Stimuli that predict the delivery of reinforcement following the appropriate response have been designated as S^D for free responding or S^+ for discrete trials situations. (An example of free responding would be a rat in a Skinner box pressing a bar for food pellets; a rat running a maze would be an example of discrete trial responding.) Stimuli associated with the unavailability of reinforcement in comparable situations are designated as S^Δ (S delta) or S^-. In classical conditioning, CS^+ and CS^- are used to indicate potential onset of the UCS.

Stimulus-Generalization Gradient

The term used to label the graphic representation of response strength given to the original stimulus and other similar stimuli is the *stimulus-generalization gradient*. It should be noted that stimulus generalization and discrimination can be treated as opposite ends of a continuum, so the amount of either stimulus generalization *or* discrimination can be evaluated from a stimulus-generalization gradient.

EXAMPLE 3. The two curves in Fig. 10-1 are stimulus-generalization gradients. One illustrates widespread stimulus generalization (Fig. 10-1*a*), while the second portrays quite specific differentiation (Fig. 10-1*b*). The former represents responding to a wide variety of stimuli, while the latter shows responding to a much narrower variety.

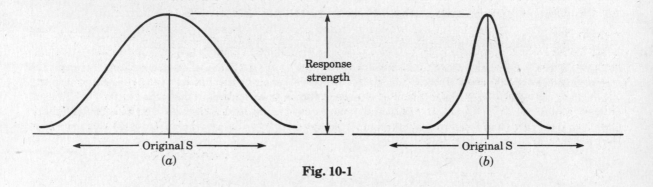

Fig. 10-1

10.2   PROCEDURES AFFECTING GENERALIZATION

A major determinant of the response strength obtained in a given generalization setting may be the procedure used. Several important variables in the design and presentation of discriminative-learning procedures are discussed here.

Simultaneous vs. Successive Stimulus Presentation

Essentially, any test of stimulus generalization or differentiation consists of a comparison. The two basic forms of comparison are to have both stimuli present at the same time, called *simultaneous presentation,* and to present only one stimulus at a time, called *successive presentation.* Simultaneous presentation typically involves reinforcing a response made to one of the stimuli (the positive stimulus) but not to the other (the negative stimulus). In successive presentation the organism is free to respond or not respond as each stimulus appears.

Single- vs. Multiple-Stimulus Testing

When testing for stimulus generalization or discrimination, the organism may compare the original stimulus and one additional stimulus (*single-stimulus testing*) or the original stimulus and several additional stimuli (*multiple-stimulus testing*). Interestingly, single-stimulus testing usually produces stimulus-generalization gradients that are unique for the particular stimulus comparison, while multiple-stimulus testing appears to mask unique properties and produce gradients with almost identical slopes regardless of the value of the initial training stimulus (see Problem 10.8).

Selection of a Measure

There are at least two ways in which any change in the measure of generalization can be reported. The first, called *absolute generalization,* refers to the difference between the actual amount of response strength reported when the test stimulus is presented compared to the actual response strength shown when the original stimulus was used. *Relative generalization,* the second method of reporting a change, refers to the percentage relationship between the response strengths given to the original and test stimuli.

EXAMPLE 4. If subject A has a response strength of 30 units to the original stimulus (however the response is measured) and 18 to the test stimulus, the absolute generalization is 18, while the relative generalization is 60 percent. When subject B shows a response strength of 40 to the original stimulus and 20 to the test stimulus, B's absolute generalization is greater than A's (20 vs. 18), but the relative generalization is less (50 vs. 60 percent). Differing conclusions might be reached depending upon which measure was selected.

In attempting to judge the extent of generalization, psychologists must also take into account *multidimensionality,* the possibility that more than one aspect of the stimulus situation may affect response strength. It may be that some unforeseen aspect of a multidimensional stimulus—and not the aspect supposedly showing generalization—is what cues a response.

EXAMPLE 5. Suppose that the "pie" diagram in Fig. 10-2a is the original stimulus, and that the subjects being tested show a certain amount of stimulus generalization; test stimulus "pies" with slightly smaller portions shaded or slightly larger portions shaded (as in Fig. 10-2b) also yield responding. In general, responding should decrease as the size of the shaded area of the test stimulus diverges more and more from that in the original stimulus. But what about a "pie" stimulus such as the one shown in Fig. 10-2c? It is an exact "negative" of the original; its white area is the same size as the shaded area in Fig. 10-2a. As a test stimulus, Fig. 10-2c might yield an unexpectedly high rate of responding because in some way it is more like the original stimulus than Fig. 10-2b is.

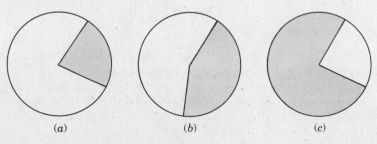

(a)   (b)   (c)

Fig. 10-2

10.3 UNIVERSALITY OF GENERALIZATION

It has already been pointed out that generalization and differentiation can be expected to occur in both classical and instrumental conditioning situations (see Chapters 3 and 4). Generalization can also be observed in many natural settings and it can be put to use in a wide variety of learning procedures, which leads some learning psychologists to describe it as "universal."

Generalization in Natural Settings

While many instances of generalization have been demonstrated in experimental laboratories, perhaps just as many can be found in natural settings. Applying the principles of generalization to such human problems as racial prejudice or abnormal patterns of behavior is of particular interest to psychologists.

EXAMPLE 6. Suppose a clinical psychologist has to deal with a patient who shows a phobic reaction to running water. The phobia may have developed long ago, in response to something that happened at a waterfall, but because of generalization the fear or anxiety is now shown in the presence of showers, hoses, water running into a sink, and the like. The psychologist's aim would be to teach the patient to better differentiate the original stimulus (the waterfall) from the others and thus to recognize the source of the phobia.

Generalization of Extinction

During extinction conditions there is no reinforcement for responding. If a stimulus similar to the original training stimulus is presented repeatedly during extinction, later tests of response strength using the original stimulus will show a diminished value when compared with the original (acquisition) strength. This phenomenon, called *generalization of extinction,* helps support the universality of the concept of generalization.

10.4   EXPLANATIONS OF GENERALIZATION

Several proposals have been put forth to try to explain generalization and differentiation. No one explanation is universally accepted; each has special strengths and weaknesses.

Previous Learning: Differential Reinforcement

One proposal suggests that responding to the original stimulus or other similar stimuli will be a function of previous experience, particularly whether or not the previous responses were reinforced. Reinforcing some responses and not others in some systematic manner is called *differential* (or *selective*) *reinforcement.*

EXAMPLE 7. Differentiation is often shaped (see Chapter 4). A young child learns to discriminate which man is "Daddy" and which is "Uncle Fred" by being selectively reinforced for responding appropriately. Continued reinforcement of the response pattern leads, in this case, to strict differentiation rather than generalization.

Functional vs. Physical Explanations

Another way to explain generalization has been to emphasize experience without focusing on the reinforcement conditions. A *functional explanation* asserts that learning to recognize the relevant (or irrelevant) components of the stimulus is what enables an organism to generalize. Differential reinforcement may play a role in this learning, but it is not seen as the only, or even the necessary, condition for learning.

Physical explanations have been based upon the concept of *cortical irradiation.* The proposal is that some sort of "spread" occurs within the cortex, and the breadth of its spread will determine the extent to which generalization will occur. Originally proposed by Pavlov, this explanation has since been generally discounted.

10.5   VARIABLES AFFECTING THE GENERALIZATION GRADIENT

A number of factors have been found to affect the slope of obtained generalization gradients (such as those in Example 3). Some of the most important are presented in this section.

Predictiveness of the Stimulus

One variable that will to a large extent determine the slope of a generalization gradient is the *predictiveness* of a stimulus—a measure of how strong the original S-R association is in comparison to other S-R associations.   In general, the more certain the original S-R association, the less likely will be associations with "competing" stimuli, unless independent or separate associations have been established.   (The certainty of a particular response following a particular stimulus is also identified as the amount of *stimulus control.*)

Amount of Training

Research has shown that increased *training*, like increased predictiveness, generally leads to greater steepness of the generalization gradient slopes—in other words, to greater differentiation.   Two related proposals attempt to explain this finding.   One suggests that the increased training helps strengthen the appropriate or relevant S-R bonds.   The second proposes that extinction of irrelevant S-R bonds takes place during the intertrial intervals.

Partial Reinforcement

The rate of response generated by a particular schedule of reinforcement appears to affect the slope of the generalization gradient.   In general, the higher the rate of responding, the steeper the gradient's slope.   The proposed explanation of this finding is that faster rates focus attention upon external stimuli—such as the generalized stimuli being linked to the response.   Slower response rates allow attention to be diverted to internal cognitive stimuli, or to stimuli irrelevant to the learning task.

Reward and Punishment

Typical findings are that increased amounts of reward during acquisition will produce steeper generalization gradient slopes (greater differentiation).   Increased punishment of responding during acquisition produces flatter generalization gradient slopes (greater generalization).   In some extreme instances, the strength of response to the test stimulus may be greater than that given to the original stimulus if a punishment condition has existed.

EXAMPLE 8.   In some social situations the strength of a response may be increased as a result of punishment.   Suppose Anne is the love of Charlie's life, but she punishes his amorous advances by ridiculing him in public.   When a new (generalization) stimulus appears in the person of Mary, Charlie may direct his advances toward her and become even more fervent and persistent in his pleas.

Training-Test Time

The greater the delay between training and a test of generalization, the greater the expected generalization.   In other words, delay of testing tends to produce flatter generalization gradient slopes.   One explanation proposed for this is that forgetting of stimulus components is more likely to occur during the delay period than response forgetting is.

Motivation

The effect of motivation upon the slope of a generalization gradient depends upon *when* the motive condition is at a high level.   Greater motivation levels during acquisition generally produce flatter slopes for the generalization gradients later obtained during testing.   However, increased motivation during testing can be expected to generate steeper slopes for the obtained generalization gradients.

Brain Stimulation

Psychologists have made interesting findings relating to the introduction of brain stimulation during the time between acquisition and subsequent testing. In lower organisms such stimulation appears to steepen the slopes of the generalization gradient. At present, this result is not well understood. (This research illustrates one way to use subhuman organisms in an attempt to identify physiological determinants of generalization or differentiation.)

10.6 EXCITATION AND INHIBITION

Influences that affect generalization or differentiation may be either favorable (excitatory) or aversive (inhibitory). Both factors appear to be important, although the single most important consideration determining selective responding appears to be when a S^Δ or S^- becomes recognizably aversive.

Peak Shift

One phenomenon that illustrates the relationship of excitatory and inhibitory factors is called *peak shift*, the finding that response strength may move "away from" the direction of an S^- (which is presumed to have aversive properties) and beyond an original S^+, even though the S^+ continues to maintain its properties. Figure 10-3 illustrates peak shift.

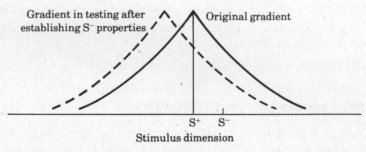

Fig. 10-3

EXAMPLE 9. Politics provides illustrations of the peak-shift phenomenon. Suppose a man supports a candidate who is slightly more conservative than the candidates he usually likes to support. Later, after the candidate is elected and is actually functioning as a legislator, the bills she proposes and votes in favor of are extremely conservative—a fact that serves as a strong aversive condition to the voter. In the next election, the man may shift, not back to his original position, but actually beyond it to support a candidate whom earlier he would have judged too liberal.

Behavioral Contrast

Suppose two separate (but perhaps related) S-R bonds exist in the person's behavior repertoire, and extinction conditions are introduced for one of the S-R bonds. *Behavioral contrast* will be illustrated if the frequency of response for the other S-R bond increases *above* its previous maximum level although reinforcement for that bond does not increase.

EXAMPLE 10. Laboratory research demonstrates behavioral contrast. One study trained a pigeon to respond on a VI schedule of reinforcement by pecking an illuminated disc. During the initial stage of the study the disc was illuminated with either a red or green light—which color was irrelevant. Once the response rate was well established, responding to one of the colors was extinguished. Behavioral contrast was shown when the response rate to the other (nonextinguished) color increased, even though the VI conditions were maintained for that stimulus.

Transposition

The concept of transposition was originally borrowed from music; a transposed melody is one that does not change except for the fact that it is played in a different key. In a stimulus-generalization situation, *transposition* refers to responding to the relationships between stimuli rather than the absolute properties of the stimuli. For example, if an organism is trained to respond to a dim light followed by a bright light, it will be showing transposition if the value of "dim" and "bright" change but responding continues; it is not the absolute dimness or brightness that keys the response, but the dim-bright relationship.

Errorless Discrimination

A procedure used to test the excitatory value of one stimulus while not allowing aversive value to develop for another has been called *errorless discrimination*. Subjects are presented with both stimuli, usually with the S^+ having full strength and the (potential) S^- having very weak intensity. Responses to S^+ are reinforced, but the subject makes no nonreinforced responses to the other stimulus. Gradually, the strength of the second stimulus is increased, always without allowing responding that would be unreinforced. Eventually, if the procedure is well controlled, both stimuli will be at full strength and the subject will show complete differentiation without ever having made any responses (unreinforced or error responses) to the S^-.

Errorless discrimination has been used to support a conclusion mentioned previously—that the phenomena of peak shift and behavioral contrast depend upon the subject recognizing the aversiveness of the S^-. Neither peak shift nor behavioral contrast will be shown when a differentiation is established using the errorless-discrimination procedure. The discrimination is formed without the frustration associated with nonreinforcement of a response to the S^-. And if no frustration is experienced, there will be no frustration to serve as a motivation and provoke additional responding to the positive stimulus.

10.7   FACTORS INFLUENCING DISCRIMINATION

The variables presented in this section influence generalization as well as discrimination; they are set apart here only because they are almost always studied in the context of the latter.

Selective Attention

Attention to the relevant properties of the stimulus situation in part determines whether or not discrimination will develop. When the environment is relatively uncomplicated and the time for observing is adequate, recognition of the relevant stimulus properties should not be difficult. As the environment becomes more complex or as the time allotted for observation decreases, the subject will need to show more and more *selective attention*, "blocking out" or ignoring irrelevant stimuli and concentrating on those that are relevant.

EXAMPLE 11. Conductors of symphony orchestras have been trained to discriminate among the various components being contributed by the players of different instruments. During a rehearsal, the conductor must be able to identify these individual parts even when the entire orchestra is playing. This requires selective attention to the particular instrument's sound within the entire framework of the orchestra playing.

Transfer of Training

Transfer of training (to be discussed more thoroughly in Chapter 12) describes situations where the learning of one task influences the later acquisition of some other task. It has been shown that learning a relatively easy differentiation before trying to learn a related, but much more difficult, discrimination will make acquisition in the second task easier.

A second example of transfer of training in differentiation tasks has been called *discriminative-learning sets* or *learning to learn*. The subject appears to learn a general principle of how to go about responding that can then be applied in any number of specific situations.

EXAMPLE 12. Students often demonstrate they have learned a discriminative-learning set when taking notes in a lecture class. General principles, such as "Anything said more than twice really must be important" or "Ignore the puns, they're just fillers," can be applied regardless of who is lecturing.

10.8   THEORIES OF DISCRIMINATION

Attempts to explain discrimination have fallen into two basic categories—continuity (associative) theories and noncontinuity (cognitive) theories.

Continuity Theories

Continuity theories of discriminative learning, which were among the earliest attempts to explain the phenomenon, propose that the strength of a discriminative response is a function of cumulative experience in which there was a gradual buildup of S-R associations. The discriminative response strength is seen to result from these accumulated S-R associations. The problem with such a theory is that it does not account for phenomena such as the peak shift, in which the change in response strength cannot be explained by a simple adding or subtracting of the predictiveness of the various stimuli.

Noncontinuity Theories

The use of problem-solving abilities and the learning of relationships are emphasized in *noncontinuity theories*. These are also often called cognitive theories of discrimination.

Cue-reversal studies. In an attempt to determine which of the above theories might better explain discrimination, psychologists developed a procedure that involves reversing the cues during training. This could be as simple as switching horizontally striped stimulus cards from S^+ to S^- and vertically striped cards from S^- to S^+. Results of these studies seem to depend upon both when the cue-reversal takes place and what organism is being trained.

Cue-reversal early in training seems to support a continuity explanation. Acquisition is retarded, seeming to indicate that some learning has taken place and that those associations would have to be unlearned before the new association could develop.

Cue-reversal late in learning (e.g., after overlearning) provides results supporting noncontinuity theories. Acquisition of the new task—that is, making the switch—actually develops *more* rapidly than for a control group. This finding has been called the overlearning reversal effect. No adequate explanation for this finding has been developed, especially because it has only been produced when rats were the subjects. The early reversal effect has been shown with several different organisms.

"Blocking" studies. Another type of study used to try to test the continuity and noncontinuity theories is called *blocking*. A three-step procedure is used. In the first step, a stimulus-response-reinforcement sequence is presented repeatedly. For the second step an additional stimulus is presented (while the first is maintained). This second stimulus also "predicts" the eventual reinforcement. In step three, the second stimulus is presented alone to determine whether or not the response will be made.

Results of these studies tend to support a stimulus-predictiveness explanation. If the addition of the second stimulus (step two) is accompanied by some other change (such as increased reinforcement), the S-R association between the second stimulus and the response develops. However, if there is no change from the initial situation, the original S-R bond remains predominant, and the test in step three will show no association between the new stimulus and the response.   It appears that the subject *does* attend to the second (or new) stimulus, but judges its relevancy: If it adds no additional information, it is ignored.

10.9   SPECIAL CASES OF DISCRIMINATION

Several of the previously presented principles (such as errorless discrimination or blocking) may be considered as special cases, but they also fit to some extent within the section where they were presented.   This section presents two aspects of research that do not seem properly included in any of the previous sections.

Discrimination in Verbal Learning

Studies of discrimination in verbal learning use a procedure of presenting pairs or sets of words, asking for a choice of response, and reinforcing correct responses (see Chapter 6).   When understanding of a pattern for responding is possible, gradual learning of the discrimination usually develops.

Learning without awareness.   One verbal discrimination-learning procedure is called *learning without awareness.*   In conditions where (perhaps subtle) reinforcement is given for a particular kind of response, the subject may (supposedly) increase the frequency of such responses without being aware of why.   Research in this area has been considered debatable because of the difficulty of determining awareness.

Insoluble Discrimination Problems

Two types of discrimination tasks are considered insoluble, although in theory a solution exists for one.   The entirely insoluble problem presents reinforcement in a totally random manner; that is, responses have absolutely no effect upon reinforcement.   The second type of insoluble task supposedly has a correct response, but the difference in stimulus values is so small that it becomes unrecognizable for most subjects.

Both of these procedures create unusual response patterns. The first often leads to a fixation response that will persist even when the reinforcement contingency becomes obvious. (This is similar to learned helplessness, described in Chapter 8.)

The second situation, in which choice is extremely difficult, will produce what has been called *experimental neurosis.*   Overtaxing the organism's abilities and requiring continued responding generates distress, confusion, and possible abnormal patterns of behavior.

EXAMPLE 13.   Experimental neurosis was first investigated by Ivan Pavlov, whose dogs were required to try to distinguish between stimuli with successively closer and closer properties.   When the differentiation surpassed the dogs' ability, they often showed what Pavlov described as neurotic behavior, such as whining, refusing to enter the experimental room, attempting to bite the handler, or extreme passiveness.

Solved Problems

10.1   Suppose Pearl is taking a drivers' education class.   One day, the instructor tests the students' recognition-reaction times by presenting a series of stimuli and asking for a response that explains the meaning of each stimulus.   Interestingly, when Pearl is presented with an eight-sided red sign, her reaction time is much slower than when she sees an eight-sided sign painted black but with the word STOP in white letters.   What explains the difference between Pearl's two responses?

The extent to which and the way in which a subject attends to stimuli play an important part in determining how well the subject will learn about the stimulus properties.   In this case Pearl has apparently attended to the white lettering STOP, but has not attended to the color of the background.   Additional tests could be conducted to determine if Pearl recognizes that an eight-sided sign means stop, a triangle means yield, etc.   Eventually, the significant (or attended to) aspects of each stimulus could be identified.

10.2   Consider again the situation described in Problem 10.1.   Imagine that Pearl shows rapid recognition of the painted words STOP, YIELD, and DETOUR, but virtually no recognition of the different sign shapes.   Describe her behavior in terms of the major topics of this chapter.

Being able to distinguish the various words represents discrimination (differentiation).   Pearl's inability to distinguish the various signs and shapes illustrates stimulus generalization.

10.3   Suppose Pearl (Problems 10.1 and 10.2) *always* distinguishes every word but shows absolutely no distinction among the sign shapes.   Sketch the generalization gradients that would be obtained.

The two gradients represented in Fig. 10-4 would be straight lines, representing the extremes of value that can be obtained.   In the case of words, Pearl shows complete (or strict) differentiation; thus the curve shows responding at one point only (Fig. 10-4*a*).   On the other hand, Pearl shows complete generalization with regard to sign shapes, responding to all of them equally; response strength is equal for all shapes, no matter how far they diverge from the shape (stimulus) being tested (Fig. 10-4*b*).

Complete differentiation means that Pearl would respond correctly to each word stimulus, never confusing any.   Complete stimulus generalization means that she might give any response to any one of the sign shapes.

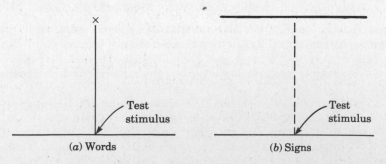

(a) Words   (b) Signs

Fig. 10-4

10.4   Summarize Pearl's situation in terms of stimulus control.

Stimulus control is a concept suggesting that particular aspects of a stimulus situation will determine what responses will be made.   In Pearl's case, stimulus control appears to be exclusively a function of the word presented, while the shape or color of the sign has no bearing on her responses. Stated another way, the words are the discriminative stimuli determining the responses made.

10.5   Pearl's responses are the result of previous learning.   Distinguish attention and responding that are the result of previous learning from attention and responding that are the result of innate factors.   Give an example of a differentiation based upon innate factors.

Previous learning would most likely involve reinforcement for recognizing and distinguishing one stimulus from others.   This depends upon experience in the form of practice or training.   Attention and responding controlled by innate factors are a result of the particular heredity of the organism and require no practice or training in order to be manifested.   For example, it has been found that a male robin will make attack responses toward the red breast of another male (or even toward crude stimuli that approximate the red breast) without any previous training.

10.6   Pearl's friend Petra, who was raised in West Germany and only recently moved to the United States, is also taking the drivers' education class.   When shown the eight-sided red sign, Petra responds by saying "Halt! ...   Oh, I mean, Stop."   What principle does Petra's response illustrate?

When the same stimulus elicits several comparable responses, response generalization is said to have been shown.   In this case, "Halt" is the German equivalent of the English word "Stop."

10.7   Pete has two older sisters, Betty and Dotti.   As a baby, Pete often had his sisters as babysitters, sometimes together and sometimes one at a time.   As his language skills developed, Pete learned to call each of his sisters by name correctly, distinguishing one from the other.   The girls often had him practice this when they baby-sat.   Distinguish the two procedures that apparently were used.

Pete was exposed to a *simultaneous-differentiation* task when both sisters were present; the differentiation involved *successive* stimuli when one or the other was there alone with him.   Comparable laboratory circumstances have been used in many experiments, with simultaneous stimulus presentation requiring a choice response, while successive stimulus presentation means only one stimulus is present at any one time and requires a yes-no response or (as in this case) appropriate labeling.

10.8   Two groups of pigeons are trained to peck a lighted disc in order to receive a food reinforcement.   For one group the disc is illuminated in a shade of yellow, while for the other group the disc is blue.

Following training, both groups are divided into two subgroups.   For each, one subgroup is tested during extinction to the original stimulus and one generalization stimulus.   The other subgroup of each original group is tested during extinction to the original stimulus and three other generalization stimuli.   Wavelength deviations for the generalization stimuli are matched for the two groups.

How comparable will the generalization gradients obtained be for the single-stimulus subgroups?   For the multiple-stimulus subgroups?

In a single-stimulus comparison, the slope of the stimulus generalization gradient is likely to be unique for each comparison.   This appears to result from the greater discriminability of wavelength differences in different parts of the wavelength dimension.

In multiple-stimulus comparisons, the slopes of the generalization gradients will be almost identical regardless of the initial stimulus values.   The additional test stimuli appear to create some sort of interaction that produces generalization around the extinction stimulus, such that the pigeons respond in the same manner regardless of the initial training-stimulus value.

10.9   Why is the measurement of generalization (or differentiation) difficult?

Generalization can be measured in either absolute terms or relative terms.   For example, suppose two tests of generalization are conducted, with the response-strength value for one test being 20 originally and 8 later, and the response values in the other test being 40 originally and 20 later.   The absolute changes would be 12 and 20, respectively, while the relative changes would be 60 percent and 50 percent.   Thus, using absolute values, it would appear that there is a greater drop shown in the latter test, while the relative value shows the opposite.   It is not possible to state conclusively which testing procedure shows the greater drop in generalization (or the greater increase in discrimination).

10.10   A subject in a discriminative-learning task is being trained to respond to an audible tone of 440 Hertz (Hz) and not to certain selected tones of other frequencies.   After numerous training trials, the subject is presented with tones of considerably higher and lower frequencies.   As tones with frequencies closer and closer to 440 Hz are presented, the response strength increases.   These responses are then charted on a generalization gradient that slopes off steeply from the highest response at S-440 to virtually no response at either S-330 or S-660 (the lowest and highest ends of the stimulus scale).   The discriminative-learning procedure has apparently been effective.   However, when the experimenter extends the stimulus scale to a maximum value of 880 Hz and a minimum of 220 Hz, something peculiar occurs: the curve of the gradient no longer descends in two smooth slopes.   Indeed, the levels of responding to S-220 and S-880 are almost as high as the response level at S-440.   What has happened?

   The experimenter has chosen a multidimensional stimulus—one that can be interpreted in more than one way.   In the dimension of physics, a sound wave of 330 Hz is "closer to" or "more like" the S-440 than a sound wave of 220 Hz is.   In the musical dimension, however, S-440, S-220, and S-880 are all designated as the note (or pitch) A.   (S-220 is one octave below S-440, S-880 is one octave above.)   By extending the stimulus scale to include S-220 and S-880, the experimenter has made it more likely that the subject will respond to the stimuli in the terms of (or dimension of) music, and not of the physical properties of waves.

10.11   The extent of generalization effects is illustrated by generalization of extinction.   How is generalization of extinction demonstrated?

   While the usual definition of generalization is that responding occurs not only to the original stimulus but to other similar stimuli, generalization of extinction is illustrated when *not* responding occurs not only to the original stimulus but also to other similar stimuli.   In other words, the extinction effects "spread" from the stimulus used during extinction to other similar stimuli.

10.12   Why are physical and functional explanations of generalization considered both different and similar?

   The difference between physical and functional explanations of generalization rests in the locus of the effect.   Physical explanations propose that some sort of spread occurs within the cortex; this has been called cortical irradiation.   Functional explanations stress the learning of the relevant (or irrelevant) dimensions of the stimulus.   Instead of attributing generalization to a particular physical process, functional theorists emphasize selective reinforcement of responses.
   The two explanations are similar in that they both depend upon experience.   Frequently, psychologists have suggested that some combination of physical and functional explanations is needed to completely explain the generalization effect.

10.13   Explain how the predictiveness of the stimulus appears to be a most important factor in determining the slope of the generalization gradient.

   Research has shown that the relative strength of a stimulus controlling a response is a function of how predictable the S-R relationship is. The more certain a particular S-R bond is, the less likely that any other stimuli will evoke the same response (unless such stimuli have independently been bonded to the same response).

10.14   What accounts for the increased steepness of the generalization gradient slopes that result from increased amounts of training?   Do different schedules of partial reinforcement seem to affect this result?

In general, the finding that increased training produces increased steepness of the generalization gradient slopes requires two explanations.   One proposes greater conditioning of the S-R bonds. The second suggests that extinction of irrelevant S-R bonds occurs during the intertrial intervals. (*Note:* At the beginning of training, an initial increase in responding is sometimes found.   This apparently results from the organism's testing the extent of success the response will have.)

Partial-reinforcement schedules will affect the results described above.   Schedules that generate high response rates through the manipulation of external (exteroceptive) stimuli will generate steep generalization gradient slopes.   The slopes will be relatively flat when the schedule produces slow responding with long interresponse pauses.   In these latter cases, subject-produced (interoceptive) stimuli appear to control the responding, thus making the exteroceptive S-R bond relatively unimportant.

10.15   Do reward and punishment have the same effect upon generalization?   Explain.

Reward and punishment seem to have opposite effects upon responding in generalization tests. In general, the greater the amount of reward during acquisition, the less the amount of generalization.   However, punishment of a response tends to increase the amount of generalization.   (*Note:* In some cases, punishment of a response actually produces *greater* responding for one of the generalization test stimuli than for the original stimulus.   This is considered a form of *displacement,* with the tendency to respond viewed as the summation of response strength and inhibition effects.)

10.16   If two groups are given identical training on Monday, with group A being tested for generalization on Tuesday and group B having their generalization test on Thursday, which group should show a flatter slope for the generalization gradient?

Assuming all other conditions remain the same, group B should show the flatter generalization gradient.   In general, the greater the amount of time between training and test, the greater the generalization.   Results such as these are often attributed to differential forgetting, which suggests that the stimulus components are forgotten while the responses learned are retained.

10.17   What is the relationship of motivation to the slope of a generalization gradient?   What effect has brain stimulation had on generalization gradients?

In general, the slope of the generalization gradient will be steeper with increasing levels of motivation during the test situation.   However, greater motivation during response acquisition seems to produce greater generalization.

While not specifically identified as a motivational variable, introduction of brain stimulation, after acquisition of a response but before the test of generalization, appears to produce steeper gradients of generalization.   Although not well understood, this procedure illustrates an attempt to determine physiological characteristics of learning phenomena.

10.18   Edwin has two close friends toward whom he shows approximately equal "friendly" responses.   However, one of the friends joins a social group, establishes new friendships, and begins to snub Edwin.   What can be expected to happen to Edwin's frequency of "friendly" responses?

The principle that probably will operate here is called behavioral contrast.   In the past, both stimuli (friends) provoked responding (friendly responses) and these were reinforced.   Now, one set of responses is being extinguished.   It can be expected that these responses will diminish in strength *and* that the frequency of friendly responses toward the other friend will increase above their previous baseline value.

10.19 Suppose that Kathryn has grown up revering the University of North Carolina Tarheels but disliking the Duke Blue Devils. She thinks the light blue of the UNC uniforms gorgeous and the deeper blue of the Duke uniforms ugly. If Kathryn were to illustrate the peak-shift phenomenon in choosing a new blue skirt, what type of blue would she pick?

The peak-shift phenomenon implies that the choice (essentially a generalization response) is made in the direction *away from* the S^- (Duke's blue) and beyond the S^+ (UNC's light blue). Therefore, Kathryn would choose a blue slightly lighter than UNC blue.

10.20 Both the peak-shift phenomenon and the phenomenon of behavioral contrast seem to have similar elements. What explanation appears generally to account for both phenomena?

Both phenomena appear to occur because the S^- acquires a recognizable aversiveness. In circumstances where this is not allowed to occur (as in Problem 10.25, following) the phenomena are not revealed.

10.21 Using a continuity theory of discrimination, sketch the positive, negative, and net gradients that ought to be found for the "blues" example presented in Problem 10.19.

See Fig. 10-5.

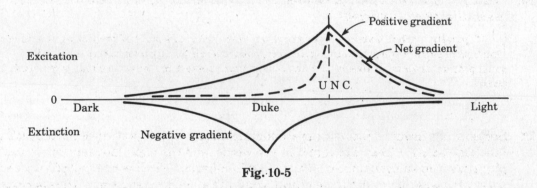

Fig. 10-5

10.22 Suppose Kathryn (Problem 10.19) were shown the Duke blue and an even darker shade of blue. What would the principle of transposition predict of Kathryn if she had to make a choice between the two?

Transposition occurs when relative rather than absolute properties are learned. Therefore Kathryn, having learned that "lighter blue is better," would be expected to choose the Duke blue rather than the darker shade. However, it might be possible that Kathryn would recognize the darker shade as that of Navy and respond to the absolute properties rather than the relationship, saying, "Well, I like Navy better than Duke."

10.23 What factors determine whether or not selective attention will occur in a discrimination-learning situation?

The two factors that appear to determine the onset of (or need for) selective attention are stimulus overload and the amount of time available for attending. If the amount of information being presented in any given time unit exceeds the receiving capacity of the organism, the transition from complete attention to selective attention will occur.

10.24 If a fairly easy discrimination task has been previously learned, how will the later acquisition of a more difficult differentiation be affected?

Assuming the two tasks are similar, research evidence indicates that learning the easy discrimination first should make acquisition of the later, more difficult, differentiation easier. This is an example of positive transfer of training. (See Chapter 12 for a full discussion of transfer principles.)

10.25 Why does the procedure of errorless discrimination learning appear to be a reasonable way to train a particular response (or "not-responding") without generating negative emotional consequences?

Errorless discrimination learning is comparable to the procedure of shaping (see Chapter 4). A gradual phasing-in of a stimulus is accomplished with careful attention to allowing only appropriate responses and never allowing incorrect responses to occur. Eventually, the presence of the S$^-$ can be at full strength, yet no response has ever occurred or, therefore, been extinguished.

It is suggested that such a procedure prevents responding that ultimately proves frustrating, the kind of circumstance that can arise with the usual kind of discrimination-training procedure, in which both stimuli are presented full strength. Avoiding the frustration should help prevent negative emotional consequences. Proposals for the use of errorless discrimination-training procedures have been made for behaviors such as toilet training and thumbsucking.

10.26 What kinds of tasks have been used to study differentiation in verbal learning? What results have been obtained?

Typically, verbal learning discrimination tasks have consisted of presenting the subject with long lists of pairs of words, requiring a choice, and then reinforcing correct responses. When there is some pattern or understanding of what constitutes a correct response, gradual acquisition usually occurs.

10.27 Subjects are brought into an experimental setting on the pretext of participating in a language study. They are asked to say words, and the experimenter "reinforces" each plural noun by murmuring an encouraging "um-hmm." Tallies are kept of frequencies, to determine whether or not more plural nouns are given over successive time periods, even though the subjects are not explicitly advised of the reinforcement conditions. Do such studies, called learning-without-awareness or "um-hmm" studies, fit the verbal discrimination format?

In a sense, learning-without-awareness studies or "um-hmm" studies (where the phrase "um-hmm" is the reinforcer) are a form of verbal discrimination learning. The subject supposedly increases the frequency of a particular verbal response (in this case saying plural nouns) without recognizing that such an increase, or verbal discrimination, is being reinforced. These studies have been controversial because of the difficulty of determining just how aware the subjects were of the reinforcement contingencies. (It is difficult if not impossible to assign a value to awareness.)

10.28 If in tasks such as those described in Problems 10.26 and 10.27 the subject learns a general principle for responding, what principle is illustrated?

The principle of discriminative-learning sets (sometimes called learning to learn) is illustrated when the subject learns and then later applies a general principle for responding in differentiation tasks. For example, a sales clerk in a paint store may have learned that when a customer is having trouble selecting between two quite-similar paint chips, the better recommendation is the lighter one of the two because the paint on an entire wall usually looks darker than it does on a sample chip. Thus, the customer will more often be satisfied when the lighter of the two is chosen.

10.29   Is it possible to have insoluble discrimination tasks?   What tasks are like this?   What results are obtained in such circumstances?

There are two forms of insoluble discrimination tasks.   One simply has no consistently correct response; reinforcement is given in a purely random manner, and response choice has no bearing upon the delivery of reinforcement.   The second has a correct response, but the choice between the two stimuli presented is so difficult as to be essentially insoluble.

In the first circumstance, a result somewhat comparable to that of learned helplessness (see Chapter 8) is found.   Even if a consistent pattern of reinforcement *is* established later—making differentiation at least theoretically possible—the typical response is to continue with some form of fixation or peculiar behavior rather than to switch to the correct response.

For the second type, exceedingly difficult differentiation, the term "experimental neurosis" has been coined to describe the responses that typically develop.   The level of difficulty surpasses the organism's capability and therefore provokes discomfort, agitation, or "breakdown."

10.30   Distinguish between continuity and noncontinuity theories of discriminative learning.

Basically, a continuity theory of discriminative learning places emphasis upon the gradual buildup of habit strength and the summation of generalization gradients (see Problem 10.21).   Noncontinuity theories stress the ability of the organisms to demonstrate problem-solving abilities.   The emphasis in noncontinuity theories is often on learning relationships.

10.31   What support do cue-reversal studies with rats give for continuity and noncontinuity theories of differentiation?

The answer to this question depends on when the cue reversal occurs.   Cue reversal involves switching the S^+ and S^- cues: black was correct but now is wrong, while white was wrong but now is correct.   If cue reversal occurs early in acquisition, a continuity theory appears to be supported because acquisition is retarded.   Original associations must be unlearned before new associations can be learned.   (Such a result has been found with species other than the rat.)

However, cue reversal after overlearning does not support the continuity theories.   The switch in performance actually occurs *more* rapidly for the overlearning group than it does for the control group.   This latter finding has been called the *overlearning reversal effect*.   Various explanations have attempted to account for this result, but in general they have not been deemed satisfactory. (The overlearning reversal effect has only been produced when rats are the subjects.)

10.32   Describe a blocking experiment.   Why do results obtained from some studies seem to support an associative rather than attentional explanation of blocking?

Blocking is accomplished using a three-step procedure.   First some stimulus is solidly associated with response and reinforcement.   The second step consists of adding a second stimulus to the well-learned S-R pattern of step one.   The third step is a test of whether or not the response pattern persists when only the second, or added-on, stimulus is presented.   If the response is not given, the original stimulus is said to "block" the potential effectiveness of the later stimulus, even though the later stimulus does predict the reinforcement outcome.

Certain attempts to illustrate blocking have failed to produce supportive results.   Generally, these involve procedures where some other change (e.g., increased reinforcement) accompanies the added-on stimulus. The suggestion is that if the new stimulus does predict something new, the association will be learned.   If the new stimulus is irrelevant, no association is made.   The subject apparently *does* attend to the new stimulus, but then makes a judgment as to its relevancy.

Key Terms

Absolute generalization.   The actual difference in response strength shown for the original stimulus and the test stimulus.

Behavioral contrast.   When a subject has acquired two somewhat-similar S-R bonds and one is subjected to extinction, response strength for the other may increase beyond its previous maximum level even though reinforcement for this second S-R bond is not increased.

Blocking.   In compound conditioning, extreme salience of one CS so that no response strength accrues to the other.

Cortical irradiation.   A physiological theory proposing that some sort of "spread" of excitation in the cortex determines the extent to which generalization will take place; the theory is not widely supported.

Differential reinforcement.   Reinforcing some, but not all, responses in some systematic manner; often used in shaping some response.

Differentiation.   Another name for *Discrimination.*

Discrimination.   Responding to the original stimulus but *not* to other similar stimuli.

Discriminative-learning sets.   Learning a general principle of how to respond that can be applied in a number of specific situations.

Discriminative stimulus.   A particular stimulus that sets the occasion for or cues a response.

Errorless discrimination.   A gradual procedure whereby response strength is built up to an S^+ while no unreinforced responses to S^- are permitted; eventually, complete discrimination can be established with no incorrect responding occurring.

Experimental neurosis.   The unusual patterns of responding shown by organisms exposed and forced to respond to extremely difficult (nearly insoluble) discrimination tasks.

Generalization of extinction.   The finding that extinguishing responses to a generalized stimulus reduces resistance to extinction of the response to the original stimulus.

Learning to learn.   Another name for *discriminative-learning sets.*

Learning without awareness.   A situation where response strength changes without conscious recognition of the contingencies involved.

Multidimensionality.   The proposal that within a set of stimuli more than one aspect or set of criteria can be used to judge "differentness" or similarity.

Peak shift.   The finding that maximal response strength may move in a direction away from an S^- beyond the stimulus value for S^+ even though S^+ maintains its properties.

Primary stimulus generalization.   Stimulus generalization based upon the physical properties of the stimulus.

Relative generalization.   A percentage that contrasts response strength shown to the original stimulus and that shown to the test stimulus.

Secondary stimulus generalization.   Stimulus generalization based upon the subject's knowledge of language or some other symbol.

Selective attention.   Restricting scrutiny to only part of a stimulus complex.

Simultaneous presentation.   In testing generalization or discrimination, offering the comparison stimuli at one time.

Stimulus control.   The proposal that particular aspects of a stimulus situation determine what response(s) will be made.

Stimulus generalization.   Responding not only to the original stimulus but to other similar stimuli.

Stimulus-generalization gradient.   The graphical representation of the strength of responses made to the original stimulus and other similar stimuli.

Successive presentation.   In testing generalization or discrimination, offering the comparison stimuli one after the other.

Transfer of training.   When the learning of one task affects the later acquisition of some second task.

Transposition.   Responding to the relationship between two or more stimuli rather than to their absolute properties.

Chapter 11

Acquisition Principles

In almost all of the preceding chapters, reference has been made to acquisition, that part of the learning process during which information is attained and a response becomes a part of the behavioral repertoire. This chapter is a review of the basic principles of acquisition, but does not confine itself to the acquisition phase of any particular type of learning, such as classical conditioning, instrumental conditioning, verbal learning, and so on.

11.1 ACQUISITION vs. MEMORY

There is often some difficulty in distinguishing between the terms *acquisition* and *memory*.

Acquisition

While there is no irrefutable physiological evidence to confirm it, the most widely accepted definition holds that *acquisition* is a process that involves experiencing something, with that experience leading to the development of an ensuing trace of the event in the nervous system of the organism. Acquisition frequently is described as the *input* process of learning. Another term used to describe acquisition is *storage,* implying the establishment of the trace.

It should be noted that the word "learning" is often used to refer to acquisition. However, "learning" is also used to describe shifts in recall over a series of trials, and is, strictly speaking, a broader term than "acquisition."

Memory

The term *memory* refers to the retention of the acquired trace over some period of time. Evidence of memory is provided by some *output* process. This is often called *retrieval*. (Memory and retrieval are discussed in Chapters 13 and 14.)

EXAMPLE 1. There have been many attempts to use sophisticated computer programs to simulate learning experiences. These programs are usually some version of the basic scheme shown in Fig. 11-1. The acquisition phase of learning is represented here by the input phase as well as the first part of the processing-and-storage section, while the next part, along with the output section, represents retrieval. Usually, some retrieval cue is necessary to generate output.

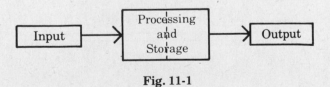

Fig. 11-1

11.2 CHARACTERISTICS OF STORAGE

Studies of the establishment of the trace during acquisition have focused on three factors basic to the storage process. These are stimulus differentiation (discussed in Chapter 10), the associations between stimuli and responses, and response learning (also interpreted as the availability of the response). All three aspects are considered important, but response learning is recognized as the absolutely essential element.

Learning Curves

The acquisition process is graphically represented by a learning curve, on which is plotted the learner's response performance for several acquisition trials. (A curve showing response change during any *one* trial would represent acquisition; if the curve shows response levels attained over a series of trials, it is a representation of learning.)

EXAMPLE 2. Figure 11-2 shows a typical negatively accelerated learning curve. It is negatively accelerated because the acquisition progresses from trial to trial at an ever slower *rate;* in other words, the curve always continues to rise, but less and less with each successive trial.

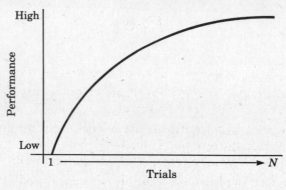

Fig. 11-2

Plateaus. Occasionally during the period of acquisition there will be an interval of little or no progress. Such a period is called a *plateau.*

EXAMPLE 3. The learning curve in Fig. 11-3 shows a plateau within the overall acquisition sequence.

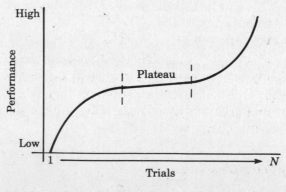

Fig. 11-3

Asymptotes. Often the process of acquisition slows and appears to reach an upper limit, perhaps because of the nature of the task or the capabilities of the subject. The final portion of a learning curve representing this situation will level off as it approaches the *asymptote.*

EXAMPLE 4. Figure 11-4 shows an extension of the learning curve presented in Fig. 11-2. The last portion of this curve is approaching the asymptote. (Another way to describe this situation is to say that the organism responds asymptotically after a number of trials.)

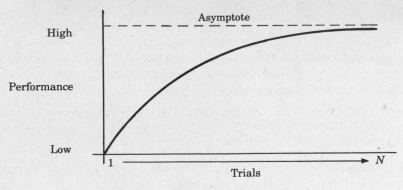

Fig. 11-4

Arousal and Attention

In its simplest form, *arousal* is the level of alertness displayed by the organism. More generally, the term is used as a synonym for motivation.

The relationship between arousal and acquisition is described by an inverted-U curve (see Fig. 11-5 and Chapter 17). Within the concept of arousal, psychologists often study *attention*, that is, whether or not specific recognition of a distinct stimulus has occurred.

Research has shown that some minimal levels of arousal and attention are necessary for acquisition to take place, although arousal and attention are not enough by themselves to guarantee that acquisition will occur.

11.3 MEASURES OF RESPONSE STRENGTH

This section presents some of the variables frequently studied as measures of response strength during acquisition. (Some of these variables could be used as measures of retention as well; see Chapters 13, 14, and 15.)

Amplitude and Magnitude of Response

Both *amplitude* and *magnitude* of response are measured as the difference between some preacquisition (or baseline) level of responding and the response value given during acquisition. They differ only in that amplitude is measured on every trial, including those with zero difference, while magnitude is measured only on those trials when a discernible difference between the baseline and acquisition levels is observed.

Frequency or Probability of Response

In discrete or limited acquisition trials the possibility of response per unit of time is controlled by the experimenter. The presence or absence of the response in a series of such trials is recorded as the *frequency of response.* In free-responding circumstances, the number of responses per unit of time determines the *probability of response.* Both frequency and probability are interpreted as indicators of acquisition strength—greater frequency or greater probability is taken as evidence of better or more thorough acquisition.

EXAMPLE 5. A jogger who has worked her way up to running four miles a day at least five days a week shows a higher probability of the running response than her husband, who also jogs four miles a day but seldom more often than three times a week. The woman's response, because of its greater probability, is interpreted as evidence of more thorough acquisition.

Latency of Response

Latency of response is defined as the time elapsed between the onset of a cue stimulus (such as a CS) and the beginning of the response.   In general, a shorter latency of response indicates better or more thorough acquisition.   (Another means of evaluating acquisition is to determine the *total time* for responding—that is, the time from signal onset until the entire response is *completed*.)

Resistance to Extinction

If an acquisition period is followed by a period of extinction, the total time or the number of trials required to reduce response strength to its original or baseline value is sometimes used as a measure of the strength of acquisition.   This measure is called *resistance to extinction*.

Associative Strength

The concept of *associative strength,* most frequently used in verbal learning situations, refers to the likelihood a particular stimulus will be followed by a specific response.   (Associative strength has been used to measure both acquisition and long-term retention.) Any increase in associative strength, just like any increase in the other variables discussed so far, is interpreted as an indicator of greater acquisition strength.

Associative reaction time.   Associative strength in a verbal learning task can itself be measured by the latency of the verbal responses: the shorter the latency period, the greater the associative strength.   This special instance of latency, known as *associative reaction time,* will vary according to a number of factors, including whether the response is free or controlled: If the subject is allowed to make any response to the stimulus presented, the procedure is called *free association.* If the response is constrained in some way—for example, if the only acceptable responses are synonyms, pronouns, or words containing the letter *m*—the procedure is called *controlled association.*

It should be noted that verbal responses given with the shortest associative reaction time are also the responses given most frequently.   This link has been described as *Marbe's Law* (named after an early researcher of this correlation).   In general, both greater frequency and shorter associative reaction time are thought to indicate greater strength of acquisition.

Associative commonality.   Certain tendencies or predictable patterns of verbal responding are bound to develop in a culture.   The measure of how frequently the subject produces such culturally determined or encouraged responses is called *associative commonality.*   It is necessary to keep up-to-date tallies of culturally popular verbal responses in order to distinguish between them and any responses that are the result of a verbal learning procedure.

Paraphrasing.   Measuring acquisition response strength in verbal learning tasks becomes more difficult as the verbal responses being trained become more complex.   One reason for this is that the responses given by a subject may be equivalent in meaning to the desired responses but expressed in a different way.   Such transformation of the actual responses, but not the meaning, is called *paraphrasing.*   (See also the discussion of surface structure vs. deep structure in Chapter 18.)

EXAMPLE 6.   Suppose the stimulus in a verbal learning task is the phrase "The boy was . . ." and the original response consisted of ". . . arrested for stealing two tomatoes from his neighbor's garden." If the subject's test for acquisition produces a response of ". . . picked up for stealing vegetables from his neighbor," there is some question as to whether or not the response should be scored as correct.   Although the general sense of the original message is found in the paraphrased response, the wording has been changed.

11.4   EXTERNAL VARIABLES INFLUENCING ACQUISITION

Although it is difficult in some cases to distinguish between external and internal variables that affect acquisition, the general proposal is that *external variables* are those aspects of the materials or learning environment that arise outside the individual while *internal variables* (see Section 11.5) are generated within the individual.   There is much research evidence to indicate frequent interaction between external and internal variables affecting acquisition.

The Total-Time Hypothesis

One of the most important variables affecting acquisition is simply the time available for acquisition to take place.   Research results have been summarized in the *total-time hypothesis*, which states that acquisition is a function of the amount of time available for learning.   In general, the greater the span of time available for acquisition, the greater the acquisition.

The Spew Hypothesis

A second important external variable has been called the *spew hypothesis*.   It states that verbal units experienced most frequently are the ones most likely to be produced as responses and therefore the most likely to become part of associations.   In other words, acquisition of associations may be a function of previous experience with the potential response members.

EXAMPLE 7.   Because the word "red" is used much more frequently than the word "scarlet," the spew hypothesis would predict that a naive observer might look at the uniforms of a football team that were labelled by the school as "scarlet and gray" and respond that the uniforms were "red and gray."   The greater availability of the response "red" makes it more likely to become part of the association keyed off by the uniforms.

Intentional vs. Incidental Instructions

Another important variable often manipulated by some external agent is the organism's *intention* to learn.   Learning that is intentional because the subject has been given explicit instructions to learn usually results in superior performance.   Learning that takes place incidentally—without any instruction indicating that the task is a learning task—tends to produce somewhat lower levels of performance.   However, when the incidental instructions happen to focus attention upon the relevant aspects of the responses, response learning apparently takes place and the differences between the performance of the intentional and incidental groups tends to diminish.

Whole vs. Part Acquisition

Acquisition tasks may be constructed so that the organism being trained acquires the entire task at one time; this is called *whole learning*.   If an organism acquires components of the task before putting them all together, *part learning* has taken place.   The latter type of acquisition can be divided into *pure part* acquisition, where each task component is acquired independently before the entire task is "assembled" at the end, and *progressive part* acquisition, where the first component is learned, then continues to be rehearsed as the second is added.

EXAMPLE 8.   A student could use whole learning, pure part acquisition, or progressive part acquisition in memorizing Shakespeare's Sonnet 73:

That time of year thou mayst in me behold
When yellow leaves, or none, or few, do hang
Upon those boughs which shake against the cold,
Bare ruined choirs where late the sweet birds sang.
In me thou seest the twilight of such day
As after sunset fadeth in the west,
Which by and by black night doth take away,
Death's second self that seals up all in rest.
In me thou seest the glowing of such fire
That on the ashes of his youth doth lie,
As the deathbed whereon it must expire,
Consumed with that which it was nourished by.
This thou perceiv'st, which makes thy love more strong,
To love that well which thou must leave ere long.

The poem consists of four sentences. Each of the first three sentences is four lines long (a *quatrain*) and contains some extended metaphor of death or dying: the first quatrain makes use of the image of a tree late in the fall, the second an image of dusk, and the third the image of a glowing fire. The fourth and final sentence of the poem is two lines long (a *couplet*).

A student would be using a *whole* learning technique if he memorized the poem by reading it over and over from start to finish. If he first memorized each sentence independently—first quatrain one, then quatrain two, then three, and then the couplet—before "assembling" them, he would be using *pure part* acquisition. And if the student first memorized quatrain one, then one and two, then one and two and three, and then the whole sonnet, he would be using *progressive part* acquisition, continuing to rehearse each learned part while acquiring progressively more and more of the material.

(*Note:* Although the whole vs. part distinction is listed under external variables because it may be generated by the nature of the task or by instructions, it could easily be considered internal if it was the subject who made a conscious choice to act in a certain manner. In other words, one could say that a student who used pure part learning to memorize the sonnet did so because he organized the material mentally and selected the most effective learning strategy. One could just as easily say, however, that the very structure of the sonnet dictated the use of pure part acquisition.)

Distribution of Practice

External constraints may force acquisition tasks to be "massed" into a short period of time or "distributed" over a longer period of time with periods of rest interspersed. In general, although there are numerous exceptions, research results indicate greater ease of acquisition and better retention when distributed practice rather than massed practice is used. (*Note:* Again, the use of massed or distributed practice could be considered a matter of personal or internal choice rather than the result of external constraints or promptings.)

Confirmation vs. Prompting

When acquisition is being guided by some outside agent, such as a teacher, correct responses may be either confirmed or prompted. *Confirmation* involves asking for a response to be made, followed by verification of whether or not the response was correct. In *prompting* the correct response is presented, and the subject is then asked to repeat it. The choice of either confirmation or prompting is often determined by the type of material being learned and the stage of acquisition.

EXAMPLE 9. An instructor teaching the computer language Fortran might at first use prompting techniques to introduce the basics: "Multiplication requires an asterisk between the pair to be multiplied; $(a - 7)$ times $(b - 7)$ is written $(a - 7) * (b - 7)$. Now, how do you write $(a - 7)$ times $(b - 7)$?" Later the instructor may switch to a confirmation technique, simply asking the students how multiplication is designated in Fortran, then either confirming or disconfirming the response.

Meaningfulness

Quite frequently, verbal learning experiments involve the selection of materials to be learned according to the *meaningfulness* value of the material—the extent to which the verbal unit has meaning for the subject.   (*Meaningfulness* and *meaning* are *not* the same; *meaning* refers only to whether or not the verbal unit has specific objective referents, while *meaningfulness* includes any subjective associations evoked by the material to be learned.)

EXAMPLE 10.   In the English language, neither GUL nor XAG has meaning; both are nonsense syllables. Yet GUL has been found to have high meaningfulness ratings (perhaps because it looks and sounds like the word "gull"), while XAG has been judged much lower in meaningfulness.   (See also Chapter 6.)

11.5   INTERNAL VARIABLES AFFECTING ACQUISITION

The variables found in this section arise primarily within the individual.   As mentioned before, these variables often interact with external variables such as those presented in Section 11.4.

Practice and Rehearsal

Common sense would seem to imply that greater amounts of *practice* (exposure or trials involving the materials to be learned) and *rehearsal* (performance of some response using the materials to be learned) should lead to greater acquisition.   Research results tend to show that such expectations are not always supported.   The findings are that practice facilitates acquisition if the subject has the intention to learn and focuses upon the appropriate responses.   Rehearsal is seen to benefit acquisition when the process involves relevant aspects of the materials to be learned and does not interfere with other strategies the subject might use for acquisition (see Problem 11.18).

Secondary Organization

Almost all the other variables to be presented in this section can be classified as representative of *secondary organization,* defined as any arrangement or organization imposed by the subject on the materials to be learned.   (*Primary organization* is any arrangement present or inherent in the materials to be learned.)

EXAMPLE 11.   Suppose the following list of words is to be learned:

> coffee   winter   station   window   party
> market   college   island   machine

A subject who learned the words in order—"coffee, winter, station . . . etc."—would be showing the effects of primary organization (in this case, a serial organization).   Secondary organization would be shown if the subject acquired the words by grouping them in some other way—perhaps by using them in a sentence: ". . . bought a *coffee machine* at the *market* before going to the *party* given by his *college.* . . ."

Acquisition strategies.   The various forms that secondary organization can take are called *acquisition strategies.*   These strategies may be very simple (for example, the subject may simply repeat the response to be learned over and over).   They may also be very sophisticated, involving information or organizational skills the subject has learned previously.

Clustering and coding.   Other terms used to represent acquisition strategies are "clustering" and "coding."   While these terms are sometimes used interchangeably, *clustering* usually refers to "grouping" materials to be learned because they are judged to be members of the same category, and *coding* is a more general term referring to some active technique used to modify materials into more easily acquired units of information.

Clustering is dependent upon the subject recognizing or identifying some category within the materials that can be used to organize them.   Coding occurs when the subject actively imposes some kind of order on the materials.   (Coding may be accomplished through a number of different procedures, including stimulus selection, rewriting materials, component description, and component elaboration.)

EXAMPLE 12. Suppose subjects are asked to memorize the following series of digits: 1, 8, 2, 7, 3, 6, 4, 5. Subjects who acquire it by *clustering* might notice that the series is made up of a reorganized version of the set of digits from one to eight: the first, then the last, then the second, then the second-to-last, and so on.   Subjects who acquire the series by *coding* might "rewrite" the material, storing it as a date and two 2-digit numbers: "eighteen twenty-seven, thirty-six, and forty-five."

Mnemonic devices.   In some instances of learning a person may make use of *mnemonic devices,* another type of acquisition strategy.   In such situations, the subject acquires an organizational scheme of some sort, then later uses that previously-learned scheme as a basis for acquiring additional (new) materials.

. A fairly well known mnemonic device involves learning a sequence that begins, "One is a *bun*, two is a *shoe,* three is a *tree,* four is a *door*." Once this is committed to memory, any sequential set of materials can be associated to these "*pegwords*" and therefore learned in its appropriate order.

EXAMPLE 13.   Suppose the task was to learn in correct order the words previously presented in Example 11.   A subject could use the mnemonic device described above to recall the words in their correct sequence: "Coffee and buns, a shoe in the winter snow, a railroad station beside a big tree, a house with four doors . . ."

Mediation.   The use of clustering, coding, or mnemonic devices is usually classified under the general heading *mediation,* which refers to some "go-between" material that links a stimulus and response or more than one response.

Imagery.   The quality of a stimulus that generates some sort of "mental" representation is called its *imagery potential.*   Subjects may generate mental "pictures" (iconic imagery), mental "sounds" (echoic imagery), or perhaps symbolic imagery—using words to represent some event.

Study techniques.   Many of the principles of secondary organization can be applied to study situations.   Some other variables that may help as well include *warm-up* (as a preparation for acquisition), an *active* (rather than a passive) approach to the learning task, and *overlearning,* (practice beyond initial acquisition).

Measurement of Secondary Organiziation

Attempts to determine if *secondary organization* (the influence of internal variables upon acquisition) has occurred usually involve repeated random presentations of the materials to be acquired.   The pattern of response during the trials is inspected to determine if some organizational arrangement can be noted.   However, it should be recognized that identification of some arrangement may reveal what has transpired without necessarily demonstrating why those results were obtained.

Solved Problems

11.1   Distinguish among the terms "acquisition," "learning," and "memory."

Acquisition is the process of experiencing something and, as a result, developing some sort of trace of that event.   The term "learning" is often used to mean acquisition, although it is also used to describe changes in recall over successive trials.   "Memory" refers to what is retained from any one experience.

11.2   How do storage and retrieval relate to acquisition and memory?

Basically, storage refers to the input aspects of learning while retrieval describes the output from memory.   Storage, then, is an acquisition process.   Retrieval is the process necessary to extract or use information from memory.

11.3   Acquisition (or storage) has been broken down into three general components.   What are they? How do they appear to affect acquisition?

The three components of acquisition are stimulus differentiation, response learning (or availability) and the association between stimuli and responses.   While all three aspects are considered very important in the acquisition process, response learning is essential if acquisition is to take place or later retrieval is to be demonstrated.

11.4   In general, what effect does arousal appear to have upon acquisition?

The relationship of arousal to acquisition is best described as an inverted-U curve (see Fig. 11-5).   Maximum acquisition takes place when arousal levels are moderate to fairly high, while both very low and very high levels of arousal typically have a deleterious effect upon acquisition.

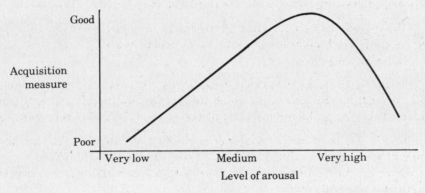

Fig. 11-5

11.5   If the relationship described in Problem 11.4 is accurate, why is there a fairly big business devoted to selling equipment that is supposed to "help you learn while you sleep"?

Such businesses are concerned with making money, not enhancing acquisition.   Controlled research studies to determine the possibilities for learning while asleep have shown that investment in such equipment is unwarranted and that attempts to learn while asleep are almost totally unsupportable.

11.6   Is attention the same thing as arousal?

Generally, attention is considered more specific than arousal.   "Arousal" refers to a relatively broad evaluation of the motivational level of the subject being studied, for example, in the most basic case determining whether or not the subject is awake.   "Attention" describes whether or not the subject recognizes or somehow indicates observance of particular stimuli.   It should be noted that while both a sufficient arousal and appropriate attention are considered necessary for acquisition to take place, they are not sufficient conditions to assure that it will (see Problem 11.16).

11.7   Sketch a learning curve to represent the following acquisition situation: After an initial warm-up period, a student learning a verbal task sees her performance improve markedly, then level off, then improve again, then level off at some final level.   Label the portions of the learning curve you sketch.

See Fig. 11-6.

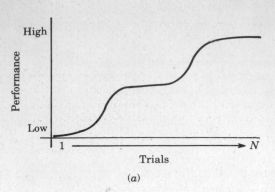
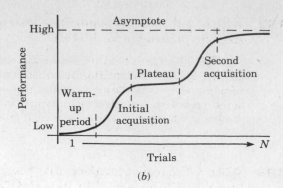

Fig. 11-6

11.8   Determination of whether or not acquisition has taken place requires some measure of response strength.   What are some of the more commonly used measures of strength of response?

Amplitude of response, magnitude of response, frequency of response, latency of response, probability of response, total time for responding, and associative strength are all commonly used as measures of response strength.   Psychologists choose which measure(s) to use according to the type of response involved and the acquisition procedure employed.   (See Chapters 3 and 4 for a discussion of many of these measures.)

11.9   Suppose as part of an experimental task you are asked to think of the first word you can that means the opposite of the stimulus word presented.   What measure of strength of response is being used?

There may be more than one correct solution to this problem.   One possibility is that your performance is being evaluated for associative strength.   In this case, the measure would be of controlled association, because the instructions limit your response to opposites, rather than free association, where you would be asked simply to give the first response generated.

A second possibility is that the variable being measured is latency of response, the time between onset of the stimulus and production of the response.   (This might have to be additionally checked against whether or not the response given really was an opposite.)

11.10   The measure of latency of response mentioned in Problem 11.9 has a particular label.   What is it?   What is assumed when it is used as a measure of response strength?

Measure of latency of response in an association test is called the associative reaction time.   It is assumed that the shorter the latency of response, the greater the strength of the association.   It has been found that, in general, those words given most rapidly in word-association tests are also those given most frequently.   This relationship is often called *Marbe's law*, after an early investigator.

11.11   Are associative strength and associative commonality the same thing?

Associative strength is simply a measure of how likely it is that a particular response will be made to a particular stimulus.   Associative commonality is a measure of how frequently a subject is likely to produce a particular culturally determined or encouraged response to a particular stimulus.   Thus associative commonality is a special case of associative strength: it measures the likelihood of those responses that are popular in a culture.

11.12　Why is it that as the acquisition task becomes more complex, measurement of response strength becomes more difficult?

　　　The difficulty is that the responses required may contain several or many components.　The psychologist must (often arbitrarily) determine how many of the components have to be present in the response before it can be judged as being present, complete, or correct.　A particularly good example of this occurs when a subject paraphrases the content of a prose passage: the ideas but not the exact contents of the passage are presented, and the psychologist must determine if this response is acceptable.

11.13　When asked to give an associative response to the stimulus word "musician," you respond by saying "Bernstein."　Explain your response according to the spew hypothesis.

　　　The spew hypothesis predicts that input frequency—that is, which verbal units are experienced more frequently—determines the order of use of the units in a free-recall situation.　Because the units are more likely to be experienced, they are therefore more available to enter into associations. In this case, it would be suggested that greater experience with the response unit "Bernstein" would make that response more likely to have become paired with the stimulus ("musician") than some other response, such as "Previn" or "Ozawa."

11.14　Explain what is meant by saying that acquisition may be affected by external variables, internal variables, or both.

　　　The two major aspects of acquisition are the materials to be learned and the techniques or means employed for acquisition.　Any variables that modify the materials but that are not generated by the subject are considered external to the individual.　Those variables affecting acquisition and generated by the individual are considered internal.　In many cases, the particular materials and the acquisition techniques employed interact to affect acquisition.

11.15　Perhaps the most important external variable manipulated by experimenters studying acquisition is time.　What is the major hypothesis that has been developed to explain the effect of time on acquisition?

　　　The general proposal is that acquisition is a function of the amount of time available for learning; that is, the greater the amount of time devoted to acquisition, the greater the acquisition.　This seems to hold despite the use of a wide variety of procedures and has come to be identified as the *total-time* or *invariance* hypothesis.

11.16　Challenging the total-time hypothesis for importance in influencing acquisition is the variable of intention.　Yet interpretations of intention have focused upon attention, which previously was described as a necessary but not sufficient condition for acquisition.　What interpretation of attention resolves this difficulty?

　　　There is a large body of research comparing intentional and incidental acquisition situations, and the majority of the data indicates that intentional groups show superior acquisition.　However it appears that when the incidental task focuses upon the relevant aspects of the stimulus situation, this difference disappears.　Intention to learn centers attention on the relevant aspects, thus providing the superiority usually found.

11.17　Give an example of how the external variable of meaningfulness and the internal variable of coding might interact to affect acquisition.

　　　There are any number of possible solutions to this problem.　In one, the subject could be asked to learn nonsense syllables such as NEH or LEF: Attempting to give more meaning to these stimuli, the subject may recognize they can be coded as the words HEN and ELF.　This may help with acquisition.

It should be noted that such coding procedures may facilitate the initial acquisition, but can create problems with later retrieval of the item if there is difficulty decoding from the meaningful associate to the original nonsense syllable.

11.18 Many children are raised by parents who repeatedly encourage them by saying, "Practice makes perfect."   Cite at least two reasons why this statement may be wrong.

One reason was presented in Chapters 3 and 4: If the children experience partial reinforcement for an incorrect or inadequate response, that response may become very resistant to extinction.

A second reason is the intention of the children during practice.   It can be expected that if the children do intend to learn, practice will facilitate acquisition.   The lack of intention, however, usually means that repeated trials will have little or no effect upon acquisition.

A third possibility involves the concept of rehearsal.   While the research results are mixed, it has been found that forced rehearsal may facilitate acquisition if it focuses attention upon relevant aspects of the stimulus, but may result in a decrease in acquisition if it interferes with the acquisition strategies the children would usually use.

11.19 In Problem 11.18, one part of the solution mentions acquisition strategies.   When verbal materials are being learned, what range of acquisition strategies is available to the learner?

Strategies for acquisition of verbal materials range from no strategy ("I don't know, I just learned what I was told to learn") to syntactical strategies in which the materials to be learned are incorporated into a phrase or sentence.   An example of this latter strategy (using the nonsense syllables presented in Problem 11.17) would be to say, "I changed NEH to HEN, added an imaginary T to LEF, and then thought the HEN LEFT recently."   Other strategies that are thought to fall somewhere in between these two include simple repetition, use of single- or multiple-letter cues, formation of words, or establishment of some superordinate relationship.

11.20 Suppose the subject is asked to recall the names of all the major league baseball cities in the United States of America.   What acquisition and recall strategy would be likely to operate here?

The strategy involved is called clustering.   Both for original acquisition and later retrieval, clustering may facilitate performance.   In this case, the subject may first learn the names of cities with American League teams, then the cities with National League teams.   (Clustering might be taken a step further by organizing the cities into clusters of National League Eastern Division, then National League Western Division, and so on.)

11.21 Some introductory psychology textbooks include a section on how to study.   Based upon the principles presented in this chapter, what do you expect some of the major recommendations of such a section would be?

"How to study" sections often suggest some or all of the following: Take an active rather than passive approach to the material—this is sometimes expressed as utilizing a recitation technique rather than just silently reading the material.   Allow for a warm-up period if necessary.   Distribute the study sessions to avoid fatigue, either for any given day or over a period of several days.   Try to acquire the knowledge according to a sensible pattern of parts or wholes, depending upon the nature of the materials to be learned.   Utilize imagery, mnemonic techniques, or other memory devices as necessary.   Continue acquisition techniques beyond the minimum acceptable acquisition level to establish the overlearning effect.

11.22 Many of the principles presented in this chapter might be summarized under the label "secondary organization." What general procedure has been used to determine if secondary organization has occurred?

The procedure used to investigate secondary organization has been to present a set of materials in some random order, ask for free recall, present the materials again in some *new* random order, again ask for free recall, and continue in this manner. If the subject is using some secondary-organization acquisition (and recall) strategy, it should be revealed by the pattern of responses that will appear in the successive recalls. However, this procedure may show that secondary organization exists, but not reveal which type is being used or why it is being used.

11.23 In an earlier discussion of secondary reinforcers (see Chapter 7), it was pointed out that they may bridge the time gap created by delay of reinforcement, thus serving as the mediator between response and reinforcement. Explain how mediation may also be considered an example of a secondary organization acquisition technique.

Depending upon the type of material to be learned, the use of mediators may facilitate acquisition. For example, learning the name of the former Cincinnati third baseman might involve the sequence: Cincinnati *Reds*—Pete *Rose,* with the nickname (the color red) serving as the mediator.

11.24 A teacher of French says to his class, "Repeat after me, *Voici la plume,*" and the class recites the same phrase. Is the teacher using prompting or confirmation?

The teacher's technique is prompting rather than confirmation. The students are given the correct response and expected to repeat it. A confirmation technique would involve the teacher asking, "How do you say 'Here is the pen' in French?" and then confirming the correct response or disconfirming any incorrect responses. Research indicates that either technique may improve acquisition, depending upon the materials to be learned and the pace involved.

Key Terms

Acquisition. The phase of learning during which information is attained and a response becomes part of the behavioral repertoire.

Amplitude of response. The difference between the preconditioning, baseline value of a response and the measured CR; the value is measured for all trials.

Arousal. The level of alertness shown by an organism.

Associative commonality. A measure of the frequency with which subjects produce culturally popular responses.

Associative reaction time. Latency of response for verbal association.

Associative strength. A measure of how likely it is that a particular stimulus will be followed by a specific response.

Asymptote. The apparent upper limit of performance in the acquisition phase.

Attention. Specific recognition of a particular stimulus.

Clustering. Grouping or categorizing items in a presented list according to some characteristic inherent in the list; the smaller units or groups thus formed are then more manageable, or easier to acquire.

Coding. Actively imposing an order or organization on a group of materials to be learned in order to make them easier to acquire.

Confirmation. Asking for a response, then verifying whether or not the response was correct.

Controlled association. Limitation of the range of subject response following presentation of a cue stimulus.

Free association. Allowance of any response following presentation of a cue stimulus.

Imagery. The "mental picture" generated by some verbal unit.

Input. The reception and consequent acquisition of information.

Latency of response. The time between the onset of a cue stimulus and the beginning of a response.

Learning curve. The graphic representation of acquisition performance.

Magnitude of response. The difference between the preconditioning, baseline value of a response and the measured CR; the value is measured only for trials where a difference exists.

Marbe's law. The tendency for associative responses with the shortest latency to be given most frequently.

Meaningfulness. The average number of associations a verbal unit elicits.

Mediation. In verbal learning, association of two items because they share some third thing in common.

Memory. The storage and later retrieval of a response that was previously acquired.

Mnemonic device. An easily learned organizational scheme that is acquired and then can be used to acquire and retrieve materials learned later.

Output. Responses that indicate what has been retained from input and storage.

Overlearning. The amount of practice occurring after a performance criterion has been reached.

Paraphrasing. Making a verbal response not in the exact words originally used but without changing the meaning of the response.

Part learning. The acquisition of discrete components of a task before all components are linked as a whole.

Plateau. An interval of little or no progress during acquisition, preceded and followed by periods of improvement in responding.

Primary organization. Arrangement of acquisition materials according to any arrangement or organization inherent in the materials to be learned.

Progressive part learning. An "add-on" form of part learning; when the first unit has been acquired, it continues to be practiced while the second is acquired, and so on.

Prompting. Presenting a correct response, then requiring the subject to repeat that correct response.

Retention. The process of storage; the period from acquisition until retrieval.

Retrieval. In learning, the phase when information is produced as a response from storage.

Secondary organization. Arrangement of acquisition materials as determined by some choice on the part of the subject.

Spew hypothesis. The proposal that the availability of verbal units is a direct function of the frequency of experience with those units.

Storage. In learning, the phase when information is retained.

Total-time hypothesis. The proposal which states that acquisition is a function of the amount of time available for learning.

Warm-up. Any activity used as preparation for acquisition.

Whole learning. Acquisition of an entire task at one time.

PART IV: *Retention: Memory*

The chapters in this part focus on the storage-retrieval aspects of the aquisition-storage-retrieval sequence described earlier. Retention and memory imply that what has been previously acquired is held in storage for some period of time and then somehow retrieved from that storage.

The chapter on transfer of training (12) provides the transition between those focusing on acquisition and those concerned with retention. Retention of one task is necessary before the acquisition of the second task can be effected.

Chapter 13 emphasizes measurement of retention and various interpretations of memory, while Chapter 14 deals with forgetting. This latter topic is viewed as a failure to show retention, and variables producing forgetting are discussed.

A recent development in the study of retention and memory has been the increased use of computers to study information processing and output. These topics along with attention to input are explored in Chapter 15. Finally, Chapter 16 presents three interesting viewpoints that are relevant for the entire learning sequence. Cybernetics, a mathematical stimulus-sampling approach, and signal-detection theory are presented briefly.

Chapter 12

Transfer of Training

The belief that learning one task may affect the learning of some second task has existed for a long time. Indeed, long before psychology was established as a separate discipline, philosophers and teachers firmly believed in the concept of "mental faculties" that could be developed. They held that training certain of these faculties would make a person a better "thinker," and that the learning of one sort of mental task would greatly enhance a person's ability to perform other, more sophisticated tasks. This idea—that the learning of one task can facilitate or otherwise influence the learning of another task—has been widely studied by psychologists, who refer to the phenomenon as *transfer of training*.

12.1 TRANSFER-OF-TRAINING DESIGNS

Investigations of transfer of training have largely taken place in experimental reseach settings—the "laboratory." Several widely accepted experimental designs for studying transfer of training have emerged. All of these designs contain at least two steps in order to determine what effect the learning of a task in the first step has upon the acquisition of the second-step task. Here is a basic design:

Group	Step one	Step two
Experimental	Learn task 1	Learn task 2
Control	Put in time	Learn task 2

Comparison of the two groups' performance in step two allows the researcher to determine if the learning of task 1 has had any effect upon the acquisition of task 2. During step one, the control group usually is kept busy with some task that is *not* related to either task 1 or task 2. Performance of this allegedly unrelated task, called "putting in time," should require of the control group the same expenditure of energy and level of arousal found in the experimental group's performance of learning task 1. In other words, the activity involved in putting in time should account for (or *neutralize*) such extraneous variables as *warm-up* or *fatigue*.

EXAMPLE 1. Imagine that task 1 involves solving fairly difficult mathematical problems. Subjects in the experimental group may suffer "mental fatigue" that could carry over to task 2. If this is a concern, the researcher may want to have the control group perform a comparably difficult (but unrelated) task, perhaps something like searching for the "hidden pictures" within a large drawing. By pretesting, the researcher could predict that both groups would then approach task 2 with somewhat equivalent fatigue, and differences in performance could be attributed to the effects of task 1 acquisition rather than to fatigue, which in this experiment is an extraneous variable.

Additional designs. The design given above is the one most frequently used to study transfer of training, but this is by no means the only one. A few other basic designs are listed here:

(1) To determine if learning task 1 has more effect upon learning task 2a than it does on learning task 2b:

Group	Step one	Step two
I	Learn task 1	Learn task 2a
II	Learn task 1	Learn task 2b

(2) To determine whether learning one task before learning another may have some facilitative or inhibitory effect:

Group	Step one	Step two
I	Learn task 1	Learn task 2
II	Learn task 2	Learn task 1

(3) To determine whether or not time between learning the first and second tasks affects the transfer effects:

Group	Step one	(Intervening time)	Step two
I	Learn task 1	(Time period A)	Learn task 2
II	Learn task 1	(Time period B)	Learn task 2

EXAMPLE 2. The first design above assumes the two tasks being learned in step two are equivalent—that is, if the learning in step one had not taken place, task 2a and task 2b should be equally difficult to learn.   It also assumes that equal amounts of learning have taken place in step one.   Making these assumptions, an experimenter could conduct a study such as the following:

Group	Step one	Step two
I	Learn French	Learn Spanish
II	Learn French	Learn Italian

This study might help determine if learning French would be of more benefit to those going on to learn Spanish or those going on to learn Italian.

Mixed vs. unmixed tasks. In the second step of a transfer-of-training experiment, the subjects may be asked to learn several types of materials (a *mixed task*) or a single type of material (an *unmixed task*).   In the former case the subjects serve as their own controls while in the latter there are several control groups.

Task similarity.   The resemblance between elements of different tasks or between those of a single task are called respectively *intertask similarity* or *intratask similarity*. Variation of task similarity may have pronounced effects upon the transfer effects obtained (see Section 12.5).

Experimental purposes.   Most transfer-of-training investigations are conducted to determine if the acquisition of or learning of the first task will have some effect upon the acquisition of the second task.   However, these studies can sometimes serve a second purpose, that of determining just what was learned during acquisition of the first task.   Using properly chosen second-step acquisition tasks, analysis may reveal specific elements that formed the basis of the first learning.

EXAMPLE 3.   Suppose several paired-associate learning tasks are tested for transfer of training.   One object of the study might be to see how the learning of one series of nonsense syllables and their appropriate responses influences the learning of another series of nonsense syllables paired with the same responses.   A simplified version of the design is shown in Table 12-1.   It is likely that the learning of task 2a will be facilitated more than the learning of task 2b because the initial letters in task 2a series of syllables are the same as those in task 1.   (In task 2b, it is the middle letters that are identical to their counterparts in task 1.)   Thus, such an experimental design suggests that task 1 facilitates task 2a more than it does task 2b. Additionally, this transfer of learning suggests that it is the initial letters in a series of nonsense syllables that are the most salient elements of the nonsense syllable, and the more likely to produce positive transfer of training.

Table 12-1

Group	Step one	Step two
I	Learn task 1:	Learn task 2a:
	FEH—R_1	FOL—R_1
	VOP—R_1	VAS—R_2
	PAC—R_3	PIB—R_3
II	Learn task 1:	Learn task 2b:
	FEH—R_1	LEC—R_1
	VOP—R_2	POL—R_2
	PAC—R_3	CAS—R_3

12.2   TRANSFER-OF-TRAINING EFFECTS

As mentioned in the preceding section, most transfer-of-training studies investigate the effects of one learning upon the acquisition of a subsequent task.   Three results are possible.

When the learning of the first task facilitates learning of the second task, *positive transfer* is said to have taken place.   *Negative transfer* means that the learning of the first task has in some way hindered or interfered with acquistion of the second task.   *Zero transfer* (also sometimes called neutral transfer) means that learning the first task had no effect upon second-task acquisition.

It should be noted that determining that some transfer effect has taken place does not necessarily indicate why that effect occurred.   Many different explanations of transfer of training have been proposed.   Some of these are explored in the materials following.

EXAMPLE 4.   Learning to play the clarinet may have both positive and negative transfer effects when the subsequent task is learning to play the oboe.   Because the clarinet is a single-reed instrument with a mouthpiece, there would be negative transfer to the double-reed, no-mouthpiece arrangement of an oboe. However, the oboe and clarinet require similar fingering patterns, so positive tranfer could be expected as well.   (It might also be pointed out that learning to play the clarinet probably would have no transfer effect to a later memorization of passages from the works of Camus, for example.)

12.3   MEASUREMENT OF TRANSFER

Investigators of transfer of training have presented their results in several different ways.   No one measurement technique is considered to be *the* way to present data, but three types of measurement—absolute transfer effects and two measures based upon percentage of transfer— are the most frequently used.

Absolute transfer.   The difference in the responding by the experimental and control groups in step two yields an *absolute transfer* measure.   The reseacher must be careful to determine what response measure is being used before deciding *if* some transfer effect has been demonstrated.

EXAMPLE 5.   Suppose the response measure used in determining second-step performance is the number of errors made on the task.   If the experimental group had a total of 75 and the control group had a total of 125, the absolute difference will show the control group with 50 more responses than the experimental group. However, because the measure used in this case is the number of *errors*, the results will be interpreted as evidence of positive transfer.

Percentage of transfer. Two formulas have been used quite frequently to represent the percentage of transfer from one task to another. These are:

$$(1) \quad \text{Percentage of transfer} = \frac{E - C}{C} \times 100$$

$$(2) \quad \text{Percentage of transfer} = \frac{E - C}{E + C} \times 100$$

where E = experimental group performance
        C = control group performance

EXAMPLE 6. Using the data presented in Example 5 (and remembering that these were error data), the percentage of transfer according to each of the above formulas is as follows:

$$(1) \quad \text{Percentage of transfer} = \frac{75 - 125}{125} \times 100 = -40\%$$

$$(2) \quad \text{Percentage of transfer} = \frac{75 - 125}{200} \times 100 = -25\%$$

Extent of testing. Because it is often difficult to determine *when* transfer effects may be revealed, tests for transfer (the acquisition of the second task) are generally carried out over a fairly long period of time or a great number of trials. This helps ensure that if any transfer effects exist, they will be identified.

12.4 GENERAL VARIABLES INFLUENCING TRANSFER EFFECTS

Variables that influence the obtained transfer effects are usually categorized as *general*, or found for many different tasks, and *specific*, or limited to a particular type of task. Three of the most widely studied general variables are warm-up, fatigue, and learning to learn.

Warm-Up

Especially when the first and second tasks of a transfer experiment are conducted in close temporal sequence, participation in the first task may create a mental or physical preparation for acquiring the second task materials. Such an effect is called *warm-up*.

EXAMPLE 7. The research design that would allow for determination of warm-up effects is as follows:

Group	Step one	Step two
I	Learn task 1	Learn task 2
II	Put in time	Learn task 2
III	Rest only	Learn task 2

If the study is concerned with positive transfer effects, it is possible that group I performance may be superior to that of either Group II or Group III. However, if there is some benefit from warm-up included in the step-one task, it should be revealed by better performance in Group II than in Group III.

Fatigue

A second possibility is essentially the opposite of warm-up. The activity of step one may create either mental or physical fatigue that will hamper the acquisition performance on the second step. (*Note:* If this is a concern, the design presented in Example 7 might be used to reveal such an effect.)

Learning to Learn

An additional general influence upon transfer effects has come to be called *learning to learn* (or, sometimes, *learning sets*). This influence is "general" in the sense that the subject appears to learn how to go about doing tasks, then applies these general rules to various specific situations.

EXAMPLE 8. Several years ago American automobile manufacturers introduced a standard security ignition system that locks the steering wheel when the key is removed. All American cars after that point had the ignition switch on the steering column, so that someone who learned to locate and operate the ignition switch in one car could operate it in other cars. This is different from the situation 20 years ago, when cars' starter buttons were located in many different places and specific learning was required for each variation.

12.5   SPECIFIC VARIABLES INFLUENCING TRANSFER EFFECTS

Many transfer tasks have been analyzed in terms of their specific components. Generally, these analyses fall into one of the three catagories: stimulus factors, response factors, or S-R association factors.

Stimulus Differentiation

If the task in step one requires the subject to distinguish among several different stimuli, *stimulus differentiation* is involved. When the task in step two entails the same differentiation, positive transfer can be expected. In general, the amount of transfer obtained is a function of the difficulty of discriminating among the various stimuli of task one. The greater the learning involved in step one, the more pronounced the transfer effects in step two.

EXAMPLE 9. When learning about selling clothes, a novice clerk may have to differentiate among many different characteristics, such as fabric, cut, collar length, or matching of plaids. Such stimulus differentiation could be expected to transfer to a "new version" of the same line of clothes. (*Note:* Using the *principles* learned, rather than the properties of a specific line of clothes, to evaluate a different brand, would represent learning to learn.)

Response Learning

Explanation of the influence of *response learning* is very straightforward: when the subject has learned something about the responses during step one, and the same responses are required in the second task, positive transfer can be expected. Response learning in step one simply saves that much time and effort in step two.

S-R Association Factors

Two types of association have been proposed. If the association is between the presented stimulus and the subsequent response (S→R) it is called a *forward association*. If the reponse acts as a stimulus to provoke recall of what was the original stimulus, a *backward association* (R→S) has been shown.

EXAMPLE 10. Several years ago, a popular television game show demanded that contestants make backward associations. The players were presented with the answers and won money if they were the most rapid in giving an appropriate question for the answer.

Specific associations in verbal learning tasks are studied frequently. These are presented in Section 12.6.

Task Difficulty

Any one or any combination of the specific factors just discussed may produce varying levels of task difficulty. Although the determination of task difficulty may be somewhat subjective, agreement is often reached.

One interesting finding regarding task difficulty is shown when the following design is used to test transfer effects:

Group	Step one	Step two
I	Practice difficult task	Difficult task
II	Practice easier but related task	Difficult task

While theory predicts that maximum positive transfer of training should be generated by performing exactly the same task in both steps (group I), results from studies such as this have shown group II achieving higher levels of positive transfer. A progressive or gradual approach—from a somewhat easier task to the more difficult task—appears to yield best performance, especially when difficult differentiations are the eventual goal.

EXAMPLE 11. The principle of this section is illustrated by the teaching of letters of the alphabet to young children. Initial tasks should be easy and perhaps exaggerate—for example, distinguishing x and o. Step-by-step progression might later lead to distinction between m and n and ultimately differentiate between b and d.

Concept of Similarity

Much of the importance attached to the principles presented above can be attributed to or explained by the concept of *similarity*—that is, how alike stimuli, responses, or associations are judged to be. Similarity can be divided into two types (comparable to the divisions of stimulus generalization): *physical similarity*, based on the actual physical properties of the two events being compared, and *learned similarity*, judged according to the verbal meaning of the two events.

Functional Fixedness

When the subject is unable to recognize alternate uses for a particular implement or object and persists in using it only for its original purpose although an alternate use may be required, *functional fixedness* has occurred. In general, functional fixedness produces negative transfer.

EXAMPLE 12. Suppose a couple leaves their house carrying umbrellas because they heard a weather report that predicted thundershowers. If during their walk they complain because the sun is so hot and they cannot find any shade, they are showing functional fixedness. Thinking of umbrellas as devices for warding off rain but not bright sun exemplifies the principle.

12.6　TRANSFER IN VERBAL LEARNING

One of the most popular means for investigating transfer-of-training effects has been to use human subjects in verbal learning studies, especially using paired-associate tasks. Several designs have been developed. For each, the standard control condition is represented as A-B, C-D, meaning two S-R paired-associated tasks of totally new or different materials. (See illustrations of other designs in Examples 13 and 14.)

The A-B, A-D Design

To investigate the effects of attaching new responses to the same stimuli, the experimental group is tested with an A-B, A-D sequence. In general, negative transfer can be expected.

EXAMPLE 13. Consider the experiment described in Table 12-2 in which an A-B, A-D design is used to test for the transfer of training between several paired-associate tasks. (In each task, the stimuli are the nonsense syllables and the responses are the numbers.) In step two, the experimental group is tested for transfer to a task that links "old" (original) stimuli to "new" responses. The control group, in step two, attempts to link "new" stimuli to the *same* "new" responses. In general, it can be expected that the control group will perform better in step two than the experimental group will. This is interpreted as evidence the old-S–old-R learning of task 1 by the experimental group interferes with its learning in task 2, which involves making an old-S–new-R association. In other words, negative transfer has taken place for the experimental group.

Table 12-2

Group	Step one	Step two
	Learn task 1:	Learn task 2:
Experimental	VED—17	VED—25
	MUQ—80	MUQ—53
	FOH—38	FOH—14
	Learn task 1:	Learn task 2:
Control	VED—17	QUY—25
	MUQ—80	MIP—53
	FOH—38	PEJ—14

The A-B, C-B Design

To investigate the effects of attaching the same responses to different stimuli, the experimental group is tested with an A-B, C-B sequence. In general, response learning from the first task carries over to the second and produces positive transfer of training effects.

The A-B, A-Br Design

When the experimental group is tested with an A-B, A-Br sequence, the same stimuli and the same responses are used in all trials, but the pairings are rearranged. (The letter *r* in Br stands for rearranged.) Usually, this produces considerable negative transfer, because of interfering associations carrying over from the first task to the second.

EXAMPLE 14. An A-B, A-Br design would be set up as shown in Table 12-3. In all likelihood, the control group would perform considerably better in step two than the experimental group would, showing significant negative transfer for the experimental group.

Table 12-3

Group	Step one	Step two
	VED—17	VED—38
Experimental	MUQ—80	MUQ—17
	FOH—38	FOH—80
	VED—17	QUY—25
Control	MUQ—80	MIP—53
	FOH—38	PEJ—14

The Effect of Meaningfulness

One additional variable that may operate in all of the above designs is the *effect of meaningfulness*. (See Chapter 6 for discussion of meaningfulness.) In general, it can be said that as the meaningfulness of the items used in the tasks drops, response learning becomes more important and association learning becomes less so.

EXAMPLE 15. When the subject is required to learn a pair such as "Table"-"Visit," it is presumed that little or no response learning is necessary and the concentration of effort will be on making the appropriate connection between the two words. On the other hand, if the pair is "Island"-"Torpor," the unfamiliarity of the response term may require more response-learning effort than would the preceding pair.

12.7 SPECIAL INFLUENCES ON TRANSFER OF TRAINING

Three principles presented earlier are reintroduced here in the context of transfer of training.

Sensory Preconditioning

In some classical conditioning situations, two neutral stimuli are paired together for a number of trials. One of these stimuli (CS_1) is then used as the CS in the conditioning procedure. The transfer effects of the initial pairing can then be determined by using the other stimulus (CS_2) in the conditioning situation and comparing the acquisition of the CR for this group to the performance of an appropriate control group. This has been called a *sensory preconditioning* procedure.

Stimulus Predifferentiation

When the subjects are taught to make different responses to several different stimuli before those stimuli are used in some acquisition task, *stimulus predifferentiation* is said to have taken place. In general, the greater the relevancy of the initial (differentiating) responses to the later acquisition task, the greater the positive transfer effects expected.

EXAMPLE 16. Suppose that subjects in a driver education experiment are divided into two groups. During predriving classroom preparation, group I is presented with a paired-associate task that has the shapes of traffic signs as stimuli and the appropriate driving rules as responses. One such S-R pair would look like Fig. 12-1.

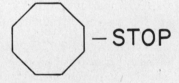

Fig. 12-1

Meanwhile, group II is presented with a paired-associate procedure that links the same traffic sign shape with their geometrical names. (For example, the sign shape in Fig. 12-1 would be associated with the response "octagon.") Later, when both groups are being tested for their responses to the sign shapes in an actual driving situation, group I would be likely to show better performance. This is because the differentiation learned by group I in the classroom paired-associate task is more relevant to acquisition of the later driving task than that learned by group II.

Familiarization

Familiarization is a term usually used to refer to the manipulated frequency with which a subject experiences a particular stimulus or response. Familiarization is often manipulated during an experimenter-controlled pretraining period, in which materials that are later used as part of the transfer task are presented before actual training. Facilitation or interference may result, depending upon the subsequent task involved. (The familiarity of a particular stimulus or response can also be measured by having the subjects "rate" how familiar each stimulus or response is; the problem with this, of course, is that the experimenter must then rely on the subjects' ratings.)

12.8   THEORIES OF TRANSFER OF TRAINING

In keeping with the orientation of this book, the following theories of transfer of training are presented only in brief version.

Association Theories

Association theories of transfer of training are based primarily on extensions of conditioning and verbal learning principles. Transfer is explained as a function of stimulus generalization, response generalization, and/or mediation.

Encoding Variability Theory

Based on the concept of stimulus encoding, the encoding variability theory stresses that the functional stimulus in a transfer situation may differ from the nominal stimulus. This difference would then modify stimulus differentiation or association predictions and, in some cases, help account for results that were contrary to the original conceptions.

Cognitive Theory

Emphasis on development of cognitive strategies or rules is the major thrust of cognitive theory. The learner is viewed as actively trying to develop and comprehend such rules or strategies, then to apply them to new circumstances.

Solved Problems

12.1   A leading psychologist once stated that there was "no more important topic in the whole of the psychology of learning than transfer of training. [It] is basic to educational theory." Explain why such a statement represents a "traditional" viewpoint.

Traditional educational theorists emphasize the fact that learning experiences are built upon previous learning—the basic premise of transfer of training. In particular, they believe that the mind can be trained and that training in certain areas (such as Latin or arithmetic) will help a student acquire knowledge in other areas (such as English grammar or algebra). This kind of specific transfer of skills is not all the traditionalists propose, however: They also believe the mind can be "exercised" in a general way and "trained to think."

12.2   Describe the "basic" experimental design for testing transfer of training, including the tasks performed by one experimental group and a control group.

Testing transfer of training involves a two-step experimental design, as follows:

Group	Step one	Step two
Experimental	Learn task 1	Learn task 2
Control	Put in time	Learn task 2

Comparison of the two groups' performance in step two allows the researcher to determine if learning task 1 has had a favorable influence, an unfavorable influence, or no influence upon the acquisition of task 2. During step one, the control group "puts in time," which means that it is kept busy performing a task not related to task 1 or task 2. The purpose of the "putting in time" activity is to ensure that the control group experiences approximately the same amount of warm-up or fatigue as the experimental group does in task 1. (In order to fully "neutralize" or account for the fatigue and warm-up variables, the experimenter may do extensive pretesting of the "putting in time" activity or use more than one control group during testing.)

12.3   The experimental design presentation in Problem 12.2 is the most frequently used for studying transfer of training.   However, other designs are possible.   Which of the "other" designs might be used if the experimenter was interested in determining in which order students at a computer school should learn two different programming languages?

The research design necessary to solve the problem would be as follows:

Group	Step one	Step two
I	Learn language 1	Learn language 2
II	Learn language 2	Learn language 1

The students, divided into two groups that were as alike as possible before the experiment began, would learn the languages in opposite order.   If the time necessary for acquiring both languages was the measure of learning used, the group that needed less time for acquisition would be demonstrating the better transfer design.

12.4   Suppose the head of the computer school (Problem 12.3) was also concerned about whether or not both programming languages should be taught in the same semester.   What transfer of training design would have to be used in order to also answer this question?

The design presented in Problem 12.3 would have to be expanded to incorporate two more groups as shown in Table 12-4.

Table 12-4

Group	Step one	Step two
I	Learn language 1 first semester	Learn language 2 first semester
II	Learn language 1 first semester	Learn language 2 second semester
III	Learn language 2 first semester	Learn language 1 first semester
IV	Learn language 2 first semester	Learn language 1 second semester

12.5   Explain what it means to say that a researcher has chosen to test transfer of training using low intertask similarity and an unmixed task in the second step of an experiment like the one described in Problem 12.2.

Suppose the initial (step-one) task involves some sort of S-R association.   Testing for transfer in step two might mean altering the stimulus in some manner while retaining the same responses, altering the responses while retaining the same stimuli, or altering both the stimuli and responses.

If the task in step two acquisition is an unmixed arrangement, it means the subjects will experience only one of the above conditions.   In a mixed condition, more than one of the variations might be included in the step-two acquisition.   Additionally, low intertask similarity means that the components varied for the second task will differ noticeably from their counterparts in step one. (*Note*: Intertask similarity refers to a comparison between tasks, while *intra*task similarity would refer to the similarity of components within a single task.)

12.6   What does it mean to say that the most common purpose for conducting a transfer-of-training experiment is to test the cumulative effects of practice?   What other purpose can be served by a transfer-of-training experiment?

In essence, a test of the cumulative effects of practice asks whether more practice on the task in step one will have some effect upon the acquisition of the task in step two.   This is by far the most frequent concern of transfer-of-training experiments, but such experiments can serve a second purpose.   Properly designed, transfer-of-training investigations can be used to try to answer the question, "What *was* learned in step one?"   Comparable training for all groups in step one, followed by carefully selected second-step tasks, may allow the experimenter to identify the particular components that were predominant in the step-one learning (see Example 3).

12.7 Suppose that the teacher at the computer school (Problem 12.3) found that learning language 1 speeded up acquisition of language 2. What type of transfer would be demonstrated? What type of transfer would be demonstrated if learning language 2 resulted in no shortening of the time necessary to learn language 1?

The first result (indicating that language 1 learning makes language 2 learning easier) represents positive transfer; that is, learning one task facilitated acquisition of a second task. The second result, in which the order of the learning is reversed, illustrates zero transfer; that is, acquisition of one task had no effect upon acquisition of the second.

12.8 What kind of result would have to be found to illustrate negative transfer in Problem 12.7?

If the learning of one language made it more difficult to learn the second, negative transfer would have occurred. (*Note*: This does not mean both tasks would not or should not be learned. If computer students *must* learn both languages, some other presentation sequence or teaching technique may be necessary to eliminate the negative-transfer effects.)

12.9 Results from a transfer-of-training study show that the experimental group's performance in the second task equalled 40 response units, while the control group's performance was 60 response units. Compute three different measures of transfer of training using these data.

1. The absolute transfer-of-training score is -20 response units, indicating negative transfer has occurred.

2. A percentage formula for transfer of training is

$$\frac{E - C}{C} \times 100$$

which in this case yields

$$\frac{40 - 60}{60} \times 100 = -33\%$$

again indicating negative transfer.

3. Another percentage formula for transfer of training is

$$\frac{E - C}{E + C} \times 100$$

which yields

$$\frac{40 - 60}{100} \times 100 = -20\%$$

also indicating negative transfer. There is no universal agreement accepting any one of these measures as better than any of the others.

12.10 Explain why many studies of transfer of training use extensive test tasks in the second step of the procedure.

Extensive test tasks are used in the second step of a transfer-of-training procedure because, in a sense, there is no guarantee of when the transfer effects (*if* they exist) will manifest themselves. Although it generally can be expected that transfer effects are going to show up at the beginning of the second-step test task, this may not always happen, as when several trials are necessary for a warm-up period. By extending the test task, the experimenter can be more certain of identifying any transfer effects that may exist.

12.11 In Problem 12.2 mention was made of both warm-up and fatigue effects.   Explain why these are considered general transfer effects.

Both warm-up and fatigue effects result simply from participation in a task.   Warm-up is thought of as a facilitative effect yielding positive transfer-of-training effects.   Fatigue is inhibitory and should produce negative transfer-of-training effects.   Because such effects are possible, it is necessary, when testing for specific transfer-of-training effects, to involve the control group in a step-one task that provides comparable general effects to those being presented to the experimental group.

12.12 Law enforcement officials learn a "routine" for investigating criminal cases.   What principle of transfer of training is illustrated by such practice?

Learning how to go about doing a task, such as an investigation routine, represents learning to learn—that is, learning general principles that may be applied to many different specific situations.

12.13 As a test of nonspecific transfer-of-training effects, one researcher presented successive trials to subjects, with three lists to be practiced for five trials on five consecutive days.   (All lists were considered to be of equal difficulty, and the order of their presentation was varied from group to group of subjects.)   The results obtained are presented in Fig. 12-2.   Add labels or identifying marks to the graph to represent the nonspecific transfer effects obtained in this study.

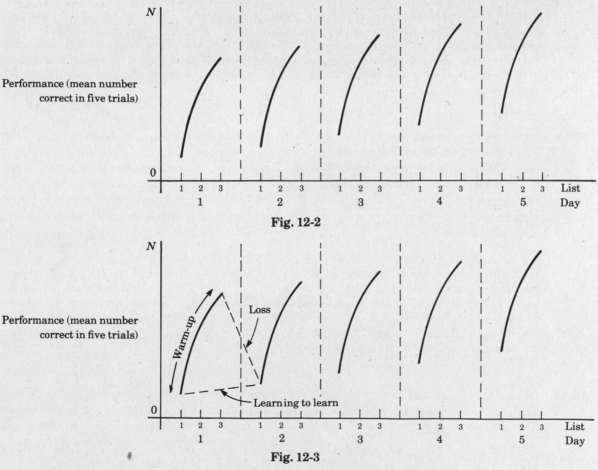

Fig. 12-2

Fig. 12-3

See Fig. 12-3.

Improvement from trial one to trial three for any given day represents warm-up.   Improvement from trial one of one day to trial one of the next day represents learning to learn.   The difference in performance from trial three of one day to trial one of the next day illustrates loss of the warm-up effect.

12.14 Tennis and badminton are considered by some to be quite similar, while baseball is considered quite different from either of them.   Design a transfer-of-training study that would help determine specific and general transfer effects from learning the rules of tennis and baseball to learning the rules of badminton.

The solution of this problem would involve a three-group transfer-of-training experiment, as follows:

Group	Step one	Step one
I	Learn tennis rules	Learn badminton rules
II	Learn baseball rules	Learn badminton rules
Control	Put in time	Learn badminton rules

As examples of what may be found, the specific rules regarding a force-out in baseball should have no effect upon learning badminton rules, while the specific rule in tennis about alternating courts for service could transfer.   Correspondingly, the more general principle stating that a ball hitting a line remains in play (service or out-of-bounds line in tennis, foul line in baseball) also could transfer.   (*Note:* Such a general principle may create negative transfer in learning the rules of other sports; for example, when learning the rules of football, where a ball or foot on the line is considered out-of-bounds.)   Even more generally, the learning of the inviolability of an official's judgment might be a general principle that would apply in all cases, although the specific rules might differ considerably.

12.15 New to her job as office supervisor, Elaine decides that she must first learn the names of her employees, and she therefore practices pairing the appropriate name with the respective face.   After several days, she feels fairly confident of responding with the correct name, but realizes that she must also know each person's responsibility in the office. Therefore, she starts to try to put the correct label or title with each person.   Why should her first learning of face-name combinations probably provide positive transfer to the second acquisition task?

In the initial learning task, one of the aspects in Elaine's learning is developing differentiation of the physical features of the various employees.   This same differentiation should prove helpful when Elaine attempts her second learning of face-job pairings.   The stimulus differentiation of the first task transfers to the acquisition of the second task.   (*Note:* Greater amounts of positive transfer can be expected when the employees look very much alike.   Just as with verbal tasks showing high intralist similarity, the initial differentiation may be fairly difficult, but once learned it should help the learning of the second task considerably.)

12.16 In Problem 11.25, the French phrase "Voici la plume" was used, and translated as "Here is the pen."   Suppose the student who learned this phrase later must identify the implements of colonial America and is able to learn quickly that the feather dipped in ink and used as a writing instrument was sometimes called a plume.   What transfer principle may be demonstrated?

There are at least two solutions to this problem.   One involves response learning—having learned the response "plume" in French class, the student has no need to learn that response again, and carry-over might be expected.

A second possibility involves establishment of the mediator "pen." The student may learn the second association as

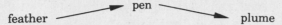

feather   →   pen   →   plume

with "pen" serving as the mediator for the "feather"-"plume" association. (Mediation has been suggested as a theoretical explanation for some transfer of training.)

12.17   Refer again to the situation described in Problem 12.15. Under what circumstances would learning of forward associations create negative transfer for Elaine at some later date? When would backward associations be likely to create negative transfer?

     Negative transfer from a forward-association learning might occur if one of Elaine's female employees married and chose to use her husband's last name. The face-name association previously learned would now be inappropriate and could interfere with the new learning.

     Negative transfer from a backward association could result from learning a particular face-name combination (name-face as a backward association), then having a new employee hired who had the same name. Elaine might have to find some way to distinguish the two employees—for example, by calling one Bob and the other Robert.

12.18   In teaching an interior decorating class, Arthur has found that the students seem more able to learn the names of various shades of color within a particular color range if they first practice distinguishing the several broad color ranges. Therefore, he trains them to respond appropriately to category stimuli such as "yellow-orange" or "red-orange" before trying to differentiate ochre, amber, and umber, other names for shades of orange. What finding regarding transfer of training does Arthur's technique reflect?

     In certain learning situations, the ultimate task to be learned is so difficult that initiating practice using that task may create confusion or despair. In such cases, it has been shown that practice on an easier task provides the appropriate foundation for going on to acquire the more difficult task—an instance of positive transfer of training. Arthur's technique applies this finding to a practical situation. Broad category names are learned (easy task), then specific distinctions are acquired for variations within those categories (difficult task).

12.19   The similarity of items to be learned is an important consideration in studies of specific transfer effects. What are the ways similarity may be evaluated?

     Broadly, similarity may exist because two stimuli or responses have common physical properties or because there is some degree of learned likeness. (This is comparable to the concepts of primary and secondary stimulus generalization; see Chapter 10.)

     Physical similarity may depend on the number of discrete units that are alike (e.g., XUF and YAF have one similar letter) or on how close two stimuli are in some continuum such as color or tone. Learned similarity results from verbal meaning or the possibility of some mediator linking the stimuli.

12.20   Explain why functional fixedness may be particularly noticeable if there has been a high degree of overlearning.

     Overlearning refers to continued practice of an already learned task. If the subject has used an object for a specific purpose many times more than necessary for minimal understanding, it is very possible that the subject would be unable to "see" other possible uses for the object and not make the type of transfer necessary to solve the problem at hand.

12.21 Transfer of training frequently is studied in verbal learning by using paired-associate tasks (see Chapter 6).   Create a table that presents the basic designs studying transfer of training in verbal learning and indicating the expected effects.

See Table 12-5.

Table 12-5   Basic Transfer Designs (Verbal Learning)

Design		Stimuli	Responses	Usual transfer effect
Step one	Step two			
A-B	C-D	Different	Different	Control
A-B	A-D	Same	Different	Negative
A-B	C-B	Different	Same	Positive
A-B	A-Br	Same	Same (rearranged)	Much negative

12.22 Although the table just presented in Problem 12.21 indicates that much negative transfer can be expected in the A-B, A-Br design, studies using responses of very low meaningfulness have *not* supported such predictions, yielding zero transfer or even some positive transfer.   Develop an explanation for such findings.

The explanation requires use of both response-learning and association principles.   It is proposed that using responses with high meaningfulness in the first-step (A-B) acquisition involves little or no response learning and that most effort is concentrated upon learning the associations (both forward and backward).   On the other hand, low meaningfulness responses require much response learning, leaving relatively little effort to be devoted to association learning.   Therefore, when the second-step (A-Br) task is undertaken, orientation toward the associations produces negative transfer for the subjects using the high-meaningfulness responses, but the subjects using low-meaningfulness responses benefit from the response-learning process and show more positive effects.

12.23 Apply the same interpretation given in the solution to Problem 12.22 to the A-B, C-B design to estimate transfer effects.

While Table 12-5 indicates that the usual transfer effect in the A-B, C-B design is positive, it can be predicted that there will be greater positive transfer when response meaningfulness is low.   Using the same type of interpretation as that given in Problem 12.22, low response meaningfulness means that the subject would concentrate upon response learning rather than association learning—particularly the backward association B-A.   In the second step, the response learning has a positive transfer effect for acquisition of the C-B pairs, while D-A backward associations could create some negative transfer effects.

12.24 Contrast sensory preconditioning and stimulus predifferentiation.   Which of these usually is thought to represent familiarization?

Sensory preconditioning is a procedure used before conditioning is undertaken.   Generally, two stimuli simply are presented together for a number of trials, developing a seeming equivalency that may transfer to a later task.

Stimulus predifferentiation essentially is an opposite procedure.   If two or more stimuli are presented before the experimental acquisition tasks, the subjects are trained to give distinguishing responses for each stimulus.   Thus, rather than a developing equivalency, as in sensory preconditioning, stimulus predifferentiation creates a discrimination among stimuli.

Typically when the concept of familiarization is used in verbal learning studies, it refers to the stimulus-predifferentiation model.   Transfer is facilitated by learning distinctions among stimuli.

12.25   A subject learning paired-associate tasks has the pair JOKE-GUX in the first task and the pair JEST-GUX in the second task.   Briefly interpret the potential transfer using each of the theories presented in this chapter.

There are two varieties of association theories.   The first, based upon generalization, would evaluate the potential for generalization and perhaps note that both stimuli start with *J*, implying positive transfer should result.   The second, based upon mediation, might recognize that JEST and JOKE do have a similar meaning (secondary stimulus generalization), but that JOKE is more familiar.   The result may be a second-step learning represented as JEST = JOKE, goes with GUX.

The theory of encoding variability emphasizes the possibility that stimulus encoding will change the nominal stimulus to some other representation.   In this situation, the subject may concentrate upon the middle letters of the first stimulus and code the pair as OK-GUX.   If this happens a negative transfer might be expected.

Cognitive theories stress potential strategies or rules for learning.   Encoding, such as that described above, may be one version of a cognitive strategy, but other variations are possible.   For example, the subjects could develop some retrieval strategy or rule while acquiring the pairs that may or may not apply to the second task.

Key Terms

Backward associations.   Generally speaking, any association formed such that a later-presented item prompts retrieval of an earlier-presented item; more specifically, an R → S association.

Familiarization.   The manipulated frequency of a subject's experience with a particular stimulus or response.

Forward associations.   Generally speaking, any association formed such that an earlier-presented item prompts retrieval of a later-presented item; more specifically, an S → R association.

Functional fixedness.   Inability to recognize alternate uses for an implement or object and persistence in using the implement only for its original purpose.

Intertask similarity.   The resemblance of elements of two different tasks.

Intratask similarity.   The resemblance of elements within one task.

Learning to learn.   Learning a general principle of how to respond that can be applied in a number of specific situations.

Negative transfer.   When the learning of one task makes more difficult the later acquisition of some second task.

Sensory preconditioning.   A learning situation in which there are repeated pairings of two potential CSs before one is used in classical conditioning; then later presentation of the other (nonconditioned) CS produces a CR-type response.

Stimulus predifferentiation.   Training distinguishing responses to several different stimuli before those stimuli are used in some acquisition task.

Transfer of training.   The effect that learning one task has on the later acquisition of some second task.

Warm-up.   Any of a number of experiences that prepare an organism for the performance of a response or the acquisition of a task.

Chapter 13

Memory Processes

Any measure of the quality or quantity of the learned material stored by an organism over a period of time is a measure of *retention*.   There are several different ways the subject of retention can be approached.   For one, it can be discussed in terms of *forgetting* (Chapter 14)—for example, the amount of previously learned material an organism *fails* to demonstrate in a given situation. Additionally, retention can be understood in terms of *information processing* (Chapter 15)—as the middle stage in a kind of input-storage-output sequence.   Retention can also be described in terms of *memory processes,* the subject of this chapter.

13.1   ANALYSIS OF MEMORY

Memory can best be discussed by referring to the the acquisition-storage-retrieval process described in Chapter 1 and elsewhere.   In studies of memory, the emphasis is on the second and third stages of this process.

EXAMPLE 1.   Suppose an elementary school student is to learn the statement "2 plus 2 equals 4."   The first stage, acquisition, may involve practicing this statement repeatedly.   In studies of memory, the main (but not exclusive) focus would be on the second and third stages, storage and retrieval: The child, once a period of time has elapsed after practice, might be asked to respond to the question, "How much is 2 plus 2?"

A number of different interpretations of this acquisition-storage-retrieval sequence have been put forth.   Some of the most important of these are presented in later sections of this chapter. However, it is first necessary to discuss how data concerning retention are gathered.

13.2   MEASUREMENT OF RETENTION

Attempts to measure retention fall into several major categories, which are presented in this section.

Recall

When subjects are given some minimal cue, such as a question or instruction that directs their attention to the right materials (but not any specific answers), a *recall* measure of retention is being used.   Recall measures are subdivided into *free recall,* in which the responses can be produced in any order the subject pleases, and *serial recall* (also called ordered recall), which requires the subject to respond with the items in the order they were previously presented.

Recognition

If the subject is presented with the correct answer and must only judge the correspondence of that answer to some already stored trace, a *recognition* measure of retention is being used.   Recognition measures also take two forms—presentation of only one item, to which the subject responds yes or no, or exposure to several items, from which the subject selects the correct item or items.

EXAMPLE 2.   Suppose Shirley has attended a very important horse race—one which you really wanted to be present for, but simply could not attend.   Afterwards, you question her about the race.   The four possibilities for measuring retention would be illustrated by the following questions:

1.   Free recall: Tell me the names of all the horses in the race.
2.   Serial recall: Tell me the names of the horses in their post positions.

3. Recognition (a): Did Treasurariat run in the race?

4. Recognition (b): Were any of these horses in the race—Treasurariat, Atturned, Seacracker, or Sightation?

Both recall and recognition are considered *direct measures* of retention, attempting to determine not only how much has been retained, but also the properties of what is retained.

Relearning

A third general measure of retention has been called *relearning*. It is measured as the difference in time or effort needed to restore previously learned material to the criterion used for original learning, divided by the time for the original learning. In experiments where time is not a reasonable measure to employ, effort (e.g., the number of experimental trials needed) is often evaluated instead.

Attempts to quantify relearning usually are presented as a *savings score,* using the following formula:

$$\text{Savings score} = \frac{\text{original learning} - \text{relearning}}{\text{original learning}} \times 100$$

EXAMPLE 3. At the end of his high school career, Brice had a chance to be selected for an all-expenses-paid trip to France. The only requirement was that he present a talk to number of community groups—in French! Brice developed the talk, translated in into French, and then spent two weeks memorizing his presentation. Brice was very well received, so following his freshman year in college he was asked to return to France to give his talk to other groups. He gladly accepted, then found he could give the talk perfectly after only four days' practice. Brice's savings measured about 71 percent:

$$\text{Savings score} = \frac{14-4}{14} \times 100 = 71\%$$

Perceptual Memory (Reproduction)

In one additional method of measuring retention, called *perceptual memory* or *reproduction,* the subject is asked to recreate the stimulus as it was originally sensed. Because such a measure often requires artistic or musical skills, and because these talents often vary considerably from one person to another, this type of measure is not used frequently; it is too difficult to determine whether or not the response given is a function of retention or talent.

EXAMPLE 4. Suppose several subjects are shown the stimulus in Fig. 13-1a and told to study it for 10 seconds. If the stimulus is removed and the subjects are told to sketch what they saw, they might come up with drawings like those in Fig. 13-1b and c. The experimenter in this case would have at least two major problems. First, it would be difficult to determine how close to the original a sketch would have to be in order to be considered a successful reproduction; in other words, (c) is closer to the original (a) than (b) is, but is it "correct"? Second, should "incorrect" answers be considered as evidence of a lack of retention or as a lack of sketching skill?

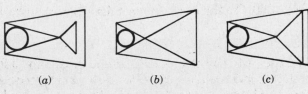

(a)   (b)   (c)

Fig. 13-1

Accuracy of Measurement

The measures of retention given above may produce varying results. For example, recognition measures should always produce some indication of retention simply because of chance correct responses (Example 5), while savings-score measures may produce a negative score (Example 6).

EXAMPLE 5. Suppose students are taking a 50-question (100 point) multiple-choice exam, a type of recognition test. Each question is accompanied by four choices, and guessing is not penalized. If Angela knows the answers to 42 of the questions, she is assured of a score of 84. Of the remaining eight questions, she is likely to get two correct, since the odds of guessing correctly are one in four. Thus her total retention score may well be 88 in spite of the fact that she knew only 84 percent of the answers.

EXAMPLE 6. Suppose that the original learning of a task requires 40 trials, while relearning takes 50 trials. The relearning measure of retention, or savings score, would come out as a negative percentage:

$$\frac{40 - 50}{40} \times 100 = \frac{-10}{40} \times 100 = -25\%$$

This result is difficult to grasp: How should we understand a negative savings score—is it an indication that the original learning inhibited relearning? That is, can the learning of some task actually impede later performance of the same task? It is more likely that some interfering learning takes place between the time of original learning and the relearning test. (This problem is discussed in the next chapter, under the heading "Retroactive Inhibition.")

Measurement of retention is thus influenced by whatever concept of memory is used by the investigator. It is very possible there may be many characteristics of retention not being measured or even recognized as potentially measurable. As a result, caution should be exercised when interpreting any single measure of retention.

13.3 SINGLE-PROCESS THEORIES OF MEMORY

A single-process theory of memory proposes that all retention can be explained according to one set of principles. The two most widely accepted single-process theories of memory are association theory and trace theory.

Association Theory

The association theory of memory proposes that repeated S-R connections form the basis for memory. The greater the number of repetitions of an S-R event, the stronger the association. Memory is thus viewed as habit.

Trace Theory

Trace theory proposes that all memory results from some residual engram, or trace, left in the nervous system as a result of experience. (See Chapter 20 on the physiology of the nervous system.) Many trace theorists believe that the trace is an actual physiological change. And in all trace theories, each new experience interacts with previous traces to either solidify or modify them.

Debate regarding the acceptability of these two positions has generated considerable research. Changes in memory theory are discussed in this chapter. The association-insight dispute that developed is presented in Chapter 19.

13.4 DUAL-PROCESS THEORIES OF MEMORY

The most common distinction used in dual process theories is between *short-term memory (STM)* and *long-term memory (LTM)*. In general, STM is thought to be relatively transitory in nature, lasting for perhaps 30 to 60 seconds, and to have a limited capacity. LTM usually is thought of as relatively permanent, with an indefinite length and unlimited capacity. In addition, it is usually proposed that LTM may have greater depth of memory processing when compared to that of STM.

EXAMPLE 7. A classic example of the distinction between STM and LTM is made when recalling telephone numbers. Frequently used numbers are "permanently" stored and may be recalled for many years. Even after a certain number is no longer in service, a person may respond by saying, "Certainly I remember—first we had Parkside 7072, then Circle 0443, then that was changed to TF9-0443, and finally it became 839-0443 when the telephone company stopped using letters." Such a response may span 30 years of telephone numbers, but when the same person is asked to repeat the number of the television repair shop he called only one hour before, he is likely to say, "I don't have any idea." The repair shop's number was held in STM long enough to be used, but never processed into LTM.

Another dual-process proposal distinguishes between *primary memory* (essentially STM) and *secondary memory* (LTM). While the particular terminology may not provide any additional understanding of memory, an accompanying proposition, suggesting that a memory event might be held simultaneously in both primary and secondary memory, is important. In effect, this implies that STM and LTM are not necessarily separate processes, but rather, may overlap.

Yet another dual-process position distinguishes *semantic memory* from *episodic memory*. Semantic memory is abstract and associative; language is required to encode the material to be stored and later retrieved. Episodic memory is the nonassociative and sequential storage of particular occurrences as they happen—perhaps involving visual imagery or other sensory information.

Physiological Suspicions of Dual Process

Most of the early dual-process theories of memory arose within physiological psychology but definitive chemical or physical evidence has yet to be obtained. The first basic proposal was that STM was a trace held impermanently in a reverberating neural circuit, while LTM involved a permanent physiological change. Changes in the synapses of the central nervous system or modification of molecules of ribonucleic acid (RNA) are possible explanations of the LTM changes.

Clinical Evidence of Dual Process

Studies of amnesia have provided clinical evidence supporting a dual-process interpretation of memory. Accidents or brain surgery, for example, may produce conditions where the client is unable to remember recent events (STM), but has no difficulty recalling events from some time ago (LTM).

Experimental Evidence for Dual Process

As might be expected, the bulk of evidence for dual-process theories of memory has come from experimental research. Some of the most important studies are presented here.

One frequently used STM verbal learning task is called the Peterson (or Brown-Peterson) procedure, after the investigators who developed it. A three-part item (or triad) such as the series X-Q-T, is presented briefly, and the subject spells out the response. Then the subject is asked to perform some "filler" task during the retention interval before being asked to spell out the three-part item again. Retention intervals typically range from 0 to 30 seconds. Frequently it is found that retention drops from nearly 100 percent with a 0-second interval to less than 20 percent correct when the interval is 15 seconds or more. The conclusion is that if rehearsal of the three-part response is prevented (by the "filler" task), the STM is lost very quickly.

A second verbal learning task that has provided support for the STM-LTM distinction is that of free recall of serially presented items. (See Chapter 6 for a discussion of this task.) When a 30-second delay is introduced before recall, retention of the last items in the list (the recency effect) is very poor, unlike the results obtained with immediate free recall. It is proposed that the 30-second delay is sufficient for loss of these items from STM.

Many more studies supporting the STM-LTM differentiation are discussed below.

STM Processes

Attempts to test the STM-LTM distinction have included studies trying to delineate STM processes. The results of one such study are presented in Fig. 13-2.

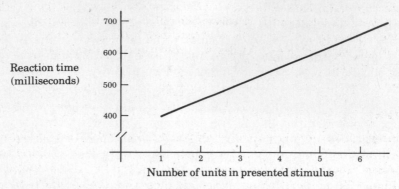

Fig. 13-2

The independent variable in this experiment was the complexity of the stimulus—ranging from the most complex (a stimulus consisting of six items) to the least (a stimulus consisting of only one item). In each trial, brief presentations of these stimuli were made to subjects and then removed. Shortly afterwards, the subjects were presented with a "target unit" and asked to answer simply yes or no to the question, "Was this target unit part of the stimulus just presented?" Not surprisingly, the more complex the stimuli became, the longer it took for the subjects to answer the question. This suggested to the experimenter that in searching out stimuli in STM, subjects scan items successively (one by one) rather than simultaneously (in a "parallel" fashion). Incidentally, such a conclusion lends weight to the idea that the memory processes involved in STM are qualitatively distinct from those involved in LTM, thus lending support to a dual-process theory of memory.

LTM Processes

Comparable studies have been conducted to try to determine the search properties involved in retrieving material from LTM. Evidence indicates that LTM may be organized in a hierarchy, and that responses from LTM may have to be processed according to that hierarchy.

EXAMPLE 8. The order in which questions are presented can be manipulated to demonstrate the influence of the LTM hierarchies. If the subject is asked to name a large city that starts with D and that has a professional basketball team, the reaction time may be slower than if the order is reversed. Giving the concept of professional basketball first narrows the area of LTM that the subject must search, since the set of all professional basketball cities is much smaller than the set of all cities with names that begin with D.

Coding Process

Dual-process theories are given further support by evidence that demonstrates the existence of different coding processes for STM and LTM. Simply stated, *coding* is the way in which traces are put into memory. The many different types of coding processes identified include various types of *sensory coding* (often associated with STM) or *semantic coding,* based upon the meaning of a word and often thought to be an important factor in LTM.

EXAMPLE 9. The man who could not recall the telephone number of the television repair shop (Example 7) had stored the number in STM. Nonetheless, he had to remember the number for a certain length of time—for however long it took him to turn away from the phone book and toward the phone and to complete the dialing. For this type of short-term storage, acoustic coding—for example, the man repeating the number under his breath until he completed the task—was sufficient. This type of acoustic coding would not be enough to place the trace in LTM, however, and obviously the man did not spend 30 years repeatedly murmuring his own various telephone numbers.

Level of Arousal

Level of arousal appears to affect the ability to encode information. In general, higher arousal yields better coding and later retention.

EXAMPLE 10. Research dating back to the work of Ebbinghaus has shown that there are better times of the day for acquisition of certain kinds of skills. Humans generally perform verbal or mathematical tasks best in the late morning, but apparently perform motor-skills tasks best in the late afternoon. School schedules are often arranged to take advantage of this knowledge, with academic classes scheduled for morning and athletic practice for the late afternoon.

Memory Attributes

One way to interpret memory is as a collection of *attributes,* which are the significant aspects of events that are encoded and later provide the means for retrieving and differentiating memories. Attributes have been classified as independent and dependent, i.e., those characteristics that are general and evaluated for many different events and those that are specific to the event.

EXAMPLE 11. Recollection of a particular party can involve both independent and dependent attributes. The memory may include the time of year (June), the place (along the Rhine River), and the reason (a birthday). These would probably be classified as independent attributes. However, the memory might also include attributes such as the sun's reflection off the water (a visual code) or the sound of the barges on the river (an acoustic code) that were dependent upon the particular event.

Retrieval Cues

An aspect of memory that has received extensive consideration is that of *retrieval cues,* which are those stimuli used to provoke the response from memory. A number of psychologists consider selection of retrieval cues to be the most significant part of memory. They believe that the same event may possibly be encoded in memory according to differing *retrieval tags* (labels) and that these will differ in accessibility or ease of recollection depending upon whether or not the cues used correspond with the tags.

EXAMPLE 12. The misinterpretation of a cue may elicit a totally inappropriate memory. Consider the case of a usually well-behaved child who is being especially bothersome at a difficult moment. Her father, trying to fix a lamp, says, "Wait in the corner for the present." What is your interpretation of that phrase? The child may misinterpret the word "present" and go off to the corner to await the arrival of a gift. The child interprets the ambiguous phrase as a memory cue for something she desires very much, and she is shortly disappointed.

Tip-of-the-Tongue (TOT) Phenomenon

Sometimes the retrieval of information from LTM involves several approximations of the correct response before it is finally hit upon. This type of responding is called the *tip-of-the-tongue (TOT) phenomenon.* The subject feels ready to give the correct response, but is able to produce only approximations of it—perhaps responses with a similar sound, a similar meaning, or some other similar attribute. Often, "sticking with it" eventually leads to the production of the correct response. The tip-of-the-tongue phenomenon illustrates the importance of retrieval cues (in this case self-generated), and lends support to the idea of memory as a collection of attributes.

EXAMPLE 13. People who play "trivia" games sometimes show tip-of-the-tongue responding: If the player is asked to name Clark Kent's girlfriend, the response may be something like, "Lois Page—no, that was a girl I dated in college . . . Della Street—oops, that's Perry Mason . . . How about Lois Street? . . . Just a minute, not Street, but Lane—Lois Lane!" Notice the number of attributes that show up in the response sequence, including the correct first name, the appropriate number of syllables, and the street-lane similarity. This is typical of tip-of-the-tongue responding.

13.5 THREE-PROCESS THEORIES OF MEMORY

One major distinction and several minor modifications distinguish three-process theories of memory from the dual-process proposals already presented. *Three-process theories of memory* introduce an initial, extremely short phase within the memory process called *sensory storage* (or *sensory memory*) that precedes *short-term storage* and/or *long-term storage*.

Sensory Storage

Three-process interpretations of memory begin with *sensory storage,* a very limited memory held in the sensory receptors or sensory nervous system. The trace held in sensory storage must be processed rapidly into either short-term storage or long-term storage, or it will be irretrievably lost.

EXAMPLE 14. Sensory storage is readily demonstrated when one recalls Independence Day celebrations. After dark, when one of the children lights a sparkler and then runs with it through the yard, the image is not of a point of light (or spray of lights), but rather of a "streak" of light extending for some distance. The very brief retention of this image represents sensory storage.

Short-Term Storage

Comparable to STM of dual-process theory, short-term storage is thought to last for a brief period of time, have a limited capacity, and require active treatment of the materials being held if they are not to be lost. The limited capacity of the short-term storage has been called the *rehearsal buffer.* It is presumed that rehearsal is necessary for maintenance or additional processing of the trace. Furthermore, loading the rehearsal buffer usually results in the loss of some material.

Long-Term Storage

Long-term storage is comparable to LTM of the dual-process theory. It is thought to have unlimited capacity and may hold traces for indefinite periods of time. Perhaps the most important characteristic of long-term storage is how the traces are encoded. The more stable and resistant to interference the coding processes are, the more likely the memory will be retained.

Figure 13-3 presents a simplified diagram of a three-process theory of memory. It should be noted that responses can be generated out of either short-term or long-term storage, that those two storage processes can interact, and that outside influences may modify activity within any one or all of the three processes.

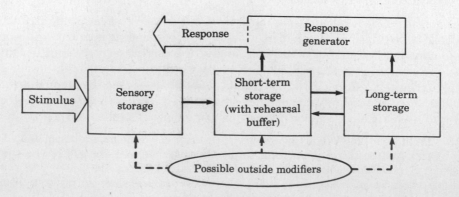

Fig. 13-3

13.6 ALTERNATIVE EXPLANATIONS OF MEMORY

Theories such as those presented above have generated some controversy.   There are continuing debates as to which theory is most acceptable, and while each has its advantages (such as the economy of explanation in single-process theories or the generation of research from three-process explanations), no one theory has gained preeminence.

Some memory theories cannot be categorized in any one of the ways described so far in this chapter.   Proponents of these theories claim that a totally different frame of reference is necessary for explaining memory.   Perhaps the most widely known of these theories has been called the *levels-of-processing* approach, which emphasizes coding, rather than some sort of storage or memory mechanism, as the most important process.   Durability of memory results from the depth of processing accomplished by a limited capacity central processor.   While such a theory does present an alternative to the storage theories presented above, it has been criticized as being unproductive in terms of generating research and unable to account for data generated in other theoretical frameworks.   These controversies are likely to continue for some time while additional studies are conducted.

Solved Problems

13.1   Describe how all three stages of learning—acquisition, storage, and retrieval—play a role in memory processes.

Acquisition refers to experiencing something and, as a result, developing some sort of trace of that event.   "Holding" that trace describes the process of storage.   When some stimulus provokes an output, or response, based on that trace, retrieval is said to have taken place.   Responses generated in the retrieval stage serve as evidence that memory exists—that is, that acquisition and storage occurred previously.   (While the main focus in memory research is on storage and retrieval, acquisition is studied as well—for example, when various acquisition procedures are tested in order to determine which results in the most complete or accurate memory.)

13.2   Explain what is meant by saying that evidence indicates a lack of accuracy and accessibility of information in human memory.

Research has shown that the three processes of acquisition, storage, and retrieval do not necessarily produce either accurate or accessible memories.   Inaccuracy may result from faulty acquisition, modification of the trace during storage, or inappropriate retrieval.   Lack of accessibility appears to be mostly a retrieval phenomenon.   Information may be stored but not easily recovered from memory.   (Possible explanations for why this happens are presented later.   However, to test this point, the reader need only try to recall something once memorized in school—perhaps a poem or the names of the capitals of all 50 states.   The information may once have been stored and it may be retrievable but not be readily accessible at this time.)

13.3   The retention measure of recall is mentioned in Problem 13.2.   Why is the measure of recall thought to represent acquisition, storage, and retrieval, while recognition measures supposedly involve only the first two mechanisms, but not retrieval?

Recall measures involve the presentation of some minimal retrieval cue, in response to which the subject provides all the additional information.   This means that following acquisition and subsequent storage of the material, the subject must perform some sort of retrieval process in order to give evidence of retention.

Recognition measures do not require a search or retrieval process for evidence of retention to be present.   The correct answer is given to the subject, who merely needs to identify a correspondence between the item and some trace held in storage.   Retrieval does not seem to be involved.

13.4   Why are recognition measures sometimes called judgment measures?

As pointed out in the solution to Problem 13.3, because the correct answer is present, recognition measures seemingly do not require retrieval, but rather identification of the correspondence of a presented item to some item in storage.   However, recognition measures often involve simultaneous presentation of both correct items and distractors.   The subject must compare each presented item with the stored material and judge whether one, some, or all of the potential answers correspond to information within storage.

13.5   Why is the retention measure of relearning called an indirect measure, while recall and recognition are considered direct measures?

Relearning does not involve asking a "What do you know?" or "What do you recognize?" question, but instead makes a comparison between the time or trials involved in original learning and the time or trials for relearning.   As such, no measure is made of *what* was retained, only an estimate of *how much* was retained (often called the amount of savings).   Both recall and recognition measures attempt to identify both how much *and* what was retained, and thus are considered direct measures of retention.

13.6   Eloise has developed the reputation of being a "quick study," especially helpful when summer stock shows are being presented in rapid-fire order.   One of the directors has said, "Why, she must remember 90 percent of her part from one year to the next.   If it takes her three weeks to learn that part originally, she can get it in three *days* the next summer."   Assuming the director's second statement is correct, how accurate is the first statement?

The answer to this problem can be determined by computing the savings score.   Accepting the idea that Eloise studies her part every day of the week during the original learning period, and therefore converting three weeks to 21 days, the retention indicated is equal to approximately 86 percent.

$$\text{Savings} = \frac{21 - 3}{21} \times 100 = 85.7\%$$

It appears that the director's first statement is reasonably close to the percentage of Eloise's retention from one year to the next.

13.7   Many psychologists regard attempts to measure perceptual memory as foolish or fruitless.   Why?

Measurement of perceptual memory is often accomplished by reproduction, meaning the subject is asked to reproduce the visual or auditory stimuli that have been stored.   A major problem with such measurement is the question of talent—some subjects simply have better artistic or musical skills than others and may create "better" answers on that basis rather than because their retention of the material is better than that of the other subjects.

13.8   The reader is asked to answer the next two questions honestly: (1) Do you have a pet name for a loved one?   (2) If you were asked to give the name of that loved one, would you reveal the pet name or would you report the more conventional name?   Now explain why these two questions are examples of a major problem that could arise in any recall measure of memory.

The two questions asked in this problem raise important issues that must be faced by any investigator in a study of learning.   First, the investigator must realize that a subject, for whatever reason, may not report all the responses he or she has to a particular situation.   For example, when asked to report all her associations to the word "husband," a woman may report her husband's surname (Keith) but not his pet name (Panda).   Secondly, the experimenter may not even be aware of the variety of associations a subject may have to a particular stimulus, and in designing an experiment may neglect to provide stimuli that will elicit the full variety of associations. It may not even occur to the experimenter mentioned above, for example, that husbands and wives often have pet names for one another. Consequently, any conclusions about what a person does or does not have stored in memory must be regarded very cautiously, pending other findings in which the subject has additional opportunities to retrieve material from storage.

13.9 Trace and association theories of memory are both alike and different. Cite the major similarities and differences between these two approaches.

The major similarity between trace and association theories of memory is that both are single-process (one-process) theories. This means that supporters of either theory believe that all memory events are acquired, stored, and retrieved in accordance with a single set of principles.

The major differences between the two theories are as follows: in association theories memory is viewed as developing from the repetition of S-R events, with associations eventually taking the role of habits. Trace theories propose that some change in the nervous system occurs with the development of memory. These traces may become relatively stable, compact, or regular if the conditions allow.

13.10 Driving in a strange city, Stephen stops at a filling station to get directions to a friend's house. That evening at dinner, the friend asks Stephen how he came into town and how he found the house. Stephen replies that he stopped to ask directions, but cannot remember now what streets he took to get to the friend's house. What possible explanation is there for Stephen's loss of retention?

There are many possible solutions to this problem, but the most likely one is that Stephen held the information in short-term memory (STM) only until it had been used, but never processed it into long-term memory (LTM).

13.11 Distinguish between STM and LTM. How do these concepts compare to primary memory and secondary memory?

The major distinctions between STM and LTM involve comparisons of the duration and stability of the memory, the amount of information that can be held in the memory, and the depth of processing that can occur. In general, STM has a much shorter duration—in many cases, less that 30 seconds—and is thought to be less stable that LTM. Evidence indicates, on the other hand, that LTM may last indefinitely and show extreme stability. STM is thought to be a limited-capacity memory (immediate-memory span judged to be 7 ± 2 chunks of information), while LTM appears to have un-limited capacity. Finally, processing of memory seems to occur in greater depth for LTM when compared to STM.

The terms STM and LTM correspond respectively to primary memory and secondary memory. The introduction of the latter pair of terms was important to the psychology of learning because it pointed out that a particular event may be represented in both primary memory and secondary memory simultaneously. This means the two systems are not considered to be mutually exclusive.

13.12 Explain the Peterson procedure. Sketch a graph of the typical results obtained when using this procedure.

The so-called Peterson procedure (also sometimes called the Brown-Peterson procedure) involves presentation of a three-part response item or triad (such as the letters X-F-M) followed by a 3- to 18-second retention interval filled with a counting task (for example, counting backwards by 3s from 406). This is followed immediately by a test for retention of the triad. Typical results obtained in such a study are shown in Fig. 13-4.

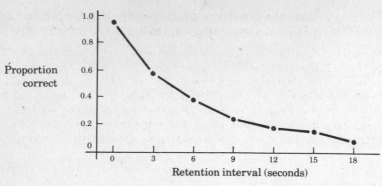

Fig. 13-4

13.13 Why do studies like the one described in Problem 13.12 generate interest in STM as a process separate from LTM?

   The implication of the results shown in Fig. 13-4 is that there could be some transient memory that lasts for a very short period of time but that dissipates almost completely in less than 20 seconds if rehearsal is not allowed.   This may be seen as evidence for STM as distinct from the much longer-lasting LTM events studied previously.

13.14 Describe the physiological proposal that corresponds to the STM-LTM distinction.

   Basically, the proposal is that physiological processes would be of two types.   The first includes short-term reverberating circuits within the nervous system that either receive additional processing or are irretrievably lost (STM).   The second involves permanent modification of the nervous system, perhaps in the form of changes at the synapses that create enduring physiological traces (or engrams) of the memory (LTM).   (Although considerable research has been conducted attempting to support such proposals, there is no unqualified evidence for them.)

13.15 One implication of a proposal such as that presented in Problem 13.14 is that repetition of an event might be more likely than a single presentation to generate the permanent modification of the nervous system.   Studies attempted to investigate this and obtained results like those shown in Fig. 13-5.   The group whose responses are represented by the solid line was presented with identical tasks on every third trial; all other trials for this group were different.   The control group, whose responses are represented by the dashed line, was presented with a new and different task on each trial.

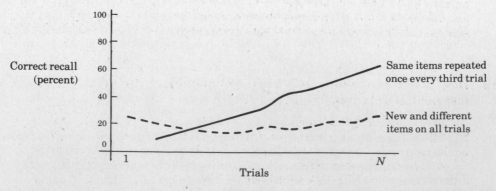

Fig. 13-5

Why do such results seem to support the physiological theory proposed above? How might the concept of learning to learn at least partially negate this support?

One must assume that the learning in each task creates a physiological trace. If the trace fades prior to the next presentation of the same task, the expected recall should be the same as that for nonrepeated tasks. However, such results are not obtained, indicating possible support for some sort of synaptic changes. The more frequently the task is repeated, the better the performance.

The concept of learning to learn complicates the explanation, however, because it is possible (and indeed has been demonstrated in other research studies) that repeated trials may produce a non-specific transfer effect that will lead to better acquisition of later-presented tasks (see Chapter 12).

13.16 The serial-position curve for immediate free recall is presented again in Fig. 13-6. (See Chapter 6 for a discussion of free recall.) Also, in the figure is a serial-position curve for a 30-second delayed free recall. How does the dual-process concept of memory appear to be supported by the differences between the two curves?

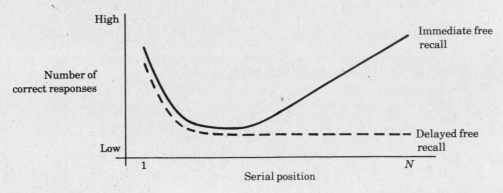

Fig. 13-6

The interpretation supporting a dual-process theory of memory suggests that the last items presented (position N and those just preceding) are held very briefly in a short-term storage and "reported out" almost immediately. This *recency effect* is thought to represent STM. When a 30-second delay is introduced, the recency effect disappears. The interpretation of this is that the STM is unprocessed and therefore lost.

13.17 How have reaction-time data been used to indicate that recall from STM involves successive scanning rather that simultaneous scanning?

Essentially, the solution to this problem is to state that the research using reaction time as the measure of response indicates that as the number of items held in a particular STM is increased (for example, from 1 to 7), the reaction time preceding correct responding increases. If the subject were using simultaneous scanning of the items, such a progressive increase would not be found.

13.18 How have reaction-time data been used to indicate that recall from LTM may involve hierarchical processing?

Studies investigating reaction time for correct responding to sets of stimuli show that if the stimuli are presented in a hierarchical manner, the reaction time will be shorter than if the order is not hierarchical. This means, for example, that a presentation like "It's a vegetable; it begins with C" will produce a correct response more quickly than the reverse order (C, vegetable). While the differences are less than 1/10 second, the evidence points to a conclusion that LTM is searched in a hierarchical fashion to produce the correct response.

13.19   Showing slides to her classmates, Julia makes a remark about one that pictures a dessert called Black Forest cake: "That was really good.   You can see how beautiful it looked, but I can remember how great it tasted, and how it smelled, and even what the sounds were like at the restaurant that day!"   What do Julia's comments illustrate about memory?

An important consideration of memory is that there may be several different ways of coding the responses acquired.   In this case, Julia has indicated memory codes based on several different sensory processes.

13.20   How does semantic coding differ from the sensory memory codes described in Problem 13.19?

Semantic coding is dependent not on the sensory properties of the stimuli but on the meaning represented by the code.   It is possible that there may be many interactions among different memory codes.   For example, the words "Black Forest cake" or the German equivalent "Schwarzwalder-kuche" may elicit very different memory codes, depending on a person's familiarity with the two languages and the actual dessert.

13.21   What has research indicated about the effect of arousal upon strength of encoding?

Like many other performance characteristics, strength of encoding seems to be a function of arousal, with better memory codes developing when the levels of arousal are higher, and little or no memory developing under very low arousal conditions.   (It should be noted that research on "learning while asleep" indicates that such a procedure is fruitless.   Equipment that allegedly teaches you while you sleep is a waste of both time and money.)

13.22   If the subject seems more likely to confuse the words "four" and "floor" during a retention task rather than the words "opal" and "ruby," which memory process is more likely to be operating?

The confusion appears to result from similarity in acoustic (auditory) coding rather than semantic coding.   Many researchers have proposed that acoustic coding is primarily an STM phenomenon, while semantic coding is primarily an LTM event.   Therefore, this subject's difficulties would apparently be occurring in STM.

13.23   Studies like those described in the preceding problems might give support to a definition of memory as a collection of attributes.   What does this mean?   What are some examples of attributes?

Attributes are the prominent characteristics of stimulus events that are judged to be important in coding processes.   The accumulation of attributes differentiates one memory from another and serves as the basis for memory retrieval.

Attributes can be grouped broadly into two categories: those independent of the nature of the stimulus event—such as time, space, and the mode or frequency of the event—and those dependent upon the nature of the event—such as visual, acoustic, or semantic properties.

13.24   Suppose the subject asked to recall the name of Mad Ludwig's hunting lodge in Bavaria responds by saying, "Oh, that was Lindell . . . no, wait, that's not it . . . it was Lindelhaupt . . . no, Linderhaupt . . . almost, let me see . . . oh . . . Linderhof!"   What phenomenon is illustrated by such a sequence?   How does this appear to support an explanation of memory as a set of attributes?

The responses illustrate what has been called the tip-of-the-tongue phenomenon.   Subjects often respond with partially correct answers that approximate, according to first one attribute and then another, the final correct response.   In this case, the series reveals recognition of the first letter and first correct syllable, then a need for an additional syllable to reach the correct length, and finally correction of the later syllables to produce a totally correct response. Such a sequence seems to support the concept of memory as attributes in that the final response appears to result from an add-on of characteristics.

13.25 If the subject in Problem 13.24 had been asked to name the King's hunting lodge in Germany, the response might have been much poorer. Why?

A seemingly important aspect of memory is the retrieval cue that is given. The question asked here is less specific, and therefore likely to produce more incorrect responses. ("Bavaria" is more specific than "Germany"; "Mad Ludwig" is more specific than "King.") Both the retrieval cues given to the subject and the "retrieval tags" the subject has employed in storage may be crucial in determining how fast the correct response is produced or whether it is produced at all.

13.26 Three-process theory is based on the concept of storage. What are the various storage mechanisms suggested? How do they differ?

Three-process theory proposes sensory storage, short-term-storage, and long-term-storage processes. Short-term and long-term storage are approximately the same as STM and LTM presented in earlier problems. Sensory storage is an extremely short trace held by the sensory receptors or sensory nervous system. It is viewed as a preliminary memory stage, accounting for reception of the signal. If the signal is not processed into short-term or long-term storage, it will be lost.

13.27 In three-process theory, what keeps information from being lost from short-term storage? Under what circumstances will information be lost from the short-term store?

It is proposed that rehearsal keeps information active in short-term storage. Rehearsal regenerates the trace and, in effect, serves as a control process.

There are two major reasons why information may be lost from short-term storage. One is that rehearsal processes are either not initiated or are discontinued. The second is that the short-term store is viewed as a limited-capacity system (sometimes called the rehearsal buffer) and may become full. Then, if additional information is taken into the short-term store, some material already there will be forced out and therefore lost.

13.28 What controls the amount and accessibility of information in long-term storage?

Because it is proposed that long-term storage has virtually unlimited capacity, the amount and accessibility of information are not limited by size of the store nor rehearsal per se. Rather, the ability of the subject to code the information in some highly stable and interference-resistant manner appears to determine the properties of materials housed in the long-term store.

13.29 What kinds of controversy exist regarding the various theories of memory processes?

Essentially, there are two major controversies regarding the theories of memory processes. One is the debate as to which of the various theories should be accepted. For example, a recent presentation pointed out how three-process theory could be readily adapted to, and therefore explained by, a single-process association theory.

The second debate is whether or not *any* of the theories should be accepted. (At least one alternative to all of the preceding theories has been presented, suggesting that memory results from the depth of analysis occurring in a limited-capacity central processor.) To date, research has resolved neither of these debates.

Key Terms

Acquisition. The phase of learning during which information is attained and a response becomes part of the behavioral repertoire.

Coding. In verbal learning, a general term referring to active techniques used to modify materials into more easily acquired chunks of information.

Free recall. A measure of retention in which the subject may recall in any order desired.

Long-term memory (LTM). Retention of some response for more than 30 seconds; materials from sensory or short-term storage are processed into this type of memory.

Memory. The storage and later retrieval of a response that was previously acquired.

Perceptual memory. A measure of retention in which the subject is asked to recreate the stimuli as they were sensed originally.

Peterson procedure. Presentation of a three-part response item (or triad) followed by some short-term filler task, then a signal requesting recall of the response.

Primary memory. Another name for short-term memory.

Recall. A measure of retention in which a subject is given only a minimal cue and must produce the requested materials.

Recognition. A measure of retention in which the correct answer is presented along with others to the subject; the subject must select the correct answer from among several alternatives.

Rehearsal. Repetitive drill of some acquired item.

Rehearsal buffer. A term describing the limited capacity of short-term memory and implying the need for processing to maintain the storage.

Relearning. A measure of retention in which the time or trials necessary for the second learning of a task are compared to the time or trials necessary for original learning.

Reproduction. The subject's recreation of a stimulus in a perceptual-memory task.

Retrieval. In learning, the phase during which information is produced as a response from storage.

Retrieval cues. Stimuli used to provoke a response from memory; may correspond to the various retrieval tags (labels) according to which memories are encoded.

Reverberating circuit. The proposed neural pathway in the cortex that carries a repeating signal.

Savings score. A percentage that indicates the difference between time or trials necessary for relearning a task as opposed to the time or trials necessary for original learning.

Secondary memory. Another name for long-term memory.

Semantic coding. Coding based upon the meaning of a word.

Sensory storage. The very brief retention of a signal in its unprocessed sensory form.

Serial recall. A measure of retention in which the subject must recall in a specific order.

Short-term memory (STM). Retention of some response for a 1-to-30-second period; during this period some initial processing may take place.

Storage. In learning, the phase during which information is retained.

Tip-of-the-tongue (TOT) phenomenon. The situation in which retrieval (usually verbal) from long-term memory seems almost possible, but cannot quite be accomplished; approximations of the correct response are often given.

Chapter 14

Forgetting

As with many other very important concepts in the psychology of learning, *forgetting,* defined as a loss of retention, cannot be measured directly. Measurement of forgetting is made by determining the difference between maximum possible retention and actually observed retention. It is assumed that what was not retained was forgotten.

When data are presented to show this loss of retention, they frequently form what has been called the curve of forgetting (See Fig. 2-1). This curve represents a general finding about forgetting: As the time since the completion of learning a task increases, performance of that task will decrease. Refinements of and exception to this general principle will be discussed later in this chapter.

14.1 FORGETTING RELATED TO MEMORY PROCESSES

In Chapter 13 memory was analyzed in terms of acquisition, storage, and retrieval. This section presents these three general learning principles as they relate to forgetting.

Acquisition

There is only one important principle relating acquisition to forgetting: The material cannot be forgotten if it never was acquired. This may occur because of a failure to attend to certain stimuli, a misinterpretation of stimuli, or many other reasons.

EXAMPLE 1. Suppose a college teacher asks one of her students if he remembers the name of the Spanish explorer who sought the Fountain of Youth in Florida. The student might respond by saying, "No, I was raised in Canada, and we never studied Spanish explorers in our history classes. I guess I never learned it." It would not be correct to say this student had forgotten the name of the explorer because something not acquired cannot be said to be forgotten.

Storage

Once a memory has been acquired, it is thought to be held in storage until it is retrieved. If for some reason there is a modification of the stored memory or if it disappears altogether, forgetting is attributed to *storage failure.*

Retrieval

Attempts to use stored memories may not always prove successful. In such cases, forgetting is attributed to *retrieval failure.* The various explanations of retrieval failure include the presentation of inappropriate retrieval cues and interference from some other, competing memory.

EXAMPLE 2. A small child may show retrieval failure when asked to name his father's sisters and brothers. The *retrieval tag* the child uses for these people is "aunts and uncles." The retrieval cue presented does not prompt the appropriate responses, thus creating the appearance of forgetting.

Two additional points need to be made: First, inappropriate retrieval cues and interference are only two of several proposed explanations for both storage failure and retrieval failure. Second, some psychologists believe that all instances of forgetting should be attributed to both storage failure *and* retrieval failure.

Change in Context

If the general physical setting in which retrieval is attempted is very different from the setting in which retention first took place, a subject may give evidence of forgetting. Even though storage has been accomplished and the appropriate retrieval cue is presented, the change in the context—or general stimulus conditions—may be enough to prevent retrieval. If this is the case, the subject is demonstrating *state-dependent learning*.

14.2 BASIC THEORIES OF FORGETTING

Several interpretations of forgetting have been proposed. This section presents the basic theories of forgetting; more detailed treatments of each theory are presented later in this chapter.

Decay Theory

A very early explanation of forgetting, called the *decay theory*, proposed that acquired traces deteriorated solely because some period of time had elapsed since acquisition took place. Forgetting was simply attributed to the passage of time. The other theories presented in this section are, in a way, reactions to the inadequacies of decay theory. (There were too many results that could not be adequately accounted for by decay theory, and other theories were created in attempts to overcome these inadequacies.)

Trace-Change Theory

Arising from the work of gestalt psychologists, *trace-change theory* emphasized perceptual principles thought to result from physiological processes. Summarized as *laws of good organization*, the principles cited most often were *closure*, the tendency to close an open figure, *symmetry*, the tendency to create balance for a figure, and *good figure*, the tendency to establish a more perfect figure. These perceptual tendencies were believed to be built-in physiological functions, and later retention could be expected to reflect the operation of one or more of these effects.

EXAMPLE 3. The gestaltists proposed that subjects who viewed a stimulus such as the one shown in Fig. 14-1 would tend to recall it later as a rectangle, thus reflecting the effect of closure.

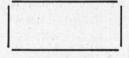

Fig. 14-1

Evidence supporting trace-change in retention has been mixed. One contrasting position has been that *consolidation* of the trace rather than trace-change takes place. Consolidation means that a trace becomes less "fragile"or susceptible to disturbances or interruptions that would normally produce forgetting. Consolidation can be enhanced or made more likely by encoding the appropriate retrieval tags, arranging acquisition trials in some special way, or allowing rehearsal of the learned materials.

Motivated Forgetting: Repression

The concept of *repression,* or *motivated forgetting,* was developed by Sigmund Freud as part of his psychoanalytic theory. The forgetting of especially anxiety-provoking memories was seen as a defense of the ego and a way to reduce conscious stress. Freud believed that repressed memories could continue to create unconscious motives that might influence behavior, however.

Retrieval-Failure Theory

Retrieval-failure theory emphasizes the inability of the subject to get a memory from storage. This is often attributed to the presence of inappropriate or conflicting retrieval cues. Such a situation is thought to make the memories temporarily inaccessible rather than permanently lost.

One special case of retrieval failure, called *switching,* occurs when some of the multiple stimuli associated with one learned response are presented along with some of the multiple stimuli associated with another learned response.

EXAMPLE 4. Suppose a dog has been trained to make a withdrawal response to the presence of a light in sessions conducted by experimenter A in the morning. The same light is used in afternoon sessions by experimenter B to train a salivation response. With repeated practice, the dog acquires both responses. But if A appears in the afternoon or B in the morning, it is likely the dog will try to perform *both* responses. The switching of some of the external contextual stimuli creates retrieval confusion.

Interference Theory

The basis of *interference theory* is the belief that learning one group of materials may inhibit the retrieval of some other learned materials. Interference theory really consists of two sub-theories, usually referred to as *retroactive inhibition* or interference *(RI),* and *proactive inhibition* or interference *(PI).*

Retroactive inhibition (RI). The assumption of RI is that something learned later may interfere with the retention of something learned before. The experimental design used to test RI is as follows:

Group	Step one	Step two	Retention interval	Step three
Experimental	Learn A	Learn B		Test retention of A
Control	Learn A	Put in time		Test retention of A

EXAMPLE 5. If relearning is used as the measure of retention when investigating RI, it is possible that the savings score may have a negative value. For example, in step one, learning a serial list of nonsense syllables might take 15 trials. After the intermediate (step two) learning of some other, interfering list of nonsense syllables, reacquisition of the original list might take 20 trials. In such a case, the savings score would be approximately −33 percent.

$$\text{Savings score} = \frac{15 - 20}{15} = -33\%$$

Proactive inhibition (PI). The assumption of PI is that something learned before may interfere with the retention of something learned later. The experimental design used to test PI is as follows:

Group	Step one	Step two	Retention interval	Step three
Experimental	Learn A	Learn B		Test retention of B
Control	Put in time	Learn B		Test retention of B

EXAMPLE 6. Suppose the subjects in an experiment are told to memorize a list of nonsense syllables (list A) on the first day of a four-day experiment. On the second day, they are tested for the retention of list A and then told to memorize list B. On the third day they are tested on list B and told to memorize List C. On the fourth day they are tested on list C. Even though the lists of nonsense syllables are of equal length and are designed to be of equal difficulty, the percentage retained (reported correctly) by the subjects will drop off from day to day. That is, the retention of list A (measured on day two) will be higher than that for list B, which in

turn will be higher than that for list C.   Proactive inhibition apparently can have a cumulative effect, making the learning of each subsequent list more and more difficult.   (The rate of decline in retention is not usually steady, however.   The drop-off in correct responding between days one and two is likely to be more than the drop-off between days two and three, and so on.   Eventually, the interference effect of PI can be expected to flatten as it approaches an asymptotic level of incorrect responding.)

Release from proactive inhibition.   Experimenters studying proactive inhibition do not always use responses of low meaningfulness (as was done in Example 6).   One very interesting learning phenomenon, called *release from proactive inhibition,* has been found in experiments where the learned materials consist of word lists rather than lists of nonsense syllables.   Such experiments, which make use of the Peterson procedure (see Section 13.4), show that the interference caused by proactive inhibition in part depends on the similarity of the learned lists.

EXAMPLE 7.   A "release from PI" experiment might consist of five trials.   In trial one, the subjects have two seconds to look at a list of three words flashed on a screen.   The three words are in the same semantic category—perhaps the color names "orange," "blue," and "pink." As soon as this list disappears, the subjects are kept busy with a "filler" task (such as counting backwards), which prevents them from rehearsing the list of colors.   Then, at the end of a set interval, the filler task is terminated and the subjects are tested for retention of the list.   The second trial then begins, with a new list of words in the same category—perhaps "red," "yellow," and "violet"—followed by another filler task and another test of retention.   Trials three and four would be run in the same manner, and the experimenters would most likely observe the results of PI: Retention of the list in trial one will be quite high; for trial two retention will drop off considerably; and trials three and four will show further reductions in retention (See Fig. 14-2).   The "release" from PI could then be shown in trial five if the semantic category of the list to be memorized is changed.   For example, half the subjects in trial five could be presented with "duck," "cow," and "horse" while the other half (acting as a control group) are presented with "green," "purple," and "grey."   The group presented with the animal list will show a much higher retention rate in trial five than the group that continues to memorize a color list.   (It is interesting to note that subjects are often unaware of the change in semantic category that results in increased retention; they are not conscious of the change from one type of list to another.)

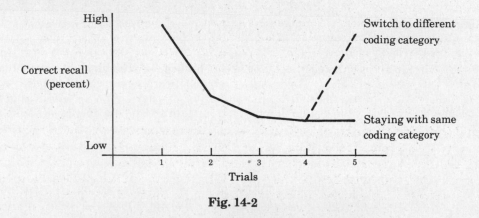

Fig. 14-2

14.3   EXPLANATIONS OF INTERFERENCE

Attempts to explain how interference leads to forgetting have fallen into two general categories, an independence hypothesis of interference and a two-factor (or unlearning) theory.

The Independence Hypothesis

The crucial aspect of the *independence hypothesis* is the concept of *response competition,* in which a stimulus elicits more than one response, and these responses compete with each other for predominance.   The independence hypothesis does *not* predict that learning new materials will influence the strength (memory) of some previous learning (thus the label independence).   Interference is attributed solely to response competition.

Two-Factor (Unlearning) Theory

Two-factor theory accepts the principle of response competition as one possible contributor to interference, and therefore forgetting, in more than one manner. First, as the amount of practice for new learning increases, there are more opportunities for old responses to be made and not reinforced. These are the conditions for extinction of old learning responses. However, assuming extinction does occur, it can also be predicted that spontaneous recovery of the old responses will occur during the retention interval. Varying the retention interval should affect the results found in a third step, test of retention. Data obtained in several research studies have supported this two-factor interpretation of interference.

The MFR procedure. One research procedure developed to investigate the two-factor position has been called the *modified free recall,* or *MFR,* procedure. Subjects trained with an A-B, A-D paired-associate sequence were then tested for retention by being asked to give the first response that came to mind when the stimulus was presented.

The MMFR procedure. A variation of the MFR procedure has been called the *modified MFR,* or *MMFR,* procedure. In this case, following A-B, A-D training, the subjects are asked to try to recall both of the previously learned responses.

Both the MFR and MMFR procedures have generated results that show a decline in the strength of the B responses as the amount of A-D practice increases; additionally, both procedures show some evidence for spontaneous recovery of B responses. Such results provide support for the two-factor theory, and the MMFR procedure tends to negate the response-competition hypothesis because both responses could be given.

EXAMPLE 8. Suppose a teenage boy who has not seen his uncle for several years goes to visit him for a week. When the uncle greets the boy by saying, "Hi, Buster," the boy blushes and says, "Please, I'm not Buster any more. Call me Bill." This situation represents an extinction trial of the "Buster" response and a practice trial for the "Bill" response. After a week with his nephew, the uncle would most likely make only the "Bill" response. However, if some time passed before they saw each other again, some spontaneous recovery of the "Buster" response could occur; at a subsequent meeting, perhaps a year after the one just described, the uncle might greet his nephew by saying "Hi, Buster" once again.

Response Suppression

Although response-competition and unlearning concepts are the two most widely accepted explanations of interference, at least one other position, called the *response-suppression hypothesis,* has gained some support. This interpretation of interference developed from research using a recognition test of retention following the A-B, A-D sequence. In such studies, the stimulus and both responses are available to the subject, and both can be appropriately paired with the correct stimulus. Apparently, extinction or unlearning of the B responses has not occurred. In an attempt to explain why B responses are not produced in the recall tasks, the concept of response suppression has been put forth. It is proposed that the subject restricts responses to those from the more recent or more appropriate list. This appears to be a case of cognitive choice determining response production.

The Associative-Probability Paradox

In some cases, the same principles may predict both interference and facilitative effects. Such a situation has been named the *associative-probability paradox.* The many associations generated by a highly meaningful item may be expected to interfere with or facilitate learning a new task. The key to explaining which effect is found is called *mediation.* Associates that create mediational chains by linking responses facilitate new learning, while those that do not set the conditions for unlearning.

EXAMPLE 9. Using an A-B, A-D test design, the response members can be varied to generate conditions that may produce either facilitation or unlearning. Facilitation through mediation could be expected if the sequence involved learning YOF-bandit, YOF-robber, while learning YOF-bandit, YOF-athlete would be more likely to produce errors and unlearning rather than mediation.

The Skaggs-Robinson hypothesis. One attempt to explain the effects of similarity on facilitation or interference has been called the *Skaggs-Robinson hypothesis,* after early investigators in this area. Figure 14-3 shows the results generally predicted by this hypothesis.

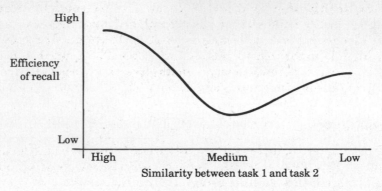

Fig. 14-3

It can be seen that intermediate levels of similarity are predicted to produce maximum interference with later retention, while best retention (facilitation) is generated when there is maximum similarity between the two tasks. (Of course, measuring accurately the degree of similarity is not always possible.) Results such as those illustrated in Fig. 14-3 are more likely to be obtained, however, with serial-recall tasks rather than with paired-associate tasks.

Degree of Learning

Another variable important in the consideration of interference effects is *degree of learning* of each of the tasks involved. In general, greater learning of the task to be tested will reduce interference effects, while greater learning of the interfering task will generate greater inhibition.

Temporal Factors

One more element that cannot be totally controlled in the study of interference effects is the time between the various steps in the procedure. These variables are generally referred to as *temporal factors,* and investigators have come to realize that no one time period is completely independent of all the others in the procedure. Figure 14-4 shows the three major time periods involved. Changing any one affects at least one other.

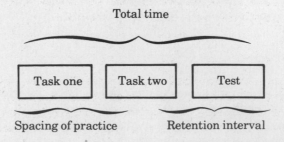

Fig. 14-4

14.4 OTHER THEORIES OF FORGETTING

Interference is not the only variable proposed as an explanation of forgetting.   Three other variables that have been proposed are presented in this section.

Independent Retrieval

Supporters of the concept of independent retrieval believe that interference theory predicts a reciprocal or inverse relationship for B and D learning.   (According to independent retrieval theorists, interference theory requires that the strength of B must decrease as the strength of D increases in a pair of learning tasks following the A-B, A-D pattern.) The supporters of independent retrieval theories claim that experimental results do not bear out this inverse relationship, and as a result they reject interference theory.   In its place, they propose that some factor such as suppression or differential encoding causes forgetting.

Differential Encoding

As mentioned in Chapter 13, there may be a difference between the nominal stimulus and the functional stimulus.   This difference may produce differential encoding effects that either heighten or reduce the inhibition effects observed.

EXAMPLE 10.   Using the A-B, A-D test sequence, it would be possible to establish pairs such as BEFIL-arm and BEFIL-cup.   The wise investigator might avoid such pairings because of potential problems.   If they are used, it is possible a subject might transform the nominal stimulus by concentrating only on the first three letters when learning the first pair and only on the last three letters when learning the second pair.   Thus, the functional pairs would become BEF-arm (beef-arm) and FIL-cup (Fill-cup).   The retrieval cues actually used may differ from those the experimenter believes are being used.

Cognitive Boundary Strength

One additional proposal suggests that retention should be viewed as cognitive resistance to interference.   The label used for this is memory *boundary strength*.   Highly practiced or relatively unique memories are more likely to develop strong boundaries—that is, high cognitive resistance to interference from other events.

EXAMPLE 11.   While one's eighth grade English class may not have been very memorable, the day that Ken dropped a one-pound bag of flour into the air circulation system may still be recalled in vivid detail.   Proponents of cognitive boundary strength would suggest that that particular memory had high resistance to interference because of its uniqueness and that the strong cognitive boundary would be likely to remain intact.

14.5 SPECIAL CONSIDERATIONS OF FORGETTING

It is beyond the scope of this book to discuss all the special considerations of forgetting.   This section presents three that have received substantial attention.

The Kamin Effect

The *Kamin effect,* at first thought to be an unusual result, has been shown to be a stable effect obtained following aversive conditioning.   Retention of a response trained with aversive conditioning is good immediately following acquisition and relatively good for long retention intervals.   However, retention of the response is noticeably poorer for retention intervals of intermediate length.   Although the Kamin effect has been demonstrated to be a reliable phenomenon, no one explanation for the results has been substantiated.   It should also be noted that a comparable effect is *not* obtained when using nonaversive conditioning.

Amnesias

In the clinical sense, *amnesia* means a complete absence of a memory.   In the psychology of learning, the term is used in a more general sense—to refer to retention losses produced by some traumatic event. Of particular interest has been the study of the time between acquisition of the memory and the occurrence of the subsequent amnesic agent; this is called the study of *retrograde amnesia*. Also investigated have been the variety of traumatic events that may produce amnesia—including electroconvulsive shock, brain stimulation, hypothermia, psychological stresses, and many other events.

EXAMPLE 12.   Many clinical case histories present reports of amnesias.   A fairly common type involves physiological damage to the brain (e.g., destruction of part of the frontal lobe) followed by evidence that memories of long ago can still be produced, but memories of the immediate past—that is, new information—cannot be retained.

Aging

A different kind of temporal consideration related to forgetting is the topic of *aging*.   This has been studied in several different manners—in developmental terms, in physiological perspective, and from clinical viewpoints.   Particular interest has been directed toward *infantile amnesia*, the inability to remember anything from before about age three.   Although many different proposals have been put forth, no special explanation for the effects of aging on retention has gained favor.

EXAMPLE 13.   Demonstration of infantile amnesia is a simple matter.   Ask yourself, or a group of friends, to recall the earliest memories possible.   Almost without exception, these will be from age three or four or later.   (It should be noted that many psychologists believe that personality characteristics are established from events that will not be remembered.)

Solved Problems

14.1   Why is it not correct to say that psychologists measure forgetting directly?

It is impossible to measure forgetting directly.   (Think of how you would answer the request, "Tell me all you forgot.")   What psychologists measure is retention, then assume that what has not been retained has been forgotten.

14.2   Suppose a person is asked to name some of the "The Boys of Summer" and professes ignorance.   The questioner then says, "Oh, you remember, the Brooklyn Dodgers of the late forties and early fifties.   With that, the respondent names Campanella, Reese, Robinson, Furillo, Cox, and Roe very quickly.   In terms of the learning variables presented in Chapter 13, which explanation of forgetting appears to best account for the initial inability to respond?

Of the three possibilities (acquisition, storage, and retrieval), the initial inability to respond seems to be a failure to retrieve the information from storage.   In this case, the cue ("The Boys of Summer") has not been encoded as a retrieval tag accompanying the names, and therefore does not cue the appropriate set of responses.   When the second cue is presented, it "fits" with a retrieval tag and responding occurs.   The responding supports the above interpretation because it indicates that there was *not* a storage failure.   (*Note:* Forgetting should not be explained as an acquisition failure; what is not learned cannot be forgotten.)

14.3   Following the respondent's quick recitation of the six names in Problem 14.2, the questioner asks, "But who was the first baseman?"   The answer given is, "I really do know that, but I just cannot remember."   What is the difference between the inability to respond in this case and the inability described in the previous problem?

Both of these instances of forgetting can be attributed to retrieval failure (rather than storage failure), but they differ significantly as well.   In Problem 14.2 the initial forgetting occurred because the respondent failed to use an appropriate retrieval cue, whereas in this situation forgetting appears to be the result of interference—retrieval of the correct response ("Gil Hodges") is somehow blocked or inhibited, perhaps by some other memory.

14.4   Pursuing the subject, the questioner of the previous problems (14.2 and 14.3) says, "You know, the center fielder on that team was Duke Snider.   What was his real first name?" The respondent says "Edward!"   Later, this response is corrected by a listener who remarks that the name was not Edward, but Edwin.   This incorrect response may indicate what forgetting process?

The response "Edward" instead of "Edwin" may represent a storage failure.   In this case, it is not a total destruction of the response, but rather a modification.   (It should be noted that some psychologists feel that forgetting may be the result of simultaneous storage and retrieval failure.)

14.5   Regardless of the explanation used to account for loss of retention, the pattern of loss is similar for most tasks.   Describe this "curve of forgetting."

As first described by Ebbinghaus (see Chapter 2, Fig. 2-1), the typical curve of forgetting shows the most rapid loss of retention in the period soon after acquisition, followed by an increasingly gradual decline in retention as the time since learning increases.

14.6   It is sometimes suggested that students who sit in bed and study with the stereo on may have difficulty when taking examinations in a quiet classroom.   Explain this.

Such students may benefit from the effects of state-dependent learning if the context in which acquisition occurred is the context most likely to elicit high performance.   Change in context, either by removal of previously present cues (as in this case) or by introduction of some novel stimulus, does not really change either storage or retrieval processes, but does appear to have a general, usually detrimental effect on performance.

14.7   Why is the simple decay theory of forgetting not generally accepted?

Decay theory, which proposes that forgetting occurs simply because of the passage of time, is not generally accepted because there is a wealth of evidence indicating that something more than decay must be happening.   Theories that have developed to try to explain this "something more" can be categorized as trace-change, interference, retrieval-failure, and motivated forgetting theories.

14.8   Give an example of trace-change in retention illustrating one of the gestalt principles of good organization.   Then suggest how trace-consolidation might have prevented this.

The gestalt principles of good organization include closure (the tendency to close an open figure), symmetry (the tendency to balance a figure) and good figure (the tendency toward a more perfect figure).   All of these were thought by gestaltists to operate relatively automatically.   An example of trace-change in retention might occur when the subject is presented with a stimulus that looks like Fig. 14-5a and later responds by sketching (or selecting from several choices) a drawing that looks like Fig. 14-5b.

However, if the subject "sets" the memory trace, perhaps with a series of spaced practice trials or by encoding it (as a "lopsided arrowhead," for example), the response may be the same as, or much closer to, the original stimulus.   This would represent trace-consolidation.

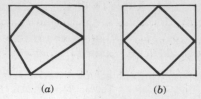

(a)   (b)

Fig. 14-5

14.9   Explain the concept of repression.

A psychoanalytic concept developed by Sigmund Freud, repression is most simply defined as motivated forgetting.   Freud suggested that repression occurred as a defense for the ego, in the sense that the failure to remember a particularly anxiety-producing memory would result in less conscious stress.   (Freud also believed that these repressed memories could continue to influence behavior as unconscious motives.   Therapy could bring these memories to a conscious state, where they would be dealt with and the anxieties alleviated.   For greater detail, consult a personality or abnormal psychology textbook.)

14.10   To test the theory of forgetting as retrieval failure, the experimenter selects two groups randomly, then instructs them to try to recall the brand names of as many different car manufacturers as possible.   One group is simply given paper and pencil.   The other group is given several sheets of paper, each headed with a category such as "Foreign Cars," "American Cars," or "Cars No Longer Made."   Predict which group will make more correct responses, then explain your prediction.

The solution to this problem could take two paths.   If you do *not* accept the theory of forgetting as retrieval failure, you would predict equal performance for the two groups.   Such a prediction would assume that the retrieval cues did not affect recall.   However, there is a good deal of research that would make the alternative prediction plausible—i.e., that provision of appropriate retrieval cues will facilitate recall.   The prediction that the second group will show better recall than the first is likely to be substantiated.

14.11   Lance, at age eight, has become accustomed to waving goodbye to his parents each morning as they back their car from the driveway and toot the horn twice.   Lance also has had several experiences, when riding his bicycle, of having a car coming toward him sound the horn to warn him to get out of the way.   One afternoon, Lance is riding his bicycle in the driveway as his parents pull in.   They toot twice as the car approaches Lance.   If Lance illustrates the principle called switching, what is he likely to do in response?

Switching is shown when the stimuli presented are associated with more than one response; that is, the stimuli provide part of the context for two or more different responses.   Research has shown that when switching takes place, subjects may try to perform both (or all) of the responses.   In this case, Lance may try to get out of the way *and* wave at the same time.

14.12   Suppose students in an experiment are required to learn two tasks (task A and task B) that are potentially incompatible.   How would a psychologist determine the extent to which learning each task interferes with learning the other?

Because interference may be either proactive or retroactive, it would be necessary to have the subjects learn the tasks in both orders (first task A followed by B, then B followed by A).   Then the psychologist could test for the retention in each situation.   In designing the experiment, the psychologist would have to use eight groups.   Groups 1 through 4 can be considered experimental and groups 5 through 8 are control groups.   See Table 14-1.

Table 14-1

Group	Step one	Step two	Step three
1	Learn A	Learn B	Test A
2	Learn A	Learn B	Test B
3	Learn B	Learn A	Test B
4	Learn B	Learn A	Test A
5	Learn A	Put in time	Test A
6	Put in time	Learn B	Test B
7	Learn B	Put in time	Test B
8	Put in time	Learn A	Test A

14.13 Three groups of subjects are gathered for a five-trial test of "release from proactive inhibition." In each of the first four trials the groups memorize a list of fruits, and during the retention intervals are kept busy with a rehearsal-prevention task. (See a description of the Peterson procedure in Section 13.4.) What would be the most likely result if on the fifth trial one group switches to memorizing a list of sports, another group switches to a list of vegetables, and the third (control) group is presented with another list of fruits to memorize?

The results, summarized in Fig. 14-6, show that highest retention rate is demonstrated by the group that switches to the "sports" list, a semantic category distinctly different from "fruits." The group that switches to the "vegetables" list shows somewhat less release from proactive inhibition because of the similarities that exist between the semantic categories "vegetables" and "fruits." (The two categories are similar in the sense that both are foods.) The third group, which receives yet another list of fruits to memorize, has the lowest retention score, reflecting the continuing buildup of PI.

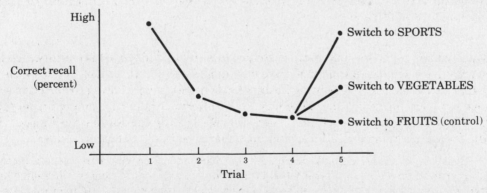

Fig. 14-6

14.14 Explain the response-competition hypothesis of retroactive inhibition. Then show why a two-factor theory of retroaction appears to better account for the RI effect.

The response-competition hypothesis was predicated upon the idea that learning new materials in no way affects the strength of previous learning. Interference exists only in the form of response competition. For example, paired-associate tasks in the A-B, A-D format could be followed by a test presenting A and asking for B responses. The independence hypothesis would suggest that competition between the B and D responses would create the interference and thus the apparent forgetting.

A two-factor theory developed when research results showed that as the number of interfering (interposed) tasks increased, the number of intruding responses produced in later recall of the B responses at first increased, but then decreased. At some point, response competition no longer contributed the major effect. Researchers attributed the apparent absence of or reduction in response competition to unlearning or extinction of the A-B list associations. Thus, the factors of response competition *and* unlearning, used together, seemed to provide a more complete interpretation of retroactive inhibition.

14.15 How would the two-factor theory suggested in Problem 14.14 be applied to PI effects?

The same two factors can be applied to a PI experiment. It is assumed that unlearning of the first-task materials occurs while the second task is being learned. If there is an immediate test of retention of the second task, greater unlearning and less response competition can be expected. If the test of retention for the second task is delayed, however, the effect of response competition will increase and the effect of unlearning will decrease.

Presumably, spontaneous recovery of the first-task materials can occur during the retention interval preceding the test of retention, and PI may increase as a consequence. However, studies have not always supported this prediction, making it necessary to use both unlearning and response competition to account for PI.

14.16 Both the MFR and MMFR procedures provided support for the two-factor theory. Briefly explain these procedures and the results that appeared to support the two-factor theory.

In MFR (modified free recall), A-B, A-D learning steps are followed with a recall step where the subject is asked to recall the first response that comes to mind. In MMFR (modified MFR) the subjects are asked to try to recall both previously learned responses (B and D).

Results using the MFR procedure showed that as the number of trials of the interpolated task increased, recall of the B responses decreased. It was also shown that as the retention interval increased, there was some evidence to support spontaneous recovery of the B responses.

Recall of B responses using the MMFR procedure also decreased as the number of A-D learning trials increased. Because both responses could theoretically be used in the MMFR procedure, this finding also seems to support the two-factor theory.

14.17 How did use of a recognition test of retention present evidence that contradicted the two-factor theory suggested in the last two problems?

Given a recognition test of retention, most subjects are able to pair appropriate S-R pairs for either of the two lists. Unlearning does not appear to have occurred. Researchers using this procedure have proposed that a suppression of the response rather than an extinction process takes place. The recognition procedure overcomes this suppression, and correct responding is possible.

14.18 Explain the concept of facilitation. How does facilitation play a part in the associative-probability paradox?

Facilitation refers to the fact that learning one set of materials may eventually help with the retention of some other set of materials. It is possible to measure both proactive facilitation and retroactive facilitation.

The associative-probability paradox exists because it is possible to predict both interfering and facilitating effects in certain research studies. For example, high meaningfulness of verbal items can predict either inhibition (because of the interference of associations with new learning) or facilitation (because of mediation effects). The important factor seems to be whether or not the items link responses in mediational chains. If so, facilitation can be expected; if not, interference will probably occur.

14.19   Give an explanation for a statement such as, "I had more trouble remembering the ones that were sort of like those I used to know than the ones that were totally different.   Of course, the ones that were the same were easy."

   The statement expresses results that have been accounted for by the Skaggs-Robinson hypothesis, which indicates that maximum inhibition is obtained when there is an intermediate degree of similarity between the two tasks involved.   Exact similarity produces maximum retention.   (Essentially, the subject practices the same task twice.)   Totally different tasks create no confusion because there is no overlap.   (However, it should be noted that results may vary considerably depending upon the type of tasks being studied.)

14.20   What kinds of predictions relate degree of learning to PI or RI effects?

   In general, the predictions are: (1) the greater the degree of learning of the task to be tested, the smaller the inhibition effect observed; and (2) the greater the degree of learning of the interfering task, the greater the inhibition effect observed.   Most research results substantiate these predictions.

14.21   Why is it impossible to eliminate procedural difficulties when trying to test the effects of temporal (time) factors upon either PI or RI?

   The problem is that there are three possible temporal factors that may be varied, but they cannot be varied independently.   For example, if the experimenter wishes to test the effects of varying the retention interval between the second task and the test of retention, the time between the first task and the retention task will also automatically change.

14.22   The concept of state-dependent learning (see Problem 14.6) is one example of the effect of context upon retention.   Encoding has been proposed as a second type of context effect.   Explain why encoding might increase or decrease the observed inhibition effects in an experiment.

   The solution to this problem points out (once again, as in Chapter 13) the difference between a nominal stimulus and a functional stimulus.   The investigator may establish conditions expected to produce an inhibition effect, but if the subject perceives the conditions in some other manner, such effects may not be obtained.

14.23   In Problem 14.17, suppression of the response was suggested as an alternative to the unlearning hypothesis of the interference effect.   Give an alternative label for response suppression, and then briefly present the countering argument developed by the proponents of two-factor theory.

   Another way to interpret the results—showing that there is not an inverse relationship between learning of the second task and unlearning of the first—has been labeled the independent-retrieval phenomenon.   This is the label used to represent the finding that recall of B (in an A-B, A-D test paradigm) is just as likely when D is recalled as when D is not recalled.

   Supporters of the two-factor theory believe that the independent-retrieval phenomenon ignores the crucial aspect of unlearning.   They argue that it is *not* response replacement (or lack of it) that is proposed as unlearning—that is, more D learning does not replace B responses.   Rather, the unlearning of B happens when B occurs as an unreinforced response during A-D learning.   The greater the opportunity for those conditions, the greater the unlearning of B responses will be.

14.24 Whitney is preparing to leave the house to go to the grocery store to buy eggs and bread.   As he is leaving the house, Eleanor shouts, "Get some lettuce, some soup, and a half-gallon of ice cream."   Arriving at the grocery store, Whitney is unable to recall all five items.   In terms of cognitive boundary strength as an explanation of interference, which items are most likely to be remembered?   Why?

It is most likely that Whitney will remember the eggs and bread.   According to cognitive explanations of interference, retention is the resistance to interference and is expressed by the concept of boundary strength.   Because it is likely that Whitney had practiced the responses "eggs" and "bread" more than the other responses, they are thought to be more resistant to interference from competing systems.   (*Note:* If Eleanor had asked for some unusual purchase, such as half a pound of tongue, the cognitive system should be distinct, or separate, from the others and Whitney would show a high probability of response.)

14.25 Trained on an avoidance task involving electric shock, a group of rats later demonstrates the Kamin effect.   Sketch a graph that illustrates the results that would be obtained.

The Kamin effect is a nonlinear retention function showing that following aversive conditioning, retention will be relatively poor for intermediate retention intervals, but quite good either very soon after conditioning or after relatively long retention intervals.   Thus, the solution to this problem should look like the curve in Fig. 14-7.

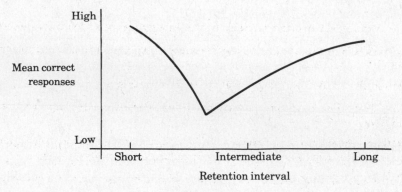

Fig. 14-7

14.26 Describe, in general, the types of memory losses identified as amnesias.   To what causes are these amnesias usually attributed?

Although frequently summarized under the single term "retrograde amnesia," amnesias often are studied in terms of a temporal dimension.   A distinction is made between loss of memory of immediately preceding events and loss of memories acquired some more considerable time before.   A most common cause for amnesias is some sort of physiological trauma.   Another cause sometimes cited is psychological trauma, although this is considered more difficult to identify or describe than physiological trauma.

14.27 What general conclusion can be reached regarding the relationships of aging and retention?

Research has shown that very young and very old individuals are most likely to show deficits in retention, especially after short retention intervals.   The inability to retain memories from before about age three has been called *infantile amnesia*.   However, identifying these relationships does not explain why they exist.   Lack of synaptic development, lack of verbal conceptualization, pathologies of old age, lack of appropriate experimental procedures, and other difficulties make explanations hard to establish.

Key Terms

Amnesia.   Complete failure of a memory.

Associative-probability paradox.   The possible use of the associates in one learning task to predict both interference and facilitation for some new learning.

Boundary strength.   A concept used to describe cognitive resistance to interference; the stronger the boundary, the less likely it is that interference will affect retention.

Closure.   In perception, the "completing" of an incomplete stimulus or piece of information.

Decay theory of forgetting.   A theory that attributes forgetting to the mere passage of time and the accompanying deterioration of memory storage.

Facilitation.   The aid that the learning of one task provides in the retention of some other task.

Forgetting.   Loss of retention; never measured directly, but rather indirectly on the basis of measurable failures of retention.

Infantile amnesia.   The relatively complete forgetting of the experiences of the first 3 to 5 years of life.

Interference theory of forgetting.   A theory that attributes forgetting to the blocking of one task's retention by the retention of some other task.

Kamin effect.   In aversive conditioning, the finding that retention of the trained response is good immediately following conditioning and also for long retention intervals, but relatively poor for retention intervals of intermediate length.

Mediation.   The association of two different items because they share some third characteristic.

MFR procedure.   In an A-B, A-D paired-associate procedure, testing retention by asking for the first response that comes to mind.

MMFR procedure.   In an A-B, A-D paired-associate procedure, testing retention by asking for both responses.

Proactive inhibition (PI).   The assumption that something learned earlier may reduce the retention of something learned later.

Release from proactive inhibition.   In a repetitive STM task, the noticeable increase in performance when a novel stimulus (or a stimulus from a new category) is introduced after several trials.

Repression.   A defense mechanism used to keep anxiety-producing memories from consciousness; motivated forgetting.

Retrieval failure.   An explanation of forgetting attributing inability to respond to the presentation of inappropriate retrieval cues and/or interference.

Retroactive inhibition (RI).   The assumption that something learned later may reduce the retention of something learned before.

Retrograde amnesia.   The finding that amnesia recovers in a reverse temporal sequence, with most recent occurrences being the last to be recalled.

Skaggs-Robinson hypothesis.   The prediction that efficiency of recall will be better when similarity between two tasks is either high or low, but not when it is in some medium range.

State-dependent learning.   The association of learned materials with the environment in which they were learned.

Storage failure.   An explanation of forgetting that attributes inability to respond to some modification or destruction of a stored memory.

Switching.   Changing the external contextual stimuli for two tasks (but not the tasks themselves) when testing retention; often produces responses appropriate for both circumstances.

Trace-change theory of forgetting.   A theory that attributes forgetting to the alteration of memory storage resulting from physiological processes.

Unlearning.   An explanation of interference based upon the principles of extinction and spontaneous recovery.

Chapter 15

Information Processing

The retention stage of the learning process can also be understood in terms of *information processing*, a broad term meant to include a wide variety of cognitive approaches to the study of memory. The basic assumption of most information-processing models is that human mental processes, like computer processes, can be best understood as the input-processing-output sequence that the human mind follows in encoding, storing, and retrieving information.

15.1 TERMINOLOGY

Many different information-processing models are based on computer models, and much of the special vocabulary of information processing is drawn from computer programming.

Input-Processing-Output

Input refers to the reception and consequent acquisition of information. *Processing* describes the storage of information, along with any transformations or losses of learned materials that may occur. *Output* refers to the responses that indicate what has been retained from input and processing. In the language of computer operations, this sequence can be described as follows: The input is called the *read-in*, each series of manipulations or processing represents the *routine* or *subroutine*, and the output is the *read-out*.

Information

Even the term *information* requires definition. In the most general sense, *information* refers to any events such as stimuli, data, programs, and so forth that make up the input, or read-in. But this is not a satisfactory explanation because some stimuli add nothing to the overall amount of information put in storage. (Such stimuli are considered either *irrelevant* or *redundant*.)

A more acceptable definition of information is that it is any event that reduces uncertainty. A corollary is that the greater the amount of uncertainty that is reduced, the greater the amount of information that has been transmitted.

EXAMPLE 1. Unusual names reveal the principle of uncertainty reduction. Students in schools may be easily identified if either their first or last names are unusual, while uncertainty is likely to be much greater if the student's name is relatively common. Thus, "Pennilyn Forestburger" would be thought of as a name that transmitted more information than "James Johnson."

Simulation

Some information-processing theorists have made attempts to construct computer programs that can mimic human performance. This process is called *simulation*. It is thought that the computer programs may reveal the underlying principles that determine human performance. Generally, simulation research is considered to approach behavior from a relatively broad perspective when compared to the more limited (S-R) studies that characterize the behaviorist approach.

Artificial Intelligence

A second aspect of information processing is called *artificial-intelligence* research. In these cases, rather than try to imitate what humans actually do, the computer programs are designed to maximize performance of a particular task. Research of this sort may aid scientists in determining where humans fall short and, possibly, what might be done to modify human performance to better accomplish certain goals.

EXAMPLE 2. A psychologist might use one of at least two information-processing approaches in order to study the training and performance of air traffic controllers. If the researcher in this area creates programs to reflect how people in this profession actually perform, the studies are attempts at simulation. However, if the programs are designed to outperform the human, the investigation is classified as one of artificial intelligence. Either simulation or artificial intelligence can be used to redesign training programs and on-the-job performance routines.

15.2 PROPERTIES OF THE COMPUTER

In order to understand the information-processing approach, it is necessary also to be familiar with the major working characteristics of computers. This section explores some of these.

Hardware vs. Software

The term *hardware* is used to describe the physical parts of the computer, including a central processor and the memory elements. It is impossible for the computer to operate beyond the limits of its physical structure—for example, the size of the memory store or the speed of operation.

Additional limitations upon operation are created by the *software*, or programs, that are used in the computer. Usually it is possible to write many different programs for any computer, but whichever program is used will determine the eventual input-output relationship. In other words, extremely sophisticated hardware does not by itself guarantee sophisticated output; both the hardware and software place limitations on what a given computer can do.

EXAMPLE 3. Computer hardware and software can be thought of, respectively, as analogous to the human's central nervous system and thought processes. The mutual dependence of physiological and cognitive processes is seen as bearing a resemblance to the interaction of hardware and software.

Computer Uses

Two of the major uses of computers in the study of the psychology of learning, simulation and artificial intelligence, were discussed in Section 15.1. In addition to these applications, computers have been used in both data collection and analyses. For example, computers can be used to initiate stimulus presentations with great accuracy (such as magnitude or timing), to record responses, and to summarize and analyze the results collected.

EXAMPLE 4. Some psychologists estimate that every minute of analysis performed by an advanced computer is worth one week of hand calculation, and that the accuracy will be much better. This speed of analysis has made possible very rapid modification of ongoing processes that would never have been possible in pre-computer times.

Reservations regarding computer uses should be recognized. Using a computer does not assure that a correct answer (or for that matter, any answer) will be found for a particular problem, especially in psychology. It is possible that not all behaviors are amenable to computer analysis, that not all programs are truly accurate, and that more than one program may produce exactly the same result.

Memory Store

The digital computers typically used for research in information processing make use of a binary (two-digit) system that reports each element of information as either present (1) or absent (0). A report of any condition other than 1 or 0 represents error.

The *memory store* is simply the location of information in the hardware. Both data and program instructions may be held in the memory store and are essentially the same in character. Use of information held in the memory store is called *processing* (for example, computation using the data available and a computation program).

EXAMPLE 5.   It is important to realize that programs can be treated as data as well as executed.   Programs can be evaluated, analyzed, and modified before being reinserted into a memory store—thus being treated as data rather than simply as processes.   This may be very important when the research is designed to try to find the "best fit" between the program and some actual performance.

The size of the memory store available and the sophistication of the programs prepared will often determine the processing that will occur.   In general, the relationship between the two can be viewed as reciprocal; that is, the greater the amount of information held in the memory store, the less processing that will be required, or vice versa.

EXAMPLE 6.   Humans using encoding processes for retention parallel this processing—memory store reciprocity.   It is possible to memorize definitions for every word encountered (memory store) or rules that allow interpretation of newly confronted words (processing).   The greater the size of the memory store or vocabulary, the fewer the number of words that will be considered new.

Timesharing

When the computer is programmed for *timesharing,* it will be able to oscillate or shift from one task to another.   The computer can be programmed to hold the information from the inactive task in memory store, so that return to that task can be achieved without any loss of data or storage modification.

Multiple Processing

If the hardware of the computer allows it, more than one processing mode can be used simultaneously, which is called *multiple processing.*   Thus, two or more tasks may be undertaken by the computer at the same time.

EXAMPLE 7.   Humans show behavior comparable to both timesharing and multiple processing.   Timesharing can be illustrated by the person who takes time out from preparing a cake recipe to answer the phone, returns to the cake preparation, and continues with the next appropriate step.   It should be recognized, however, that while the computer can be expected to show perfect timesharing, the human may not.   After the phone call the human may add salt a second time, apparently not retaining a memory of performing that operation the first time.

Humans also are capable of showing multiple processing, as long as the control systems required are not in conflict.   An illustration of this is the person who listens to records while painting the woodwork in the house.   Two tasks are being completed simultaneously but are not in conflict.

Memory Search

One property of computers that is of particular interest to psychologists studying learning and retention is the means by which information is "called up" from the memory store.   This is called *memory search.*   Basically, memory search occurs when the central processor in some manner inspects the memory elements and activates those appropriate for the instructions currently operating the processor.

Access to elements.   To release or activate information held in a memory element, the central processor must send a probe signal (comparable to a retrieval cue) that gains access to the appropriate stores.   Quite often this is accomplished by sending the probe along a sequential data path shared by all elements.   Called a *bus* arrangement because it follows a specified route, the probe identifies those elements containing the requested information and initiates the call-up.

Sequential vs. random access.   When information is stored in a built-in-sequence, the entry or extraction of data by the central processor is accomplished by the probe simply counting along the sequence to the appropriate location and performing the necessary function.   Called *sequential access,* the time involved is directly dependent upon the size of the sequence and the "distance" the probe must travel along the sequence to complete its operation.

Random access depends upon a device that decodes an *address* for the memory elements involved.   More intricate to establish, random access will usually be faster than sequential access in actual operation.

EXAMPLE 8.   Trying to identify the location of a particular letter within the alphabet may be used to illustrate both sequential access and random access.   Ask yourself which letter occurs three before S.   Determine how you answer the "probe."   It is likely your initial reaction was one of random access; for example, S is toward the end of the alphabet.   The probe therefore directs you away from starting with A, B, C and may have you begin with M.   The second step might then require sequential access, first in a forward serial manner (M, N, O, P, Q, R, S), and then counting back to identify P as the correct answer.

Another way to distinguish sequential and random access is to consider sequential access as *nonassociative* in nature (that is, nonconnected or recorded by order in time) and random access as *associative* (connected by some encoding).   Most computer memories contain both.   Still another way to consider access is to compare *content-addressable* memory (what is in it) versus *location-addressable* memory (where is it held in memory store).

Response from memory.   Once the access to memory has taken place, the information called up may take several different forms.   If the probe simply asks if there is information there (yes-no), the response mode is called a *poll*.   When the probe determines where the information is located in memory, the response mode is referred to as a *return address*.   A *contents response* to the probe actually presents the information of the memory store.   When a contents response also contains additional instructions (to continue or expand the probe), it is called an *actor*.

EXAMPLE 9.   Students learning how to administer individual psychological tests to children soon learn to phrase their questions (probes) to elicit contents responses rather than a poll.   For example, they find it best to say, "Tell me more about that," rather than "Can you tell me more about that?"   The latter question can be adequately answered with a yes or no, but would not then accomplish the purpose of the test.   The first question should call up additional information if it is available.

Memory Hierarchy

Computer memory elements often are set up in several stores comprising a *memory hierarchy*.   Such hierarchies are usually organized according to the size of the store and the speed with which the information can be recovered from the store by the central processor.

EXAMPLE 10.   One memory hierarchy that has been used in computers designates its levels as register memory, cache memory, main memory, and secondary store.   This four-level hierarchy is arranged in order of speed of access as well as memory-store size, with each stage being somewhat slower and somewhat larger than the previous.

Partial Match

The probe of a memory store may be capable of identifying that the elements sampled only partially satisfy the probe requirements.   If the probe finds such elements, the resultant *partial match* can operate in one of two manners.   If the probe is fairly general, many more memory elements may be called up than are necessary for solution to the problem (answer to the probe). On the other hand, if the probe is extremely specific, no elements will be sampled—even those that are nearly correct and could have been considered appropriate responses.   Use of a large number of memory elements with relatively great flexibility helps overcome the problems presented by partial match.

15.3 INPUT

The properties of computers described in Section 15.2 function only in terms of the information received—that is, the input.   Recognizing this, several psychologists have concentrated their research efforts on trying to determine what controls input into humans, either by studying humans directly or by simulating human performance using computers.   This section looks at several of the important points investigated.

Attention

The major consideration of any input is that the person *must* attend to the stimulus if it is to be received and have any possibility of becoming part of the information stored in memory. Several researchers have devoted their efforts to studying what controls attention.

Voluntary vs. involuntary attention.   One question that psychologists studying attention try to answer is whether control rests with the individual or is a result of the stimulus properties. When the individual chooses the focus of attention, it is called *voluntary attention*. If the properties of the stimulus appear to force attention, it is called *involuntary attention*.

EXAMPLE 11.   Suppose you are sitting in a booth at a restaurant. You realize that the couple in the next booth is having a rather heated discussion about something. By choice, you can eavesdrop, thus showing voluntary attention. However, if by chance there is an exceedingly loud clap of thunder, your attention will be diverted by the sound, an example of involuntary attention.

Filter theory.   One major proposal developed in an attempt to explain attention is called *filter theory*. Basically, the concept is that either physiological properties of the individual and/or choice mechanisms incline the individual to attend to certain stimuli while disregarding others.

Many different forms of research support the basic premises of filter theory—that receptors in the reticular activating system (the control core of the brain stem) show a certain amount of selectivity in transmitting signals to higher cortical areas. These filters, called *sensory gates*, determine whether or not a signal will be attended to by an individual. Perceptual studies have shown that both the type of signal and the number of other signals present will influence how the sensory gating process operates in a given case. In some instances, researchers have shown that they can manipulate circumstances to make an individual completely filter out signals that would otherwise be attended to.

EXAMPLE 12.   Researchers have used various learning tasks in order to test the filter theory of attention. In one such study, which employed a *divided attention task,* subjects were presented with two aural messages at the same time (one headphone channel to each ear). The subjects were also asked to repeat immediately the message from one of the channels each time it was presented (this is called a *shadowing task*). These subjects remembered almost nothing of the message in the other channel, as measured by a test of retention given 30 seconds after the end of the stimulus presentation, thus giving weight to the filter theory of attention.

Attenuation filter.   One modification of filter theory has been called the *attenuation filter* approach. Some studies do not produce results showing the absolute, all-or-none type of filtering described in Example 12. Instead, these studies show that all messages are given an evaluation when they arrive, and that full or partial shifts of attention may occur, depending on the type and number of messages. If there is no reason to alter reception behavior, the filter operates as usual. However, if a novel, special, or particularly important message arrives in one of the "blocked" channels, reception may occur. The context and content of all stimuli are viewed as being important.

EXAMPLE 13.   Attenuation is supported by what is called the "cocktail party phenomenon." At most such parties, there are several conversations going on simultaneously and therefore several messages that could be received. Usually, all but one are filtered out. However, it has been shown that a person will shift attention to a previously blocked message if that person's name is mentioned in it. In other words, if someone mentions your name, the message priorities change (the filter adjusts) and a new channel of attention is opened.

15.4   INFORMATION

Research on what is actually placed in the memory store and how much can be handled at one time has provided understanding of the concept of information. (Remember the definition from Section 15.1: information is any event that reduces uncertainty.)

The Bit

In Section 15.2, any element of information in a memory store was described as being either present (1) or absent (0). From the use of this kind of computer memory store has emerged the term *bit* of information, an abbreviation of *bi*nary digi*t*. One bit of information is defined as the amount of information that allows a decision between two equal alternatives. (A general rule: As the number of alternatives is increased by a factor of two, one additional bit of information will be required to make a decision. Thus, four (2^2) equally likely alternatives require two bits of information, while eight (2^3) alternatives would require three bits.)

EXAMPLE 14. The concepts of information and bit can be demonstrated easily using a grid. Suppose your problem is to select the one "correct" square from the sixteen equally likely alternatives represented by the four-by-four grid shown in Fig. 15-1.

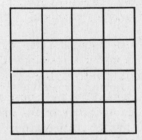

Fig. 15-1

There are several ways to approach this problem. You might just take a shot in the dark and select a square, saying, "Is it this one?" If you select the correct one, all uncertainty is removed and maximum information is transmitted. If the answer is incorrect, however, only one-sixteenth of the uncertainty is reduced. That is, much less information is conveyed.

A second approach would involve "halving." Each successive question would provide one bit of information. Thus you might say (1) Is it in the upper half of the grid? No. (2) Is it in the right half of the bottom two rows? Yes. (3) Is it in the right two of the four remaining squares? No. (4) Is it the upper one of the two remaining squares? Yes. These four bits of information (or comparable appropriate ones) will be enough to assure your knowing the correct answer, and thus to reduce the uncertainty to zero. This binary process of elimination is shown in Fig. 15-2.

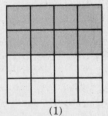 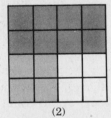 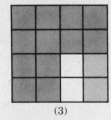 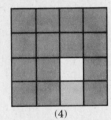

(1)   (2)   (3)   (4)

Fig. 15-2

Immediate-Memory Span

As mentioned in Chapter 13, research has shown that the *immediate-memory span* for humans is generally capable of processing 7 ± 2 units of information at one time. The size of the unit of information being processed may vary, depending upon the encoding techniques being used, the properties of the information being received, and so on. One way in which the capacity of the immediate-memory span can be increased is called *chunking,* where several units of information are grouped together because they possess some attribute in common. The several units of information can then be processed as one chunk.

Immediate consciousness. Some psychologists agree that the immediate memory spans 7 ± 2 units of information, but they add that the actual attention to or processing of information is limited to a single unit at a time. These psychologists discuss mental processes in terms of *immediate consciousness,* in which only one unit of information is being processed at any one moment. (*Note:* This concept implies that even the immediate-memory span requires timesharing and rehearsal.)

15.5 INFORMATION-PROCESSING RESEARCH

Computers are basic to information-processing research; this section mentions only a few of the ways in which they are used.

Algorithms and Heuristics

There are two general methods of searching for answers to problems in information-processing research. The first is to use an *algorithm,* which consists of a set of rules that *guarantee* solution of the problem. All alternatives are considered, thus exhausting all possible solutions and allowing determination of the correct one. *Heuristics,* on the other hand, are "rules of thumb" that propose promising or economical approaches to solving the problem. Because these are nonexhaustive, there is no assurance a correct solution will be found. Yet, because heuristics are usually selected on some rational basis, they may prove much more efficient than algorithms.

EXAMPLE 15. There are many examples of algorithms found for solutions to mathematical problems. Applying the appropriate sequence of rules to multiplication or long division problems will guarantee that the correct answer will be obtained. On the other hand, if an attempt were made to use algorithms to solve certain more advanced problems, such as diagnosing a disease, the exhaustive search might prove tremendously time-consuming and inefficient. In such cases, the use of heuristics could avoid many "dead end" searches, allowing the physician to make a rapid diagnosis and begin treatment as soon as possible.

Games-Playing

A particularly intriguing line of information-processing research has arisen out of the study of *games-playing.* Using simulation studies and investigations of artificial intelligence, researchers have tried to determine the processing and output sequences associated with the inputs of games such as tic-tac-toe, checkers, or chess. While this may at first sound foolish, the limits of the games create excellent opportunities for determining the types of searches and evaluations (heuristics) that prove either successful or unsuccessful and lead to self-improvement at the task.

EXAMPLE 16. Computer programmers have designed tic-tac-toe programs that make it impossible for the computer to be beaten. The sequence of choices in this case would efficiently cover all possible situations a player might face and can be learned by humans. It is believed that similar attempts will provide greater understanding of intellectual processes and, at the same time, help advance the study of the ways in which computers can be used.

The General Problem Solver (GPS)

Another interesting line of research in information processing has been the development and use of the *General Problem Solver (GPS)* by Allen Newell and Herbert Simon and their associates. The GPS is a program containing a core set of processes which simulate human problem-solving behavior.

The GPS is used to study a variety of problems. Two basic processes are repeated until a solution is determined or the problem is judged insoluble. The first process establishes subgoals that may help solve the problem. This is called *problem-solving organization.* The second, *means-end analysis,* then tries to use heuristics that will achieve that subgoal. The process is repeated until a total solution to the problem is accomplished.

Extremely sophisticated, the GPS can monitor the ongoing processes and discard what appear to be the least fruitful processes being generated. While human capabilities probably are not mirrored exactly, research using the GPS or similar programs has helped identify the kinds of processes and decisions that seem to be a part of human problem solving.

Solved Problems

15.1 Presented with repeated trials of a serial-list learning task, the subject can be said to show the acquisition-storage-retrieval sequence described in the previous two chapters. However, this task can also be interpreted according to the information-processing viewpoint. Describe this second interpretation, relating it to the first and to the task.

The information-processing approach interprets the learning format as an input-processing-output sequence. In this case, presentation of and learning the items of the serial list represent input, processing accounts for storage, and output represents the retrieval (retention test) of the items of the list.

15.2 Why can it be said that newspaper headlines illustrate the concept of information?

The definition of information often is given as the reduction of uncertainty. The less common or typical the material presented, the more the uncertainty is reduced and therefore the greater the information provided. Thus, the more unusual the message transmitted by a newspaper headline, the greater the amount of information it transmits. For example, a headline saying "Ordinary Day in Heidelberg" would not be considered to transmit as much information as the headline "Flooding Strikes Heidelberg."

15.3 Suppose a researcher attempts to design a program that will track a satellite's path and send correction signals when necessary. Is this program representative of simulation or artificial intelligence? Explain.

Most likely this would be an instance of artificial intelligence rather than an example of simulation. The intent of the researcher's work is probably to create a program that will perform in the best manner possible. It is probably not an attempt to mimic the human's behavior exactly. Work such as this, which emphasizes maximum efficiency regardless of how a human might perform, is representative of artificial intelligence.

15.4 The solution to Problem 15.3 indicates that simulation research is likely to produce a program that is less than maximally efficient. What then are the advantages of doing simulation research?

Since human mental processing is often less than maximally efficient, so are computer simulations of it. Research on simulation does have its benefits, however: It allows analysis of how good human mental performances are, where they might be modified, and what underlying processes produce them. Simulation also helps psychologists test various theories of learning and representations of "higher" mental processes. This latter point is of particular importance to the psychology of learning, because it means psychologists now have a technology that allows them to study elaborate and complex learning theories.

15.5 Computers used in both artificial-intelligence research and simulation studies follow the input-processing-output sequence described above. How do the terms hardware and software define the limitations of these computers?

Hardware refers to the physical components of the computer, which place limitations on the speed with which the computer can function, the number of memory stores the computer can contain, and the capacities of those memory stores. It is impossible for any computer to exceed its own physical limitations.

Software is the term used to describe the programs written for the computer. While it is usually possible to write many different programs for any one computer, the program used determines the relationship that will exist between the input and the eventual output.

15.6   Describe the analogy between the hardware-software distinction given in Problem 15.5 and human behavior.

The hardware of the computer can be said to represent the physiological capacities and limitations of the human, while the software or programs are comparable to the thought processes or strategies humans use to process information. (*Note:* Accepting this analogy means that the ultimate success of physiological psychology will be to describe where thought processes occur, but prediction of which behavior will occur necessitates also knowing the strategy being used—that is, the "why" of the thought process.)

15.7   Learning psychologists use computers in simulation studies and artificial-intelligence research. What other major uses for computers do they have?

On a more basic level, computers have brought about tremendous changes in the processes of data collection and analysis. For example, computers allow very precise presentation of stimuli and recording of responses. They also provide rapid, accurate, and relatively inexpensive analyses of the data once the collection is completed. It should be recognized, however, that none of these processes can be carried out any more efficiently than the program, which of course is written by humans. A good program may accomplish many tasks without error, but a poor or misused program can introduce error into any study.

15.8   Why has it been said that there is no guarantee that all components of human thought are amenable to computer analysis or explanation?

Two lines of evidence indicate (at least at present) that there is no guarantee that human thought can be completely analyzed or explained using computers. One is that some behaviors simply have not "fit" any program, or perhaps one should say that no program has been created to fit certain behaviors. The second line of evidence is almost a mirror image of the first: In a number of cases, more than one program can produce exactly the same output, implying that more than one thought process may yield exactly the same behavior. In this latter circumstance, identification of the process in use for any given response may be impossible.

15.9   What property of the computers used for research in psychology of learning inclines investigators to view retention as an all-or-none process rather than an incremental process?

The digital computers represent information as either present or absent; that is, the state of any given memory store is either 1 or 0. Any middle-range value between 1 and 0 is considered an error condition. This yes-no representation fits an all-or-none interpretation of learning and forgetting, but does not fit an incremental viewpoint.

15.10   Explain how the terms "data," "programs," "memory," "processing," and "computation" relate to each other.

Basically, memory is a place where information is kept. In the computer, this is called the memory store and may hold data, the facts used by the processor, or programs, the instructions to be followed. In this sense, programs are not fundamentally different from data. Processing refers to the execution of the program being used. Often the processing takes the form of computation, although many other forms of processing also exist.

15.11   How does memorization of multiplication tables for values greater than 9 times 9 represent a trade-off between memory and processing?

The trade-off between memory and processing refers to the amount of initial effort and subsequent information to be stored versus the later effort required to produce information. For example, if multiplication tables are memorized up to 12, the person will store as information that "9 times 12 is 108" and be able to produce that information relatively quickly. The same result could be produced using the sequence of rules showing that "9 times 2 is 18, record the 8, carry the one, 9 times 1 is 9 plus 1 is 10, so the answer is 108." The initial learning of a general rule requires less time and effort, but the later use of the rule for one particular task takes much longer than the simple retrieval of the same answer. Thus, any given circumstance such as this will require a decision regarding how much initial effort will be expended in memorizing particular facts rather than just learning rules to be used later.

15.12 The problems above have dealt with only one action at a time, yet both humans and computers can perform more than one mental act in close sequence or at the same time. Describe the two common means for handling more than one task, comparing humans and computers.

The two common means for acting upon more than one task are called timesharing and multiple processing. Timesharing essentially consists of switching back and forth between more than one task, while multiple processing refers to simultaneous performance of more than one task.

When a human shows timesharing, the quality of performance will depend upon how well information from one task can be held in short-term storage while attention is devoted to the other task. Computers can be programmed to do this perfectly.

Humans show multiple processing when performing two tasks requiring different control systems—for example, when knitting and humming a tune simultaneously. For computers to do this, more than one processing system must be built into the hardware, and appropriate programming must be developed.

15.13 How are memory elements stored in computers? How are they probed? What responses are possible to the probe?

Memory elements can be stored according to a sequential access or random-access organization. Sequential access means the items are stored in a built-in sequence along which the central processor can step in either direction. Random-access organization uses a symbolic address code which the central processor uses to determine which stores to call up. Random access requires a decoding network, and thus there is more complexity in establishing it. However, random access is generally faster than access to a sequential organization.

The probe of memory stores is done by the central processor sending a signal along a common data path shared by all the elements. This is often called a *bus,* which travels the route (however arranged) and determines where the information (if any) is held.

The responses may take the form of a *poll* ("Yes, it's here," or, "No, it isn't"); a *return address* ("It's here; you'll have to get it"); the *contents* ("Here's what you asked for"); or what has been called an *actor* ("Here's what you asked for, and let's see what else can be found").

15.14 Why do many computers have storage for many memory elements of a rather particular nature rather than fewer, more general stores?

This is in order to overcome the problem of partial match. If the probe (bus) activates many elements because there is some general "closeness" or similarity, a great deal of unwanted information may be summoned from storage. When there are many elements with more particular characteristics, the probe can be more selective, and less unneeded information will be called.

15.15 Computer memories have been described as hybrid memories. Explain this term by distinguishing between location-addressable and content-addressable representations.

Computer memories have been described as hybrid memories because they tend to combine nonassociative and associative memories. Nonassociative storage refers to simple location within the memory store and requires a sequential probe. Such information is called location-addressable. Associative storage refers to indexing more than one item according to some symbol. The probe is programmed to elicit all locations with contents containing the same or similar related information, and the information is thus considered content-addressable. As mentioned above, memory representations depend upon the program used for probing.

15.16 Describe a computer memory hierarchy that is considered somewhat comparable to the actual operation of human memory.

The solution to this problem requires the reader to recall the designations used in previous chapters to distinguish different levels of memory.   Accepting that human memory has at least two levels (short-term and long-term), a comparable computer hierarchy can be developed.

One such hierarchy contains four levels: a register memory, a cache, a main memory, and a secondary store.   The register memories are very small and very fast, holding only a single computer word.   The cache is also quite small, holding the information being worked upon at the moment.   It is relatively fast, using content-addressable probes.   The main memory is randomly accessible, reasonably fast, and may hold materials not currently being used but likely to be called.   The secondary store is the slowest, holding a great deal of information that is usually kept in a sequentially addressable representation.   Information taken from the secondary store may be moved to one of the other memories, and information taken into any one of the other memories may also be placed in the secondary store.

Although there are more than two memory stores described for the computer, it can be seen that the speed of activity and the size and duration of memory are quite comparable to the levels of memory suggested for humans.   The first two are roughly comparable to STM, the latter two to LTM.

15.17 Before information can be held in memory, it must be accepted as input.   What is the key concept controlling input?   What major proposals have developed regarding input?

Input is a function of attention.   The information cannot become part of a memory store unless it has somehow come under attention.

A major proposal regarding attention is that some attention is involuntary, or stimulus-determined, while other stimuli are attended to as a result of choice.   Both of these concepts can be subsumed under the more general heading of selective attention: that is, the particular stimulus attention (input) shown may result from the properties of the stimulus or the receiver.

A related proposal has been called filter theory.   This suggests that physiological mechanisms and conscious choice may predispose the organism to attend to certain stimuli while ignoring others.   This proposal has generated a great deal of research that has attempted to determine the properties of the filter.

15.18 What physiological evidence seems to support the filter theory concept?

At least two types of physiological evidence support the proposal of a filter theory.   One shows how the reticular activating system (RAS) selectively "passes on" stimulus inputs—and especially those that are sudden, novel, or important for survival—to higher cortical areas.   At both the RAS and higher cortical levels, there is evidence for selectivity that has been described as *sensory gating*.

A second relevant line of evidence is that there appear to be specialized receptors that are particularly likely to respond to certain stimulus properties (e.g., horizontal, angular, or corner properties).   These receptors have been called *feature-detector mechanisms*.   These mechanisms, which are specialized to respond to particular stimulus features, operate in a manner similar to the filtering concept described above.

15.19 In addition to physiological evidence, what other lines of research have supported filter theory?

Filter theory has been supported by results obtained in perceptual-analysis studies, scanning studies (such as those mentioned in Chapter 14), shadowing studies, and research on divided attention (also called listen-and-report studies).   All of these have demonstrated the selectivity of attention proposed by filter theory, suggesting input may be a function of many different properties of the environment and the receiving organism.

15.20   What is the major difficulty with filter theory?   What kinds of research point out this difficulty?   Describe an alternative proposal that tries to account for the difficulty.

Filter theory usually suggests an all-or-none reception of information.   Thus, if a shadowing study has the subject report one channel of information, filter theory would propose that information in another channel would not receive attention.   However, not all research results support this proposal.   Subjects will show some attention to and reception of information in the second channel, for example, when the second channel message includes the subject's name.

An alternative proposal is called the attenuation filter.   This suggests that all incoming messages are analyzed to some extent and compared to some threshold of reception.   "Special" messages (for example, those containing the subject's name) will be received even though instructions indicate some other channel should predominate.   Context and content become important in determining attention and help explain why reception is not always filtered on an all-or-none basis.

15.21   What term is used to describe a unit of information?   What limits do humans appear to show regarding the number of items of information they can process at one time?

A unit of information has come to be called a bit—the amount of information needed to make a decision between two equal alternatives.   (Bit is a contraction of *bi*nary digi*t*.)

Research on immediate memory span has indicated that humans can hold 7 ± 2 items of information to be processed at any given time.   Because of the ability to chunk information into relatively large components, immediate memory may contain many units of information.   It has been proposed that actual attention—that is, immediate consciousness rather than memory span—may be limited to a single unit of information at any given time.   However, what constitutes a unit of information may vary with the complexity of the task.   The nature of processing information may change from task to task.

15.22   Describe how computer programs can be written to simulate human chunking behavior.

Humans can increase the absolute size of the immediate-memory span by recoding the materials into larger blocks, or chunks, of materials.   If an appropriate program is written, the computer can simulate this.   The computer may group several stimuli because they share some common feature.   The computer may also encode materials according to some rewording process.   In either case, the computer mimics the way humans chunk materials.

15.23   Distinguish between algorithms and heuristics.

Algorithms are sets of rules or procedures which, if followed, are certain to lead to the solution of a particular type of problem.   Every possible alternative is considered.   Heuristics are suggestions of how to attack a problem.   They are guides that may prove efficient or successful, but there is no guarantee a solution will be reached.

15.24   Scientists have programmed computers to play chess at a very sophisticated level.   Are these chess-playing programs based on algorithms or heuristics?

The programs for chess-playing depend upon evaluating each move, weighing the effects of alternative solutions, and recalling experiences with board moves encountered in preceding games.   As such, they cannot provide absolute guarantee of an eventual winning solution, and thus represent heuristic methods rather than algorithms.   However, by trying different heuristics and continuing to improve the program, scientists have made the computer a very worthy chess opponent, capable of competing with master players.   (*Note:* It has been suggested that because of the many possible combinations of moves in chess, a complete, exhaustive, and guaranteed winning search for a single game could not be completed within a human lifetime, even using the fastest computer now available.)

15.25   For what purpose was the General Problem Solver (GPS) developed?   What are the basic processes of the GPS?

The General Problem Solver was developed to try to simulate what humans do when solving problems.   By attempting to find components common to many different problem-solving tasks and using them in one model (the GPS), it was hoped that the strategies or tactics of human problem solving could be identified.

There are two basic processes that repeat in cycles until a problem is solved or abandoned as too difficult by the GPS.   The first, called problem-solving organization, consists of setting subgoals that might help solve the problem at hand.   Having selected a subgoal, the program moves to the second process, called means-end analysis.   Here the attempt is to use appropriate heuristics to achieve the subgoal.   If this latter process fails, new subgoals are sought.   If successful, the next subgoal is set and the process repeats.

Key Terms

Algorithm.   A set of rules that guarantees a solution to a problem.

Artificial intelligence.   The construction of computer programs to maximize performance of a task.

Attenuation filter.   A physiological filter affecting attention which is thought to perform an evaluative operation.

Bit.   The amount of information that allows a decision between two equal alternatives; abbreviation for *bi*nary dig*it*.

Chunking.   Grouping or blocking together items of information in order to consolidate them.

Filter theory.   The proposal that either physiological properties or choice mechanisms of the individual create selective attention.

General Problem Solver (GPS).   A program intended to simulate the core processes used by humans in problem-solving behavior.

Hardware.   The physical components of a computer.

Heuristics.   Promising, economical approaches to problem solving; "rules of thumb" for attacking a problem.

Immediate consciousness.   Actual attention to or processing of information.

Immediate-memory span.   The amount of material that can be held in immediate memory at one time; believed to equal 7 ± 2 units of information.

Information.   Any event that reduces uncertainty.

Input.   The reception and resulting acquisition of information.

Means-ends analysis.   The use of heuristics to try to reach a goal or subgoal established by problem-solving organization.

Memory search.   Inspection of the memory store by the computer, followed by activation of elements appropriate for the program.

Memory store.   The location of information in the hardware of a computer.

Multiple processing.   Simultaneous performance of more than one task.

Output.   Responses which indicate retrieval from storage.

Poll.   A yes-no response mode indicating whether or not the information is present.

Processing.   Storage of information; transformation or loss of information may occur during this stage.

Random access.   Memory search by a computer program that uses a symbolic address code to determine which elements to probe; also called associative or content-addressable memory.

Routines.   The manipulations or processing of information by a computer.

Sensory gates.   A name for physiological filters affecting attention; essentially all-or-none operation is attributed to these.

Sequential access.   Memory search by the computer program along a built-in sequence in memory store; also called nonassociative or location-addressable memory.

Simulation.   The construction of computer programs to imitate (mimic) human behavior.

Software.   Programs written for a computer.

Timesharing.   Switching back and forth between two tasks; success depends upon how well the nonprocessed task can be held in STM.

Chapter 16

Acquisition and Retention:
Other Viewpoints

The last five chapters have dealt with the most widely accepted theories of acquisition and retention. This chapter briefly presents three more approaches that have gained some favor, although not as much as the previously discussed theories. In general, these three approaches have a somewhat more mathematical or mechanical basis than those discussed before.

16.1 CYBERNETICS

One approach to acquisition and retention has stressed the importance of *feedback* in learning. Called *cybernetics,* this proposal adopts an input-processing-output format similar to that described in the last chapter. It differs, however, in that emphasis is placed on a "feedback loop," where output is evaluated as part of subsequent input, and adjustments are made accordingly. Figure 16-1 illustrates the basic feedback loop proposal.

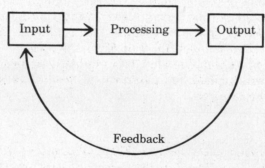

Fig. 16-1

The combination of the new input and the feedback is considered to determine subsequent processing, so the organism is *self-regulating*. In other words, the organism will continue to function until environmental conditions indicate that performance should be stopped or otherwise modified. (*Note:* Any system that "shuts off" automatically after a prescribed period of time is called *regulated,* as opposed to self-regulated.)

EXAMPLE 1. A well-trained race car driver illustrates the feedback principle stressed here. The input from environmental conditions brings about reactions such as steering adjustments or braking. These reactions, in turn, create new environmental conditions (such as changes in speed or direction) that are evaluated and acted on by the driver. In other words, the driver responds not only to external inputs (such as weather conditions or curves in the road) but to his own previous responses as well (including his own steering, braking, and accelerating responses).

The TOTE Sequence

The TOTE sequence, standing for *T*est-*O*perate-*T*est-*E*xit, includes all the basic processes of a feedback system. Developed by George Miller and his associates, the TOTE sequence is really the simplest form of what may be a more elaborate sequence. When the first test indicates some operation is necessary to bring conditions into synchronization with some environmental standard, the operation is made and followed by a second test. However, if the second test indicates the appropriate condition has not been achieved, another operation-and-test sequence will occur. Only when the appropriate conditions are reached will the exit phase, or termination, occur. Thus, the sequence may appear as TOTOTOTE, for example.

EXAMPLE 2. Suppose a gardener wants to have a weed-free bean patch. Upon arriving at the garden, she first tests to determine if there are any weeds present. If she spots some, an operation (weeding) is necessary. When the operation is complete, a second (later) test is made to discover if any weeds were missed. If some are located, the operation-test sequence is repeated. If no weeds are found, the gardener exits.

Plans and images. The operations made during a TOTE sequence are thought to be a function of *plans* and, indirectly, *images.* Plans are defined as the human counterpart of a computer's program—that is, the format for responding and the standards used for judging the success or failure of the results of those responses. Images are the accumulated knowledge the organism has about itself and its environment. Images help determine the plan chosen or alternates to be tried if the first plan is not successful.

16.2   STIMULUS SAMPLING THEORY

William Estes developed a mathematical approach to learning based to a great extent upon the work of Edwin Guthrie, discussed in Section 2.4. This approach has been referred to as a *stimulus sampling theory.* Like Guthrie, Estes believed that the contiguous occurrence of stimulus and response, even in the absence of reinforcement, was enough for conditioning to take place. He simplified Guthrie's proposals by considering responses only as productive or non-productive—that is, on the basis of whether or not an outcome was achieved. Estes believed that stimuli consisted of many elements, but that identification of the elements was not important. He did try to estimate what proportion of stimulus elements might be sampled on any given trial. The probability of a response being made was a function of how many stimulus elements had been paired contiguously with the response.

Theta (Θ)

Perhaps the most important assumption of Estes' stimulus sampling theory (other than the acceptance of S-R contiguity as sufficient for conditioning) is that a proportion of the total number of stimulus elements will be sampled on each trial, and that this proportion can be estimated. Estes labelled this proportion *theta* (Θ). When the value of theta is 1, all learning would take place in one trial; as the value of theta approaches 0, more and more trials would be required. The likelihood of responding (because of S-R conditioning) was seen as a function of the number of stimulus elements sampled.

Estes believed that the change in the number of elements sampled for any given trial was a function of the proportion of elements so far left unsampled at the beginning of that trial. Estes used the following formula to summarize this relationship:

$$\Delta X = \Theta(S - X)$$

The formula states that the change in the number of stimulus elements sampled (ΔX) will be equal to the difference between the total number of possible elements (S) and those already sampled (X) times whatever value has been assigned to Θ.

EXAMPLE 3. Suppose that a psychologist believed that on each trial a subject would sample one of every ten elements in a stimulus complex of 50 elements. Because the theta value is 0.1, five elements would be sampled on the first trial, four or five on the next, and four on the next. At the same time, the likelihood of responding would increase correspondingly.

Trial one:	$\Delta X = 0.1(50 - 0)$	$= 5$
Trial two:	$\Delta X = 0.1(50 - 5)$	$= 4.5$ (4 or 5 elements sampled)
Trial three:	$\Delta X = 0.1(50 - 9.5)$	$= 4.05$ (4 elements sampled)

After trial one, a total of five elements would have been sampled. After trial two, the total would be nine or ten, and after trial three it would be 13 or 14.

Estes also developed a formula to predict the likelihood of responding. In it, the change in the likelihood (ΔP) is equal to the estimated proportion of stimulus elements sampled on each trial (Θ) times the difference between 1 (perfect responding) and P (response probability on the previous trial).

$$\Delta P = \Theta(1 - P)$$

EXAMPLE 4. Using the same assumed theta value as that of Example 3, the change in probability of responding can be calculated for each successive trial.

$$
\begin{aligned}
\text{Trial one:} & \quad \Delta P = 0.1(1 - 0) & = 0.1 \\
\text{Trial two:} & \quad \Delta P = 0.1(1 - 0.1) & = 0.09 \\
\text{Trial three:} & \quad \Delta P = 0.1(1 - 0.19) & = 0.081
\end{aligned}
$$

Thus, the probability of responding after three trials would be 0.271, the sum of the change in probability determined for the three trials.

EXAMPLE 5. If Examples 3 and 4 are compared, it can be seen that the two approaches produce comparable results:

Trial	Elements sampled	Stimulus complex	Probability (one trial)	Total elements sampled	Cumulative probability
one	5	50	0.1	5	0.1
two	4.5	50	0.09	9.5	0.19
three	4.05	50	0.081	13.55	0.271

Learning Curves

Estes' formulas can be used to predict the pattern of responding in an acquisition task. In many cases, the predictions obtained with these formulas are quite close to the learning curves obtained under actual testing conditions.

Relationship of Stimulus Sampling Theory to Other Variables

Attempts have been made to use stimulus sampling theory to account for major principles originally suggested by other theories. Some of the most important are presented in this section.

Stimulus generalization. The number of elements common to the original stimulus and the test stimulus will determine the amount of stimulus generalization obtained.

Differentiation. Differentiation occurs when there are no overlapping or common elements. However, research has shown that subjects can differentiate stimuli that appear to share common elements that should lead to some generalization. An explanation of this has to assume that the common elements are ignored or combined in differing fashions with the nonshared elements to form distinctive patterns.

Extinction. Stimulus sampling theory explains extinction as learning not to respond—that is, pairing stimulus elements with not responding.

Spontaneous recovery. To account for spontaneous recovery, stimulus sampling theory has to propose that not all the stimulus elements of conditioning are present or functional during extinction. Then, after a period of rest, these elements become part of the stimulus environment, thus provoking a response in proportion to the amount of the total stimulus complex they represent.

Forgetting. A similar explanation accounts for forgetting. Stimulus sampling theory proposes that the stimulus elements presented during the retention test somehow differ from those of the conditioning period, and therefore the response is not produced.

Reinforcement. The sole function of reinforcement in stimulus sampling theory is the determination of which responses are conditioned to which stimulus elements. There is no concern with concepts such as arousal or drive reduction.

EXAMPLE 6. The concept of stimulus sampling is often illustrated using drawings such as those in Fig. 16-2. For these particular representations, one could expect about 30-percent response strength in a test of stimulus generalization, based on the 6 (of 20) common elements shown for the two stimuli.

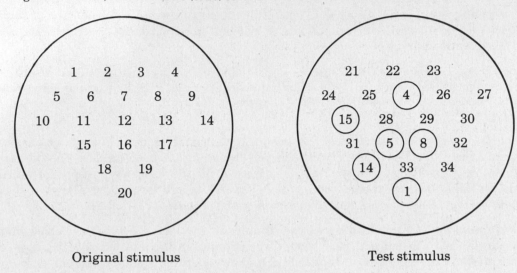

Original stimulus   Test stimulus

Fig. 16-2

16.3 SIGNAL-DETECTION THEORY AND DECISION THEORY

Judgments as to whether a stimulus is present or absent are not always easy to make, and two approaches to studying the problem have developed in the psychology of learning. When the major concern is with perceptual learning, the research has been summarized under the heading *signal-detection theory.* Investigations concerned with the decision-making processes have been called *decision theory* research. Both, however, have concentrated upon the same basic processes.

EXAMPLE 7. The difference of interpretation between signal detection and decision theories can be illustrated by examining how each is used to describe the same situation: During World War II, a major concern of the armed forces was the soldier's or sailor's ability to identify an approaching enemy craft. In one sense, being able to spot the enemy craft is simply a matter of detection—the more sensitive the observer, the better the detection process. In another sense, however, each detection really involves a decision: Is the stimulus (the enemy craft) really there, or would it be a mistake to say it was (and sound an alarm, for example)? The first interpretation above suggests signal-detection theory; the second suggests decision theory.

Detection vs. Threshold

In early perceptual research, the concept of *threshold* was very popular. Two aspects were considered. One, *absolute threshold,* was defined as the stimulus value that could be detected 50 percent of the time. The other, *difference threshold,* was defined as the minimum amount of change in a stimulus value necessary to be detected as a change. This latter value was often called a *just noticeable difference (j.n.d.).*

More recent research on signal detection has shown these concepts to be relatively unsophisticated. Both absolute and difference thresholds may vary, depending upon several different variables, which are described below.

Detection (Decision) Research

The research design for studying detection (decision) processes is quite simple.   For each trial, subjects are asked to respond "yes" or "no" regarding the presence (or change) of a stimulus.   To be certain that subjects do not respond arbitrarily, some trials involve no stimulus presentation. These are called *catch* trials.

There are four possible results in any given trial.   When the stimulus is present and the subject responds "yes," a *hit* response is made.   If the subject says "no" when the stimulus is present, it is called a *miss*.   For catch trials, a "no" represents a *correct reject,* while a "yes" is called a *false alarm.*

EXAMPLE 8.   Suppose a novice SONAR operator pushes the button to sound "battle stations" when he hears an audio signal produced by a whale.   By mistaking this signal for that made by an enemy submarine, the operator has responded with a false alarm.   Recognizing the signal from the whale for what it was would be a correct reject.

Proportion of hits and false alarms.   Assuming other variables are held constant, the number of hits and false alarms will vary with the percentage of catch trials used in the research design.   As the proportion of catch trials is increased, the number of yes responses decreases accordingly.   This, in turn, means there will be fewer hits and fewer false alarms.   In other words, both hits and false alarms depend in part upon the *probability of the stimulus* occurring.

Signal intensity.   The probability of the stimulus is only one of several variables that can affect performance.   The subject's sensitivity to the stimulus is also affected by *signal intensity,* a term that refers to the strength of the stimulus and how distinguishable it is from surrounding (extraneous) stimuli.   In this type of research, irrelevant stimuli are often referred to as *noise.* The difference between a signal and the surrounding noise is considered to have psychological dimension, and is represented by the label d'.   As d' increases, accuracy of performance increases.

Receiver-operating-characteristic (ROC) curves.   Manipulation of the value of d' (the relationship of the signal to noise) and the proportion of catch trials will create an interaction that will determine the hits and false alarms obtained.   Such interactions have been graphically illustrated as *receiver-operating-characteristic (ROC) curves.* (Figure 16-3 shows several ROC curves.) It can be seen if d' is equal to 0, performance is determined exclusively by the proportion of actual stimulus presentations to catch trials.   As the d' value increases above 0, performance changes and the interaction becomes more and more noticeable.

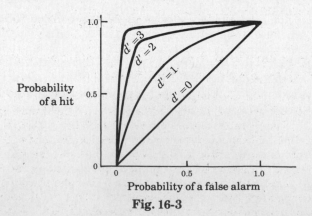

Fig. 16-3

Motivation.   One additional variable, that of the subject's *motivation,* has been found to be important in determining detection or decision processes.   Motivation has been studied in terms of *payoffs* (what it is worth to make a correct detection or decision) and *costs* (the penalty that will be invoked if an incorrect decision is made).   As the ratio of payoffs and costs varies, performance will change accordingly.

EXAMPLE 9.   It is fairly easy to understand how motivation might affect decision making.   The situation where any correct detection leads to a payoff while an incorrect decision is not penalized would produce "yes" responses any time there was a suspicion of a signal.   For example, an assistant who is told, "Call the supervisor at any time of day or night if you think the critical value may be reached," will be more likely to make false alarm responses than one who is told, "Do not bother the supervisor unless you are *certain* a critical value is reached."

Decision Processes as Learning Behavior

The research and theories described above have been interpreted as aspects of learning behavior.

Acquisition.   Because attention is a major consideration in any study of acquisition behavior, detection processes are considered important.   If the subject does not detect the signal, learning cannot take place.   Therefore, the variables affecting detection are important to acquisition.

Retention.   Comparably, detection of a correct answer can be an important part of retention. For example, when a recognition measure of retention is used, the d' value can be interpreted as the subject's sensitivity to correct memories as opposed to incorrect (distractor or noise) memories.

There are several different ways response selection may be interpreted. The *threshold-decision rule* states that a response will not be selected unless its strength of association with the stimulus (retrieval cue) exceeds some threshold value.   A variety of this is called the *high-threshold rule*.   This states that when the circumstances involve an extremely large number of response alternatives, the subject will respond only when the strength of association exceeds some high threshold value.

The *maximum-decision rule* is suggested for circumstances where more than one response may exceed threshold value.   In this case, the response with the greatest strength of association is demonstrated.   The maximum-decision rule is likely to be applied to situations having a defined number of response alternatives and a lower criterion for the threshold value—that is, circumstances unlike those where the high-threshold rule is applied.

EXAMPLE 10.   The judges in a beauty contest probably apply a maximum-decision rule of some sort when making their choice regarding the winner.   It is likely that all of the contestants surpass the threshold criterion.   Therefore, selection must be made on the basis of which contestant has the maximum values.

Solved Problems

16.1   Many psychologists have used the example of a household thermostat to illustrate the concept of cybernetics.   Explain how this can be done.

Cybernetics refers to the application of feedback theory to the study of human learning.   Performance is judged to be a result of internal regulations that result from both input and observation of subsequent output.   The operation of a thermostat mirrors this concept nicely.   Input, in the form of a temperature reading, indicates whether or not a particular standard is being met.   If it is (for example, if the room is warm enough), the feedback indicates the furnace should be off.   If the standard is not met, the furnace should be activated until an appropriate level, received as feedback by the thermostat, is reached.   (The reader will recognize the similarity of this approach to the information processing theory presented in Chapter 15.   This additional presentation is given only to indicate how some psychologists have stressed the feedback aspect of the sequence.)

16.2   Explain how a person who sat on some splinters might demonstrate a TOTE sequence.

The TOTE sequence represents basic feedback operation.   Standing for Test-Operate-Test-Exit, the expression describes the self-regulated feedback series that will be followed until a problem is resolved.   In the problem at hand, the initial test would be to determine if splinters were implanted.

If located, a removal operation would occur.   A second test would then be made to discover if they all were removed.   If not, the operation-test sequence would be repeated.   When the test indicated all splinters were gone, the exit phase, or termination of the sequence, could occur.

16.3   How do plans and images play a part in the TOTE sequence?

Essentially, a plan establishes both the behavioral sequences to be used and the standards against which the results will be judged.   Images, the total "programming" of a person's experiences, contribute by helping to determine the plan that is selected or by providing additional ways of approaching the problem if the plan must be modified.

16.4   Explain how the stimulus sampling approach of Estes is similar to Guthrie's contiguity theory.   What major modifications did Estes make in the contiguity approach?

The core of the mathematical approach developed by Estes was that the mere contiguity of responses and stimulus elements was sufficient for conditioning to occur.   This is comparable to Guthrie's viewpoint, but differs because Estes concentrated only on the result of the responses made: he categorized responses only on the basis of whether or not they produced a particular outcome. This two-class division of responses was unlike Guthrie's explanation of responses as acts composed of many components (movements).   Additionally, although Estes accepted the concept of many stimulus components, he did not show concern for identifying them.

16.5   Based upon the differences cited in the solution given in Problem 16.4, show how Estes presented a precise mathematical representation of the contiguous-conditioning principle originally suggested by Guthrie.

Guthrie's theory emphasized that the contiguity of stimulus elements with response components was sufficient for conditioning to occur on any given trial.   This was all-or-none conditioning, but because there were many stimulus elements and many response components to be connected, the conditioning of an act (the total response) might require many trials.

Estes simplified the interpretation of the response to either responding (producing an outcome) or not responding (not producing an outcome).   All stimulus elements are linked by conditioning to one of these two states.   The amount of change from one state to the other was represented by the number of connections between stimulus elements and the response made on any given trial.   This number of connections or responses made could be compared to the total number of stimulus elements that could be sampled on any given trial, and the resultant proportion could be calculated.   (Estes labelled this proportion theta, or Θ.)   Therefore, the likelihood of responding is a function of the total number of elements linked to a response (or sampled) during conditioning.

16.6   If Θ equals 0.2, what would be the likelihood of responding on the third trial of conditioning?

For the first trial, 0.2 of all the stimulus elements would be sampled and linked to the response, leaving 0.8 unsampled.   The second trial would have 0.2 of the remaining 0.8 sampled (0.16), and a total of 0.36 would have been sampled.   On the third trial, 0.2 of the remaining 0.64 would be sampled (0.128), bringing the total of sampled elements, and therefore the likelihood of responding, to 0.488.

16.7   Show how substituting P for the ratio of already conditioned stimulus elements (X) to all possible stimulus elements (S) produces the basic probability-of-responding formula in Estes' stimulus sampling theory.

As described in the preceding two problems and their solutions, the likelihood of responding can be evaluated as the number of stimulus elements sampled at any given moment in conditioning. The number sampled for any trial can be expressed by the formula $\Delta X = \Theta(S - X)$, with X representing the already sampled elements and S all the stimulus elements possible.   The change in the number of elements sampled on any given trial is equal to the proportion of elements that can be sampled multiplied by the number of elements not yet sampled.

If the probability of responding is represented as $P = X/S$, substitution into the formula above produces the equation $\Delta PS = \Theta(S - PS)$, which when reduced by (divided by) S on both sides becomes $\Delta P = \Theta(1 - P)$.   The change in the probability of responding for any given trial is equal to the theoretical proportion selected (Θ) times whatever increase in response probability is still possible.

16.8   Using the stimulus sampling theory, explain generalization and differentiation.

Stimulus sampling theory provides a satisfactory framework for explaining stimulus generalization: the more stimulus elements the original stimulus and the test stimulus share in common, the greater the likelihood of responding.   The theory is not as satisfactory for explaining differentiation, however, especially if perfect discrimination is shown in the responding to two stimuli that share some common elements.   It is necessary to assume that the subject somehow either ignores the overlapping elements or else responds to some pattern of stimuli rather than just elements.   Both of these assumptions have a cognitive "flavor" and may, once again, point to the distinction between nominal stimuli (what they appear to be) and functional stimuli (what actually operates in this situation).

16.9   How does the distinction between nominal and functional stimuli fit with explanations of extinction, forgetting, and spontaneous recovery that are made using stimulus sampling theory?

In stimulus sampling theory, extinction simply becomes a counterconditioning situation.   The subject learns that *not* responding to the stimulus elements is appropriate.   However, both spontaneous recovery and forgetting require the nominal-functional distinction indicated above.   It is suggested that spontaneous recovery occurs because stimulus elements that were not part of the functional stimulus during extinction (but *were* during conditioning) reappear, thus provoking the response in proportion to the total number of elements.   Forgetting may occur when the nominal stimulus used as a retrieval cue is seemingly the same as during conditioning, but the functional stimulus actually differs from that of conditioning.

16.10   What function does reinforcement serve according to the stimulus sampling theory?

The only effect of reinforcement considered important for stimulus sampling theory is that it determines which responses become conditioned to which stimulus elements.   Other considerations, such as drive reduction or optimal arousal, are not thought to be important.

16.11   Explain why detection and decision are basically the same process when studied experimentally.

Several threads of research brought detection studies and investigations of decision processes together.   Detection studies were originally concerned with identification of perceptual threshold values or practical applications in transportation or war situations.   (For example, is there a "blip" on the radar screen?)   These gave way later to studies that attempted to determine the factors that affected why the subject might say yes or no—that is, made a particular decision.

16.12   Sketch the two-by-two matrix that represents the "typical" research design for studying decision theory (signal-detection theory).   Explain how each quadrant would be studied.

The usual research design for studying detection theory is represented in Fig. 16-4.   The subject makes a correct response in quadrants 1 and 4, identifying appropriately the presence or absence of a stimulus.   In quadrants 2 and 4 a catch trial is used, with no stimulus presented.   When the subject says yes to a catch trial, this inappropriate response is called a false alarm.   In quadrants 1 and 3 the stimulus is present.   If the subject says no, a miss has occurred.   Several reasons (presented below) may account for the miss.   It should be noted that even the most sincere and well-trained subjects make both misses and false alarms.

Stimulus

		Present	Absent
Response	Yes	Hit 1	False alarm 2
	No	Miss 3	Correct reject 4

Fig. 16-4

16.13   Subjects in one group (A) of an experiment were given 90-percent stimulus-present trials and 10-percent stimulus-absent (catch) trials.   Subjects in a second group (B) received 75-percent stimulus-present trials and 25-percent catch trials.   Motivation and stimulus intensity were held the same for both groups.   Which group should show the highest hit percentage?   Which group should show the highest false-alarm rate?

Group A will show both the highest hit percentage and the highest false-alarm rate.   Repeated research studies have shown that as the number of catch trials is increased, the proportion of yes responses diminishes accordingly—for both correct and incorrect circumstances.

16.14   What term describes the graphical representation of the results described in the solution to Problem 16.13?   What variable affects the shape of the curve obtained?

The graphical representation of the relationship between the probability of hits and the probability of false alarms is called a receiver-operating-characteristic (ROC) curve.   The shape of the ROC curve will depend upon the signal intensity value used and how that signal contrasts with surrounding noise.

16.15   Describe, by sketching distributions, a high-noise and a low-noise situation.

The subject's sensitivity to a signal can depend, in part, on the amount of interference or noise that exists to impede reception or recognition of the stimulus.   Interference is less in a low-noise situation, as sketched below in the distribution shown in Fig. 16-5(a).   Interference is much greater for the high-noise situation, shown in Fig. 16-5(b).   The value d' indicated on the sketches represents sensitivity differences—or in some studies may be thought to represent memory strength for two different S-R situations.

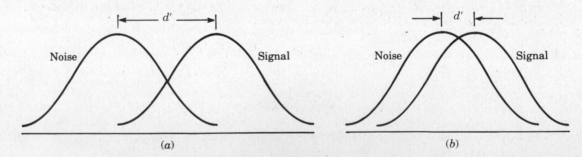

Fig. 16-5

16.16   In the last two problems, stimulus intensity, noise, and the probability that the signal will occur are all seen to affect the detection (decision) process.   What other major variable has also been found to be very important in determining this process?   How is this usually described in research on this topic?

In addition to the probability of the signal, the intensity of the signal, and the difference between the signal and surrounding noise, the subject's motivation has been found to be important in determining the detection (decision) process.   In research on this topic, motivation often is studied in terms of the payoffs and costs of the decision made.

16.17 Multiple-choice (recognition) tasks often have a single correct answer and three "distractor" items. Explain how the calculation of hit and false-alarm rates could be used to determine how "close" to the correct answer the distractors were judged to be.

Using the hit and false-alarm rates, d' can be calculated.   This can be viewed as the difference in average memory strength for the correct items compared to the distractors.   Said another way, one can determine how much noise the distractors create.   Regardless of the criterion a subject establishes for accepting an answer, the d' value allows an estimate of both recognition memory strength and the effectiveness of the distractors.

16.18 Distinguish between the maximum rule for recognition memory and the high-threshold rule.

The maximum rule for recognition memory is applied when there are a defined number of alternatives from which to select the response. Simply stated, the subject chooses the response having maximum familiarity.   When there appears to be an unlimited or at least poorly defined number of response choices available, the high-threshold rule may apply.   This states that a response is selected only if the S-R association strength exceeds some high threshold.

16.19 If students taking an exam use the maximum rule, what type of error is most likely to be made?   What type of error would be most likely if the high-threshold rule is applied?

Because the maximum rule is more likely to be used in conjunction with lower threshold values, the errors made are going to be errors of commission—that is, selection of incorrect alternatives.   On the other hand, when the high-threshold rule is applied, the errors made are more likely to be errors of omission—that is, no response.   (*Note:* Instructors sometimes encourage the use of one or the other of these rules by establishing some standard regarding the penalties for guessing.)

16.20 Summarize the principles of signal-detection theory by explaining why the word threshold really means some flexible or "sliding" standard against which judgments are made.

Early theories in perception proposed both absolute thresholds (present-absent) and rigid difference thresholds (just-noticeable differences).   But the research in signal-detection situations has shown how the decision threshold varies according to the probability the signal will be present or absent, the amount and quality of distraction compared to the strength of the signal, and the payoffs and costs associated with correct and incorrect responding.   Any statements regarding detection or memory probably should be preceded by a phrase such as, "given the following circumstances . . ." This would take into account the variables mentioned above.

Key Terms

Absolute threshold.   The lowest value at which a stimulus is detected 50 percent of the time.

Correct reject.   In detection research, the situation that occurs when the stimulus is not present and the subject responds that it is not.

Cost.   The penalty that will be administered if an incorrect decision is made in detection research.

Cybernetics.   A description of any learning system that contains a feedback loop.

d'.   The value representing the relationship of the signal to noise.

Difference threshold.   The minimum amount of change in a stimulus value necessary to be detected as change.

False alarm.   In detection research, the situation that occurs when the stimulus is not present and the subject responds that it is.

Feedback. Knowledge of the consequences of a response or series of responses; may modify subsequent responding.

Feedback loop. The technique of including evaluation of output from one trial as part of the input for the next trial.

High-threshold rule. In detection research, when there are many possible responses, the finding that a response will not be given unless the S-R association value for that response exceeds a particularly high criterion.

Hit. In detection research, the situation that occurs when the stimulus is present and the subject responds that it is.

Image. In feedback theory, the accumulated knowledge the organism has about itself and its environment.

Just noticeable difference (j.n.d.). Another name for difference threshold.

Maximum-decision rule. In detection research, when more than one S-R association value exceeds the criterion, the finding that the response with the greatest strength of association will be demonstrated.

Miss. In detection research, the situation that occurs when the stimulus is present and the subject responds that it is not.

Noise. In detection research, any irrelevant stimuli.

Payoff. In detection research, what it is worth to make a correct decision.

Plan. In feedback theory, the human counterpart of a computer program; the format for responding and criteria for judging the success of the responses.

Receiver-operating-characteristic (ROC) curves. The graphical representation of the relationship between the probability of hits and the probability of false alarms.

Theta (Θ). In stimulus sampling theory, the (estimated) proportion of stimulus elements that can be sampled in any one trial.

Threshold. The level of stimulation necessary for reception to occur.

Threshold-decision rule. In detection research, the finding that a response will not be given unless the S-R association value surpasses some criterion.

TOTE sequence. Representing Test-Operate-Test-Exit; all the basic processes of a feedback system.

PART V: Extensions of Acquisition and Retention

Many psychologists feel that the acquisition-storage-retrieval sequence cannot be treated as a static process. The three chapters of this part present some of the principles illustrating how learning can be dealt with as a dynamic process.

Chapter 17 presents the major delineations of motivation and assesses the effects of motivation on performance. A number of important variables are considered in an attempt to show the widespread influences of motivational variables on learning.

Chapters 18 and 19 deal with what are often called the cognitive aspects of learning. In Chapter 18 the basic considerations of language learning are presented in terms of both perception of speech and acquisition of language skills. Chapter 19 focuses on the nature of thinking and mental operations, then goes on to present some aspects of problem-solving behavior. Certain characteristics of tasks used to study these topics are also discussed.

Chapter 17

Learning and Motivation

This chapter emphasizes only one of the two major relationships between learning and motivation studied by psychologists: the effects of motivation on learning. Psychologists study the effects of learning upon motivation as well, but such an approach to the topic is more appropriate for a book concentrating on motivation.

17.1 MOTIVATION AS A CONCEPT

Motivation is often defined as any internal condition that initiates, guides, and maintains a response. It must be treated as a concept because motive properties cannot be observed directly. Motivation is inferred from antecedent conditions and consequent responses.

EXAMPLE 1. Suppose that by mistake a family leaves its dog, Princess, alone in the backyard for the entire day. When the family members realize what they've done, they worry because they know that Princess will be "hungry" and "thirsty," words which represent motive conditions. And later in the day, when Princess is offered food and water and heartily consumes both, the assumption that she was motivated appears to be supported. It should be recognized, however, that the terms "hungry" and "thirsty" are labels that summarize conditions and predict subsequent reactions. What the dog's exact motivational condition is—either physiologically or psychologically—cannot be determined.

Motivation as Arousal

Perhaps the most common view of motivation is that it is a function of *arousal*—the general level of alertness and muscular tension in an organism. Arousal may be either appetitive or aversive.

Appetitive arousal. Conditions that initiate and maintain behaviors attempting to achieve goals are evidence of *appetitive arousal.*

Aversive arousal. Conditions that initiate and maintain responses attempting to avoid unpleasant or negative conditions are evidence of *aversive arousal.*

EXAMPLE 2. A man who consumes milkshakes and heavy desserts even though he does not enjoy them might be responding to aversive arousal in the form of a feeling that he is too thin.

It should be recognized that appetitive and aversive arousal may each generate either positive or negative emotions.

EXAMPLE 3. The man described in Example 2 may indeed react to an aversive arousal (feeling too thin) and judge added weight favorably. At the same time, however, there may be negative emotional components associated with the responding, such as resenting the amount of money that he must spend to buy all the calorie-laden foods.

Motivation as Drive Reduction

The only difference between this interpretation and that of motivation as arousal is that *drive reduction* focuses on the consequences of the actions rather than the activation of the behavior. *Drive* is treated as a physiological or psychological state resulting from some *need,* a physiological or psychological deficit or imbalance. Reactions to motivation are made to reduce the drive condition.

Motivation as Incentive

A more complex interpretation of motivation involves the concepts of drive and reinforcement (any event that increases or maintains the strength of a response). *Incentive* is defined as the combination of a drive and some associated reinforcement. Motivation is the desire to arrive at the incentive. Satisfaction comes from doing so, rather than from drive reduction.

Motivation in Operant Conditioning

Yet another way to interpret motivation is to use the operant conditioning approach. In this case, motivation is any condition that makes a stimulus reinforcing. The emphasis is on the effects of reinforcement (for example, increasing or maintaining response strength), and not on the actual motivational condition.

17.2 MEASUREMENT OF MOTIVATION

Although attempts are made to estimate the strength of the motive conditions operating in a given situation, motive strength cannot be measured directly. Some of the indirect methods of measurement are presented here.

Motivation Measured by Amount of Deprivation

A desire to quantify the measurement of motivation has frequently led to the use of *amount of deprivation* as a way of estimating motivation. Deprivation (meaning doing without) is measured as the time since the last satisfaction. Even this is difficult, however, because the last reinforcement may or may not be sufficient to produce *satiation* (complete satisfaction). Care must be taken to determine all the possible influences upon the measurement of deprivation.

EXAMPLE 4. Research on motivation often uses hours of deprivation as the measure of motivation. Groups of subjects are divided equally before the deprivation period begins and then are tested at varying intervals later. Each subgroup experiences a different amount of deprivation and, presumably, a different level of motivation. Variables such as hunger or thirst are the ones studied most frequently with this type of procedure, although it could conceivably be used to measure the motivational strength that has developed since the last party one attended, since one's last sexual experience, or since one was last out of debt.

Motivation Measured from Behavior

Certain motives cannot be measured in terms of deprivation. It is necessary to observe the subsequent responses and infer the motive conditions from them.

EXAMPLE 5. A phrase describing a child as showing an "especially high level of aggressiveness" implies there is a motive of aggressiveness. Devising a way of measuring such a characteristic in terms of deprivation would be unwieldy, but the assumption of such a motive from observation of the child's behavior is both possible and reasonable.

Respondent and Operant Components of Motivation Measurement

Identification and measurement of motives may be at least partially dependent upon previous respondent or operant conditioning. When the stimulus components have been previously paired with a particular interpretation of their meaning, reintroduction of the stimuli may yield that same interpretation. Additionally, the responses of recognizing and labelling a stimulus situation may be reinforced as operants.

EXAMPLE 6. In the first few months of life, a child's smile is almost certainly elicited—i.e., it is a respondent component of the child's response to pleasure. As the child grows older, however, smiling may become an operant, demonstrated in situations where smiling is reinforced. Thus, even though the child may not like to have Aunt Ruth affectionately pinch his cheek, he may smile dutifully because such a response will be reinforced.

17.3 RELATIONSHIP OF MOTIVATION AND PERFORMANCE

Regardless of the particular motivation-performance combination, research supports a general finding that performance will increase with increased level of motivation up to some fairly high level, but that exceedingly high levels of motivation produce poor performance.

EXAMPLE 7. Students who are first-time members of a large lecture class may experience the reaction of "clutching" when the instructor calls upon them to recite in class. Previous experience in small classes has not provided sufficient background for the possibility of having to speak in front of so many peers, and although the motive level to do well may be exceedingly high, the subsequent performance is often poor.

The Yerkes-Dodson Law

The *Yerkes-Dodson law* (named for the investigators who developed it) states that as a task is judged more difficult, lower levels of motivation are required to produce maximum performance. Combining this finding with that stated above produces results such as those shown in Fig. 17-1. Note that the curves for all tasks show the characteristic inverted-U relationship between level of motivation and performance, with the position of the peak varying as a function of the difficulty of the task.

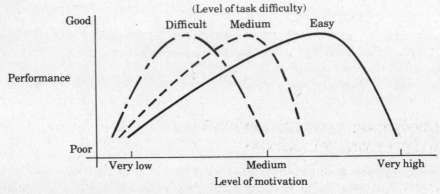

Fig. 17-1

Amount of Reinforcement

While the relationship between motivation and performance appears to be well established, differences in performance can be obtained when different reinforcement values are used. In general, it can be expected that *if* the level of motivation is the same for two comparable subjects (or groups of subjects), performance will be better for those receiving a better or higher level of reinforcement.

Contrast effects. One interesting variation of the effects of reinforcement is shown by the *contrast effects* illustrated in Fig. 17-2. Note that when the level of reinforcement is shifted, performance shows a tendency to "overreact." That is, it shifts to a level somewhat beyond what would otherwise be expected. When the change goes beyond an improved level of performance, this is called *positive contrast.* Dropping below the expected poorer performance is called *negative contrast.* Both positive and negative contrast are often transitory states.

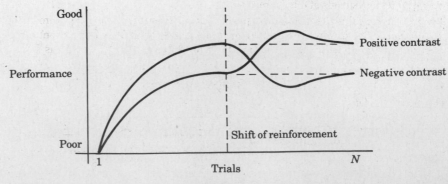

Fig. 17-2

EXAMPLE 8. Several groups of rats were trained to run a straight runway to receive differing levels of reinforcement (measured as the number of food pellets found in the goal box). After training, test trials were conducted in which all rats found only one food pellet in the goal box. Figure 17-3 shows that as the difference between training and test conditions increased, running speeds varied accordingly. This illustrates the negative contrast effect.

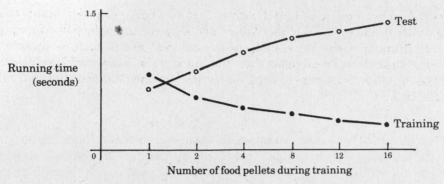

Fig. 17-3

17.4 STUDIES MEASURING THE EFFECTS OF MOTIVATION ON LEARNING

The previous section has shown that changes in motivation can be expected to produce changes in performance. This does not necessarily mean that the changes in motivation affect learning (habit strength). In general, to determine this, *transfer* designs are used to discover if the relatively permanent effects of the original learning influence the responses in some new situation.

Types of Transfer Designs

Several variations of transfer designs have been used. Training may be started under one level of motivation and then continued with some other level. Alternatively, training may be conducted using one level of motivation, followed by extinction using some other level, with resistance to extinction being the measure of learning. Training under one level of motivation also may be followed by a period of rest (a "forgetting" period), and then reconditioning with a different level of motivation may be used to measure the transfer from the first learning.

EXAMPLE 9. The experimental design represented by the 2 × 2 chart in Fig. 17-4 illustrates the second procedure described above. A study such as this allows determination of both acquisition and extinction drive conditions in responding. The totals at the end of each row show the sum of all subjects' responses at the end of 2 hours' training (Σ 2 Tr.) or 20 hours' training (Σ 20 Tr.). The totals at the bottom of each column show comparable sums for periods of extinction.

The differences in the column totals reflect performance differences resulting from differences in motivation during *extinction*. The differences in the row totals reflect relatively permanent effects resulting from motivation differences during *training*. These latter differences can be thought of as learning differences.

Hours of deprivation in extinction

		2	20	
Hours of deprivation in training	2	$\Sigma(2,2)$	$\Sigma(2,20)$	Σ 2 Tr.
	20	$\Sigma(20,2)$	$\Sigma(20,20)$	Σ 20 Tr.
		Σ 2 Ex.	Σ 20 Ex.	

Fig. 17-4

Problem of Response Differences

Although the designs described above present ways of determining the effect of motivation upon learning, they make one assumption that may not be supported. The differing motivation conditions are supposed to be affecting the *same response,* but this may not be true. A number of research studies have indicated that subjects may be learning different forms of the same response. In such cases, comparisons of different groups may reveal the effects of motivation on learning different responses rather than the effects of motivation on the same response.

EXAMPLE 10. Rats trained to run through a maze may show different responses when performing under different levels of motivation. Those with low drive may engage in many extraneous responses. Those under high drive are likely to eliminate any competing or extraneous responses and concentrate on running the pattern that leads to the reinforcer.

Competing Responses

Yet another difficulty with measuring the effects of motivation on learning may result when the tasks used encourage the learning of competing responses. In general, subjects with low levels of motivation will do poorly in such circumstances, while those with higher levels will usually do about as well as they would in single-response tasks.

Effects of Fixed-Interval Schedules

The effects of a change of motivation during training may be masked if a fixed-interval (FI) schedule of reinforcement is used. Performance for subjects trained with a FI schedule typically illustrates the "scalloping" pattern of responding, with little or no responding at the beginning of the interval. Change in motivation may not affect such a pattern of responding because the schedule effects surmount those caused by the level of motivation.

17.5   VARIABLES INVESTIGATED RELATING LEARNING AND MOTIVATION

The relationship of motivation to learning has prompted many different types of studies investigating various variables connecting the two. Some of these are presented in this section.

Satiation

A number of studies have attempted to investigate the concept of *satiation,* the reduction of a drive level to zero. Several interesting results have been obtained. One indicates that for a number of different motivating conditions (hunger or thirst, for example) there may be *satiation centers* in the brain that signal when sufficient consumption has occurred. (These centers can indicate satiation before actual tissue satisfaction has been achieved.) Another study indicates that internal cues may be overridden by external cues so that responding will continue even after satiation has occurred.

A third type of study has shown that achieving satiation may not be the important consideration. Interpretations of motivation in terms of incentive rather than drive reduction show that maximizing positive incentives (pleasurable changes) may be more important than minimizing drive states. (Comparable findings have been suggested for negative incentive conditions.)

EXAMPLE 11. The incentive interpretation appears to be highly relevant when discussing sexual behavior. The responding to create a *transition* from a higher to a lower drive state seems to create greater pleasure than the lower drive state itself.

The Placebo Effect

A *placebo* is an inert substance that is administered as if it were active. If the subject responds in a manner that indicates a belief that the substance was active, the *placebo effect* has been shown.

EXAMPLE 12.   Dealers in illicit drugs have been known to take advantage of the placebo effect.   A person may ingest or smoke some substance with the expectation of achieving a drug effect.   Although the substance is actually inert, the person achieves a "high" anyway.

Functional Autonomy

When a response that was originally performed to satisfy some other motive becomes motivating in and of itself, *functional autonomy* exists.   In other words, the responding generates itself, even in the absence of the motive condition that first initiated it.

EXAMPLE 13.   The behavior of a miser can be used to illustrate the concept of functional autonomy.   Often the person may at first accumulate money in order to gain financial security or to satisfy some social motive, such as peer acceptance, through the accumulation of wealth.   In time, the responding itself may become motivating and, indeed, may become so important that the responses are made even when the original motives are no longer satisfied.   (The miser may keep his money in a mattress, which offers little security, and may through his actions earn the hatred of his peers rather than their acceptance.)

Cognitive Dissonance

When a person has two different feelings about the same stimulus or has two opposing items of information, *cognitive dissonance* is said to exist.   Studies in this area have shown that responses will be made to try to *reduce* the dissonance.   In other words, cognitive dissonance is motivating.   Generally, the greater the discrepancy, the greater the strength of motivation believed to exist.   However, the greater the justification for supporting the dissonant positions, the less the reduction of dissonance that can be expected.

EXAMPLE 14.   Suppose a woman believes that holding ethnic prejudices is incorrect, and she dislikes ethnic jokes.   She finds, however, that certain of her coworkers expect her to laugh at such jokes.   This creates cognitive dissonance.   The importance to the woman of acceptance into the working group will probably determine the amount of dissonance reduction.   If for her it is terribly important to be accepted, it will be much easier to accept the dissonance, and little reduction can be expected.   If acceptance is not very important to her, much greater dissonance reduction can be expected; for example, she may not even pretend to laugh when an ethnic joke is told.

Conflict

The effects of competing motive conditions upon behavior include *conflict*.   Usually, conflicts are resolved when the person chooses one of the competing motives as most important and responds according to it.

Approach-approach conflict.   When the person must choose between two motive conditions that have positive value, an *approach-approach conflict* is said to exist.

Avoidance-avoidance conflict.   If the competing motive conditions both have negative value, choosing which to respond to is called an *avoidance-avoidance conflict*.

Approach-avoidance conflict.   When a single stimulus has both positive and negative values, the choice of whether or not to respond to it (or how to respond) is described as an *approach-avoidance conflict*.   The situation is called a *multiple approach-avoidance conflict* when there is more than one stimulus involved, and each stimulus has both positive and negative values.

EXAMPLE 15.   Deciding whether or not to jump into a swimming pool may represent an approach-avoidance conflict.   The positive value is the pleasure of swimming and the cooling effect it will have.   The negative value is the shock of the radical change in temperature that must be experienced when one first enters the water.

Stress

One area of motivation that has been widely studied is *stress,* the experiences that follow noxious stimulation.   In general, research has shown that stress motivation will facilitate the learning of and continued performance of responses that alleviate the stress.   However, if the stress conditions break down, performance will be impaired.

It should be noted that stress often includes the concepts of anxiety and fear. While both are thought of as emotional reactions, anxiety is usually considered less definitive and weaker than fear.

Learned Helplessness

A particularly interesting area of research in motivation is that of *learned helplessness*. When the subject has been in an unpleasant or noxious situation for some time, and no coping response is possible, a change of the circumstances that allows successful escape or avoidance *does not* lead to the appropriate behavior. Apparently, once the subject learns that responding is futile, the behavior pattern carries over to the later stimulus situation.

EXAMPLE 16. Unusual family circumstances may lead a child to develop learned helplessness. When the parents punish the child regardless of what response is made, the child may soon learn that there is no coping response—that is, punishment is inevitable. Once these circumstances are changed (perhaps after court action and referral to a foster home), the child may continue to exhibit depression and an inability to cope even though responses would now be successful. (In many cases, it may be necessary to force such a child to recognize that coping behavior will work.)

Latent Learning

Originally studied in animal learning research, the principle of *latent learning* has now been demonstrated for many different species, including humans. Basically, the principle states that learning (the acquisition of responses) may take place but not be translated into performance unless there is an appropriate incentive.

Innate Responses

Several different areas of research have attempted to determine the effects of motive conditions on innate (unlearned) responses.

Instincts. Unlearned responses that are stimulus-specific, species-specific, and automatic when a *releaser stimulus* is present are called *instincts*.

Species-specific defense reactions (SSDRs). *Species-specific defense reactions (SSDRs)* are also unlearned. However, they are made to learned stimuli that have been identified as either safety signals or danger signals.

Brain stimulation. Implantation of electrodes into the brain and subsequent use of these to deliver electric shock may serve to generate both motivation and reinforcement (or aversive conditions). Apparently no learning is necessary for these effects to be produced.

EXAMPLE 17. Research using rats has shown that self-stimulation—for example, pressing a lever so that a mild and pleasant electric shock is delivered to the brain—may be positive and so dominant that the rat will ignore food even after a prolonged period of food deprivation. In some cases the rats are so involved with self-stimulation that they ignore the food that is set before them and starve to death.

Solved Problems

17.1   During a practice session in typing class, Philip works slowly and makes numerous errors. Two days later, when given a test of typing skills, Philip's performance is considerably faster and the number of errors he makes is considerably reduced. Give two interpretations of Philip's change in performance—one that attributes it to motivation and one that does not.

The solution to this problem makes two important points about motivation—first, that a change in performance *can* be attributed to some change in motivation, and second, that other variables must be accounted for before such an attribution is made.

Using a motivational interpretation, one might say that the change in Philip's performance results from a heightened desire to perform well (a change in motive strength). A nonmotivational interpretation might attribute the change to a considerable amount of practice or learning that went on during the period between the practice session and the test. Not until variables such as these latter ones have been accounted for can a motivational interpretation be accepted.

17.2   Why is it said that one can never observe a motive?

Motivation is a concept (a hypothetical construct). The characteristics of behavior observed in natural settings or experimental studies make it possible to infer motivation. But the behavior observed, such as changes in performance from one time to another or differences in the simultaneous performance of two different subjects, simply suggest the presence of a motive. They do not present direct evidence of that motive.

17.3   If motivation must be treated as a concept, or hypothetical construct, why do psychologists study changes in performance such as Philip's (Problem 17.1) as motivational investigations?

The solution to this problem is that there may be no alternative. Although the motive may not be directly observable, it may be necessary to explain a behavior in the absence of any other variables (such as learning or maturation) that could be used as explanations.

17.4   Distinguish between appetitive and aversive arousal definitions of motivation. Is it possible to think of each as capable of producing both positive and negative emotional components?

Appetitive arousal (or activation) is an internal condition that initiates and maintains a response that is aimed at achieving some goal. Aversive arousal results in attempts to avoid unpleasant or negative goals. Appetitive and aversive arousal may each produce both positive and negative emotional components. For example, although water may be thought of as a positive goal, the appetitive arousal to seek water may have negative emotional components: a person who is lost in the desert and feels there is no hope of finding water may become desperate or depressed. Correspondingly, even though it is accompanied by pain, a spanking may be considered pleasant by the child who regards it as a sign of a parent's interest and attention.

17.5   In Problem 17.4, both appetitive and aversive arousal can be interpreted as motives that promote behavior that will be drive-reducing. Explain the concept of drive reduction. Then describe the operant interpretation of motivation and differentiate it from the drive-reduction approach.

Drive reduction implies that the organism is experiencing some condition that provokes a behavior which will reduce some need—i.e., some physiological or psychological imbalance. The responses are made to achieve some goal that will lower (or eliminate) the need. For example, the seeking, finding, and consuming of food reduces the hunger drive.

Proponents of an operant interpretation of motivation discount the importance of drive reduction, defining motivation as any condition that makes a stimulus reinforcing. The emphasis is on the reinforcement effects (increasing or maintaining response strength) rather than on the motivational conditions. Motivation is important only as a part of the technology of behavior control.

17.6   Educational "enrichment" programs were started as attempts to offset the effects of poor learning environments. Relate such programs to concepts of motivation.

The basis for establishing enrichment programs was the belief that many children were living in deprivation conditions—that is, they were doing without the conditions necessary for learning experiences. Amount of deprivation is one way of measuring motivation. In this case, it was proposed that providing appropriate environmental circumstances to overcome the deprivation would promote successful learning experiences. The general principle is that deprivation creates motivation, while creating an environment that allows relief from that deprivation will lead to learning the responses needed.

17.7   Suppose two children seem to have comparable swimming skills, but when they attend a special summer training camp one improves markedly while the other continues to perform at precamp levels. Make a behavioral inference concerning the motive conditions operating in this situation.

If it can be presumed that other conditions are equivalent (this is a difficult assumption to make), the performances would seem to indicate that one child is more motivated to learn and improve than the other. Making inferences about motivation from behavior probably is less certain than measuring motivation in terms of deprivation, but such inferences are necessary when dealing with motive conditions that are not easily quantified in terms of deprivation.

17.8   Explain how the name of a motive may represent an operant response.

An operant of naming exists when an individual labels a motive and is reinforced for making that response. For example, a child may be rewarded by her parents for saying, "I'm sleepy." This reinforcement usually occurs only when the situation and the observable behavior of the person appear to be appropriate to the label given. It should be realized that unobservable stimuli also may be a part of the situation but will not contribute to the reinforcing agent's judgment of whether or not to deliver reinforcement.

17.9   How can the external environment establish stimulus control over the naming of a motive such as hunger?

The names of motives come to be responses to external environmental conditions as well as internal stimuli. In the case of hunger, the person might be much more likely to say, "I'm hungry," at a buffet dinner party than at a meeting of a weight-control group, even if the internal cues present were essentially equal for both occasions.

17.10   Consider this sentence: "I'm going inside to get warm." Does it illustrate the concept of need or the concept of drive?

It is probably safe to say that the sentence represents both concepts. Need is defined as a physiological or psychological imbalance or deficit. Drive is the physiological or psychological state resulting from the need. This sentence reflects both a physiological need (a lack of warmth) and a drive state to overcome that deficit.

17.11   Distinguish among the terms "reinforcement," "punishment," and "incentive."

A "reinforcement" is any event that increases or maintains the strength of a response. This may be the presence of some pleasant or appreciated stimulus (positive reinforcement) or the removal or termination of some aversive stimulus (negative reinforcement).

"Punishment" refers to the delivery of an aversive stimulus because a response that is judged inappropriate is made, leading to the aversive or unpleasant circumstance.

The term "incentive" is used to describe the combination of a drive and a related reinforcer. Thus, water is a reinforcer for thirst, but only serves as an incentive when the organism is actually thirsty.

17.12 If one accepts the definition of incentive given in Problem 17.11, what interpretation of motivation can be made using the concept of incentive achievement?

Motivation can be considered as the desire to attain the incentive, with the resultant satisfaction being the pleasure of achievement rather than the reduction of drive. In other words, the organism is not seeking to place itself in a driveless state as much as it is trying to achieve the pleasure associated with drive satisfaction.

17.13 Elizabeth is taking Biology 432 as an elective on a pass-fail basis; she needs to make only a minimum passing grade in order to get credit, and a high passing grade will get her no more credit than a low passing grade. Gregory is a Biology major in the same course, needing to make a good grade in order to "round out" his already high grade-point average in his required courses. Mark is taking Biology 432 for the third time, having withdrawn from the class during the two previous attempts. He knows he *must* do well or he will be disqualified from the premed program. Sketch the curve relating motivation to performance, then designate the places on that curve where each of the three students mentioned above might fall.

The relationship of motivation to performance is shown by the inverted-U curve illustrated in Fig. 17-5. The three students are shown in their predicted positions. Elizabeth, with low motivation, is expected to do moderately well at best. Gregory, with strong but controlled motivation, should do well. Mark, with exceedingly high motivation, will probably do quite poorly.

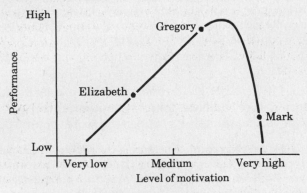

Fig. 17-5

17.14 If it can be said that Biology 432 (see Problem 17.13) creates a difficult task for Mark, what prediction would the Yerkes-Dodson law make regarding optimal performance by Mark?

The Yerkes-Dodson law proposes that as task difficulty increases, the optimal motivation level for maximum performance decreases. In Mark's case, the attempt should be made to find some way to reduce his level of motivation. Such a reduction should yield better performance levels.

17.15 Using the concepts of positive contrast and negative contrast, explain the effect that the amount of reinforcement will have upon performance levels.

Positive contrast and negative contrast involve shifts in levels of performance that occur when the amount of the reward is shifted. Positive contrast is "overshooting" and then adjusting to the higher (better) level of performance expected when the amount of reinforcement is higher. Negative contrast is "undershooting" and then adjusting to a lower (poorer) level of performance expected when the amount of reinforcement is lower. Basically, assuming comparable motivation conditions, performance can be expected to be better when reinforcement levels are higher; and will adjust, after a period of "contrast," when reinforcement amounts are changed.

17.16 Suppose a teacher is unsatisfied with the apparent progress of learning in a particular class. He announces that rather than taking biweekly exams, the class will have quizzes given every other day. The teacher then determines whether or not this change in technique has an effect upon the progress of learning. Which type of design studying the effects of motivation upon learning does this most closely illustrate? What other designs are often used?

  The teacher's change in pattern may be presumed to change the students' motivation (or at least the cycle of the students' motivation). This design involves a change in motivation during continued practice. Alternatives to this procedure include (1) training under one motivational condition and extinguishing the learned responses using some other level of motivation, and (2) training under one motivational condition, allowing some "forgetting" period to pass, and then reconditioning using a different level of motivation.

17.17 When asked later about the teacher's decision to change the pattern of class (Problem 17.16), one student remarks, "I didn't have to learn the same things." Why does this comment point out a difficulty with experiments that try to evaluate the effects of motivation upon learning?

  Simply stated, the effects of two different levels of motivation may be to inspire the learning of one response under one condition and the learning of some other response in the other condition. This is not modifying the *same* response according to the two different conditions. Thus, quizzes every other day may emphasize rote memory of definitions, while biweekly exams could stress relationships among principles. (There is no assurance that any one of the designs suggested in the solution to Problem 17.16 would avoid such a difficulty.)

17.18 Suppose the teacher in Problem 17.16 announces that exams will be given after randomly determined periods of time. (These would be "surprise" or "pop" quizzes.) What effect would motivation levels most likely have upon the scores obtained?

  The solution to this problem requires accepting the concept of competing responses. In other words, if different types of responses are demanded by different types of questions, studying one type may create problems for learning another. The expectation for low-motivation students is that performance will be poorer in this situation than it would be in situations where they need to learn only one type of response. For highly motivated students, performance will be about the same under either condition.

17.19 The parent observing a child happily seated in front of the television set says, "You must not be very motivated if you're sitting there! What about the term paper you have due?" Describe some circumstances that would make the parent's first sentence correct and some that make it incorrect.

  The parent probably is correct if the paper is not done yet and due tomorrow. However, if the due date is two weeks away, the student may be highly motivated, but showing the pattern of responding typical of a fixed-interval (FI) schedule. Research in laboratory situations has shown that well-established FI conditions can, in some cases, override the potential motivation effects during the initial states of the interval.

17.20   Using the incentive interpretation of motivation, explain why the transition from a higher drive state to a lower one may be more important than the satiation of the drive.

The incentive interpretation of motivation emphasizes the pleasure of drive satisfaction rather than the achievement of a driveless state. Drive satisfaction is accomplished by the transition from higher to lower drive state, while a driveless state exists when satiation has occurred. Thus, terminating the drive is not considered as important as the conditions leading up to that point. Sexual drives are one example that fit this interpretation.

17.21   What kind of evidence exists regarding the signalling of satiation?

It is recognized that actual (physiological) satiation of drives such as thirst or hunger cannot take place rapidly enough to account for the cessation of responding that is often observed. Evidence tends to indicate that there are areas in the brain (called *satiation centers*) that somehow evaluate responding and indicate when sufficient "intake" activity has occurred. The exact location of such centers remains to be established.

17.22   Clinical observations of grossly obese individuals have indicated that external cues such as the availability and quality of food appear to play a very important part in determining their eating habits. Explain this in terms of satiation.

These individuals appear to ignore signals of internal satiation. Instead, their behavior is dominated by external indicators of satiation ("Is there any good food left?"). Obesity can thus be interpreted as a result of the dominance of external cues.

17.23   Why is the placebo effect another example of the importance of external cues?

By definition, a placebo is an inert ingredient that is administered as if it were active. When the subject believes that the placebo will be active and responds accordingly, the placebo effect has occurred. Generally, the placebo effect will result from convincing external cues. If the subjects monitor internal cues carefully, they might recognize the lack of effect. But subjects who show the placebo effect do not monitor internal cues and, instead, rely upon the external stimuli.

17.24   Many children learn to read by completing a series of reading assignments. Reinforcement comes from the completion of the work and the subsequent grade received. What term describes the fact that some children continue to read purely for the enjoyment of reading?

The term that describes the changeover from performing an action to satisfy some motive to performing that action because it is motivating in and of itself is *functional autonomy*. Reading that is done just for the pleasure of reading can be said to illustrate functional autonomy.

17.25   Consider the often-heard remark, "Anyway, it wasn't *that* important." How does it illustrate the resolution of cognitive dissonance?

Cognitive dissonance exists when a person has stored two contradictory items of information. It is thought that such contradictions will motivate the person to act to reduce the contradiction, or dissonance. The remark given above is one way of doing so: If one of the items is no longer thought of as being terribly important, the contradiction can be lessened and therefore the dissonance reduced.

17.26   In some circumstances the individual is confronted with competing motivations. What term describes such situations? How is this situation resolved?

Competing motivations are referred to as conflict situations. In general, resolution of a conflict occurs when the individual decides that one of the values is the most important and responds accordingly.

17.27 Eli cannot decide whether to wash his car or cut the lawn.   Assuming that he would really rather play tennis, identify the type of conflict Eli is experiencing.   What are other common forms of conflict?

Eli's conflict can be called an avoidance-avoidance situation.   He must choose between two negatively valued chores.   Other conflicts involve approach-approach circumstances (where the selection is between positively valued choices), approach-avoidance situations (where one stimulus has both positive and negative values), and multiple approach-avoidance arrangements (where one must choose from several stimuli, all of which have both positive and negative values).

17.28 Distinguish among the concepts of fear, anxiety, and stress.

Fear and anxiety may both be thought of as emotional reactions.   Fear is usually considered more intense than anxiety and is associated with specific stimuli; anxiety is often weaker and relatively vague.   Stress is a more general term that encompasses both fear and anxiety.   Stress refers to the consequences experienced following noxious stimulation.

17.29 What effect upon performance can be expected when stress conditions are introduced?

The solution to this problem depends upon the response being measured.   In most cases, if the response provides escape from or avoidance of the stress-producing circumstances, performance can be expected to improve rapidly and then maintain a high level.   However, when the stress disrupts the performance situation (for example by allowing for competing responses to be made), performance can be expected to deteriorate.

17.30 Based upon the principle of learned helplessness, use a graph to sketch the results that might be expected from a group that is naive and one that has previous experience with unavoidable electric shock when both groups are given the opportunity to escape.

The solution to this problem is represented in Fig. 17-6.   Notice that the experienced group, which has previously encountered unavoidable electric shock, makes no attempt to escape during the entire 40-second duration of each trial, while the naive group shows rapid improvement in performance toward an asymptotic (rapid) value.

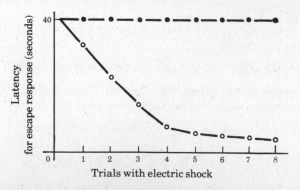

Fig. 17-6

17.31 In Problem 17.7, two children were described as responding quite differently to training at a swimming camp.   Suppose the one whose performance did not improve returned home and entered a swimming meet where many of her friends were competing.   If she showed a remarkable improvement in performance during this meet, what explanation might be given?

The principle used to explain sudden, dramatic improvement in performance has been called latent learning.   In this case, the responses had been learned but were not shown until an appropriate reinforcement was anticipated.   This is typical of latent learning circumstances and points out the need to determine what motive conditions may be operating in any given situation.

17.32   How are the concepts of instinct and species-specific defense reactions (SSDRs) comparable?   How do they differ?

>   Both instincts and SSDRs are defined as innate or unlearned acts that are characteristic of a particular organism.   They differ, however, in that instinctive responses are thought to be produced automatically whenever a releaser stimulus for that instinct is present, while SSDRs are made in the presence of learned cues called danger signals or safety signals.

17.33   Using the definition of incentive given in Problem 17.11, explain why intracranial self-stimulation can be considered as an incentive.

>   The evidence from research on brain stimulation indicates that the delivery of electric shock to the brain provokes both drive and reinforcement (or, in some cases, drive and aversive conditions).   Responses that result in intracranial self-stimulation apparently achieve the pleasure of attaining the incentive.

Key Terms

Appetitive arousal.   Conditions that initiate and maintain behaviors directed toward achieving goals.

Approach-approach conflict.   A situation in which a person must choose between two stimulus situations, both of which have positive values.

Approach-avoidance conflict.   A situation in which a person must choose whether to go toward or away from a single stimulus situation that has both positive and negative values.

Aversive arousal.   Conditions that initiate and maintain behaviors directed toward avoiding unpleasant or negative conditions.

Avoidance-avoidance conflict.   A situation in which a person must choose between two stimulus situations, both of which have negative values.

Cognitive dissonance.   A condition in which a person has two different feelings about the same stimulus or has two opposing items of information.

Conflict.   In motivation, the experiencing of two or more competing motive conditions at one time.

Contrast effects.   The finding that a switch in the level of reinforcement for a particular response will produce an overreaction in the change of performance level.

Deprivation.   Doing without; in motivation, often measured as the period of time since the motive was last satisfied.

Drive.   The physiological or psychological state resulting from some need.

Drive reduction.   In reinforcement, the lessening by a reinforcer of some need or aversive condition.

Functional autonomy.   The state that exists when a response that was made originally to satisfy some motive becomes motivating in and of itself.

Incentive.   The combination of a drive and some associated reinforcement.

Instinct.   An innate (inborn) condition that regularly provokes specific, complex responses from all members of a species when a distinctive stimulus pattern occurs.

Latent learning.   Acquisition of a response that takes place but is not revealed by performance until an appropriate incentive exists.

Learned helplessness.   The acceptance of what are interpreted as unalterable consequences of a situation, even when a countering response is possible.

Motivation.   A set of conditions that initiate, direct, and maintain responding.

Multiple approach-avoidance conflict.   A situation in which a person must choose between two (or more) stimulus situations, each of which has both positive and negative values.

Need.   A physiological or psychological imbalance or deficit.

Negative contrast.   A larger-than-expected drop in performance level as a result of new reinforcement conditions.

Placebo.   An inert ingredient that is administered as if it were active.

Placebo effect.   When the subject believes a placebo is active and therefore responds accordingly.

Positive contrast.   A greater-than-expected improvement in performance as a result of new reinforcement conditions.

Satiation.   Complete satisfaction of a drive state.

Satiation centers.   Areas in the brain thought to signal when sufficient consumption has occurred to satisfy a particular need; such signals may occur before physiological satiation occurs.

Species-specific defense reactions (SSDRs).   Proposed innate protective responses made to learned signals.

Stress.   The experiences that follow noxious stimulation; may include fear and anxiety.

Yerkes-Dodson law.   A finding that indicates that as the perceived level of a task's difficulty increases, a lower level of motivation is needed to ensure maximum performance.

Chapter 18

Language Learning

At first glance language learning may seem no different from the other forms of the acquisition-storage-retrieval sequence described in previous chapters. However, various analyses of language learning have pointed out that for at least two reasons it should be treated as a special case. For one thing, verbal behavior encompasses a huge and complex variety of responses, and no one response can be fruitfully studied in isolation. Another way of putting this is to say that the *context* of a response, the way it is combined and interacts with other verbal responses, must be considered in any study of language learning. And second, any researcher studying language must be concerned with the peculiar characteristics of each verbal response under investigation. (In other types of learning studies, the unique properties of individual responses are much less important than the general patterns or principles of responding.) This emphasis on individual responses makes language learning studies different from, say, a study of learning in which the behavior under investigation is the disc-pecking of a pigeon, where the way in which a particular pecking response is made is not nearly as important as the general pattern of responding.

18.1 THE NATURE OF LANGUAGE

Language has two major functions: to permit communication and to aid in thought processes. Probably because the first is observable and the second is not, more effort has been spent studying the ways in which languages facilitate communication.

Symbols vs. Signals

Human languages consist of symbols rather than signals. The *symbols* of languages are words, used not only to transmit information but also to express ideas and their logical implications. *Signals* also transmit information, but only in the sense that they generate some reaction from other organisms. Signals are not used in permutations and combinations, in the same manner symbols are, to develop a limitless number of ideas or propositions. (*Note:* Humans do use signals as well as symbols; such things as tone of voice and gestures may serve communicative functions. However, the bulk of human communication is accomplished with language rather than mere signs.)

EXAMPLE 1. The tail-slap of a beaver warns other beavers of potential danger. This is considered a signal rather than a symbol because although communication does occur, the signal sends one message and one message only—that there may be a present danger. The signal cannot be used in combination with other signals to send a variety of messages.

Ethology, Behaviorism, and Linguistics

Although not directly related to the study of language learning, *ethology,* the study of species-specific behavior, plays an important part in discussions about the nature of language. Many ethologists believe that much behavior is rigidly restricted by an innate genetic pattern, and they focus on the characteristics that are common to all members of a species. In a similar manner, many *psycholinguists* suggest that there are common, inherited, inborn patterns for humans that determine language learning. They propose a *preparedness,* or common specialized capacity, that controls language learning.

In contrast, the *behaviorist* position focuses on reinforcement contingencies that are unique for each individual. The behaviorist studying language learning is principally interested in establishing why particular language forms are learned; the emphasis is thus on the individual differences in language skills, and not on the species-wide characteristics of verbal behavior.

EXAMPLE 2. Pointing to the seemingly universal arrival of the /m/ sound in children's sound production, linguists stress the species-general aspect of the language acquisition. Behaviorists, however, emphasize the difference in reinforcement for production of sounds using /m/, such as the American "Mom" versus the German "Mutti."

A crucial distinction between the psycholinguists and the behaviorists is in the way they account for the production of creative phrases. Psycholinguists point out that children say phrases that have never been said before, and thus that could never have been heard or previously reinforced. This argument has weakened the behaviorist position to a certain extent, although some behaviorists claim that what are reinforced are general rules of the language rather than specific statements.

18.2 THE CONSTRUCTION OF LANGUAGE

Language construction has been studied extensively. This section presents the basic manners in which these studies have been conducted.

Language Components

One way to study language construction is to divide language into three major components—phonology, grammar, and semantics—and to determine what rules govern each.

Phonology. The study of the rules that govern the production and combination of sounds is called *phonology*. Phonologists classify the speech sounds that are used to form larger units (such as words), and thus provide the basis for the study of grammar and semantics.

Grammar. The study of the rules that determine the arrangement and modification of words is called *grammar*. Specifically, the study of the arrangement of words is labelled *syntax*, while inquiry into the rules of word modification is called *morphology*.

Semantics. The focus of *semantics* is on the rules determining word meaning. Semantics typically involves using rules of phonology and grammar and a knowledge of environmental conditions, rules of logic, and similar variables to determine meaning. In effect, semantics goes beyond the simple study of language to include philosophical and cultural investigations.

EXAMPLE 3. The sound sequence of the sentence, "How high is he?" would be studied as phonology. The rules determining the arrangement of the words would be labelled syntax, while the meaning of the words (particularly the possible multiple interpretations of the word "high") would be categorized as semantics.

A Hierarchy of Language

A second interpretation of language is essentially reductionistic, analyzing language from the relatively gross structure of a sentence through several levels to the basic sound components called phonemes. In keeping with the more common presentation of these materials, this section will be arranged in hierarchical fashion, starting with phonemes and building to sentences.

Phonemes. The smallest units of sound that can be distinguished by a native speaker of a language are called *phonemes*. In English, there are approximately 45 phonemes, including letter sounds, letter combination sounds, and stress (pronunciation) sounds.

EXAMPLE 4. Using the letter sequence "perfect," differences in phonemes can be illustrated. Consider how you read the word—as an adjective ('pur-fickt), or as a verb (pur-'fect)? Stress and pronunciation alter the same letter sequence to represent two different concepts, thus demonstrating how a phonological analysis can in part determine the semantic interpretation of a particular word.

Syllables. Although phonemes are the smallest units of sound discernible to a native speaker, the *syllable* is the unit of speech typically perceived by either the producer or receiver of speech. A syllable may or may not compose a word and may be formed from one or more phonemes. Research indicates that identification reaction time will be faster for syllables than for phonemes, supporting the concept that the syllable rather than the phoneme is the unit of speech perceived.

Morphemes. A *morpheme* is the smallest *meaningful* unit of a language. Morphemes may be composed of one or more syllables.

EXAMPLE 5. The words "best" and "greatest" can be used to illustrate the difference between a syllable and a morpheme. "Best" is a single syllable that is also a morpheme because it does have meaning. The word "greatest" has two syllables, one of which has meaning by itself (great) while the other (est) is not a morpheme. (*Note:* The verbal unit "est" would be a morpheme for a speaker of French because the syllable does have meaning in that language. In English, "est" is sometimes called a *bound morpheme,* in that it takes on meaning only when combined with some other morpheme. In the word "greatest," "est" is a bound morpheme; in the word "best" it is not. Other bound morphemes in English are "er" and "ist.")

Words. *Words* are the symbols used in a language. The structural components of words are phonemes, syllables, and morphemes. In turn, words are used to compose phrases, clauses, and sentences.

Phrases. A meaningful combination of grammatically related words that does not contain both a subject and predicate is called a *phrase.*

Clauses. A *clause* is a syntactic construction containing both a subject and predicate and forming part of a complex or compound sentence.

Sentences. A *sentence* contains both a subject and predicate (or at least implies both) and presents a complete statement.

EXAMPLE 6. Consider the following word sequence: "Colleen braked to a screeching halt and leaped from the car, after which she waited for the bee to fly out." This statement could be analyzed in terms of phrases, clauses, or sentence form. Both "braked to a screeching halt" and "leaped from the car" are phrases. The words "after which she waited for the bee to fly out" form a clause. The entire construction is a sentence.

A complex sentence is composed of two complete clauses (each with a subject and predicate). A compound sentence contains either two subjects or two predicates. Subjects typically perceive each clause of a complex sentence separately.

18.3 PERCEPTION OF SPEECH

Psychologists have attempted to determine at which level of the hierarchy presented in the previous section speech perception occurs. The present section explores this problem and the theories proposed to explain speech perception, along with the differences between spoken and written languages.

Speech Perception as Encoding

Considerable research evidence indicates that speech is *not* perceived as a string of phonemes. Humans are capable of interpreting speech presented at a rate that is greater than their auditory capacities for single-unit reception (see Problem 18.9). The complex code that is received probably consists of syllables or morphemes or both. The proposal is that humans have speech processors that somehow abstract the syllabic patterns and/or morphemic meaning from the speech received.

Spectrographic analysis. A *speech spectrogram* is a visual recording of spoken language made by using a light-sensitive paper and a series of filters that transform the speech into the recording. Analysis of natural speech indicates that humans do not show distinct demarcations between phonemes or between syllables and words.   This would tend to support the concept that processing of speech occurs at a relatively complex level.

Motor Theory of Speech Perception

Another attempt to explain the complexity of speech perception, called *motor theory,* focuses on a proposal of *covert articulation* of the stimuli received.   The covert, or internal, representation of the speech received supposedly leads to the perceptual understanding of the message.

Advanced motor theories stress both the covert-articulation concept and the actions of the nervous system required for this to occur.   These theories indicate that decoding of the message received may take place at this higher neural level rather than simply the level of articulation.

Cerebral Dominance and Speech Perception

Another view of speech perception centers on the role played by the cerebral hemispheres. Evidence from research studies using dichotic (two-channel) listening tasks supports a proposal that speech perception is predominantly a function of the left cerebral hemisphere for well over 90 percent of those studied.   This is in keeping with the contralateral pattern found for other responses—that is, the left hemisphere controls many responses for the predominantly right-handed population.

EXAMPLE 7.   Subjects wearing earphones can be given two simultaneous messages (such as the phonetic sounds /pa/ and /da/), one in each ear.   The sound heard in the right ear will more often be reported accurately and with greater confidence than that heard in the left ear.   Apparently the contralateral pattern holds, with the message to the right ear being processed primarily by the left cerebral hemisphere.

18.4   ACQUISITION OF SPEECH

Understanding how speech is perceived is not the same as understanding how speech is acquired.   This section examines some of the major concerns of the study of speech acquisition.

"Prewiring" vs. Reinforcement

As pointed out in Section 18.1, there is a major debate about the way in which humans acquire language.   One position, held by psycholinguists, is that humans are born with tendencies to produce certain speech patterns.   These theorists believe that humans are innately "prewired" to learn languages.   Behaviorists, on the other hand, see speech production as the result of reinforcement for certain responses.   One way to resolve this conflict is to think of the capacity to produce speech as a function of innate abilities and the actual statements as a function of the environmental reinforcers that are available.

EXAMPLE 8.   If the resolution described above is accepted, it is possible to understand that totally creative statements *may* be produced (humans are "prewired" with such a capacity), but may also *not* be produced in some situations (if there will not be a reinforcement or if there will be a punishment).

Production of Sounds

The production of sounds is one aspect of language that has been studied extensively.   Behaviorists have proposed that all sounds of all languages are present in a young child's *babbling* (or prespeech) stage and that those sounds that remain in the child's speech do so because the culture reinforces the child for using them.   Linguists have found, however, that certain sounds appear before others in the babbling of the young child, apparently indicating that not all sounds are available throughout the stage.   (This finding tends to support the idea that the development of speech skills follows a hereditary pattern.)   Moreover, research has shown that certain nonverbal components of speech production—including intonations and inflections such as the rise in a voice that produces a "questioning sound"—are demonstrated by children even before they can produce the appropriate words.

Speech production and maturation.　There is some evidence that speech acquisition may be easier to accomplish during the first 12 (or prepubertal) years of life.　This is sometimes called a *critical period* for language learning.　Studies of recovery from aphasias and of second-language learning provide support for this proposal, although no convincing explanations of why postpubertal learning of a language is more difficult have been established.

18.5　GRAMMAR

As mentioned previously, *grammar* includes both syntax and morphology, although research has concentrated on the former.　In effect, the rules of grammar present a format within which the perfect speaker could create an infinite number of errorless sentences.　In reality, such behavior does not occur, although many speakers are able to distinguish many instances of grammatical and ungrammatical speech.

EXAMPLE 9.　Consider the following three strings of words:

1.　Barrier the restrictive jumped John.
2.　John jumped the restrictive barrier.
3.　John exited the inflicted associate.

It is relatively easy to recognize 1 as ungrammatical and 2 as grammatically correct.　String 3 presents words in what seems to be a grammatically correct sequence, but they are nonsensical.　Such a series is called an anomalous string of words.　Typically, recall of words will be best for 2 and better for 3 than for 1.　Presentation of the words in the form of grammar apparently aids recall, even when the words make an incongruous string.

Surface Structure

Syntax, or the study of the arrangement of words, is concerned with the pattern of language presented.　The term used to describe this pattern is *surface structure*.

EXAMPLE 10.　Consider the following two sentences:

1.　The boy cheered the old man.
2.　The boy cheated the old man.

The sentences have very similar surface structures, but the meanings differ considerably.

Deep Structure

Deep structure refers to the meaning of a sentence.　Regardless of the arrangement of words, if the meaning is the same, the deep structure is the same.

EXAMPLE 11.　It is possible to express the same meaning with several different surface structure patterns, as the following two sentences illustrate: (1) "The boy cheered the old man."　(2) "The old man was cheered by the boy."

Paraphrasing.　Example 11 illustrates the restatement of the same meaning in more than one form.　This is called *paraphrasing*.

Ambiguity.　Example 11 also illustrates the concept of *ambiguity* or multiple meaning.　If the boy applauded for the old man, one meaning exists.　On the other hand, if the old man felt better because of the boy's presence, a different interpretation exists.　The ambiguity expressed is called *lexical ambiguity* because there is more than one interpretation for a particular word.　There may also be *syntactic ambiguity,* in which the surface structure of the sentence conveys more than one meaning.

EXAMPLE 12.　Syntactic ambiguity is illustrated by the sentence, "The boys and girls did not agree."　One interpretation suggests boys against girls, while the other proposes boys and girls together against some outside agent.　Additional information would be needed to resolve the ambiguity.

Types of Grammars

While psycholinguists know that a framework exists for a given language, an actual description of that framework and an explanation of how it affects word arrangements have been very difficult to establish. This section considers several types of grammars.

Finite-state grammars. According to some theorists, the preexisting state of the person who speaks determines the choice of each word according to the word that has just occurred. This type of rule, in which the choice of a word depends on the word just preceding it, is typical of a *finite-state grammar.* (*Note:* Many theorists refuse to accept the principles of finite-state grammar, proposing instead that entire thoughts rather than individual words or phrases control the production of sentences.)

EXAMPLE 13. If the previous word was "basket" the next word will take one of several forms according to a finite-state grammar. "Filled" would be an acceptable next word, followed, in turn, by "with," etc., until the sentence was completed. A finite-state grammar theoretically would not allow the word "door" to follow.

Phrase-structure grammars. A *phrase-structure grammar* presents a series of rules that allow analysis of language from the most general set of elements to the most specific. This is done by creating a tree diagram, such as the one shown in Fig. 18-1, which is used to analyze the sentence, "The boy destroyed the lighter."

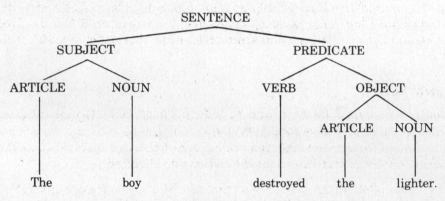

Fig. 18-1

Phrase-structure grammars may take even more sophisticated forms. For example, instead of simply having subject and predicate *nodes* (units), there might be superordinate nodes such as context and fact. Thus, a slightly longer sentence, "After quitting smoking, the boy destroyed the lighter," might be analyzed as a proposition with context and fact as shown in Fig. 18-2.

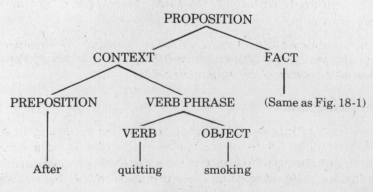

Fig. 18-2

Phrase-structure grammars are considered inefficient because there are so many different sentences that might be diagrammed in this manner and yet have totally different meanings. Likewise, two sentences with almost the same meaning may have totally different forms.

Transformations. To further complicate the interpretation of phrase-structure grammar, there can be contingent rules, called *transformational rules,* that allow symbols to be rewritten *only* under certain circumstances. The presence or absence of certain other symbols will determine whether or not a transformation can be made. (Such transformations include generating declarative or interrogative sentences, or statements in the passive or active voice, for example.) These transformations cannot be represented in tree diagrams because the context itself determines whether or not a transformation might be possible.

Semantically based grammars. As might be expected, *semantically based grammars* are controlled by meaning rather than structure. Essentially, the deep structure of a sentence is the crucial aspect, and syntactic rules exist only to provide the conditions for expressing that deep structure.

18.6 SEMANTICS

Because communication is one of the two main functions of language, and because a grammar may be based on meaning, it has become important to try to determine how the communication of meaning is accomplished. This section summarizes a few of the most important types of semantic investigations.

Holophrastic Speech

The most elementary form of speech, called holophrastic speech, consists of one-word communications that are used to convey more complex meanings. As pointed out earlier, however, it should be remembered that some understanding may be communicated by the nonverbal components of speech, such as intonation and phrasing.

EXAMPLE 14. The child's comment "Dolly" may have several different meanings, which the listener may be able to detect by knowing the context of the remark. The single word may mean, "Where is my dolly?" or, "Hand me my dolly." In either case this is an instance of holophrastic speech.

Pivot-Open Speech

A slightly more sophisticated pattern of expressing meaning, called *pivot-open speech,* involves two-word constructions. In these instances, one of the two words, called the *pivot word,* acts as a foundation for initiating a number of different phrases. The other, the *open word,* may be chosen from many that will coordinate with the pivot word. Meaning is determined by the particular combination chosen.

EXAMPLE 15. A typical pivot word for a young child would be "Mommy." Information of many sorts may be transmitted using various open words in combination with this pivot word. Thus, "Mommy happy" conveys a message very different from "Mommy tired" or "Mommy candy."

Speech as Conceptualization

More advanced (multiword) speech may be interpreted according to semantically based grammars (see Section 18.5). A *conceptualization* is thought to be a basic unit of information. The use of conceptualizations to interpret speech does not preclude phonetic or grammatical interpretations. Instead, the conceptual interpretation must be in addition to and in correspondence with the other interpretations.

EXAMPLE 16. The *tip-of-the-tongue (TOT) phenomenon* illustrates how segmental nodes of information (letters, syllables, phonemes, etc.) may be recalled even when the actual label for the concept cannot at first be recalled. Thus, while the person may not remember the name "Topeka," the train of thought may include "it's in Kansas . . . da-da-da [number of syllables] . . . two-um, Tucson . . . no, Topeka!" The subject's attempts at recall include a variety of components, including a conceptualization (the location of the city), the number of syllables, an approximation of the first syllable, and so on.

Frames. Conceptualizations allow the person to develop *frames* for speech. These frames are inferences made from two or more conceptualizations. Also called *scripts,* or *schemata,* frames house *generic memories*—that is, a class of considerations about some aspect of the environment. It is beyond the scope of this book to present all the many different types of concepts that might be held in frames. It can be said, however, that the current stimulation and the previously developed frames will affect interpretation of input and the subsequent response (speech) production.

Solved Problems

18.1 The laws of reinforcement scheduling may apply to both a rat pressing a lever and a human learning a language. Why then is language learning not grouped with other learning tasks?

Because language learning is different from other forms of learning in several crucial ways, it requires special treatment. Perhaps the most important difference is the uniqueness, or the specificity, of responses that are studied in language learning. Experiments involving rats pressing levers do not usually specify *how* the lever is manipulated; the rat may use its paw, nose, or hindquarters to press the lever. All that is required is that sufficient pressure be applied to the lever, and once that is done a response is said to have occurred. In a language learning experiment, on the other hand, the response required is much more specific or highly defined. The words that qualify as a response are not just *any* words, and not even the correct words in any order. The special properties of language, including meaning and grammar, require that a response be made in the proper form and in the proper context.

18.2 Why is language learning often described as being exclusively human?

The definition of language is that it uses symbols to express ideas, including logical relations and implications. Human language can express any number of ideas using the symbols from which it is made. By contrast, animal communication is limited to a restricted number of signals—stimuli that will arouse reactions in others of the species, but that do *not* allow unlimited permutations and combinations that result in the expression of ideas. Thus, human language is capable of creating reactions *and* creating new ideas, while animal communications accomplish only the former.

18.3 Distinguish between the positions of ethologists and behaviorists, and then apply this distinction to the interpretation of language learning.

Ethologists and behaviorists differ primarily in what they believe is most important to know about an organism. Essentially, ethologists concentrate on identifying the processes that determine the shared characteristics for all members of a species. Behaviorists, on the other hand, try to identify and study the processes and characteristics which make individual species members different from each other.

With regard to language learning, the ethologist might look for those processes that humans are especially prepared to learn and that will set the rules common to all human languages. The behaviorist would concentrate on the processes of reinforcement that establish the unique properties of particular languages, therefore differentiating among members of the same (human) species.

18.4   In what sense are many linguistic studies an outgrowth of the ethological position described in the Problem 18.3?

Many linguistic studies have focused on the concept of universal language characteristics, thus refuting the idea of exclusive reinforcement-controlled language learning. In this sense the work done in linguistics is the work of ethologists, who stress the innate, species-general properties of responding.

18.5   An African language called Xhosa includes "click" sounds produced by what is called a glottal catch. Studies of this method of sound production (unusual by Western standards) would represent which type of language investigation?

The part of language study that expresses the rules for sound production and combination is called phonology. Phonologists studying this language might, for example, investigate exactly how the sound was produced, how many different types of clicks exist, and the ways in which native speakers differentiate among the clicks.

18.6   What is the label for studies concerned with the combination of words rather than the combination of sounds?

Technically, the arrangement of words is described as syntax, and investigations of these arrangements are called syntactical studies. Generally, when both the arrangement and the modification of words are studied, the investigation comes under the heading "grammar." (The study of how words are modified in different situations is called morphology; thus, grammar consists of both syntax and morphology.)

18.7   Related to the study of both sound production and word combination is the study of word meaning. What term is used to describe this type of language investigation? Why is this area thought to be more difficult to study than either phonology or grammar?

The study of word meaning is called semantics. Unlike phonology or grammar, for which there are quite explicit rules that have specific applications, word meaning often depends not only on linguistic knowledge but also on the particular context or environment in which the language is used and on certain rules of logic. In effect, semantics involves being able to go beyond the study of language alone and into cultural and philosophical investigations.

18.8   Give an example that illustrates that phonemes are not necessarily spoken representations of the alphabet.

Defined as the smallest unit of sound that makes a difference to the native speaker of a language, a phoneme does not necessarily represent a letter of the alphabet. One commonly used phoneme in English is /th/, which consists of two letters of the alphabet that are combined in a single sound. Another example that points to the way in which phonemes, and not merely the alphabet, play a role in determining meaning is to examine the word "present" as a noun ('pre-sent) and as a verb (pre-'sent). If one considers only the spelling (disregarding the accents shown here), the words are identical. They can be distinguished, however, by reference to the phonemes of which they are constructed.

18.9   What kinds of evidence indicate that speech is *not* perceived simply as a string of phonemes tied together?

There are several different types of research that suggest that speech perception involves the reception of some kind of complex code rather than a string of phonemes. One of the most telling is a study in which "compressed speech" is presented: it has been found that receivers can follow (admittedly, with difficulty) extremely rapid presentations of speech, even at rates of 400 words per minute. That the rate of presentation far exceeds the greatest rate at which human auditory mechanisims can distinguish sounds, and yet is successful, indicates that somehow the units are being encoded.

18.10 The complex code of speech that is heard has been described by a term other than "phoneme."   What terms are most often used to describe the verbal units in which a message is actually received?

    The solution to the problem may take two different forms.   Apparently, the basic unit of speech that a listener concentrates on is the syllable, which may be composed of one or more phonemes. However, the smallest meaningful auditory unit of a language is called a morpheme, which may be composed of one or more syllables.   Thus, if the message actually received is that which is "heard," the unit of concern would be the syllable, while if meaning is crucial, the unit studied would be the morpheme.

18.11 Phonemes, syllables, and morphemes can be seen as the first levels in a hierarchy of language reception.   Complete this hierarchy.

    The remainder of the hierarchy of language reception probably should be, in ascending order, words, phrases, clauses, and sentences.   Words, the symbols of a language, are composed of phonemes, syllables, and morphemes.   In turn, phrases are built from word combinations, and may be used to create clauses or sentences.   Sentences may have several clauses, but if they do, reception generally is of each clause separately.

18.12 Suppose that some mechanical device is used to generate sounds of phonemes and that these are fed into one ear of the listener along with "chirplike" variations of the same sounds to the other ear.   (This is called a dichotic listening task.)   Would the "chirps" be judged as speech or nonspeech?

    Because the auditory reception of sounds other than speech appears to activate processors other than speech processors, the solution to this problem would depend upon the success of the speech processors in abstracting the phonemic components of the "chirps."   If these features are recognized, the sounds would be perceived as speech.   If the processors fail to recognize these features, the variations would be perceived as nonspeech.

18.13 It is apparent from the solutions to several of the previous problems (including 18.9, 18.10, and 18.12) that speech perception is quite complicated and sophisticated.   Explain how spectrographic analyses of speech seem to support such a statement and distinguish spoken language from written language.

    Speech spectrographs (visible records of spoken language) indicate the absence of identifiable boundaries between phonemes or between syllables and words.   This characteristic is obviously unlike written language, with its easily separated individual units.

18.14 While spectrographic analyses indicate noticeable differences between spoken and written language, there are a number of other important distinctions that can be identified.   Describe some of the most important of these.

    In general, spoken language is more informal than written language, with speakers making use of the repetition of words and phrases, ungrammatical arrangements of words, and compressed, or "shorthand," statements in order to communicate their meaning.   In addition, the speakers of a language have at their disposal an almost unlimited number of intonations and other ways of saying words that are not available to writers, who must rely on a limited number of graphic symbols (such as question marks and exclamation points) to convey how a particular word, phrase, clause, or sentence should be expressed.

18.15 Describe the general concept of a motor theory of speech perception. Why was such a theory developed? What distinguishes a simple motor theory of speech perception from one that is described as advanced?

> The general concept of a motor theory of speech perception is that the acoustic stimulus provokes a covert (internal) articulation of that stimulus, which in turn leads to the perceptual understanding of the stimulus. This concept was developed to try to explain the finding that speech could not be treated simply as a stream of phonemes. More advanced motor theories of speech perception emphasize not only the covert-articulation concept but also the neural involvement necessary for this so that decoding may take place at a higher neural level rather than only at the level of articulation.

18.16 Using a dichotic (two-message) task in which stimuli of equal value are presented to the two ears, predict which ear will show an advantage in accuracy and confidence of message.

> The typical finding for dichotic tasks is that the message received by the right ear will be reported more accurately and with greater confidence. It is felt that this represents dominance of the left cerebral hemisphere for the perception of speech. (*Note:* This result is found more often for right-handed people than it is for left-handed people. These results are in keeping with cerebral dominance for other types of behaviors.)

18.17 Explain why the ethology-behaviorism controversy mentioned in Problems 18.3 and 18.4 might be resolved by stating that we can know what a person is able to say but not what a person will say.

> A statement such as this combines the ethological and behaviorist positions. It allows the possibility of language ability being dependent upon an innate, specialized ("prewired") capacity, but indicates that what actually *is* said may be controlled by the reinforcers provided by the speaker's environment.

18.18 Developmental research has shown that young children in many different societies make the /t/ sound before making the /k/ sound. How does this finding seem to contradict the "babbling" theory of language learning?

> The "babbling" theory of language learning suggests that all children produce all the sounds of every language while in the babbling stage. It further proposes that exposure to the native language eventually leads to continued production of appropriate sounds (through modeling or reinforcement), while sounds inappropriate to the native language, but possibly appropriate to other languages, drop out. The developmental evidence appears to contradict the concept that all sounds are present throughout the babbling stage. If this evidence is correct, the theory loses some of its support.

18.19 What aspects of spoken language seem to be the first to develop in the babbling stage?

> Interestingly, even before the rudimentary phonemes are produced reliably, children in the babbling stage will produce sounds with noticeable and identifiably different intonations—such as those indicating a question or exclamation. In other words, the child appears to produce the rhythm and frequency of speech before generating identifiable phonemes.

18.20 How has study of recovery from aphasia seemed to support the idea of a critical period for language learning? Is there other evidence for such a concept?

> Studies of people who have suffered brain damage that has led to language loss (aphasia) show that if the patients are under 12 years of age, complete recovery of language skills is likely to be accomplished. For older persons, recovery is not nearly so likely.
> A second point of support for the concept of a critical period (birth to 12 years of age) is found in studying the acquisition of a second language. Children under the age of 12 have much less

difficulty accomplishing this than adults do. Still more support for the theory arises from the finding that language development essentially stops at the time of puberty for intellectually retarded individuals, with language skills remaining at whatever level has been reached at that time.

18.21   Why should the rules of grammar *not* be considered psychological theories?

    The rules of grammar are attempts to describe certain basic aspects of human language behaviors. However, the rules of grammar present what an ideal speaker would do under ideal conditions, not actual behavior. While the psychologist (or psycholinguist) may be very interested in the rules of grammar, the divergence of actual behavior from the rules is also of importance. Therefore, the psychologist should treat the rules of grammar as representing a structure within which (or in spite of which) an astonishingly wide variety of responses can be made, from highly creative and innovative statements to those that are simply wrong.

18.22   Consider the following word sequences: (1) "Lazy tireless clouds eat vigorously." (2) "Clouds tireless eat vigorously lazy." Which sequence of words is likely to be easier to recall, and why? Then explain why research studies on approximations of English may not study comparable forms of recall.

    The first word sequence would be recalled more easily than the second because it more closely approximates grammatical English. While the message itself is improbable at best, the format of the initial phrase is comparable to what might be found in normal speech or writing.

    Although higher-order approximations of English are more easily recalled, the retention measured may be of the individual components. The comparison of such approximations to actual English sentences may not be appropriate because the recall of sentences may be for the concepts (or "gist") of the sentence rather than the specific components.

18.23   Given the sentence "Kenton purchased a new dictionary," construct a sentence that changes the surface structure but not the deep structure. Then write a sentence that leaves much of the surface structure intact, but changes the deep structure.

    The difference between surface structure and deep structure is one of meaning. Any string of words that has the same meaning has the same deep structure, regardless of the surface structure. Thus, the solution to the first part of this problem might be, "A new dictionary was purchased by Kenton." To solve the second part, the meaning must change; for example, "Kenton sold a new dictionary."

18.24   Explain the concepts of paraphrasing and ambiguity by interpreting the sentence, "He said the dessert was really nutty."

    To paraphrase is to restate the same meaning by changing the surface structure of a sentence. In this case, if the original sentence had been, "He said the dessert contained lots of pecans" one meaning would be intended. If the original sentence was, "He said the dessert was really crazy," a totally different meaning would be implied. Thus, it can be seen that ambiguity (more than one interpretation of the sentence) exists because of the possible multiple meanings of the word "nutty."

18.25   In Problem 18.24, the ambiguity results from more than one interpretation of one word in the sentence. This is called lexical ambiguity. Define syntactic ambiguity and create an illustration.

    Syntactic ambiguity occurs when the surface structure of the sentence has more than one meaning. An example would be this sentence: "Sinking boats can be unsafe." The ambiguity of such a sentence can be seen by substituting (1) "is" or (2) "are" for the words "can be," thus making "sinking boats" either the action (1) or the object (2).

18.26 Why are finite-state grammars described as deterministic? Why are they generally rejected as an explanation for natural language?

Finite-state grammars imply that we choose one word (because of some preexisting state) and that the choice of this word determines the word chosen next. But evidence indicates that natural language is often a result of some preconceived notion—that is, we know how the sentence will end *before* starting it, and this helps determine the total structure of the sentence.

18.27 Sketch a representation of the phrase-structure-grammar interpretation of this sentence: "George bought the tickets." Then explain why phrase-structure grammar is an inefficient way for studying the syntax of a language.

The representation of the sentence given above might be sketched as in Fig. 18-3. Such interpretations are inefficient because they require a new "tree" to be constructed for each different kind of sentence. There are so many different sentence forms possible that such a task is prohibitively time-consuming.

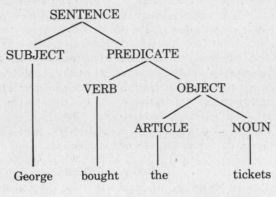

Fig. 18-3

18.28 If the sentence in Problem 18.27 had started in the same way but continued "before he left for work," what kind of semantic memory would research predict?

The new sentence, "George bought the tickets before he left for work," now includes two propositions. The probable encoding would be of each idea presented (buying tickets, leaving for work) linked by the concept "before." Research studies have shown that subjects will often recall the component propositions of a sentence but not the exact sentence (or the deep structure but not the surface structure).

18.29 Distinguish between the semantic memory concept of Problem 18.28 and the phrase-structure grammar presented in Problem 18.27.

Phrase-structure grammars present rules that allow sentences to be generated. However, the rules do allow for incorrect ideas to be expressed (for example, the rules could generate "The tickets bought George"). Semantic memories and the associated semantically based grammars emphasize meaning, and assume that syntactic or other rules serve only to convey that meaning.

18.30 As pointed out before, the study of semantics focuses on the meaning being conveyed. Describe the rudimentary forms of speech that appear to support the concept that even the initial stages of human speech represent attempts to communicate meaning.

The simplest speech consists of one-word utterances, called holophrastic speech. The one word is thought to express much more complex ideas—for example, when the child says "apple," meaning, "I want some apple" or, "Look at the apple that fell on the floor."

One step above this is pivot-open construction.   This involves two-word speech patterns, with one word serving as the base for several different ideas to be communicated.   For example, a pivot word such as "allgone" could be combined with many second words, such as "Daddy," "ball," "food," or "light."

18.31   Suppose a child says, "Apple byebye."   Explain why the pivot-open construction probably cannot account thoroughly for the intent of this utterance.

The solution to this problem is to point out that "Apple byebye" may refer to several different events.   The apple may have been eaten, rolled under a table and out of the child's view, or thrown into a field.   It is recognized that the child may have all (or any one) of these intentions, yet the pivot-open construction generates the same phrase.   It is proposed that something more, of a cognitive nature, is also occurring during this period of language development, and is revealed by later, more varied phrases.

18.32   How are conceptualizations and frame theories used to explain language acquisition and use?

A conceptualization is a basic unit of information that has been retained.   It is proposed that humans use conceptualizations to develop frames (also called scripts or schemata) that allow inferences.   The frame essentially represents what has been called generic memory—stereotypes about various components of our environment.   Inferences are made by using the information from the current situation and the frame held in memory to interpret the input and respond appropriately.

Key Terms

Ambiguity.   The presence of more than one possible meaning.

Aphasia.   Loss of language; often caused by brain damage.

Clause.   A meaningful combination of gramatically related words that contains both a subject and a predicate; often used as a part of a complex sentence.

Conceptualization.   A basic unit of information that has been retained.

Deep structure.   The meaning transmitted by a sequence of words.

Dichotic listening.   Attendance by a listener to two (or more) messages simultaneously; also called two-channel listening.

Ethology.   The study of the innate genetic patterns that produce species-specific behaviors.

Frames.   Inferences from two or more conceptualizations; used to help determine speech production.

Generic memory.   Stereotypes about various components of the environment, against which input can be judged or measured.

Grammar.   The rules determining the arrangement and modification of words in a language.

Holophrastic speech.   One-word communication.

Language.   The system of symbols used for communication and thinking.

Lexical ambiguity.   The ambiguity that exists when a single word or phrase has more than one possible meaning.

Morphemes.   The smallest meaningful units of a language.

Morphology.   The rules determining the modification of words in a language; a part of grammar.

Paraphrasing.   Restating a sentence by changing the surface structure but not the deep structure.

Phonemes. The smallest units of sound that can be discerned by a native speaker of a language.

Phonology. The rules of production and combination of sounds in a language.

Phrase. A meaningful combination of grammatically related words that does not contain both a subject and predicate.

Pivot-open speech. Two-word communication; the pivot word serves as a basis for initiating many different phrases that are distinguished by the accompanying open word.

Psycholinguistics. The study of the relationship between organisms and their language; concerned with the acquisition, structure, and usage of language.

Schemata. Another name for *frames*.

Scripts. Another name for *frames*.

Semantics. The study of what determines word meaning in a language.

Sentence. A meaningful combination of grammatically related words that contains both a subject and a predicate and that makes a complete statement.

Signal. Any stimulus that can be used for communication.

Speech spectrogram. A visual recording of speech.

Surface structure. The arrangement of words in some sequence, usually a sentence.

Syllable. The smallest unit of speech to which the receiver usually attends.

Symbol. Any stimulus that is commonly accepted as a representation for some object, event, action, or idea.

Syntactic ambiguity. Ambiguity created when the surface structure allows more than one possible meaning.

Syntax. The rules determining the arrangement of words in a language; a part of grammar.

Tip-of-the-tongue (TOT) phenomenon. The situation in which retrieval (usually verbal) from long-term memory seems almost possible, but cannot quite be accomplished.

Word. A symbol used in a language.

Chapter 19

Thinking, Problem Solving, and Concept Formation

The title of this chapter is not meant to suggest that thinking and problem solving are two completely separate processes. Most if not all thinking involves problem solving or the use of concepts. And probably all problem solving and concept formation is based upon some form of thinking. The three concepts should not be considered identical; they are alternative ways of understanding an even more elusive concept—the "mind."

19.1 THE NATURE OF THINKING

The mental activity called thinking has two major characteristics. First, it is covert, or unobservable. Second, it is symbolic—involving the manipulation or some other use of symbols. Additionally, thinking can be classified according to how conscious it is, how complex it is, and what kind of neural activity accompanies it. These variables, as well as the two most salient characteristics of thinking, are discussed in this section.

Thinking is Covert

Like other hypothetical constructs, thinking can only be inferred from an organism's performance (or behavior). It cannot be observed or measured directly.

EXAMPLE 1. Suppose a businessman brings his 10-year-old son into the office. The man introduces the boy to his secretary, who smiles at the child and says, "Hello, what's your name?" To this the boy sneers and says, "What do you think it is?" At this point the secretary may have several thoughts. One may take the form of words—perhaps something like, "If any kid of mine ever talked like that, I'd. . . ." Another thought might involve not words but images. For example, the secretary may for a moment picture a scene in which the child is being soundly spanked. The point here, however, is that the secretary's thoughts will most likely remain covert. Her boss may infer from her startled and stern appearance that she is having such thoughts. Or he may even know from his own past experience how someone is likely to feel after his son makes such a bratty comment. In either case, however, the man will not observe the woman's thoughts directly.

Thinking is Symbolic

Psychologists generally agree that thinking involves symbolic processes. The symbols used in a thought process are often words; but words in combination with images or even images alone may constitute a particular thought.

EXAMPLE 2. The woman in Example 1 might have had either of the thoughts mentioned—one verbal and one visual. She may also have had *both* of them perhaps sequentially, or simultaneously, or alternately, or in any number of complex symbolic combinations.

Subconscious Thinking

There is some evidence to indicate that thinking may take place on a subconscious level; that is, a person having a thought may be unaware of it. There is much evidence to indicate that subconscious thoughts are likely to establish themselves around memories and issues and facts with which a person has had abundant experience. It is also true that such subconscious thought patterns become a characteristic part of a person's behaviorial repertoire.

EXAMPLE 3. People in creative occupations often demonstrate the subconscious thinking processes in resolving problems. Seemingly sudden and insightful solutions to ongoing problems often follow periods when conscious thought is not being devoted to the problem at hand. Solutions developed in such apparent rest periods (often called *incubation periods*) may be the results of an ongoing subconscious thought process that is continuing to address the problem and that sooner or later will reveal itself in terms of another "sudden insight."

Complexity of Thinking

Some thinking processes are relatively straightforward, requiring a simple association between an incoming stimulus and the response to be made.   Much of thinking, however, involves the complex interaction of several (or many) symbols.   Indeed, a given person probably has the potential to employ an almost numberless variety of thinking processes in attempting to solve a single problem.

Thinking and Activation

There is general agreement among psychologists on two basic points relating to the relationship between thinking and neural activity.   First, thinking cannot take place unless appropriate neural circuits are activated, and such activation requires some effort.   Secondly, once activated, thought processes may continue even if there is no reason why they should.   Indeed, the attempt to stop the thought processes may prove fruitless, with much more information being retrieved from memory than is desired.

EXAMPLE 4.   One easy demonstration of the continuation of thought processes is to suggest successive topics, indicating that once consideration of the second topic begins, the first topic should be dropped.   Thus, consecutive reflections upon "A giraffe in a graduation cap and gown" and "An automobile wearing a baby bonnet and diapers" may produce conflicting and continuing mental images: a person may think of a giraffe wearing a baby bonnet and diapers.   Essentially the same principle applies when the chairperson in a meeting requests the group to go on to another topic, but the members keep referring back to the previous material.

Costs of activation.   It is suggested that thinking (perhaps both conscious and subconscious) can be best understood as a limited-capacity system.   This suggests that a person can only accomplish so much thinking at any one time.   Therefore, if a certain amount of the total capacity is devoted to a particular topic, that much is not available for other pursuits.

EXAMPLE 5.   Right now, as you are reading this book, some of your thought processes may be focused on some other topic—such as a conversation you had recently, the stuffed-up nose you have, or the possibility that once you finish reading you might go get a pizza.   If these concerns (or any others) intrude upon your concentration, it means that less than total concentration is being given to the materials.

Activation and physiological processes.   Although knowledge about physiological involvement in thinking is limited, there is sufficient evidence to allow certain tentative conclusions.   It is believed that thinking is a brain process, carried out primarily in the cerebral cortex.   Apparently, there are areas in each cerebral hemisphere capable of performing the same thought processes, but in an intact brain one hemisphere will dominate while the activity of the other for that particular thought process will be inhibited.   This prevents duplication of effort or the possibility of competition between the two hemispheres.

EXAMPLE 6.   Studies involving stroke victims have shown how, at least in some cases, individuals suffering damage to one cerebral hemisphere and resultant loss of responding have been able to recover the response patterns.   For example, speech patterns are generally thought to be controlled by the left cerebral hemisphere.   When that hemisphere is damaged, therapy apparently can help activate the comparable right-hemisphere areas and restore the speech responses.   (*Note:* There remains a need for extensive research in this field before any more definitive statements can be made.   Advances in both understanding and technology should allow much of the necessary investigation to be conducted.)

19.2   TYPES OF MENTAL OPERATIONS

Before attempting to designate and describe the various types of mental operations, it is necessary to make three general points: (1) In one way or another, thinking is a part of almost every area of psychology.   While certainly fitting within the psychology of learning, thinking has also been considered in disciplines such as physiological psychology, developmental psychology, the study of personality and abnormal behavior, and mathematical psychology, as well as in related disciplines such as philosophy, sociology and anthropology. (2) Regardless of the approach to thinking that has been adopted, the general nature of thinking described in Section 19.1 has been accepted, as have standards for measuring thinking in terms of a person's capacity to perform various mental processes and how much time is required for such performance. (3) Any mental operation is thought to produce some change in the state of knowledge of the person.

EXAMPLE 7. "Creative thought" is sometimes measured by showing an object to the person and asking for as many different uses as can be generated. Responses are evaluated in terms of how many different *types* of responses are made (capacity) and how *quickly* they are made (time). The *variety* of responses made is thought to be indicative of creativity.

Keeping these general principles in mind, the following sections present some ways of identifying types of mental operations.

Abstraction

When the stimulus input is coded in some condensed form, the mental operation of *abstraction* is said to have occurred. Although this is probably most frequently accomplished by using some verbal code (words) it may be achieved with iconic codes (visual images) or echoic codes (auditory images) as well.

An abstraction typically is one of two types. If several stimulus items are classified according to their general category, a *summary* type of abstraction has taken place. When a particular feature of several stimuli is attended to while other aspects are ignored, a *selective* type of abstraction has occurred.

EXAMPLE 8. Coding according to selection is illustrated when a person classified a ball, the moon, and a lampshade as round. The very disparate characteristics of these three objects are ignored, while the single similarity (roundness) serves as the focal point. A person would show a summary type of abstract thought by classifying a tennis ball, baseball, soccer ball and a football in the same category in spite of the differences among them.

Generation

Generation is considered the inverse of abstraction. It is a conceptual process in which some general instruction activates a code that leads to behaviors specific to the situation. Measurement of generative processes typically involves the two considerations stated earlier—how much capacity is illustrated by the responses given, and how much time it takes for responding to occur.

EXAMPLE 9. One time measurement sometimes used to evaluate generative processes is to determine the length of pauses between successive spoken words. In general, it is found that pauses are longest when the next word in a sequence is relatively unpredictable. Thus, in the phrase, *"He jumped off the bridge,"* pauses probably would be longer between "jumped" and "off" or between "the" and "bridge" than between "off" and "the."

Combination

Combinational mental processes require the use of two or more classes of mental operations. In a general fashion, these operations are represented by instructions involving X and Y, X and/or X but not Y. In other words, two considerations (at least) must be evaluated before the mental process is completed.

EXAMPLE 10. A simple example of a combinational mental process is an experiment in which subjects are presented with problems involving arithmetical operations. A time measurement will show that subjects will identify $5 + 2 = 7$ as correct more rapidly than they will identify $5 + 2 = 6$ as being incorrect. This is taken as evidence that the familiar combination demands less of the mental processes than an unfamiliar one does.

Sequencing

Psychologists have used computer simulation (see Chapter 15) to try to determine the processes involved in a *sequence* of mental operations.   The series of operations needed to accomplish a particular task can at least be hypothesized, although the actual representation is difficult because of the covert nature of thinking.   Time measurements, such as reaction time, also allow estimation of the number of mental operations required for a task.

19.3   PROBLEM SOLVING

A major area of study in the psychology of learning is that of problem solving.   Some psychologists treat this as a subcategory of thinking, while others see it as an independent topic.   For the purposes of this outline, it is not important to choose one of these viewpoints over the other.

The Nature of a Problem

Solving a *problem* involves determining the correct response in a unique or novel situation.   It is the *discovery* of the correct response, or solution, that differentiates problem-solving processes from other mental processes, such as creative thinking, free association, or recollecting memories.

Goals and subgoals.   Another way to view a problem is in terms of the goals or subgoals that are desired.   A well-defined problem has clearly designated goals and, possibly, subgoals—i.e., a definite end product and, perhaps, some intermediate accomplishments that a person attempts to achieve.   A subgoal is often seen as a means to accomplishing an eventual goal.

EXAMPLE 11.   Consider this problem: "How does one get home from school when the bridge usually used is closed?"   The problem has a relatively well-defined goal.   In contrast, consider this problem: "How does one make a significant contribution to society?"   Its goal is much less well defined.   The solution of either, however, might involve determining subgoals that lead to the eventual (final) goal.

Steps in Problem Solving

Typically, problem solving involves recognition and definition of the problem, generation and test of possible solutions, and finally selection of the best solution.

Recognition and definition of the problem.   In order to solve a problem, a person must first recognize that it exists.   Then, in order to understand what response or responses should be made to the novel situation, the person must define the goal (and possibly subgoals) he or she wants to achieve.

Possible solutions.   The next step in problem solving is to determine what solutions may allow attainment of the goal.   These possible solutions may be generated as hypotheses or actual responses.   On occasion, when no solutions appear to be forthcoming, the problem is set aside, only to have a sudden, seemingly insightful solution recognized some time later.   (Again, the period of time when apparent subconscious operations have occurred is often referred to as an *incubation* period.)

Some groups have adopted a technique called *brainstorming* as a way of solving problems.   In brainstorming, as many solutions as possible are generated before any judgments are made regarding their relative worth.

Test and selection of solution.   After possible solutions are generated, they are tested.   Generally, the solution which best achieves the intended goal is the one selected.

EXAMPLE 12.   Presented with the problem of transporting a very large crate full of heavy furniture, a man might first try to load it into his automobile.   When he realizes that the crate will not fit into the car, he has already recognized the problem and defined the ultimate goal: getting the furniture moved from one place to another.   Next, several subgoals may suggest themselves to him.   For example, can the pieces of furniture be taken out of the crate and transported one at a time? Or should the man hire a mover? Or is there someone from whom he can borrow a truck? Selection of the most promising alternative will, he hopes, leads to the ultimate goal.

Search for Solutions

The choice of a reasonable set of possible solutions is frequently thought of as the crucial step in problem solving. Consequently, special attention has been given to this topic. One major consideration has been to identify *search strategies,* or the ways in which one seeks solutions.

There are two basic search strategies. *Forward search* involves a beginning-to-end format, starting with a statement of the problem and progressing through steps until the goal is reached. A *backward search* starts at the goal and in reverse order determines the steps necessary for accomplishing it.

EXAMPLE 13. The two contrasting search strategies can be illustrated by the type of problem often found in newspapers or magazines and shown in Fig. 19-1. Solving the maze by following the track from Start to Goal represents a forward search, while starting at the goal and working backwards is a backward search strategy.

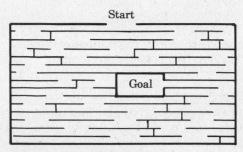

Fig. 19-1

Problem Protocol

Studies of problem solving sometimes involve asking the subjects to give a verbal report of the processes being used during the solution period. Called the *protocol,* this account helps reveal the sequence of mental operations occurring during solution. There are difficulties with depending upon protocols, however. It is unlikely that the subject will be able to express the subconscious mental operations that may take place, nor can it even be expected that an accurate representation of conscious processes will always be provided.

EXAMPLE 14. While a sample protocol will not be provided here, the reader is invited to develop one by solving the following quite widely reproduced problem: If D = 5, what are the number values for each of the other letters in the problem

$$
\begin{array}{r}
\text{DONALD} \\
+ \text{ GERALD} \\
\hline
\text{ROBERT}
\end{array}
$$

Immediately after looking at the problem, was your first reaction to say, "Well, T must equal zero"? That is the usual first step in a protocol for this problem. The solution, which can be arrived at with a variety of protocols in which numbers are substituted for letters in a trial-and-error fashion, is as follows:

$$
\begin{array}{r}
\text{DONALD} = 526485 \\
+ \text{ GERALD} = 197485 \\
\hline
\text{ROBERT} = 723970
\end{array}
$$

Variables Affecting Problem Solving

Again, it is beyond the scope of this book to present an in-depth and exhaustive discussion of the many variables that may influence the problem-solving process, and it should be recognized that many of the variables presented in earlier chapters could be studied in relation to problem solving.   Thus, the principles of acquisition, verbal learning, reinforcement, retention, forgetting, and motivation, among many others, could be investigated in any attempt to gain insight into the mental operations involved in problem solving.

EXAMPLE 15.   One learning variable that might affect problem solving is the partial-reinforcement effect (PRE), which was discussed earlier.   Given a particular problem, the subject may develop several possible solutions, select one, and find that the solution works only some of the time.   Although there may be much better solutions, this one may become a fixed part of the subject's behavior repertoire because the PRE results in great resistance to extinction.   Thus, this solution may continue to be used even in the face of evidence of its ineffectiveness.

19.4   THEORIES OF PROBLEM SOLVING

There are two major theories of problem solving, one based on S-R (behaviorist) principles and the other on gestalt psychology principles.   In addition, a third important interpretation of problem solving has been put forth by psychologists favoring an information-processing approach.

S-R Theory

The traditionally accepted S-R theory of problem solving is that solutions are reached in a *trial-and-error* manner.   One solution is tested first, and if it does not work another is used until the correct solution is found.

Some S-R theorists assume that the various solutions form a *habit hierarchy*.   It is believed that the solution highest in the hierarchy will be tried first, with subsequent attempts moving down through the hierarchy until a correct solution is found or all possible solutions have been exhausted.

Additionally, S-R theorists frequently emphasize the use of *mediation* in problem solving. They claim that internal, verbal representations of solutions precede any concrete attempts to solve the problem.   By reviewing the possible solutions verbally, a person can accept or reject each before it is tried.   (This is a covert trial-and-error process.)

Gestalt Theory

Gestalt theorists propose that problems are solved when *insight* occurs.   This is a much more cognitive approach than S-R theory; insight is revealed by the sudden resolution of a problem and performance of a correct response with little or no error preceding it.   The sudden resolution is thought to occur when the subject achieves a perceptual reorganization of the stimuli in the environment.   These new or different ways of dealing with the environment do not necessarily mean that any hierarchy of habits is involved.   (*Note:* Gestaltists admit that trial and error might be necessary in rather complex problems because the subject would be unable to perceive such a problem in its entirety and thus could not create a perceptual reorganization of it.)

Perceptual set.   A *perceptual set* is defined as the temporary tendency to respond in a certain manner.   Gestaltists have demonstrated how subjects persevere in using one form of solution even when another, better solution could be implemented.   Shown how to restructure the problem, these subjects quickly adopt the other solution.

EXAMPLE 16.   Solve the following set of problems: If *A*, *B*, and *C* represent the size of three measuring cups in ounces (oz), determine how they could be used to get the measure indicated as the desired result.

	A	B	C	Result desired
Problem 1	15 oz	6 oz	8 oz	5 oz
Problem 2	9	24	5	23
Problem 3	6	13	5	9
Problem 4	14	12	3	20

Solving Problem 1, you may realize that the result can be obtained by adding A and B ($15 + 6 = 21$) and then subtracting C twice ($15 + 6 - 8 - 8 = 5$).   The same $A + B - 2C$ set also works for Problem 2 ($9 + 24 - 5 - 5 = 23$) and for Problem 3 ($6 + 13 - 5 - 5 = 9$).   Now consider the set you would use for solving Problem 4.   If you were locked into the $A + B - 2C$ pattern from the previous three problems, you may fail to recognize the simpler (reorganized) $A + 2C$ solution.

Functional fixedness.   A special form of set has been called *functional fixedness*, the inability to recognize uses other than the most common for a particular object.

EXAMPLE 17.   The person who clutches a furled umbrella in his hand while complaining about the absence of any shade from the hot sunshine is showing functional fixedness.

Transfer of training and problem solving.   Transfer of training, the influence of some previous learning on acquisition of some new response, affects problem-solving situations in much the same way it affects other types of learning.   There may be positive transfer, negative transfer, or no transfer, and any instance of transfer may be either specific or general.

Transfer appears to be more important for reproductive (noncombinational) problems than for those requiring a productive (combinational) solution.   While the former seem to depend upon memorization and direct application of previous learning, the latter require comprehension and understanding of the problem with new and indirect uses of previous learning.   The reproductive solutions seem to fit best with S-R explanations, while the productive solutions are more in keeping with gestalt ideas.

Information Processing

Chapter 15 presented many of the basic principles of information processing as studied in the psychology of learning.   The topic is reintroduced here because this viewpoint has become an important part of the study of problem solving.

In the *input-processing-output* format, input is not seen as an eliciting mechanism, but as a material which the organism processes.   The key aspect is the study of the process, while the output (or solution) is treated simply as the result of that process.

Information-processing studies can be very efficient, handling complex problems that may be beyond the scope of simple S-R or gestalt experiments.   Algorithms or heuristics may be used as aids to understanding the problem-solving processes.   However, it is necessary, when using this approach, to be realistic in the use of the computer.   For example, computers can hold very large amounts of information in immediate storage, but using them this way is inappropriate in such a study because it does not simulate human performance.

19.5   EXPERIMENTAL PROBLEMS

This section describes some of the typical experimental problems used in problem-solving investigations.   In addition, this section reviews some of the important variables that affect problem-solving tasks.

Characteristics of Experimental Tasks

Generally, there are three important variables that may be manipulated in problem-solving tasks: stimulus factors, the responses required and strength of response expected, and possible transfer-of-training effects.

Types of Experimental Tasks

Certain tasks have been particularly popular as means of investigating problem-solving processes.   Among these are arithmetic problems, cryptarithmetic problems (Example 14), problems investigating set (Example 16), so-called insight problems requiring perceptual reorganization, search problems such as jigsaw puzzles or mazes (Example 13), and verbal problems involving anagrams (Example 18 below).

EXAMPLE 18.   In a typical anagram problem, subjects might be asked to unscramble the following sets of letters to form actual words:

ORCOL   ISBAS   ANHUM   ELHOT   ICMUS   RESPA

In addition to illustrating an anagram problem, this example shows once again how it is possible to become set to respond in a certain manner.   If the response to the sixth scrambled-letter pattern is "spare," it is likely that a perceptual set ("last three, first two") has been established by the previous five anagrams.   Other responses, somewhat less likely to be given, include "spear" or "pears."   (The last anagram is different from the first five in that more than one word can be formed by unscrambling its letters; in addition, it differs in that the word formed is always a one- rather than a two-syllable word.)

19.6   CONCEPT LEARNING

One widely studied area of thinking has been *concept learning,* the learning of specific stimulus characteristics to which responses could be associated.   Most of the research in this area has concentrated upon studies of attribute identification or rule learning.

Attribute Identification

All stimuli can be categorized according to *dimensions,* such as color, size, texture, intensity, and a number of other characteristics.   Stimulus *attributes* are the values of these dimensions.

EXAMPLE 19.   A visual stimulus might be categorized according to the dimensions of size, shape, and color.   The attributes might then be determined as follows:

Size: Large, medium, small
Shape: Square, circle, triangle
Color: Red, blue, green

Studies concerned with attribute identification generally involve acquisition of previously unknown information about the properties of the stimuli.

Rule Learning

In some cases the subject knows the stimulus dimensions, the attribute values, and the relevant attributes, yet must uncover a new relationship among the stimuli presentations.   Such a study involves *rule learning.*   The task is to identify the rule that defines the concept.

EXAMPLE 20.   Using the attributes provided in Example 19, a rule might state that reinforcement will be given for a response only when the stimulus is a blue circle.   Notice that two of the three attributes are relevant, while the third—size—does not apply as part of the rule.   The subject's task would be to determine this rule.

Conceptual Rules

Determination of which attributes are relevant and how they are used establishes *conceptual rules.*   Experimental research has concentrated on several forms of these rules, including the following.

Single attribute (present): If the stimulus has the attribute, the response should be made.   (For example, if the stimulus is blue, the response should be made.)

Single attribute (absent): If the stimulus does not have the attribute, the response should be made.   (For example, if the stimulus is anything but blue, the response should be made.)

Conjunctive: If the stimulus has two (or more) appropriate properties, the response should be made.   (For example, if the stimulus is both blue and circular, the response should be made.)

Disjunctive: If the stimulus has *one* of two (or more) appropriate properties, the response should be made.   (For example, if the stimulus is blue or circular or both, the response should be made.)

Conditional: If the stimulus event contains one dimension of an attribute, another attribute must also be present for the response to be made. (For example, if the stimulus is blue, it must also be circular for the response to be made. Perhaps, in this instance, a green stimulus might be *any* shape and be appropriate.)

Joint denial: If the stimulus has neither one attribute nor another, responding is appropriate. For example, if the stimulus is neither blue nor circular, the response should be made; the presence of either dimension makes it an inappropriate instance of the stimulus.

EXAMPLE 21. Figure 19-2 illustrates the conceptual rules presented above. A + indicates when responding would be appropriate.

		Blue	Green
Single attribute (present) (if blue)	○	+	
	△	+	
Single attribute (absent) (if not blue)	○		+
	△		+
Conjunctive (if blue and circular)	○	+	
	△		
Disjunctive (if blue and/or circular)	○	+	+
	△	+	
Conditional (if blue and circular, or if green)	○	+	+
	△		+
Joint denial (if not blue and not circular)	○		
	△		+

Fig. 19-2

Theories of Concept Learning

Three general theoretical approaches have been proposed to account for concept learning. These are association theories, hypothesis-testing theories, and information-processing theories. Each has several varieties.

Association theories. Association theories emphasize S-R bonds that develop for both positive and negative instances of a concept and the appropriate responses. These are basically passive-reception theories in the sense that the organism is not thought to be actively selecting or processing information. The only requirement of association theories is that the organism retain a memory of prior experiences.

Two variations of association theory have been called *stimulus generalization theory* and *mediation theory.* The former accounts for the correct response being given to a variety of stimuli by reason of the principle of stimulus generalization. Negative instances do not provoke the response because differentiation has occurred. The latter theory proposes that a learned internal mediating process provides equivalence for varying stimuli.

EXAMPLE 22. Mediation theory allows humans to categorize a scarf, a hat, and a jacket under one stimulus concept, "clothing," not because these objects share similar physical stimulus attributes, but because all three elicit common mediational responses, such as "protection" or "warmth" or "winter."

Hypothesis-testing theories. The basis for all hypothesis-testing theories is the assumption that the learner plays an active role in concept learning. In general, these theories assume that the subject selects a hypothesis, tests it, and either confirms or disconfirms the proposal. If a hypothesis is disconfirmed, alternates are selected and tested.

Often, this process is viewed as a sequence of decision-making events, with each decision depending on all previous decisions. In many cases, the sequence is thought to reflect some *strategy* being employed by the subject.

EXAMPLE 23. An example of strategy has been called *focusing*. Suppose the subject seeks a single attribute rule. Using the dimensions suggested in Example 19, the subject might be shown a small blue circle and told it is an example of a positive instance. The first hypothesis tested might then involve color, so that if the subject determines that a small green circle also is a positive instance, the subject knows color is irrelevant. Subsequent hypotheses would focus on the other attributes until the rule is found.

Information-processing theories. The information-processing theories of concept learning have developed primarily because of the input-processing-output analogies that have been made between human beings and computer. Researchers have attempted to develop programs to simulate the concept-learning processes shown by humans.

In general, these programs have concentrated upon rule learning rather than attribute identification. Because of this emphasis, these theories stress the processes used to select hypotheses to test and to make decisions.

Solution Shifts

One particularly interesting aspect of concept learning has been the study of solution shifts. Two varieties, reversal shifts and nonreversal shifts, have been investigated.

Reversal shifts. Also called intradimensional shifts, *reversal shifts* occur when the subject learns a particular solution, then must change to the opposite solution for the same stimulus dimensions.

EXAMPLE 24. Suppose the subject is shown four stimuli as in Fig. 19-3.

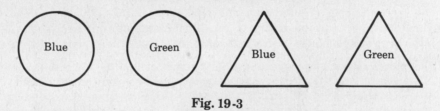

Fig. 19-3

The subject learns that regardless of color, triangles are always correct (positive instances) and circles are always incorrect (negative instances). A reversal-shift problem would require the subject to switch so that circles would always be treated as positive instances and triangles as negative instances.

Nonreversal shifts. Also called extradimensional shifts, *nonreversal shifts* occur when the subject learns a particular solution, then must ignore the dimension upon which that solution is based and learn a solution based upon a different dimension and its attributes.

EXAMPLE 25. Using the same four stimuli given in the last example and the same initial solution, a nonreversal shift would be required if the switch makes all *blue* stimuli positive instances and all *green* negative instances. The shift is from shape to color in this case, rather than within the shape dimension, as was the case in Example 24.

Studies using reversal-shift and/or nonreversal-shift procedures have provided a number of results and subsequent interpretations. The learning of associative mediating responses has been used often as an explanation for why older children perform better than younger children on reversal-shift problems, while the (relatively) verbally unskilled younger children perform better than older children on nonreversal-shift problems. But contradictory results have weakened such an explanation.

Optional shifts. Another interesting solution shift design has been called the optional shift. When the shift training occurs, more than one possible interpretation is possible. Subsequent testing helps determine what choice the subject has made.

EXAMPLE 26.   Suppose the subject is presented with the blue and green triangles and circles shown in Fig. 19-3.   The initial task involves learning that triangles are always correct.   When the shift task is presented, only two of the four stimuli are used (see Fig. 19-4).   Once the subject has learned this shift, the third step is to present a test pair of stimuli such as Fig. 19-5.   This test pair is presented alternately with the training pair shown in Fig. 19-4.

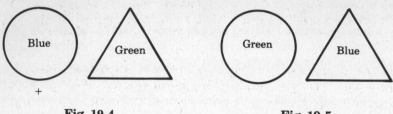

Fig. 19-4   **Fig. 19-5**

The subject's responses may show whether an option has been selected.   If the subject regularly chooses the green circle, it would appear the circle property determines the response pattern.   Since the first discrimination had triangles as the positive instance, a reversal-shift option has been shown.

If the subject chooses the blue triangle consistently, it appears that blue is the determining property.   This is known because responding continues to the alternately presented blue circle in the other pair presented during this test.   With the concentration on color rather than form, a nonreversal-shift option has been shown.

A subject who chooses neither of the two stimuli consistently is said to be making a *nonselective shift*.

Solved Problems

19.1   Before starting this problem, try to recall the name of your first-grade teacher.   Then explain why your response to this last sentence probably was representative of thinking.

There are at least two important aspects of the solution to this problem.   First, unless you actually spoke or wrote the teacher's name, your response was covert, or hidden.   (The process of thinking is considered covert—that is, thinking is defined as internal responding.)   Second, your response doubtless took the form of words.   (Thought involves the manipulation of words or other symbols.)   The characteristics of covertness and the use of symbols can therefore be used to classify your response as thinking.

19.2   Explain why the cartoon shown in Fig. 19-6 illustrates both an aspect of thinking and a component of the problem-solving process.

Fig. 19-6

An important point to understand about thinking is that much of it may take place at a subconscious level.   The sudden solution to a problem may represent a conscious recognition of thinking that has already taken place at a subconscious level.

The cartoon also represents a component of the problem-solving process in that the subconscious thinking described above has been designated as the incubation phase of problem solving.   Termination of incubation is signified by the sudden solution to a problem (see Problem 19.24).

19.3 In Problem 19.1, you were asked to try to recall your first-grade teacher's name. Why would such a thought process be considered relatively simple when compared with a problem in which you were asked to explain what went on in your first-grade class.

The solution to this problem points out that thinking may take place at many different levels of complexity. While all thinking involves covert manipulation of symbols, simple recall requires a single symbol and a basic association. But an explanation such as the one asked for here involves much more complex manipulations. (*Note:* Many terms such as "decide," "plan," "organize," and "explain" indicate that fairly complex thought processes are being asked for.)

19.4 Consider, *for a moment,* the patterns involved when birds make their winter migration. Now *stop.* Do *not* consider this topic anymore. What principle explains why you may not be able to follow the second direction given above? (Indeed, you may not yet have stopped that thought sequence.)

Many studies of thought processes have stressed the concept of activation—that is, the operation of the neural circuits necessary for conscious or subconscious thinking. Apparently, there is some effort required to get some thought process activated, but once they are started they may continue regardless of the desire to terminate them. Seemingly, memory storage works in such a way that when the symbolic manipulations of thought begin, more units of information than are either required or desired may be generated.

19.5 Reed finds that he has driven his tractor-trailer truck past the Leroyville exit, where he intended to leave the thruway. Now he must continue to the Depew exit before being able to get off. He blames this on his worries about his son, who is in the hospital. Is it possible that Reed is correct in placing the blame? What principle can be used to explain Reed's behavior?

Reed has probably evaluated the situation correctly. The activation of a thought process, particularly on a subconscious level, uses up a certain amount of the total available resources for thinking. In this case, if Reed has been processing many thoughts about his son, it is likely that the normal activity of driving has had only a small share of the resources, and thus his conscious thought processes failed to elicit the necessary behavior for exiting.

19.6 In Chapter 18, evidence was presented indicating that language processing on a simple level may be more effectively accomplished by the left rather than the right cerebral hemisphere. (Research of this nature is done when both hemispheres are active and the corpus callosum is intact.) Other research has shown that when only one hemisphere has been activated, the difference between the two hemispheres' roles is not pronounced. What does this appear to indicate about the physiological sources of thought processes?

It has been concluded that there may be dual capacities for thought processing in the two cerebral hemispheres, but that when an intact brain is operating, one of the two hemispheres will be dominant for a given type of processing. Thus, language may appear to be a function of the left cerebral hemisphere when both are active, but the right hemisphere may be *capable* of performing the necessary activities if it is the only hemisphere available. The activity of the nondominant hemisphere seems to be suppressed when both are active, avoiding duplication or competition of processing efforts.

19.7 Thinking is often characterized as covert, but it has still been possible to classify different types of mental operations and attempt to measure them. In general, what representations of mental processes have been proposed? How are they measured?

Mental processes have been classified according to philosophical considerations, developmental concerns, computer simulations, language and problem-solving aspects, physiological properties, and other approaches. Although there are many ways to attempt to categorize mental operations, measurement appears to depend upon two properties: (1) some form of capacity and (2) the amount of time required for performance of the operation.

19.8   What effect does a mental operation produce?

When the essentials of thought processing are analyzed, it can be seen that any mental operation will produce a change in the state of knowledge an individual has. Although the changes will vary according to the type of operation, the general principle appears to hold for all mental operations.

19.9   A friend says, "You must come see my office. I've really made it look great, with an azalea, an African violet, a Norfolk pine, and a miniature spruce." Your thought is, "Those *plants* really should help make the office look good." What mental operation have you demonstrated? What form of this same operation would you show if you thought, "Those flowers and evergreens will look beautiful."

By consolidating the four given names into a single category of plants, you have shown the mental operation of summary abstraction. Another form of abstraction, which is selective, would have been shown if you had discriminated between the flowers (azaleas and violets) and the evergreens (pine and spruce).

19.10   Distinguish among iconic, echoic, and verbal codes as they are used in abstraction. Is there evidence to support the idea that these are separate mental processes?

An iconic code is one which stores a visual representation (or image) of a given stimulus. Echoic coding involves storage of an auditory image. A verbal code may be either iconic or echoic, but has as its crucial property the use of symbolic representation.

Research has indicated that these processes are separate. For example, studies using split-brain subjects have shown that the verbal code may be stored in one hemisphere while its accompanying visual properties are stored in the other hemisphere.

19.11   Why is the mental operation of generation considered to be essentially the opposite of abstraction?

Generation requires the person to locate and activate previously stored specific information when given general instructions. Abstraction demands the creation of a more general representation from specific inputs.

19.12   What measurements of mental operations would be used in a study where subjects are asked to generate responses to an anagram problem? (For example, how many words can you create using the letters in the word "generation"?)

A *time* measurement would have to be used to determine how many correct responses are produced in a given period. (This is a rather gross example of a time measurement; for other responses, a specific reaction time—from the onset of a signal until the completion of responding—might be used. Responses not made during this specific period would not be counted as correct.)

The *capacity* measurement would probably be evaluated by determining the total number of words produced. Factors such as the subject's alertness, concentration, and attention may affect the capacity at any given moment, and therefore the responses produced.

19.13   Suppose an experimenter asks the subject to take the next three minutes to produce as many associates as possible to the word "plant." Suggest the pattern of responding that might be found.

It is likely that the generation process would be based upon the underlying framework created by previous learning. Thus, the specific responses prompted by the general stimulus might start with words such as ivy, tree, or vegetable; switch to more specific labels (such as miniature orange tree or eucalyptus); and then perhaps change to a new interpretation entirely (for example, words related to factories or espionage).   It would be expected that the time sequence would show relatively short pauses between words in one category, with relatively longer pauses occurring when a switch from one category to another takes place.

19.14   How is a combinational operation a more sophisticated mental operation than generation is?   Give an example of a combinational operation.

Generation simply involves the production of a response.   Combinational operations require not only response production, but some use or manipulation of the responses produced.   An example of a combinational operation might be correct identification of a product logo, requiring the person to recognize the correct shape *and* the correct color.   (*Note:* Other combinational operations might involve some sort of *and/or* or *not* determination.)

19.15   Why have reaction-time studies seemed to support the analysis of sequential operations as a predictable series of processes?

By using previously established stimulus properties (e.g., positive statements are encoded more easily than negative statements) and combining them into a particular set of reaction-time problems, recognizable patterns or sequences of mental operations have been proposed.   Thus, encoding a stimulus and judging it against a positive statement ("Is a peach a fruit?") will produce a judgmental response more rapidly than a sequence involving the need to judge the stimulus against a negative statement ("Is a peach not a vegetable?").   The additional reaction time required represents the sequencing step necessary for dealing with the negative.

19.16   Although the anagram situation presented in Problem 19.12 was treated as a generation situation, it could easily be interpreted as a problem-solving circumstance.   Using the definition of a problem, explain how this is so.

A problem exists when the subject is asked to discover the correct response in a novel situation.   It is unlikely that the subject would have practiced the anagram task presented (although similar tasks may have been practiced), thus making this a novel situation.

19.17   Suppose the subject performing the anagram task in Problem 19.12 decides to produce as many words as possible that begin with the letter *g*.   Then the subject goes on to produce words that begin with *e*, words that begin with *n*, and so on.   What problem-solving technique is this subject showing?

The goal of problem solving, as stated above in Problem 19.16, is to discover the correct response in a novel situation.   Because this task requires multiple responses, the subject apparently has established a series of subgoals that will eventually lead to the overall goal.

19.18   The boss asks you to buy a particular piece of equipment for the company at the best possible price.   Describe how you would go about doing this, using the typical steps for problem solving.

First, you must recognize there is a problem and define it correctly.   In this case, there are two components that must be considered—correct identification of the equipment to be purchased and best possible price.   Both criteria must be fulfilled to solve the problem to the boss's satisfaction.

Next, you probably should determine how to go about locating vendors of the product, and how to contact them to determine the price of the product.   You may generate several different hypotheses for this step, such as telephoning, writing letters, or driving around town to their various offices.

Finally, the single best hypothesis is selected, the information is gathered, and the product is ordered.   The entire sequence has involved correct recognition and definition of the problem, generation of possible solutions, and the selection of the best of these.

19.19 In Problem 19.18, why might an immediate selection of one solution prove inefficient?   What problem-solving technique helps overcome this difficulty?

Seeking vendors of the product, you might foolishly jump into your car and start driving around
town looking for stores that carry the product.   Your initial hypothesis proposes a time-consuming
and inefficient solution, but if you "fix" upon it, other possible approaches may be blocked.

One practical way of overcoming this danger is to use a technique called brainstorming.   The
individual (or group) is encouraged to generate as many solutions as possible, with judgments about
each deferred for the time being.   Quite often this will lead to a great quantity of solutions, with
many of them of high quality.   Delaying the choice allows for a broader range of solutions to be
considered and may (as would be true here) lead to selection of the best choice rather than one that
simply works.

19.20 Search strategies to determine solutions to a problem may be of two types.   What are they,
and how do they differ?

Essentially, a search may be either forward or backward.   A forward search tries some means of
attack, determines if progress has been made, and then progresses to the next step, eventually
reaching the desired goal.   A backward search identifies the desired end product or goal, then tries to
establish what step would have produced that goal.   When this is done, the next previous step is
determined, and so on, until the sequence (in reverse order) has been identified.

19.21 What is meant by the phrase "means-end analysis?"

The solution to some problems involves determining several steps.   The ultimate goal (the end)
probably has been identified, but the operations necessary (the means) must be determined.   What
takes place is a comparison between the knowledge at present and the goal desired.   Attempts are
made to determine the operations (means) that will eliminate any differences existing between the
current knowledge level and what is required at the end of the process.   Thus, the repeated testing of
the circumstances has come to be known as a means-end analysis.

19.22 One method of studying problem solving has been to record a subject's protocol.   What
does this mean?   What is the major drawback with this method?

A subject's protocol is the verbal description of mental operations occurring during the solution of
a problem.   Generally, the major difficulty with using this approach to study problem solving is that
the subject is unable to give a complete record of what mental operations have taken place.   There is
much evidence to indicate that subconscious influences (such as hints) may affect the strategies
employed for solving a problem but not become a part of the protocol.

19.23 Give some examples of principles of learning presented in previous chapters that can be
shown to influence the success of problem solving.

The solution to this problem could fill an entire chapter by itself.   Selecting from several
different areas, however, it can be pointed out that a particular protocol might be *modeled* after that
of someone else, that a sucessful solution may be a function of *level of motivation*, and that the speed of
solution could depend upon the *encoding* of information, the amount of information held in *short-term
memory*, or the *language* patterns employed to achieve a given goal.   The general point is that
problem solving is very much a function of many other principles of learning.

19.24 Historically, what was the major controversy regarding a subject's style of problem solving?   What resolution has been achieved?

The leading controversy regarding styles of problem solving was between S-R interpretations
and the gestalt position.   This was much like the incremental vs. one-trial controversy in that the
S-R position stressed trial-and-error learning, while the gestalt explanation emphasized sudden or
insightful solutions.

The resolution of this controversy has been to achieve a compromise—with each side recognizing value in the other's position.   For example, a seemingly insightful or sudden solution can be thought to have resulted from subconscious trial-and-error testing of possible solutions during what is called the *incubation period*.   (*Note:* The information processing approach to problem solving is yet a third way of viewing the style of problem solving employed.   This relatively recent model incorporates some features of both of the other positions.)

19.25   Explain what effect a habit hierarchy is supposed to have upon problem solving according to an S-R position.

An important belief of many of those who accept the S-R interpretation of problem solving is that the trial-and-error pattern shown will be based upon previously learned habits.   In addition, the habits are ordered into a hierarchy (sometimes called a habit-family hierarchy), with the highest on the hierarchy tried first.   The subject progresses down the hierarchy until a solution is found or the hierarchy is exhausted and the problem abandoned.

19.26   The traveler in a foreign country attempts to speak the native language, but is unsuccessful in communicating a message.   According to an S-R explanation, what effect might this have later, when the traveler faces a similar problem in a different foreign country?

The traveler would probably be less likely to try to speak the foreign language.   The S-R interpretation would suggest that mediated generalization had taken place.   The general class of responses involving attempts at speaking foreign languages would be inhibited (an extinction process is occurring), and the traveler may seek an alternative solution, such as trying to find a translator or using a pen and paper to "draw" the message.

19.27   Explain why the type of problem may affect a psychologist's choice of either the S-R or gestalt interpretation as an explanation.

The major controversy between the S-R and gestalt positions concerns the means of achieving the solution.   The S-R position accepts a step-by-step (trial-and-error) interpretation, while the gestaltists believe that solution is achieved by insight (a one-trial view).   In the past, S-R theorists tended to study problems that did *not* allow the subjects to perceive most or all of the stimulus aspects in their entirety, while gestaltists studied problems that did allow such perceptions.   Thus the theory employed was a function of the type of problem being studied.

19.28   Suppose a driver continues to use the very slow Route 161 to get from Dublin to the Olentangy River Road, even though the extension of this road now links with Interstate 270, a much faster road.   What principle might explain such behavior?

It is possible that the driver's behavior represents the persistence of set; that is, he continues to apply a solution that works badly even though a better solution is available.   Quite often, this occurs because there is a failure to understand that the situation has changed.   Achieving such understanding would then lead to establishment of a new set.

19.29   Sheldon leaves the dry cleaner carrying several sport coats on wire hangers.   When he gets to his car, he realizes he has locked his keys inside it.   Although he has left a window slightly open, he is unable to think of a way to get the car unlocked.   Finally he calls his wife to bring a second set of keys.   What should Sheldon have tried?   Why didn't he?

The solution would be to bend one of the coat hangers and try to pull up the door lock.   This may seem fairly obvious to the reader, but apparently Sheldon is unable to determine such a solution because of functional fixedness, the tendency to think of objects as having only one specific use and to ignore other possible (but less common) uses.

19.30   Why is productive problem solving thought to involve more than simple transfer of training, while reproductive problem solving is not?   What other comparison is used to describe essentially the same concepts?

Productive problem solving is held to require the combination of previously unrelated experiences.   Reproductive problem solving refers to the application of previous experiences to a new situation in a rather direct (or noncombinational) manner.   While transfer of training can be used to account for the reproductive patterns, it appears to be inadequate for productive thinking.   Transfer will not guarantee a solution for a productive-problem-solving situation; appropriate comprehension is needed also.   A second comparison that expresses much the same concept is that between memorization and understanding, with memorization being sufficient for a reproductive problem solving, but understanding being necessary in productive problem solving.

19.31   Compare the treatment of stimulus input in a problem-solving situation according to S-R theory and according to information processing theory.

For S-R theory, which is basically an associative viewpoint, the usual interpretation is that the stimulus keys-off (elicits) mediating or overt responses.   On the other hand, information-processing theory treats the stimulus as information to be acted upon, thus its name.   (*Note:* Typically, information-processing theories propose that the type of problem determines the approach that will be used to solve it; those theories typically emphasize the processes rather than the inputs.)

19.32   In a study that aims to simulate human problem-solving operations, a computer is programmed to hold a large amount of information in current storage while solving a problem.   What is wrong with such an experimental setup?

Evidence presented earlier (see Chapter 6) indicates that the immediate-memory span for humans equals approximately 7 ± 2 chunks of information.   Although the computer can hold many more units of information in short-term storage, this would not represent typical human performance, and the solution strategies achieved in this experiment would be inappropriate.   A reasonable program would incorporate typical protocols based upon factors such as serial processing, limited short-term capacity, and seemingly infinite long-term storage.

19.33   What are the major advantages in using an information-processing interpretation of problem solving?

Information-processing approaches to problem solving tend to be efficient and to allow prediction of expected response sequences.   In general, they can deal with more complex problems than can S-R or gestalt theories.   Study of algorithms, or, particularly, heuristics (see Chapter 15) are fairly limited but show potential for treatment of many of the concepts of problem solving.

19.34   What are the three major characteristics of a typical experimental problem-solving task?   Cite an example, describing how these characteristics are illustrated.

Experimental problem-solving tasks usually focus on one or more of the following: stimulus factors, response strength, and transfer-of-training effects.   If the problem involves a series of mathematical solutions, stimulus factors might include the instructions given (for example, is a set created?), response strength might refer to observation of a particular solution pattern, and transfer effects might be measured in terms of carry-over to another set of problems (positive- vs. negative-transfer or learning to learn, for example).

19.35   Distinguish between concept learning as attribute identification and as rule learning.

Concept learning is the learning of specific stimulus characteristics with which responses can be associated.   When the problem involves attribute identification, the subject's task is to acquire previously unknown information about stimulus properties.   Rule learning, on the other hand, presumes knowledge of the stimulus properties, and involves discovery of a relationship among stimulus presentations.   In attribute identification, the concept is defined by the stimulus properties, while the rule itself defines the concept in rule-learning tasks.

19.36   What is the difference between a stimulus dimension and a stimulus attribute?

A stimulus dimension is a general characteristic of the stimulus, such as size, weight, brightness, or many other properties.   Stimulus attributes are values of a given dimension—for example, heavy, average, or light for the dimension of weight.

19.37   If the chart in Fig. 19-7 represents the positive and negative instances associated with the stimuli described, name the conceptual rule that applies and describe it.

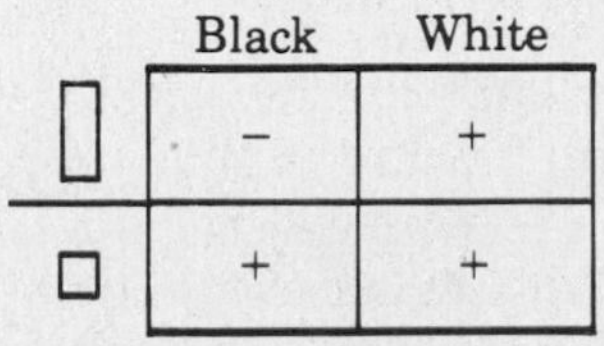

	Black	White
▯	−	+
▭	+	+

Fig. 19-7

The positive instances in the chart indicate that responses should be made if the stimulus is small and/or white.   The negative instance is only for stimulus items that are both big and black.   This is a disjunctive conceptual rule: the response is made if one or the other or both of the appropriate stimulus properties are present.

19.38   Suppose the chart given in Problem 19.37 is reversed so that the only + appears in the upper left-hand quadrant.   What rule would explain such a result?

There is more than one possible solution to this problem.   If the rule is a conjunctive rule, the positive instance would require the stimulus to be both big and black.   However, the rule might be a joint-denial rule such that any stimulus that was neither small nor white would serve as a positive instance.   In the latter case, it would not be important that the stimulus was large and black, only that it was not small and not white.   A medium-sized green stimulus could serve just as well as a positive instance for the joint-denial rule but would not satisfy the conjunctive rule.

19.39   What is the major distinction between association theories of concept learning and hypothesis-testing theories of concept learning?

Association theories of concept learning are essentially passive-reception explanations.   The only requirements are that the organism have some experience and then retain a memory of that experience.   Hypothesis-testing theories emphasize an active role for the learner.   The explanation involves the selection of a hypothesis, a test of that hypothesis, and subsequent confirmation or disconfirmation based upon the test.   This may be repeated for a number of times, forming a sequence of active decision-making events.

19.40   Why are information-processing theories of concept learning not treated as examples of hypothesis-testing theories?

The main focus of hypothesis-testing theories of concept learning is on the hypotheses selected and the decisions reached.   Information-processing theories are not considered to be examples of hypothesis-testing theories because they focus on the processes used to select the hypotheses and make the decisions rather than on the hypotheses or decisions themselves.

19.41 Suppose the subject is presented with the stimuli shown in Fig. 19-8.   Create a problem that involves learning a reversal shift.

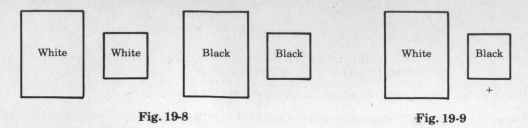

Fig. 19-8   Fig. 19-9

A reversal shift could be established by first training the subject to recognize large size as the positive instance regardless of color, then shifting to small size as the positive instance.

19.42 If the sequence of large as + and small as − is established, what change will create a nonreversal shift?

Either change that involves concentration on the color of the stimuli rather than the size will create a nonreversal shift.   This means that if either white or black becomes the stimulus indicating the positive instance, regardless of size, a nonreversal shift will have been created.

19.43 If the sequence of large as + and small as − is established, pick two training stimuli that allow subsequent testing of an optional shift.   How would the test be conducted?

If the first step is large as + and small as −, the second step of training will use the configuration shown in Fig. 19-9.

In the test step, subjects would be presented alternately with the two stimuli in Fig. 19-9 and a large black and small white stimulus.   If the subject repeatedly selects the small white stimulus as well as the small black stimulus of the training task, an apparent reversal shift has occurred.   If the subject consistently selects the large black stimulus as well as the small black stimulus, a nonreversal shift seems to have occurred.   In the latter case, the dimension of size, which was relevant in the first step, has been dropped in favor of the dimension of color.   If neither the large black nor the small white stimulus is selected consistently, the subject is said to have made a nonselective shift.

Key Terms

Abstraction.   A mental operation in which multiple stimuli are encoded in some condensed form.

Attribute.   The value of a stimulus dimension.

Attribute identification.   Acquisition of previously unknown information about stimulus properties.

Backward search.   A search strategy starting at the desired goal and working in reverse order to determine the steps necessary to reach that goal.

Brainstorming.   A problem-solving technique in which as many solutions as possible are generated before any judgment is made regarding their relative worth.

Combination.   Mental processes involving the use of two or more storage classes or units.

Concept learning.   Learning specific stimulus characteristics to which responses can be associated.

Conceptual rule.   The statement of which stimulus attributes are relevant and what relationship exists among them.

Conditional rule.   A conceptual rule under which one attribute becomes relevant in determining a positive instance only when another attribute is present.

Conjunction.   A conceptual rule under which more than one attribute is used in combination to determine a positive instance.

Dimension.   A general characteristic of a stimulus.

Disjunction.   A conceptual rule under which one attribute or another or the combination of both determines a positive instance; an "and/or" rule.

Echoic code.   The storage of an auditory representation of a stimulus.

Focusing.   A hypothesis-testing strategy by which the subject concentrates on a particular attribute, creating and testing hypotheses until that part of the rule is determined.

Forward search.   A search strategy starting with a statement of the problem and working through to the desired goal.

Functional fixedness.   The inability to recognize alternate uses for an object and persistence in using it for only its most common purpose.

Generation.   Activation of specific storage codes as a result of general input instructions.

Habit hierarchy.   In problem solving, the proposal that a best-learned solution technique will be tried first, then the next, and so on through an ordered sequence of possible solutions.

Iconic code.   The storage of a visual representation (image) of a stimulus.

Incubation period.   A phase of problem solving during which subconscious (rather than conscious) effort is expended in attempts to attain the goal.

Insight.   A seemingly sudden solution to a problem, preceded by few or no visible errors in choosing a solution.

Joint denial.   A conceptual rule under which a positive instance is determined by the absence of the two relevant attributes.

Means-end analysis.   The use of heuristics to try to reach a goal or subgoal established by problem-solving organization.

Mediation.   The association of two items not because of physical similarities but because they share some other characteristic in common.

Nonreversal shift.   A solution shift in which the subject, having learned a particular solution, then must ignore the dimension upon which that solution was based and learn a solution based upon a different dimension and its attributes; also called an *extradimensional shift*.

Nonselective shift.   In an optional-shift problem, subject choices that appear to select no stimulus dimension consistently.

Optional shift.   In solution-shift problems, shift training that allows more than one possible interpretation.

Perceptual set.   The temporary tendency to respond in a certain manner.

Problem solving.   The recognition and establishment of some goal, followed by attempts to reach that goal.

Protocol.   A verbal report of the thinking processes used during problem solving.

Reversal shift.   A solution shift in which the subject, having learned a particular solution then must change to the opposite solution for the same stimulus dimension; also called an *intradimensional shift*.

Rule learning.   Discovery of a relationship among stimulus presentations when the relevant attributes and their values are known.

Search strategies.   Ways of seeking solutions to problems.

Sequencing.   The arrangement of mental processes used in thinking.

Thinking.   Covert mental activity involving the use of symbols.

Verbal code.   The storage of a symbolic (word) representation of a stimulus.

PART VI: *Developmental Principles of Learning*

The two chapters in this part are concerned with developmental influences on learning.   They are separated in that one is primarily concerned with unlearned and physiological variables while the other focuses more on learned intellectual and personality characteristics.

Chapter 20, concerned with neurophysiology and attention, offers topics such as preparedness, attention, and the concept of a neurophysiological memory trace.   Research procedures and results are discussed briefly.

In Chapter 21, the focus is on the concept of intelligence and its relationship to the study of learning.   Additionally, the work of Jean Piaget on the development of learning and the effects of learning on personality are considered.

Chapter 20

Neurophysiology and Attention

There are many ways of trying to determine the influence of development upon learning. This chapter focuses upon perceptual and physiological aspects, while the next chapter will concentrate on the topics of intelligence and personality.

20.1 NEUROPHYSIOLOGICAL RESEARCH TECHNIQUES

Psychologists studying the neurophysiological aspects of learning have concentrated primarily on the functioning of the central nervous system (CNS). They have devoted much less attention to either the receptor or effector functions of the nervous system, assuming that these functions will be the same regardless of whether or not learning is involved.

EXAMPLE 1. Simple stimulation of a receptor like those in the retina of the eye will produce the same sequence of events regardless of whether or not it takes place in a learning situation. The physiological process that brings signals into the central nervous system is the same no matter what conditions are operating. (*Note:* An alternative interpretation is that *all* events are learning events; thus receptor and effector functions are always involved with some sort of learning.)

In light of this limitation, the following techniques are the ones most frequently used to investigate properties of the central nervous system as they relate to learning.

Naturally Occurring Events

Any number of conditions that occur in a natural (nonexperimental) setting may affect the central nervous system. Often these are events that should not or cannot be created in an experimental manner, but once they have taken place must be studied.

EXAMPLE 2. It would obviously be unethical to use an experimental procedure to create a severe concussion and the resulting brain trauma. However, automobile accidents, falls, or many other common events may have the same effect. Once such a trauma has occurred, the psychologist may want to study the effects, such as retrograde amnesia. (See below, Section 20.4.)

Electroencephalograms (EEGs)

By attaching electrodes to the skull of a subject and connecting them with a special device, psychologists have been able to monitor and record the electrical activity of the brain. This device is called an electroencephalograph, and it produces a record called an *electroencephalogram* (often abbreviated EEG). Changes in EEG patterns can be studied as a function of alterations in the stimulus environment.

Electrode Implantation

The development of sophisticated surgical equipment and procedures has allowed psychologists to implant electrodes into the brains of living organisms. These electrodes are then used for stimulation of the particular area of the brain, destruction of tissue in that region of the brain, or the recording of activity in that section of the brain.

EXAMPLE 3. One recent study showed that stimulation of a particular area of a rat's brain could be so reinforcing that the rat would respond exclusively to this stimulation and ignore other reinforcers including food, despite the fact that the rat had been almost completely deprived of food. Another study showed how memories seemingly could be "revived" by stimulation of the human brain.

Surgical Procedures

Psychosurgery, involving the destruction or removal of brain tissue, has allowed psychologists to determine the change between preoperative and postoperative conditions. Such differences, if they exist, allow "charting" of certain central nervous system functions.

EXAMPLE 4. One of the most widely known procedures is that involving the severing of the *corpus callosum,* the area of the brain connecting the two cerebral hemispheres. Used as a means to relieve severe seizures affecting some epileptic patients, this "split-brain" preparation has made possible the research on the hemispheres' separate involvements in various learning tasks.

20.2　HEREDITARY PRINCIPLES AND LEARNING

While the reader is encouraged to explore the effects of heredity upon learning in detail (perhaps by consulting a text on developmental psychology), it is appropriate to present here only several of the most important questions and findings.

Preparedness

Early investigations in the psychology of learning suggested that there might be both *stimulus equivalence* and *response equivalence.* Essentially, these concepts implied that appropriate pairing of *any* stimulus with response-producing conditions would lead to an S-R association or that *any* response that "worked" could be conditioned in a given situation.

Research studies have shown these concepts to be incorrect. Instead, species seem to inherit (perhaps as a result of evolutionary development) certain tendencies to react to certain situations. When the organism seems to be more than usually sensitive to a given circumstance, the term *preparedness* is used. Preparedness implies innate tendencies either to sense particular stimuli or to respond in a particular manner.

EXAMPLE 5. A famous study illustrating preparedness involved the study of autoshaping (see Section 7.7). Pigeons were fed when a disc was illuminated regardless of whether or not they made any response. Although no response was required, the apparent preparedness of the pigeons led to maintenance of a disc-pecking response.

Unpreparedness and Contrapreparedness

It should be recognized that innate characteristics may predispose the organism *not* to respond or to respond in a manner contrary to that required by the procedure being used. The former condition is called *unpreparedness,* while the latter is referred to as *contrapreparedness.*

EXAMPLE 6. Another quite famous study demonstrated contrapreparedness (although not intentionally). An attempt was made to train hungry raccoons to pick up tokens and deposit them in a slot so that food would be delivered. Although physically capable of making such a response, the raccoons instead would "wash" the tokens in a manner comparable to the way in which they washed their food in a natural setting. The hereditary background apparently dominated the situation, making the desired response impossible to train.

Examples of Preparedness

Although two examples have been given already, certain hereditarily controlled behavior patterns have been studied in such detail that they are treated as separate topics in the psychology of learning. This section presents several of these patterns.

Imprinting. Imprinting is an innate learning pattern demonstrated by young organisms. Typically, the response learned is one of following and attachment to a moving object (often the mother). This has been demonstrated most dramatically with young birds such as chickens or geese.

An important aspect of imprinting is that the response pattern can be acquired *only* during a limited span of time called the *critical period.* The critical period is considered a maturational variable, and differs from the concept of *readiness,* which implies that once maturational characteristics are attained, they will remain intact forever, with learning possible at any time.

EXAMPLE 7. The critical period for imprinting of a following response in birds is quite short (18 to 24 hours). If imprinting does not occur during this period, it will not occur at all. Evidence suggests that there are also critical periods for certain human behaviors, although these periods are much longer and not so well defined. Thus the report of limitations on the development of language learning after puberty (see Section 18.4) is an extension of this same concept.

Species-specific defense reactions (SSDRs). A second type of responding that illustrates preparedness is called a *species-specific defense reaction (SSDR).* An SSDR is an innate response made to aversive stimuli that occur suddenly. SSDRs are often elicited by "danger stimuli"—that is, by only those particular types of stimuli that have been learned to be aversive.

EXAMPLE 8. The importance of innate responses such as SSDRs can be seen in conditioning studies requiring a response that is not an SSDR. Because the organism seems to have the SSDR at the top of the hierarchy of responses to aversive stimuli such as electric shock, acquisition of some response that is not an SSDR cannot be accomplished until SSDRs are suppressed. This sometimes takes thousands of trials, demonstrating the strength of the inborn tendencies.

Learned taste aversions. Another series of studies has investigated the phenomenon of *learned taste aversions.* Evidence indicates that organisms are particularly sensitive to certain sensory properties associated with eating (such as odor) and will associate these properties with subsequent illness, while *not* associating other properties such as lighting. Apparently, the differential sensitivity shown has developed evolutionarily and manifests itself as a form of preparedness.

Examples such as these provide support for the concept of preparedness. As with language learning (Chapter 18), it would appear that the ethologists' beliefs in inherited behavior patterns are substantiated by the various demonstrations of preparedness, unpreparedness, and contrapreparedness.

20.3 AROUSAL

As it will be used here, the term *arousal* refers to the excitation of neurophysiological systems necessary for learning. Arousal can be attributed to both involuntary and voluntary factors.

Involuntary Arousal

Research evidence supports the concept that at least part of an organism's level of arousal is controlled in an involuntary manner. Incoming sensory signals are "filtered" in the central core of the brain stem by the *reticular activating system (RAS)* and either given precedence physiologically or ignored. Thus, arousal generated at cortical levels is partially determined by the activity of the RAS.

Voluntary Arousal

Voluntary arousal involves the conscious choice to attend to and react to particular environmental events. Likewise, the conscious decision to try to ignore some stimulation in order to lower arousal level would also be considered voluntary. The combination of voluntary and involuntary arousal has been called *sensory gating,* meaning that input is filtered and maintained within the organism's capacity.

Factors Influencing Arousal

There are several factors seen to be very important in determining arousal. This section considers the most important of these.

Biological constraints.   Certain sensory limitations are determined by inherited characteristics.   Arousal will be limited by the organism's capacities for receiving and recording sensory information.

EXAMPLE 9.   The familiar example of a "silent" dog whistle illustrates the concept of biological constraint. Although beyond the range of human hearing, the whistle frequency used is within a dog's range and will create arousal in members of that species.   Another concept, *automatic feature analysis,* appears to support the idea of biological constraint.   There is evidence backing the notion that specific cells within the central nervous system are particularly geared to respond to distinct stimulus features.   Again, neurophysiological characteristics seem to determine the nature of arousal.

Stimulus salience.   The phrase *stimulus salience* is used as a means of representing the importance of the input in arousal.   Although it must be recognized (as described above) that neurophysiological and psychological factors can affect arousal levels, it is also true that features of the input are important influences on arousal levels.   In general, new stimuli, novel stimuli, sudden-onset or pulsating stimuli, and threatening or aversive stimuli are the types that will be the most likely to generate arousal.   For a complete description of the many stimulus properties that may be relevant, the reader is encouraged to consult a psychology of perception textbook.

Learned constraints.   Conditioning processes and social learning have been studied as influences on arousal.   In general, the research has centered on *attention* to the input as a function of previous learning; that is, an organism may select which stimuli it attends to on the basis of previously established learned patterns of behavior.

The phenomenon of *blocking* illustrates conditioned attention.   In a classical conditioning procedure, a conditioned response (CR) can be firmly linked to one particular conditioned stimulus (CS).   The introduction of a second CS (forming a compound CS) does *not* later yield a CR that is as strong as the CR to the original CS.   Apparently the subject recognizes the redundancy of the second CS and does not form a strong second ("unnecessary") association.   (*Note:* If classical conditioning *begins* with a compound CS, both CS_1 and CS_2 will yield CRs of the same strength in most cases.)

The learning of social constraints has been illustrated by what is called the *cocktail party phenomenon.*   Research on multiple-message circumstances (as in the case of several simultaneously audible conversations at a cocktail party) have shown that selective attention can be maintained.   However, learned stimuli of high importance (such as one's name) can intrude and change the focus of attention from one stimulus to another.

The social learning of constraints is also at the heart of the somewhat controversial principles of *perceptual defense* and *perceptual vigilance.*   These concepts propose that the social conventions of a particular society will affect arousal and attention.   The idea of perceptual defense is that attention and arousal will diminish in the presence of socially disapproved stimuli.   Perceptual vigilance suggests that certain stimuli which are socially disapproved will increase the attention and arousal in the subject.

EXAMPLE 10.   In a poorly controlled but nonetheless interesting study, subjects were presented with "dirty" words on a tachistoscope—a device that can be used to project visual images on a screen for extremely short time periods.   (These periods of time can be very accurately manipulated by the experimenter at the tachistoscope's controls.)   Researchers found that the time needed for subjects to recognize "dirty" words was generally greater than the time they needed to recognize ordinary words of comparable length, complexity, and so on.   This finding was taken as support for the idea of perceptual defense.

Theories of Arousal

There are basically two types of arousal theories.   *Minimum-arousal* theories propose that if an organism desires a level of stimulus complexity just slightly above what has previously existed in the environment, arousal will be maintained.   In such theories, an organism's need for arousal may vary from moment to moment. *Optimal-arousal theories* propose that organisms have a fixed level of desire for arousal and that they will respond to adjust their stimulus environment in order to achieve or maintain that level of arousal.

EXAMPLE 11. Skydiving and hang-gliding can be understood in terms of optimal arousal. Those who engage in these activities can be seen as individuals who have a fixed need for a high level of arousal. A minimum-arousal theory might also be used to describe these activities, however. The hang-glider and skydiver will be quite highly aroused by a simple first jump. As time goes by and they gain more experience, however, they will most likely want to do higher or longer or more complex jumps and flights in order to maintain their original level of arousal. (It can thus be seen that the minimum- and optimal-arousal theories do not entirely exclude each other.)

20.4 THE MEMORY TRACE

A number of attempts have been made to find neurophysiological evidence of *memory traces,* or *engrams*. One general conclusion based upon these studies is that memory probably goes through some sort of *consolidation* phase after acquisition. Although it is not known how this neurophysiological permanence is developed, research has shown that consolidation is *not* manifested as *reverberating neural circuits* (hypothetical neural signal paths in the cortex). Psychologists have been less inclined to support this reverberating-circuit theory because rather than weakening with the passage of time, engrams seem to gain strength and permanence. Moreover, studies of *retrograde amnesia* have shown that the most recent memories are the *last* to be recovered following some brain traumas. This suggests that the most recent memories did not have the time to establish themselves as well as the older memories did.

EXAMPLE 12. Are engrams stored in reverberating circuits or consolidated in some kind of rigid structure? Yet another research study attempted to discount the reverberating-circuit theory by first teaching organisms a particular response and then cooling them to the point where cortical neural activity was effectively stopped. When the animals were warmed, there was no apparent loss of memory. This finding lends weight to the idea that engrams are *not* stored in reverberating circuits, which would have been stopped by the cooling process.

Physiological Explanations of Memory Trace

The concept of reverberating circuits has been rejected by many researchers, but an adequate alternative explanation has been difficult to find. The concept of consolidation suggests that engrams are "locked" into some kind of a fixed or static structure in the central nervous system, but physiological evidence of such structures is very scarce and inconclusive. Nonetheless, several tentative and very speculative physiological theories have been developed and are presented here.

Synaptic change. One proposal is that actual physiological or electrochemical changes take place at the neural synapses. Learning is interpreted as the facilitation, through these changes, of the signal transmission from one neuron to the next. The neural path that has been facilitated then becomes more likely than some other to carry an impulse, in effect creating something like a link in a circuit.

One especially controversial synaptic-change theory focuses on a phenomenon called *sprouting*. When there is damage to the central nervous system, the traumatized fibers will degenerate. It has been found that undamaged fibers that are physically contiguous will develop new fibers that move into the region previously occupied by the damaged (and now degenerated) fibers (see Fig. 20-1). The growth of these replacements (sprouting) is sometimes accompanied by the resumption of neural functions that were stopped when the trauma to the tissue occurred.

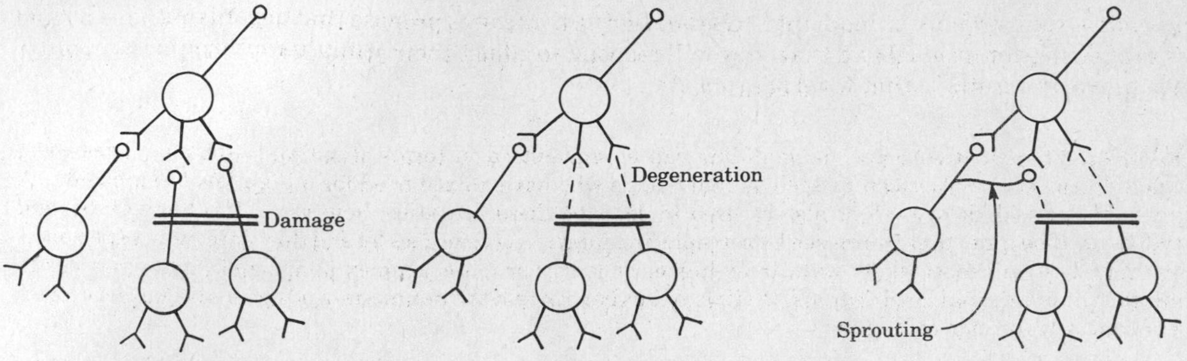

Fig. 20-1

Protein synthesis (RNA involvement).　Another theory proposes that learning situations somehow cause changes in the molecular ribbons of *ribonucleic acid (RNA)* in the nervous system.　These changes, which in turn affect the rates and types of neural firings, supposedly accompany *all* learning situations the organism encounters.

Glial models.　Another controversial idea is that acquisition does not affect neural cells directly, but instead creates some physiological change in the more numerous non-neural cells called *glia,* which influence the metabolic processes of the neurons.　Modification of metabolism can affect the firing rate of a neuron, thus changing behavior patterns.　In general, glial models have been less popular than the neural models suggested above.

20.5　LOCATION OF THE MEMORY TRACE

The previous section indicated that psychologists have been unable to settle on a single explanation of how the engram is consolidated.　Despite this, several investigations have been conducted in an attempt to determine *where* memory traces are located.　This section briefly describes some of these investigations and their findings.

Dual-Hemisphere Research

Psychologists know that the two cerebral hemispheres of the brain do not perform exactly the same mental functions.　Consequently, they have attempted to identify physiological differences between the two hemispheres that could be used to account for the functional differences.　Some of their investigations into this question are described here.

Split-brain studies.　The severing of the corpus callosum destroys all connections between the two cerebral hemispheres, making possible *split-brain* studies.　(This surgical procedure is also performed clinically on some humans in order to relieve them of some of the symptoms of epilepsy.)　Split-brain studies involving human subjects as well as others have shown that certain behavior patterns are stored in one hemisphere but not the other.　These studies have also shown, however, that one hemisphere can be trained to perform a function that previously involved only the other hemisphere.

Spreading depression.　In addition, there is evidence to suggest that psychologists can experimentally manipulate learning variables to train one, and only one, of the hemispheres in a subject who has *not* undergone the split-brain procedure.　A second way of controlling signal patterns to the cerebral hemispheres has been called *spreading depression.*　Appropriately administered electrical or chemical stimulation can effectively "turn off" one hemisphere, the other, or both.　In general, the results obtained in spreading-depression procedures are the same as those obtained in split-brain experiments.　Moreover, spreading-depression procedures have the advantage of being reversible, which is not true of split-brain preparations.

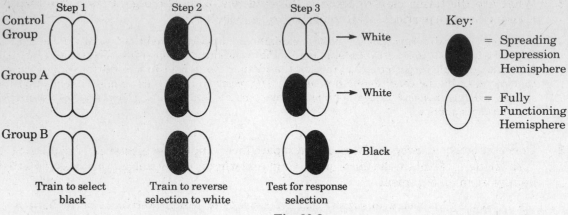

Fig. 20-2

EXAMPLE 13. A typical experiment in which spreading depression is used is illustrated in Fig. 20-2. In Step 1, all organisms have both hemispheres operating fully, and all are trained to respond to black (rather than white) stimuli. In Step 2, all groups have their left hemisphere functioning depressed and are then trained in a reversal of the previous conditioning setup: they are reinforced only for responding to white stimuli. In the test in Step 3, all three groups are presented with both a black stimulus and a white stimulus, and their responses are recorded. The control group subjects, with both hemispheres fully functional, choose white (the most recently learned response). Group A subjects, with their left hemispheres depressed, also choose white. Group B, on the other hand, does not show the effects of Step-2 reversal in Step 3: the subjects will respond only to the black stimuli because that is the only response the left hemisphere has learned.

> ***Recovery of function.*** Naturally occurring events (see Section 20.1) may provide the opportunity for study of dual-hemisphere problems.

EXAMPLE 14. Perhaps the most common naturally occurring event that allows study of dual-hemisphere problems is a cerebral arterial hemorrhage or blocking (a "stroke"). Often, this results in tissue destruction and subsequent loss of function. Being able to identify the cortical tissues affected and how and when later recovery of function is accomplished has allowed greater understanding of the operation of both hemispheres.

Solved Problems

20.1 Explain why the concepts of stimulus equivalence and response equivalence are not supported by the study of the evolutionary histories of various species. What alternative theory accounts for the great variety of highly differentiated species-specific behaviors found among organisms?

>   The concepts of stimulus equivalence and response equivalence propose the interchangeability of events in the environment—for example, *any* stimulus could serve as a CS in classical conditioning, or *any* response could be conditioned. Study of the evolutionary history of various species has shown this not to be correct, suggesting instead that each species probably has innate tendencies to respond to some forms of stimulation rather than others, and to respond with particular patterns of performance in given stimulus conditions. These tendencies to respond in certain ways are summarized by the concept of *preparedness*, which holds that species' behavioral repertoires are adapted over time to their unique environmental conditions.

20.2   What are the terms used to describe the tendency of certain organisms not to respond appropriately to particular S-R conditioning sequences?

There are two terms that are used to explain why a species might *not* condition easily or at all.   The term *contrapreparedness* implies that the evolutionary history of the species has resulted in an innate, or built-in, pattern that provokes the organism to respond in some pattern different from that required by the conditioning procedure.   The term *unpreparedness* simply implies that the species will not respond in the appropriate manner; no "alternate" or "opposite" or "contrary" responding is implied.

20.3   Concepts such as preparedness or unpreparedness imply the existence of some sort of "prewiring."   Explain the term "prewiring" and what it implies about the locus of learned behaviors in an organism.

"Prewiring" is meant to suggest that the capacity to perform certain behavior patterns is evolutionarily developed and present in every member of a particular species.   Given the appropriate stimulation, the "prewired" sequence is activated and the learned response is demonstrated.   This is generally taken by psychologists to imply that these patterns are located in the nervous system, probably in the form of neural circuits.   Whether the behavior in question is present at birth or is activated only after training, the capability, in the form of "prewired" neural circuits, is seen as innate.

20.4   Why, if the nervous system is seen as the locus of the learning process, are functions like the reception of a light flash by the retina or the activation of the muscle groups necessary for raising one's hand generally *not* studied as part of the neurophysiology of learning?

Receptor functions (sense perceptions) and effector functions (motor responses) operate in the same manner whether or not learning has taken place.   When psychologists study the physiology of learning, they distinguish between the central nervous system and the peripheral nervous system, and it is the former that they most often study, since the latter seems not to be affected by learning.

20.5   Describe the most commonly used procedures for studying the involvement of the brain in learning.

The four procedures most commonly used to study the involvement of the brain in learning processes are as follows: (1) Psychologists may make comparisons of a person's behavior before and after some naturally occurring event such as a stroke, in which there may be drastic alterations in the functioning of the central nervous system.   (2) Electroencephalograms (EEGs) have made it possible for researchers to monitor electrical activity of the brain during varying environmental conditions.   (3) Advanced laboratory procedures have made it possible to implant electrodes in the brains of a number of different organisms.   These electrodes have been used for either stimulation of the brain tissue or recording of activity within that area of the brain.   (4) Surgical procedures, and occasionally electrode implantation, have provided psychologists with the ability to pinpoint and either neutralize or destroy certain very specific areas of brain tissue (this is called tissue ablation).   Preoperative and postoperative behaviors can then be compared to determine what function that part of the brain served.

20.6   Explain why both species-specific defense reactions (SSDRs) and learned taste aversions appear to support the belief that there may be biological constraints upon learning.

Studies of SSDRs have shown that certain stimuli, called danger stimuli, appear to trigger the appropriate reactions; no other stimuli will provoke the same responses, and it is impossible to train the organism to respond otherwise in the appropriate stimulus conditions.   Apparently, the evolutionary history of the species has led to preparedness for those particular S-R sequences that are beneficial for the species.

In a similar manner, research on learned taste aversions shows that particular stimuli will come to be associated with tainted (illness-producing) food. Rats, for example, are especially sensitive to food odors associated with aversive consequences and cannot be trained to consume foods whenever such odors are part of the stimulus environment. Additionally, they can be trained to consume foods that normally have such odors if that odor can be eliminated from the stimulus presentation.

20.7 Additional evidence for neurophysiological involvement in learning has been provided by imprinting research. Define imprinting, then explain why this research seems important for the concept of critical period but not for the concept of readiness.

Imprinting is defined as the development in a young organism of an attachment or responding pattern to an object (often the mother). Typically, imprinting is observed when the object moves and the young organism follows it. Imprinting is most vividly demonstrated by young birds—particularly chickens, ducks, and geese.

Imprinting is usually restricted to a rather short period of time soon after birth. The critical period has a relatively well-defined time span during which imprinting behaviors will occur and after which they will stop; in other words, the critical period has a beginning and an ending. The neurophysiological characteristics necessary for learning are thought to exist for only a limited (critical) period of time. By contrast, the concept of readiness suggests that once certain developmental stages are attained, certain types of learning will be possible from then on, even though they may not occur until some time in the future.

20.8 A famous behaviorist, John B. Watson, once claimed that he could take any healthy, well-formed infant and, if allowed to manipulate the environment in any manner he desired, train the child for any profession. Explain why the research cited in this chapter (and the position of the ethologist, described in Chapter 18) makes Watson's claims disputable.

Basically, the concept of neurophysiological constraint contradicts Watson's position, which holds that the stimulus environment, above all else, is the determining factor in an organism's behavior. Ethologists and physiological psychologists generally believe that inherited genetic patterns make certain kinds of response learning highly likely and other kinds highly unlikely or in some cases impossible. While not denying the importance of environmental variables, ethologists and physiologists hold to the belief that there are neurophysiological constraints built into organisms that no amount of training can overcome.

20.9 Suppose a subject is totally unable to recall the letter sequences learned two hours previously as part of an experimental task. How could the subject's inability be explained in terms of intention and attention?

It can be assumed that the subject gave attention to the stimuli in order to memorize each letter sequence. It would also appear, however, that the subject did not intend to learn the sequences for anything more than the experimental task. If the subject had learned the letter sequences in anticipation of a later test of retention, he or she would probably be better able to retrieve them, and would be showing an intention to learn. By contrast, if retrieval were demonstrated by the subject even though no conscious effort was made to store the material for later use, incidental learning would have taken place.

20.10 Why might the reticular activating system (RAS) be described as the "traffic control center" of learning?

There is sufficient research evidence to indicate that the reticular activating system (RAS) acts as a sort of general filtering system for various incoming sensory signals. Even though a particular signal may be in the form and within the range appropriate for reception, the RAS may function to block its reception, sending on to the upper cortical areas only those signals that are sudden, unique, or important to the organism's survival.

20.11   Explain how the concept of automatic feature analysis also supports a neurophysiological interpretation of involuntary attention.

Automatic feature analysis is a concept that suggests that certain properties of a stimulus may be responded to selectively by specific nerve cells.   These nerve cells are thought to serve as specialized receptor mechanisms sensitive to these particular stimulus features only.   It is proposed that certain features (for example, a sharp corner in a figure or the presence of the color red) may cause these cells to fire, directing attention automatically toward that property of the stimulus.

20.12   Provide an example of voluntary attention to stimulus properties that might follow an initially involuntary attention-provoking stimulus.

There are many possible solutions to this problem.   Suppose you and a friend are taking a relaxing walk in the woods when you hear the sudden, unexpected sound of a gunshot.   It is likely that the gunshot will initiate a period of involuntary attention, which will then be followed by an active seeking out of the source of the sound.   This latter process would represent a conscious and intentional (or voluntary) form of attention, in which you would scan the woods to determine the location of the shooter.

20.13   The combination of involuntary and voluntary attentional processes has been summarized by one term.   What is this term and how does it relate to that of memory?

The overall sensitivity or attention to stimuli, including both involuntary and voluntary processes, has been summarized by the concept of *sensory gating*.   In effect, this means that neurophysiological and psychological processes determine sensory input and maintain it at a level that is within the organism's capacity.

There are several relationships between sensory gating and memory.   On the most simple level, failure to attend to something means acquisition of that material cannot occur.   At another level, attention may switch from one aspect of the environment to another, changing the understanding or interpretation of the material.   On still a higher level, attention to "old" or well-learned events requires less concentration, meaning that some process (for example, walking) may occur relatively automatically while the remainder of attention is devoted to some new learning task.   (*Note:* It must be remembered that regardless of the level of attention being used, there is a limitation to the amount of material that can be processed at any one time.   For example, see Section 6.6 for the discussion of the immediate-memory span of 7 ± 2 chunks of information.)

20.14   Distinguish between selective attention and blocking.

Selective attention is paying attention to only a part of the total stimulus environment.   This may be a result of either involuntary or voluntary processes.   Blocking is a particular form of selective attention that results from conditioning.   The subject has learned that one stimulus (CS_1) predicts a given response circumstance (CR).   When an additional stimulus (CS_2) is introduced, so that there is a compound stimulus situation, the subject does *not* learn the associations required for conditioning.   Later tests for CR strength to this second, "add-on" stimulus (CS_2), show little or no responding.   This may be explained as a form of selective attention or a realization that the CS_2 is redundant and does not predict anything more about the environment than CS_1 did.

20.15   Sam and Olivia have invited several couples to their house for dinner. The party is a pleasant one, with several conversations going at once and relaxing music playing on the stereo. Suddenly, Olivia leaves the group.   When she returns, she is asked if she is OK, and she responds, "Of course . . . I just went to check the baby.   Didn't you hear her crying?"   What aspect of selective attention does Olivia's response seem to reveal?

Olivia's response conforms to research regarding learned constraints.   Selective attention allows the individual to accept one stimulus while excluding other simultaneously occurring stimuli. This selective process is learned and apparently reduces information-processing overload.   However, introduction of an especially relevant stimulus (as in this case, the baby's cry) will override the current attentional process and change the focus of attention. Because they have not learned the relevance of the stimulus, the other people do not attend to the baby's crying.

20.16 Riding the campus bus one day, Gordon notices his shoe is untied. He bends to tie the laces, but breaks the lace and mutters, "Well, son-of-a-buck." Sitting behind him, Frances and Chuck both apparently hear what is said, yet when Frances says, "Did you hear that *awful* thing that fellow said?" Chuck replies, "What? I didn't hear anything." What somewhat controversial principles of selective attention may explain Frances' and Chuck's remarks?

The concepts of perceptual vigilance and perceptual defense may be used to explain these remarks. Perceptual vigilance proposes that the recipient may be especially attentive to events with particular importance. Perceptual defense suggests that the recipient may *not* perceive events that are psychologically unpleasant. In both cases, the reception may reach a point of distortion, such that Frances may have "heard" some word other than "buck," while Chuck denies "hearing" anything at all.

20.17 It can be inferred from the preceding problems that attention is dependent upon arousal. What are the suggested theories explaining arousal?

Two types of arousal theories are most widely accepted. Minimum-arousal theories suggest that if the organism desires a level of stimulus complexity slightly above what has just been experienced, arousal will be maintained. The organism's level of desire may change from moment to moment. Optimal-arousal theories propose that the organism's level of desired complexity remains constant and that responses are made to adjust arousal to meet this desired level.

20.18 What term is used to describe the idea of a neurophysiological memory trace? Why is it not possible to interpret such a trace as a reverberating neural circuit?

Neurophysiological memory traces often are referred to as engrams. Research evidence fails to support the idea that an engram is a reverberating neural circuit. Special procedures such as cooling effectively stop brain activity in lower organisms, but do not eliminate memory traces. Neither do *grand mal* epileptic seizures, when almost all of the brain is involved in the paroxysms and reverberating circuits would be disrupted. The memories are maintained despite these seemingly discontinuous brain activity patterns.

20.19 For a brief time after a severe automobile accident, Marie is unable to recall anything about her previous life. Shortly, however, some memories reappear. Marie is surprised to find that events more remote in time from the accident are recalled first and that events just preceding the accident simply cannot be recalled. How does Marie's pattern of memory restoration appear to support the consolidation theory of memory?

Consolidation theories of memory propose that the passage of time allows the neural trace (engram) to become solidified in some physiological manner. Marie's amnesia can be interpreted as resulting from the trauma of the injury. The consolidation of the most recent memories (from just before the accident) does not take place. Memories from longer ago, which had more time to become consolidated, are recovered because they are less fragile or susceptible to loss.

20.20 Briefly describe the physiological changes that are proposed as possible explanations of consolidation.

There have been several different proposals made to try to account for the consolidation of engrams. One suggests that actual physiological or electrochemical changes take place to alter the synapses within the brain. A second suggests that the molecules of ribonucleic acid (RNA) are somehow affected so that subsequent protein synthesis affects the firing of neurons to reflect the learning. A third proposes that consolidation in some way influences the non-neural cells, called glia, which in turn give some order to neural firing.

20.21 How does the phenomenon of sprouting seem to support the first of the theories given in the solution to Problem 20.20?

Sprouting occurs when there is damage to the central nervous system. If one set of fibers is destroyed, they degenerate. Undamaged neurons nearby then generate additional fibers to fill the area vacated by the damaged ones. This, in turn, seems to lead to recovery of function and restoration of the temporarily lost behavior. It should be noted that the original pathway is not restored, but rather *new* synaptic connections are formed and then used for restoration of function.

20.22 Explain why research studies using lesions, split-brain preparations, and spreading depression have shown that memory does *not* appear to have a unitary neurophysiological location.

Research conducted by Karl Lashley from the 1920s to the 1950s and the work of many other investigators in more recent years has resulted in the overwhelming conclusion that memories involve relatively diffuse areas of the central nervous system, including the cerebral cortex and/or lower brain centers. Elimination of potential connections by creating brain lesions often has little or no effect upon performance, while split-brain preparations and the use of spreading depression may temporarily disrupt performance, but not subsequent relearning and retention. None of these results could be obtained if a memory's single location were in the cortex.

20.23 Some of the research with split-brain preparations or the use of spreading depression would seem to deny the conclusion reached in Problem 20.22. Describe such research and explain how the results are not really contradictory.

Research using these techniques sometimes makes it possible for only one cerebral hemisphere to be involved in an acquisition process. When that hemisphere is later kept from being activated, the opposite hemisphere does not generate appropriate responses. This would appear to negate the conclusion reached in Problem 20.22, except that in these studies both hemispheres have not had an equal opportunity to be exposed to the original learning situation. This experimentally created artificial situation prevents the multiple representation of memory that generally appears when such experimental conditions are not imposed.

Key Terms

Arousal. The excitation of physiological systems necessary to enable learning.

Attention. Actual reception of sensory signals.

Automatic feature analysis. The proposal that certain properties of a stimulus may be automatically and selectively received by specialized receptor cells.

Blocking. In compound conditioning, extreme salience of one CS such that no response strength accrues to the other.

Central nervous system (CNS). Essentially, all the nerve tissue composing the brain and spinal cord.

Consolidation. The condensation and joining of memory traces during the storage phase.

Contrapreparedness. A predisposition in an organism to make a competing response in a situation; acquisition of the desired response is inhibited or, in some cases, impossible.

Corpus callosum. The area of the brain that connects the two cerebral hemispheres.

Critical period. A stage during which an organism is able to learn a new behavior; this stage is limited in time, with both a beginning and an end.

Effectors. Muscles or glands that make responses possible.

Electroencephalograph. A device used to measure the electrical activity of the brain.

Engram. A memory trace.

Glia. Non-neural cells which affect the metabolic processes of nerve cells.

Imprinting. The very rapid acquisition of a response during a critical period of development; characteristic of birds particularly.

Perceptual defense. Selective attention; a subject's tendency to be especially inattentive to stimuli that may be socially disapproved.

Perceptual vigilance. Another form of selective attention; a subject's tendency to be especially attentive to stimuli that may be socially disapproved.

Preparedness. A state of unusual sensitivity to a situation, during which acquisition is facilitated.

Psychosurgery. Surgical procedures which involve the removal or destruction of tissue in the nervous system.

Readiness. The state in which an organism is ready and able to learn a new behavior; once readiness is reached, the organism always has the ability to learn the new behavior.

Receptor. A specialized nerve ending that is sensitive to a particular type of stimulation.

Reticular activating system. The center of the brain stem; known to filter sensory input.

Retrograde amnesia. Amnesia that recovers in a reverse temporal sequence, with the most recent occurrences being the last to be recalled.

Reverberating neural circuit. A proposed repetitive neural signal pathway in the cortex.

Sensory gating. A concept proposing that involuntary and voluntary attention combine to allow signals to pass to higher cerebral levels in a selective manner.

Species-specific defense reactions (SSDRs). Proposed innate protective responses elicited by learned signals.

Split-brain preparation. A surgical procedure that severs the corpus callosum, thus creating independent functioning of the two cerebral hemispheres.

Spreading depression. A technique using electrical or chemical stimulation to temporarily suspend the operation of nerve cells; there is no permanent damage to the cells when this technique is used.

Sprouting. The development of new fibers in undamaged nerve cells to fill in the area previously occupied by the now-degenerated fibers of damaged cells.

Synapse. The gap between the axon of one cell and the dendrite of the next.

Unpreparedness. A state of neutrality toward a particular stimulus situation; acquisition is neither facilitated nor inhibited.

Chapter 21

Intelligence and Personality

There are several widely accepted ways of studying the development of intelligence and personality as they relate to learning. This chapter presents some of these so the reader can develop a feeling for the variety of concerns that learning psychologists address.

21.1 THE EVOLUTION OF INTELLIGENCE

Intelligence can be defined, in a relatively simple manner, as a measure of the capacity to learn. (There are many other definitions that could be used, considering the varying approaches to intelligence that are explored, but this general definition is probably the best place to start.) This capacity can be correlated with the phylogenetic scale, which links all organisms into a hierarchy—ranging from the simplest one-celled organisms at one end to humans at the other. Gregory Razran has proposed an accompanying hierarchy for learning abilities based upon the evolution of species according to this phylogenetic scale.

The lowest level of responding is called *reactive responding* and is demonstrated by virtually all organisms. There is some question as to whether the responses illustrated at this level actually represent learning. (*Note:* Examples of these responses, including sensitization and habituation, were presented as nonconditioning variables in Chapter 3.)

Next in the hierarchy is *associative learning*, including classical and instrumental conditioning. This is followed by *integrative learning,* the next step up in the hierarchy. Integrative learning can be illustrated by perceptual learning, in which the subject is able to combine several stimuli to create one comprehensible stimulus. *Symbolic learning* is next in the hierarchy. This highest level of learning is considered to be an almost exclusively human activity. Moreover, the identification of an organism's ability to learn at any one level means that learning at lower levels will also be possible in that particular organism. This suggests that learning capacity is an evolutionarily developed characteristic.

EXAMPLE 1. One possible exception to the belief that symbolic learning is exclusively human is the training of language behavior in chimpanzees. Although attempts to use spoken language have generally failed, the use of the gestures of American Sign Language or specially constructed objects to represent symbols has proved at least partially successful. Chimpanzees not only learn to repeat ideas, but have been found to generate unique messages.

The overall thrust of this proposed hierarchy of intelligence is that a species' capacity to learn corresponds with its position on the phylogenetic scale—thus, intelligence is viewed as an evolutionarily determined capability.

21.2 PSYCHOMETRIC AND EXPERIMENTAL APPROACHES TO INTELLIGENCE

Most studies in the psychology of learning are experimental and investigate variables that affect the performance of a wide variety of organisms—from laboratory rats to humans—on learning tasks. The findings of these studies have lent weight to a number of *learning principles,* such as transfer of training, generalization, and extinction, that can be seen to operate in essentially the same manner in a wide variety of species.

Investigations of intelligence, on the other hand, are generally confined to studies in which the subjects are humans. Moreover, these studies tend to be *psychometric* rather than purely experimental. Psychometric approaches emphasize the differences among individuals in their capacity to perform a certain task, rather than the general principles of learning that operate in all learning tasks. Such an emphasis on individual performance has been termed *idiographic,* in contrast with *nomothetic* approaches, which are concerned with the overall behavior of a group.

EXAMPLE 2. Early investigations into the psychology of learning were experimental, and most of the experimenters—including Pavlov, James, Skinner, and others—used only "lower" (nonhuman) organisms as subjects. On the other hand, Binet and Simon were asked specifically to develop some means of measuring human intelligence (and thus predict the capacity of humans to benefit from additional training). The orientation of the experimental approaches to learning was general, while that of the psychometric studies of intelligence was limited primarily to human concerns.

It should be noted that recent developments in cognitive research seem to have linked the experimental and psychometric traditions. Cognitive psychologists, concerned more with the *qualities* of intelligence and learning, have investigated the effects of both species membership and individual developmental status on performance.

EXAMPLE 3. To simplify considerably, a psychometrician might investigate a learning problem to determine how each member of a group of subjects performs a particular task. The psychometrician would use some kind of quantitative measure to establish an "average" (or "norm," discussed below) against which each individual's performance could be compared. Cognitive psychologists, by contrast, would tend to focus upon the *quality* of performance that separates each subject from the others. (These comparisons may or may not be among members of the same species.)

Norms vs. Criteria

Psychologists use both norms and criteria to measure intelligence. A *norm* is a measure of the average performance of a representative group. A *norm-referenced test* is one in which an individual's performance is compared to the performance of others who took the same test. A *criterion* is an absolute standard for comparison—it remains constant regardless of the groups' performance on the test. Criteria usually are created by experts in the field. *Criterion-referencing* means that performance on the test is compared to this standard, without concern for what others might have done.

EXAMPLE 4. Teachers often use one or the other of the methods described above. Grading "on a curve" essentially is using norms. (What is average performance for the group, and how far above or below it is each subject's performance?) Using percent ranges (90 percent correct = A, 80 percent correct = B, etc.) represents the use of criteria. Theoretically, everyone in the class can get the same grade when criterion-referencing is used; this is highly unlikely, however, if norm-referencing is used.

21.3 INTELLIGENCE AS AN EXPLANATION OF LEARNING

This section also could be headed "Learning as an Explanation of Intelligence," reflecting the controversy that surrounds this subject. From one viewpoint, levels of intelligence determine the quality of learning that will be shown. The opposite viewpoint proposes that a greater quantity of learning will produce higher measured intelligence.

To further complicate this issue, psychologists have debated at length the relative contributions of hereditary and environmental factors to measured intelligence (or learning capacity). A number of relationships have been suggested, usually in the form of the percentage contributed by each factor, but no one proposal has been widely accepted. It is probably safe to say that almost all psychologists believe that heredity and environment interact to affect learning or intelligence; any conclusion beyond that is not supportable.

EXAMPLE 5. The issue of the relative importance of heredity and environment is further complicated when an environmental factor, such as the administration of drugs, produces a physiological effect that appears to radically change the learning capacity or measured intelligence of the subject. While this might seem to support the idea that intelligence is physiologically determined, it does not explain exactly how. Most of the conclusions drawn from such studies are debatable, and it can be expected that much more research will be conducted in this area.

Achievement, Aptitude, and Interest

Several terms are frequently used to describe the relationship between intelligence and learning. *Achievement* refers to the measurement of some behavior at a given moment; it is assumed that achievement reflects past learning. *Aptitude* is defined as the measured capability to profit from additional training; the concern is not with past learning specifically, but rather with what the subject can be expected to do in the future. *Interests* also may be measured, but simply reflect those areas that generate attention or excitement in the subject.

EXAMPLE 6. It is possible that there may be little or no relationship among the three terms presented here. A person may have achieved nothing in terms of learning a foreign language, yet, when tested for potential to learn such a task, score very well. However, the person may have no desire to undertake such studies, thus showing no interest in the area.

Crystallized vs. Fluid Intelligence

Another way to compare learning and intelligence has been to distinguish between crystallized intelligence and fluid intelligence. *Crystallized intelligence* is described as the ability to recall or recognize previously learned content. By contrast, *fluid intelligence* is thought to be a physiologically determined capacity that allows insight into the solution of complex tasks. The relationship between these two is that some of the capacity of fluid intelligence will be devoted to the overlearning necessary to acquire information that will then become part of crystallized intelligence.

Convergent vs. Divergent Thinking

Still one more way to try to relate intelligence and learning is to characterize convergent and divergent thinking. Determining *the* correct answer to a particular problem involves *convergent thinking* processes. *Divergent thinking* refers to the more creative processes involved in generating many different solutions for a problem. It is likely that these two modes of thinking require different previous learning patterns and/or different types of intelligence.

EXAMPLE 7. A typical convergent thinking problem might involve naming opposites, for example, "Give the opposite (or antonym) for the following words: 'high,' 'big,' etc." A single answer solves each problem. A divergent-thinking problem requires (or allows) many different solutions. An anagram problem would be one example: "How many words of four or more letters can you create by using the letters in the word 'contemporary'?"

Physiological Constraints

An additional consideration linking learning and intelligence is that of physiological constraints. It is apparent that physiological structure may affect learning capacity and therefore measured intelligence, but what physiological changes, if any, accompany changes in intelligence is not clear.

EXAMPLE 8. An extreme case of physiological change best illustrates the effects that can be observed. In cases of significant amounts of brain damage, both measured intelligence and learning capacity are noticeably impaired. Researchers can determine which areas of the brain have been damaged and the resultant effects on intelligence. In less dramatic cases, however, it is much more difficult to identify physiological constraints or to predict the effects they will have on performance. Furthermore, it has not as yet been possible to identify the ways in which changes in intelligence may be reflected by accompanying physiological changes.

21.4 PIAGET'S VIEWPOINT AND INTELLIGENCE

Jean Piaget's studies of children led him to propose a cognitive theory of development in which a child is seen, over the years, to develop an increasingly complex and refined set of mental operations with which to function. Piaget's proposed stages of cognitive development have been used as a means for measuring intelligence as well, even though Piaget did not originally intend them to be.   One distinct advantage to using Piaget's system of stages is that it involves observing subjects in relatively "natural" rather than experimental settings.   (Traditional measurements of intelligence are for the most part conducted in testing or experimental settings.)

General Trends of Developmental Learning

Two general trends, adaptation and organization, appear in all the stages of the development of learning.   As experiences are amassed, the individual illustrates *adaptation* by generating a reasonable adjustment between the self and the environment.   This continual adjustment can be made because *organization* allows the individual to combine seemingly incongruous or constantly changing stimulus inputs into a manageable or coherent whole.   Adaptation and organization can thus be interpreted as the general processes by which a person copes with the world.

Assimilation and accommodation.   Within the general process of adaptation, Piaget distinguished the two subprocesses of assimilation and accommodation.   Actions that change the environment to better "fit" with the self represent *assimilation*. Actions that change the self to better adjust to the environment are called *accommodation*.

EXAMPLE 9.   Suppose three executives step out of a soundproof office into the much noisier factory area, and as they do so raise their voices considerably in order to be heard.   They have illustrated accommodation by changing the way they speak in order to adjust to the environment.   On the other hand, a person who turns down the blaring radio before answering the phone is showing assimilation.

Stages of Learning Development

Piaget's observations led him to propose four stages of learning development.   The ages accompanying the descriptions of these stages are meant to be approximate, but the sequence is believed to be relatively inflexible.

Sensorimotor stage (birth to 2 years).   The essence of the *sensorimotor stage* is that the child acts upon the world in a direct manner, but is not yet capable of creating an internal representation of the environment.   By the end of this period, the need for direct motor activity is reduced by the increased role of cognitive processes in interacting with the environment.

Preoperational stage (2 to 7 years).   During the *preoperational stage*, the child develops many basic concepts—such as those of time, space, mass, and causality—and rapidly expands the use of symbols.   This period is marked by considerable egocentrism, along with limited capacity for judgment and relatively disorganized sequences of thought.

Concrete operational stage (7 to 11 years).   The change from the preoperational stage to the *concrete operational stage* is marked by considerably better organization of thought, much less egocentrism, and a marked expansion in the range of judgments and mental processes.   However, limitations are still seen in that children at this stage rely upon observable evidence rather than abstract or imaginative approaches.

Formal operational stage (from 11 on).   The *formal operational stage* occurs when the child can cope with complex mental operations that involve concrete and/or abstract concepts.   Piaget believed that a child who had reached this stage could generate and deal with hypotheses about the world.

EXAMPLE 10.   The way that children of various ages respond to a set of keys can be used to illustrate the different stages proposed by Piaget.   In the sensorimotor stage, the child may try to grasp or shake the keys, using them as some sort of plaything.   While they may continue to be used for play by the child in the preoperational stage, the keys may also be labeled "mine," and some illogical or loosely formed ideas regarding their use may be developed.   At the concrete operational stage, the child might undertake a search to determine which locks the keys might fit.   When in the formal operational stage, the child may first formulate hypotheses regarding the uses for the keys, then test these in some logical or hierarchical manner.

21.5 LEARNING AND PERSONALITY

One area of the psychology of learning that has received relatively little attention is that of the relationship between learning and personality.   One viewpoint, however—the claim that personality is nothing more than the accumulation of learned behavior patterns—is widely held.

Definition of Personality

The definition of personality as the accumulation of learned behavior patterns is inadequate in some ways.   For one thing, the definition needs to be qualified to include personality factors such as emotion and motivation, which are not always expressed in behavior.   For another, personality is not merely an accumulation in the sense of being a simple sum of attributes; personality may change with each person's unique experiences, and the ways in which the attributes of personality interact may not be the result of learning.

Biological Constraint

Before pursuing this topic any further, it should be noted that personality characteristics can be influenced by the biological makeup of a person.   As with other comparable considerations, how much influence physiological as opposed to psychological characteristics might have is a matter of debate.

EXAMPLE 11. The very tall person will, of necessity, have to adopt certain responses into his or her behavioral pattern.   For example, tall people are often asked questions like, "How's the weather up there?" The responses to such a remark may range from saying, "Fine, thanks," to lifting up the questioner and saying, "Same as down there—see?" But whatever the response, the tall person is likely to experience such a question more than once, while the short person is not, and the effect of this repetition is likely to influence the tall person's personality.

Learning Patterns

All of the major variables presented earlier in this outline could be reviewed in this section as contributors to the personality of an individual.   However, because a detailed account would be far beyond the scope of this book, the reader is invited to review the earlier materials and generate examples of the influence of learning variables upon personality.

EXAMPLE 12. Suppose that a college student who is able to perform very well in small seminars or discussions is totally unable to speak when called upon in a large lecture section.   Several interpretations are possible.   There may have been previous classical conditioning, pairing the size of class with success or failure.   Then again, the student may be modeling these responses after those observed in some other, significant person.   It is also possible that stimulus generalization is being illustrated, in that success or failure in one large class has led to generalized patterns in other large classes.   Even the size of class may be treated as a differentiation phenomenon.   For example, is a class of 75 large or small?   As you should realize by now, the possible interpretations are endless.

Miller and Dollard's theory.   The theory of personality developed by Neal Miller and John Dollard illustrates how the principles of learning may be applied to the study of personality.   One aspect of their theory stresses the relatively rudimentary sequence of *drive-cue-response-reward* as a framework for establishing personality characteristics.   Additionally, Miller and Dollard try to point out how variables studied in learning can be seen as comparable to those proposed as psychoanalytic concepts by Sigmund Freud.

EXAMPLE 13. An illustration of how the drive-cue-response-reward sequence is applied to a clinical situation can be seen in the way Miller and Dollard would explain a neurosis such as a phobia.   They suggest that a subject may be confronted with a fear-producing stimulus (drive) that happens to occur contiguously with some other stimulus (cue).   An escape or avoidance reaction (response) is then made to relieve some of the fear (reinforcement or reward).   What happens is that the cue occurs again, the response is made, and anxiety is relieved.   When someone observes this pattern at some later time, especially if the response is being made to some generalized stimulus, it appears that the pattern is totally irrational. Miller and Dollard contend that if the original learning circumstances were known, the neurotic pattern would not be considered irrational, but rather the result of conditioning and stimulus generalization.

Conflict

Conflict is another topic often treated as an aspect of personality in the psychology of learning. Indeed, there are several different types of conflicts that have been studied—conflicts of motives, conflicts of response patterns, and the conflicts generated by certain response patterns under differing levels of motivation.

Probably the most common way of investigating conflicts has been to use the concepts of approach and avoidance tendencies. As previously presented in Chapter 17, the following conflict designations are used:

Approach-approach conflict. When an individual must choose between two positively valued events or objects, an *approach-approach conflict* is said to exist.

EXAMPLE 14. Suppose someone is told the following: "You may have one of these two attractive and valuable rings as a gift, but not both." The person is forced to choose between two positively valued objects—an approach-approach conflict.

Avoidance-avoidance conflict. When forced to choose between two negatively valued objects or events, the individual is likely to experience an *avoidance-avoidance conflict.* Typically, the less unpleasant is chosen, although situations of this nature sometimes lead to a withdrawal response.

EXAMPLE 15. As a guest at a dinner party given by her boss, Eleanor is offered a choice of fried liver or sautéed scallops for her main course. She intensely dislikes both, but realizes she must choose one. She may, however, only "nibble" at the dish she chooses, thus showing a form of withdrawal in the face of the conflict.

Approach-avoidance conflict. When a single object or event has both positive and negative values, a person confronted with it is likely to experience an *approach-avoidance conflict.* When there is more than one object or event involved, and each has both positive and negative values, a *multiple approach-avoidance conflict* exists.

EXAMPLE 16. Chester's decision whether to play football (less fun, more recognition) or soccer (more fun, less recognition) represents a multiple approach-avoidance conflict. Resolution of the conflict will require his analysis of these various properties, with the strongest motive probably predominating.

It should be recognized that all of the conflicts described above must be interpreted in the context within which they exist. Differing societal values, for instance, may produce very different evaluations of what appear at first to be exactly the same event. Indeed, conflicts may develop when values from more than one subculture compete within a particular person.

Other Learned Personality Patterns

It would be possible to point out hundreds of examples of additional personality characteristics that appear to be learned, but for our purposes, it seems appropriate simply to direct the reader to review previously presented concepts such as learned helplessness (Chapters 4, 8), learned aversions (Chapter 7), experimental neurosis (Chapter 10), amnesias (Chapter 14), or superstitious behavior (Chapter 4). In addition, the reader is encouraged to try to apply learning principles to various personality characteristics as illustrated previously in Example 12.

Solved Problems

21.1   Explain how a learning hierarchy can be used to illustrate the evolution of intelligence.

To solve this problem, one must first be willing to accept the idea that all species are tied together on a single phylogenetic scale, with humans representing the highest level.   Assuming this, species can be studied according to their capacities to learn.

Gregory Razran has proposed four levels of learning that represent increasingly higher levels of intellectual performance.   At the lowest level is reactive responding (such as habituation or sensitization), which is demonstrated even by single-cell organisms.   More sophisticated organisms are capable of associative learning (such as classical conditioning).   Still higher on the hierarchy is integrative learning, the ability to combine different stimuli into a single, understandable stimulus.   And the top of the hierarchy is symbolic learning, which is thought to be almost exclusively human.

21.2   What assumption is made regarding the ability of humans to learn all the various behaviors represented by this hierarchy?

It is generally accepted that any organism is capable of performing any of the types of learning below its highest point on the hierarchy.   Humans, who are capable of symbolic learning, are also able to learn at all the lower levels of the hierarchy.   By contrast, organisms lower on the phylogenetic scale are more restricted by innate predispositions; they will not show this full range of performance.   (*Note:* Language learning using American Sign Language has been shown by chimpanzees, although at a much more primitive level than that accomplished by humans.)

21.3   How does the developmental cognitive approach to learning seem to blend the experimental and psychometric approaches to learning and intelligence?

In general, experimental studies of learning have focused upon the characteristics of learning that are common to all species or all organisms within a species.   Although distinctions such as the hierarchy described in Problems 21.1 and 21.2 have been recognized, much more emphasis has been placed on the commonalities of learning experiences.   By contrast, the psychometric tradition developed from a need to specify individual differences.   Attempts to determine how to educate children who differed in learning ability centered attention on measurements that would allow identification of the characteristics that distinguished one from another.

Psychologists who have accepted a developmental cognitive approach to learning seem to have combined these two traditions.   They recognize there are differences in learning ability both within and between species.   At the same time, they recognize that these differences in developmental status may be the result of the subject's individual properties (such as the age of the subject), or of a species-wide characteristic (such as the organism's level on the phylogenetic scale), or both.

21.4   Using the concept of preparedness (see Chapter 20), explain why the psychologists who stress qualitative differences in performance have received wide support for their position.

The limits of performance are, at least to some extent, established by the organism's heredity.   As pointed out in the previous chapter, preparedness to respond in a certain manner may restrict the range of performance shown.   Thus, the rules that govern behavior will differ from species to species, and these rules will predict different levels of cognitive accomplishment.

21.5   Does the measurement of intelligence depend on idiographic or nomethetic approaches to evaluation?

Because intelligence is seen as an attribute of an individual, and not as a group- or species-wide phenomenon, it would seem to make sense to evaluate it idiographically.   However, intelligence is also evaluated in a nomothetic manner in order to establish norms determining the typical performance against which individual performances can be compared.

21.6   Distinguish between norm-referenced and criterion-referenced measures of intelligence.

A norm-referenced test is one in which an individual's performance is compared to the performances of others who have taken the same test.   Norm-referenced tests do not make use of an absolute standard of performance to show how close to complete the subject's mastery of the task may be.   A criterion-referenced test uses an accepted absolute standard as the comparison point for any one person's performance.   The performance of other subjects taking that same test does not affect the evaluation of the single individual.

(*Note:* Criterion referencing is considered more valuable as a diagnostic tool, and it has become more popular as the uses of intelligence testing have changed.   The use of intelligence measurements for improving learning is best accomplished with criterion-referenced tests, for example.)

21.7   Why are intelligence tests often criticized as not being useful measures of learning capacity?   How does the solution to this first question relate to the concepts of achievement, aptitude, and interests?

The difficulty with using intelligence tests to measure capacity for learning is that such measurement is not direct, but rather requires an inference of what ought to occur in the future based upon what has been measured at some given point.   Stated in another manner, intelligence tests are intended to measure aptitude for learning; that is, they are supposed to predict an individual's capacity to benefit from additional training.   However, quite frequently what is measured is achievement—the individual's accomplishments up to the time of measurement.   These tests do not necessarily take into account the subject's interest, with the result being that inaccurate inferences about aptitude may be made.

21.8   Using the hierarchy of learning proposed in the solution to Problem 21.1, suggest which level should show the highest correlation with intelligence as measured by a "traditional" IQ score.

Because intelligence tests frequently are heavily weighted with complex verbal tasks, it would be expected that IQ scores would correlate most highly with symbolic learning tasks.   Research results support this prediction, while correlations with the simpler associative or integrative tasks are considerably lower.   It would also be expected that IQ scores would show a higher correlation with anagram-solving skills than with acquisition of a classically conditioned response, for example.

21.9   Distinguish between crystallized and fluid intelligence.   How do these compare to the concepts of convergent and divergent thinking?

Crystallized intelligence is often demonstrated in tasks involving content recognition or reproduction.   By comparison, fluid intelligence is thought to be a neurologically determined capacity to bring insight into complex tasks that require creative solutions.   Crystallized intelligence may be the result of overlearning, in which repeated applications of fluid intelligence to particular tasks are continued after the task is mastered.

Convergent thinking involves the selection or generation of the single correct answer to some problem.   As such, it probably relies primarily upon crystallized intelligence, although more complex problems may require the insight thought to be represented by fluid intelligence.   Divergent thinking is more creative, and could be used to solve the type of problem that has more than one possible solution.   Crystallized intelligence probably plays some part in divergent thinking, but fluid abilities are likely to be more important for these tasks.

21.10 Does intelligence explain learning or does learning explain intelligence? Explain how physiological explanations are proposed as one way of resolving this controversy. What problems exist with this resolution of the controversy?

Some theorists believe that research will eventually show that physiological factors can account for both intelligence and learning. For example, the administration of some drugs that modify physiological processes seemingly alters the level of intelligence and the capacity to learn. However, until such studies are accompanied by findings regarding why and how these physiological changes produce their effects, the controversy will not be resolved.

21.11 Describe the major controversy regarding physiological characteristics, measured intelligence, and learning capacity.

The controversy revolves around the attempt to quantify the relative importance of hereditary factors and environmental factors to the development of intelligence and learning capacity. While almost all psychologists are willing to accept both genetic and environmental factors as influencing performance, they have not been able to agree on the percent of influence contributed by each factor. It is beyond the scope of this outline to pursue this controversy in depth, but the most prevalent opinion appears to be that while hereditary characteristics do contribute to intellectual and learning differences, the actual levels of performance achieved in a test will depend upon environmental factors.

21.12 Why have Piaget's proposed developmental stages of mental structures been suggested as an alternative means for measuring intelligence?

Piaget's proposals depend primarily upon observation of the transition from infant forms of thinking to those of the adult. The level of performance is thought to be representative of the stage of intellectual development, and examination of daily activities allows the psychologist to determine that stage. This approach means that the more artificial formats of many other measurements of intelligence are not required. (It should be noted, however, that it is not always clear just what behaviors should be observed in a "natural" setting.)

21.13 What role is played by adaptation and organization in all developmental stages of mental activity?

Adaptation is simply the tendency to create a good "fit" between the self and the environment. Organization refers to the tendency to combine several units of information to serve a single purpose. Both of these tendencies operate at all the developmental stages of learning by allowing the person to function in the environment and become better able to cope.

21.14 Piaget believed that adaptation consisted of two basic subprocesses. Name and compare them.

The two basic subprocesses of adaptation are called assimilation and accommodation. These are essentially opposite processes, with assimilation referring to behaviors that change the environment to better fit ourselves, while accommodation refers to behaviors that change ourselves to better fit the environment.

21.15 Suppose an aunt entertains her niece by hiding a ring of keys under one of several pillows, or pretending to hide them before actually placing them there. Describe the pattern of response the niece is likely to show if she is in the sensorimotor stage of development. What subprocess of adaptation is being shown?

The niece is likely to move the pillows until she finds the keys. In the sensorimotor stage the child tends to act upon the environment directly rather than create any mental representation of the environment. The subprocess illustrated is assimilation. The child changes the environment to better fit her self.

21.16 Two children playing together have the following conversation:

Betsy: My daddy got a new car.
Rob: Our house is white.
Betsy: It's a red station wagon.
Rob: We have a big patio.

Which stage of development is represented by this conversation?

These children are probably in the preoperational stage of development. One characteristic of behavior at this stage is egocentrism. Although the children play beside each other, they tend to "do their own things," concentrating upon their personal concerns even when they are talking to one another.

21.17 Although children in the concrete operational stage of development can take into account several different aspects of a problem at once, they do not show all the characteristics of adult thought patterns. According to Piaget, what additional development is needed for the children to reach the formal operational stage?

The characteristic that Piaget believed marked the transition from the concrete operational stage to the formal operational stage is the ability to deal with abstract or hypothetical situations. Stated another way, the child who has reached the formal operational stage is no longer dependent upon observable objects or events in order to perform abstract or hypothetical mental operations.

21.18 Explain why personality is thought to be a summary concept and how this idea relates learning and personality.

Attempts to characterize the personality of an individual often make use of the concept of a summative combination of all those relatively enduring behaviors, feelings, interests, motives, and other patterns that distinguish one person from another. As such, personality is a summary description of these various aspects.

One way of explaining the development of these characteristics is to suggest they are learned—that is, the patterns of response, the motives and emotions, the interests, and the other attributes that compose personality result from the acquisition-storage-retrieval pattern described earlier.

21.19 Why would emphasis on heredity be considered to be contrary to the viewpoint expressed in the solution to Problem 21.18?

As in Problem 21.11, one viewpoint that is opposed to the idea that personality is learned is the idea of biological constraints upon development of personality. For example, psychologists stressing hereditary patterns point to research results showing an apparent inborn tendency to seek variety in environmental events; this aspect of personality supposedly is not learned. As with the controversy regarding the contribution of heredity and environment to measured intelligence, this controversy continues to be debated.

21.20 Accepting for the moment the viewpoint that personality characteristics can be learned, give examples using classical conditioning, instrumental conditioning, and modeling.

One frequently studied personality characteristic is that of phobias. Generally described as neurotic behaviors, phobias are intense and compelling but irrational fears. Phobias are probably classically conditioned. Frequently they result from the pairing of some neutral stimulus with a fear-producing stimulus, such that the neutral stimulus becomes a conditioned stimulus eliciting the conditioned fear response.

An instrumentally conditioned personality pattern may be demonstrated by someone who has a long record of working as a volunteer for a political candidate. While trait theorists might describe this behavior as resulting from a personality characteristic such as "idealism," for example, an alternative explanation is possible: there may be a desire (drive) to be socially accepted, a stimulus pattern that indicates politics is the way to accomplish this (cue), the appropriate response pattern, and the subsequent acceptance (reward). Such a pattern is typical of instrumental conditioning.

Modeling can often be observed in the food preferences shown by children. A child may say, "I don't eat that cereal because my daddy says it tastes like straw!" The modeling of a personality to the attitudes and behaviors of the parents is obvious.

21.21 Cite one example of the attempts to integrate Freudian personality theory and learning theory.

While there are many possible solutions to this problem, one that has been explored is to consider *repression* (motivated forgetting) as a learned characteristic. The thoughts that are repressed are "put into the unconscious" because they are associated with punishment. As pointed out before, punishment tends to suppress responding. Therefore, the interpretation here is that repression is a suppression of thought responses because they are followed by punishing events.

21.22 If Melvin's choices for Saturday morning's activities are either raking leaves or cleaning the garage, what type of conflict is he experiencing? What are the other forms of conflict typically reported using such designations?

Both of Melvin's choices probably seem unpleasant to him, so he is most likely experiencing an avoidance-avoidance conflict. Resolution of such a conflict is usually accomplished by choosing the least unpleasant of the two (or sometimes simply "leaving the field").

Other conflicts of this type are designated as follows: *(a)* approach-approach, the choice between two positively valued objects or events; *(b)* approach-avoidance, when one stimulus has both positive and negative values; and *(c)* multiple approach-avoidance, when there are two or more stimuli, each of which has both positive and negative value.

21.23 Conflicts such as those described in Problem 21.22 are considered conflicts between or among motives. What are other designations of conflict situations that have been proposed in the psychology of learning?

Another way of viewing conflict is to see it as the competition of responses or, more likely, habits. If a multiple stimulus situation "keys off" more than one response tendency, the person seemingly must choose one response over the other. Another type of conflict combines the concept of response tendencies and motives; there may be a conflict between a weak habit operating in intense drive conditions or a strong habit operating in a weak drive condition.

21.24 Suppose Gretchen has an unresolved conflict about whether she should use some form of birth control or have more children. Explain how repeated attacks of intense abdominal distress may be neurotic symptoms associated with the conflict situation.

If Gretchen is experiencing intense stomachaches, she can anticipate that her husband will not expect to have sexual intercourse with her. No sexual intercourse temporarily resolves her conflict situation, thus providing some relief from anxiety. However, this mode of adjusting may produce other strong tensions and more anxiety and eventually lead to even more neurotic symptoms, and possibly physical illness.

21.25 Explain how the inconsistencies of society may have been responsible for Gretchen's anxiety and subsequent neurotic pattern of response.

Differing subcultural values may create a pattern of reinforcements and punishments for the same behaviors. In Gretchen's case, her religion may prohibit artificial birth control while society at large encourages limiting the size of her family. She may also have beliefs regarding appropriate responses to and with her husband, and both society and her religion may reinforce these. Such inconsistencies create conflicting expectations, and Gretchen may utilize a neurotic pattern to try to relieve some of the anxiety. Comparable examples can be found when parents are inconsistent in their treatment of children or teachers are inconsistent with students.

21.26 Explain how experimental neurosis is comparable to the pattern described in Problems 21.24 and 21.25.

Experimental neurosis is comparable to the "real life" situation described above in that both require the subject to react to excitatory and inhibitory tendencies generated by a single stimulus pattern (see Chapter 10).

Key Terms

Achievement. The measurement of responding at a given moment.

Accommodation. In Piaget's theory, a subprocess of adaptation; responses that change the self to better "fit" the environment.

Adaptation. In Piaget's theory, generating a reasonable adjustment between the self and the environment.

Approach-approach conflict. A situation in which a person must choose between two stimulus situations, both of which have positive values.

Approach-avoidance conflict. A situation in which a person must choose whether to go toward or away from a single stimulus situation that has both positive and negative values.

Aptitude. The measured capability to benefit from additional training.

Assimilation. In Piaget's theory, a subprocess of adaptation; responses that change the environment to better "fit" the self.

Associative learning. According to Razran, S-R or S-S learning.

Avoidance-avoidance conflict. A situation in which a person must choose between two stimulus situations, both of which have negative values.

Concrete operational stage. According to Piaget, the third stage of cognitive development from approximately age seven to age eleven.

Conflict. The situation that occurs when a person experiences two or more competing motive conditions at one time or also, possibly, when there are two or more competing responses.

Convergent thinking. Routine or common problem solving; seeking a single correct response.

Criterion. A standard of comparison established arbitrarily and held regardless of a particular group's performance.

Crystallized intelligence. Intelligence used in the application of already-learned materials; usually considered to be rigid or unchanging.

Divergent thinking. Unique or novel problem solving; generating many new solutions to a problem.

Experimental neurosis. The unusual patterns of responding shown by organisms exposed and forced to respond to extremely difficult (nearly insoluble) discrimination tasks.

Fluid intelligence. Intelligence used to adjust to new situations; usually considered as flexible or adaptive thinking.

Formal operational stage. According to Piaget, the fourth and final stage of cognitive development from approximately age eleven to age thirteen (cognitive adulthood).

Integrative learning. According to Razran, learning which involves the combination or condensation of several situations.

Intelligence. The measure of capacity to learn.

Interest. Any area that generates attention or excitement for a person.

Multiple approach-avoidance conflict.   A situation in which a person must choose between two (or more) stimulus situations, each of which has both positive and negative values.

Norm.   The average performance of a representative group; used as a standard of comparison.

Organization.   In Piaget's theory, combination of several units of information to serve a single purpose.

Preoperational stage.   According to Piaget, the second stage of cognitive development from approximately age two to age seven.

Psychometry.   Investigations which attempt to identify quantifiable individual differences among human subjects.

Reactive responding.   According to Razran, the lowest level of responding; single-contingency learning.

Sensorimotor stage.   According to Piaget, the first stage of cognitive development from birth to about age two.

Symbolic learning.   According to Razran, the highest level of learning; the human ability to generate unique messages by using symbols.

PART VII: *Applications of Learning*

While almost any learning situation probably could be treated as an application of learning, certain areas have received special attention.   This part presents some of these areas.

Chapter 22 is particularly concerned with modification of behavior using therapy or programmed learning.   The chapter also presents a brief look at biotechnology, the use of learning principles to modify behavior of lower organisms.

Perceptual-motor learning is the focus of Chapter 23.   Although this topic often is considered part of physical education rather than psychology, it can be considered to be an applied learning topic.   Characteristics and theories of motor learning, variables affecting motor learning, and research methods used to study motor learning are included.

Chapter 22

Behavior Technology

One can describe *behavior technology* as the application of learning principles to achieving practical goals. The examples of practical applications in this chapter are not meant to be even close to exhaustive, however. Indeed, some psychologists refer to conditioning as a basic part of our lives. The topics chosen here simply represent widely accepted examples of specific attempts to make practical use of learning principles.

Another general characteristic of the type of behavior technology in this chapter is that the objectives of the procedures should be stated explicitly—in a manner that allows for reasonably clear evaluations to be made. Generally, this means avoiding ambiguity or vagueness in developing statements of expected outcomes.

EXAMPLE 1. The two lists below contrast outcomes that are relatively precise with some that are relatively vague. Typically, it would be much easier to evaluate the success of the behavior technology used if the more precise phrases were employed in instructing the subjects what to do:

Relatively Precise	Relatively Vague
To identify	To understand
To compare	To appreciate
To solve	To recognize the significance of
To list	To know
To differentiate	To believe

22.1 BEHAVIOR THERAPY

Probably the widest application of learning principles has been in the area of *behavior therapy*, the use of learning principles to control responding in order to improve a person's well-being. This section will look at several concepts that appear to be common to many or all of the behavior therapies and some of the therapeutic applications of the learning principles presented earlier (in Chapters 3, 4, and 5 especially).

Intervention

It should be recognized that almost all behavior therapies can be interpreted as *intervention* circumstances. The therapist intervenes in an attempt to modify the patient's response pattern (thus the popular phrase "behavior modification").

Common characteristics. Typically, the intervention procedures used have several common characteristics. First, as indicated above, they use learning principles in attempts to control behavior. Second, they are aimed at alleviating human problems and improving the circumstances of people experiencing some kind of problem behavior. Third, the patient and the therapist undertake a mutual contractual agreement based upon the first and second points above. And fourth, the validity of such undertakings is evaluated frequently.

EXAMPLE 2. The third point given above is as important to the overall success of a behavior-therapy program as the other three, which are perhaps more obvious. It is not enough for the therapist to arrange conditions so that learning may take place for the patient. It is necessary for the patient to know what can be expected of the therapist, what methods of intervention will be employed, and what goals are to be achieved.To this end, an agreement of some sort may be struck between the two before therapy begins, enabling both the therapist and patient to evaluate the success of the procedure.

Counterconditioning

Regardless of the procedure employed, behavior therapies often emphasize response-replacement procedures. This is typically called *counterconditioning,* and involves the extinction of the previous, undesirable response and the simultaneous conditioning of a new, acceptable response pattern.

Classical Conditioning Techniques

Several behavior therapies are based upon the principles of classical conditioning. Among these are counterconditioning using extinction and positive reinforcement, systematic desensitization, implosive therapy, and aversive conditioning.

Classical counterconditioning. When the patient has learned an inappropriate conditioned response (CR_1) to a particular CS, extinction of that response and concurrent training of an appropriate replacement (CR_2) is called *classical counterconditioning.*

Systematic desensitization. This procedure is a modification of counterconditioning that is often used to eliminate inappropriate fear responses. Very mild forms of the CS are used at first and paired with relaxation and security conditions. Exposure to the mild CS continues until it is completely nonthreatening. Subsequent trials use CS conditions that are more and more like the original, fear-producing stimulus. (If the anxiety level gets too high, a less threatening form of the CS is reintroduced. Eventually, the original CS is paired with the relaxation conditions, and a CR of acceptance and security replaces the original CR of fear.)

EXAMPLE 3. Patients often are asked to rank a number of fear-producing cues from greatest to least. Systematic desensitization to the least fear-provoking stimulus is then started, with acceptable responses being conditioned. Each succeeding step uses the next most fear-producing stimulus. Thus, if the patient fears fires, the first stimulus might be a paragraph discussing fires, while the final steps might include viewing an actual bonfire at close range.

Implosive therapy. Another variation of behavior therapy that uses classical conditioning procedures has been called *implosive therapy* (or *flooding*). In these situations, the patient is immediately asked or prompted to imagine the highest level of the fear-provoking stimulus. (There is no gradual "build-up" to this level of aversiveness.) The exposure to this intensely aversive stimulus is combined with the realization that the fear is unfounded. This eventually eliminates the inappropriate response.

EXAMPLE 4. Implosive therapy is used frequently for patients with compulsions, such as the ritualistic washing and cleaning behaviors that might accompany fear of contamination by household dirt. The patient is made to confront the aversive stimulus and is kept from making the compulsive responses. When contamination does not occur, the patient is able to realize that the very worst stimulus does not produce the expected result, and the compulsions can be dropped.

Aversive therapy. Classical conditioning is also the basis of *aversive therapy,* in which an unconditioned stimulus that is unpleasant is used to modify the response pattern given to the CS. Typically, the aversive UCS produces pain or sickness, which in turn promotes escape, withdrawal, or avoidance.

EXAMPLE 5. The treatment of alcoholics sometimes involves aversive therapy. The patient is given a drug which has no effect unless alcohol is ingested. However, one drink taken while the drug is in effect will produce considerable nausea and vomiting. The concept is that drinking will become associated with the unpleasant sickness, and the patient will avoid the drinking response. (*Note:* This may not be terribly effective because no alternative response is being reinforced.)

Instrumental-Conditioning Techniques

Instrumental-conditioning techniques have been used in a number of different manners for behavior therapy. Table 22-1 summarizes the various types of behavior-therapy designs that make use of instrumental conditioning.

Table 22-1   Behavior-Therapy Designs

Positive-Reinforcement Designs			
Response	Reinforcement Given?	Name of Design	Result
Correct Response — made	yes	reward	strengthen correct R
Correct Response — not made	no	privation	strengthen correct R
Undesirable Response — made	no	omission	weaken undesirable R
Undesirable Response — not made	yes	cessation	weaken undesirable R

Aversive-Stimulus Designs			
Response	Aversive Stimulus Given?	Name of Design	Result
Correct Response — made	no	escape	strengthen correct R
Correct Response — not made	yes	avoidance	strengthen correct R
Undesirable Response — made	yes	punishment	weaken undesirable R
Undesirable Response — not made	no	release	weaken undesirable R

The learning principles associated with instrumental conditioning (including shaping, schedules of reinforcement, and extinction) are applicable in the situation presented in this table.

EXAMPLE 6.   Reward training probably is used more often than any of the other instrumental-conditioning techniques described in Table 22-1.   If the client has remained mute, initial reinforcements may be given for production of any types of sound.   Once the client has started making sounds reliably, shaping of closer and closer approximations of appropriate speech patterns can be used, and perhaps partial-reinforcement conditions will be introduced in order to try to make the newly acquired appropriate responses as resistant to extinction as possible.

Token economy.   One special case of behavior therapy has been labelled the *token economy* procedure.   Essentially, the client performs appropriate responses in order to earn some secondary reinforcer (such as a chip, ticket, or token) that can be "banked" and later traded in for privileges or rewards.

EXAMPLE 7. Hospitals or comparable facilities often use token economies. Patients accumulate credits that can be used for special events or some kind of treat.   Inappropriate behavior can lead to the loss of tokens, supposedly leading to the weakening of undesirable responses.

Biofeedback. Another special case of behavior therapy is called *biofeedback,* in which certain devices provide the client with information about bodily states that would not otherwise be accessible to the client.   Responses such as heart rate or blood pressure are monitored and then transformed or amplified into visual or auditory signals.   The client, receiving these signals (called *feedback*), attempts to modify the physiological states and thus the signals.   The therapist may reward successful attempts at modifications, but the modification of the signal itself may also be considered reinforcing.

EXAMPLE 8. There have been a number of studies investigating the use of biofeedback to alleviate headache symptoms that are supposedly caused by excessive blood flow to the head area.   Clients are connected to a temperature-sensing device that monitors the change in temperature in the hands or feet, for example.   Then the subjects practice raising (or learn to raise) that temperature value.   They are reinforced for modifying the blood flow so that more goes to the extremities and less to the head, which in turn relieves the headache symptoms.   The mechanical monitoring allows sensing of a bodily function that would otherwise not be readily recognized.

Response as reinforcer. One more interesting aspect of instrumental behavior therapy is the use of a *response as a reinforcer*.   Known as the *Premack principle* (after an investigator) or "Grandma's rule," the idea is that a desired response can be trained by requiring that it be made before some other response (preferred by the client) is allowed.   Basically, this is an "if you do what is requested, then you can do what you want" arrangement.

EXAMPLE 9. Allowing the patient to watch television in the dayroom only after the room has been cleaned illustrates this principle.   The preferred behavior is used as the reinforcer for the less desirable response.   It is hoped that such a contingency arrangement will encourage patterns of good citizenship within the hospital setting.

Modeling

The basic premise of using modeling in behavior-therapy situations is to present the patient with an opportunity to observe the actions of others whose response patterns may be copied later.   Observation and subsequent imitation may thus create appropriate response patterns for the client.

Vicarious extinction. Most modeling procedures consist of observing and then copying responses that are appropriate.   One exception occurs, however, when the client observes an inappropriate response that is *not* reinforced.   The client is able to perceive the nonreinforcement and, it is hoped, will choose to drop a similar response from his or her behavioral repertoire as a result of this *vicarious extinction*.

EXAMPLE 10. Observing a model who is not reinforced for socially inappropriate "bad manners" may provide the client with understanding through vicarious extinction.   This could lead to a subsequent decrease in comparable responses on the client's part.

The Problem of Generalization

One difficulty that appears to exist in all types of behavior-therapy procedures is that the pattern established in the relatively artificial therapy setting may or may not be generalized to day-to-day living situations.   It may be that the stimuli provided by daily living circumstances are sufficiently different from those in the therapy setting for the client to differentiate and not respond with the appropriate conditioned responses.   As a result, the client may return to the inappropriate patterns previously displayed.

EXAMPLE 11. An instance illustrating this problem was shown in research conducted with autistic children as patients.   When the training of social responses was confined to a single room, the responses did not generalize to outside circumstances.   It was necessary to conduct the behavior-therapy program in many different locations before the social responses would generalize to nontherapy settings.   (*Note:* This is also representative of the principle of state-dependent learning, discussed in Chapter 20.)

22.2 PROGRAMMED INSTRUCTION

A second major application of learning principles has been in the area of *programmed instruction*. Such a procedure makes use of individualized instruction and immediate feedback from sources other than the teacher in order to improve the efficiency of learning.   Some of the forms of programmed instruction include programmed textbooks, teaching machines, and computer-assisted instruction (CAI).

The advantages of this kind of instruction are thought to include (1) more frequent individual instruction, (2) immediate feedback for both correct and incorrect responses, (3) an appropriate level of instruction for each participant with correspondingly appropriate ways of shaping the responses, and (4) no personal unpleasantness (which might be demonstrated by a frustrated teacher, for example).

The disadvantages of programmed instruction include (1) the problems of establishing appropriate steps for all respondents so they are neither overchallenged nor bored, (2) the expense involved in obtaining necessary equipment, and (3) the lack of personal interaction and resultant absence of social-skills learning.

EXAMPLE 12.   The novelty of computer-assisted instruction (CAI) often attracts children to work with the teaching device.   (Some CAI machines use both visual and auditory signals to present the task and reinforce the respondent, and these signals may in and of themselves arouse and motivate the student.)   Spelling, arithmetic, and comparable tasks can be practiced at an individual pace with a high level of success and a great deal of feedback—something that cannot be provided by a single teacher.

Types of programs.   Programs usually take one of two forms—linear or branching. *Linear programs* are the same for all respondents and progress in a straight-line fashion from beginning to end. *Branching programs* direct the programs of each respondent according to the first responses made.   Branching programs are essentially individualized for each participant, but are more difficult to create than linear programs and require more sophisticated equipment.

Simulators.   An interesting variation of programmed instruction is accomplished by using *simulators,* mechanical devices that are used to imitate actual performance conditions.   Attached to a computer, the simulators can duplicate episodes that are comparable to those the respondent could expect to encounter in the "real-life" situation for which he or she is being trained.   Simulators are frequently used when either the expense, time, or risk involved in using the actual equipment is deemed to be too great (for example, in the training of airline pilots or supertanker captains).

EXAMPLE 13.   Driver education classes often use simulators as a way of introducing students to potentially dangerous situations without having to actually stage the accident conditions.   Sitting in a simulated driver's seat with all the appropriate equipment, the student can observe the "road" on a movie screen or videotape monitor and attempt to respond correctly.   All three advantages cited above are found in the use of such a training device—the cost is considerably reduced, the risk of accident is nonexistent, and a wide variety of driving situations can be presented in a short period of time.

22.3 BIOTECHNOLOGY

One other form of behavior technology—*biotechnology*—deserves mention.   It involves the training of animals to respond in ways that will make it possible for them to take the place of people or machines.   While biotechnology is quite commonly used in situations such as farming, social pressures often prevail against other applications.

EXAMPLE 14.   During World War II, psychologists developed the methodology and equipment to train pigeons to be "kamikaze bombardiers."   They were conditioned to peck at a sightlike device inside a bomb in order to direct the bomb toward its target.   A general reluctance on the part of the military to use animals in this way prevented widespread implementation of this program.

Solved Problems

22.1 Why, when a therapist begins to work with a client, is it better to state that the goal of the therapy "is to identify problem areas and develop new response patterns for coping" than to say that the goal "is to understand yourself better"?

Difficulties may arise when the expected outcomes of a therapy situation are subject to many possible interpretations. When there are fewer interpretations, the success of obtaining goals is more likely to be measurable, which in turn means that establishing the therapy program is that much easier. The same principle holds in establishing the objectives of training or educational programs: the more specific the goals, the easier they will be to evaluate.

22.2 Explain why behavior therapies are often referred to as intervention techniques.

Behavior therapies make use of learning principles in an attempt to control behavior. As such, the therapist (or manipulator) is indeed intervening in the client's life. An alternative term used to describe behavior therapies is "behavior modification" (or in the jargon, "behavior mod").

22.3 The solution to Problem 22.2 indicated that one general characteristic of behavior therapies is that they apply learning principles in an attempt to control behavior. What other characteristics appear to be common to all behavior-modification procedures?

There are three additional characteristics common to all behavior-modification procedures. One is that the control of behavior sought has as its goal the improvement of the client's functioning. The second is that the procedures involve an agreement (or contract) between the client and the therapist specifying the roles, goals, and behaviors for each. Finally, the expectation is that the procedures and subsequent results will be evaluated in an attempt to determine the validity of the techniques employed.

22.4 Counterconditioning using classical conditioning procedures has been used fairly frequently as a behavior-therapy technique. Explain how this is done when a positive-reinforcement (a positive UCS) condition is employed.

The intent of counterconditioning using positive classical conditioning procedures is to replace an undesirable response (CR_1) with a desired one (CR_2). That is, the CS-CR_1 sequence is modified to become a CS-CR_2 sequence. This is accomplished by extinguishing the CS-CR_1 pairing while reinforcing the CS-CR_2 sequence by using a UCS that will elicit a CR_2-type response.

22.5 Why are behavior modification techniques such as those that use systematic desensitization or an aversive UCS not necessarily viewed as counterconditioning?

Counterconditioning implies that an undesirable response (CR_1) is being replaced by one that is acceptable (CR_2). In behavior-modification procedures that use an aversive UCS or systematic desensitization, there is some question as to whether or not a second response has, in fact, been conditioned to the original CS. In a sense, these procedures condition a not-responding attitude. That is, the first (unacceptable) response is extinguished and replaced by not responding.

22.6 How does implosive therapy differ from systematic desensitization? How are they alike?

Implosive therapy asks the patient to make imaginative representations of some of the most anxiety-producing stimuli while the patient is in a totally nonthreatening situation. This "flooding" of anxiety in a "safe" situation forces the patient to learn that the imagined situations cannot be harmful. Implosive therapy differs from systematic desensitization in that the most anxiety-producing stimulus is used first—there is no gradual build-up. The two types of therapies are alike in that both typically employ the use of representations (rather than actual anxiety-producing stimuli) and completely nonthreatening circumstances.

22.7   What are the major considerations of contingency management in behavior therapy?

There are three significant factors of contingency management used for behavior therapy: (1) whether a correct or undesirable response is made (or not made), (2) whether a response (or no response) is followed by (or not followed by) a reinforcer or an aversive stimulus, and (3) what effect the particular combination of (1) and (2) has upon the response being studied.

22.8   Using the contingency-management situations described in the solution to Problem 22.7, explain the circumstances in which administration of a positive reinforcer affects response strength.

Perhaps the most common form of behavior therapy is that of reward training, in which performance of the desired response is followed by positive reinforcement. This should strengthen the desired response. A second use of presentation of positive reinforcement is called cessation training. Positive reinforcers are given when the undesirable response is *not* made. It is expected that this will weaken the strength of the undesirable response.

22.9   When are the punishment procedures used for behavior therapy labelled passive avoidance, and when are they called active avoidance?

"Punishment" refers to situations where the performance of a response leads to some aversive stimulus; that is, the aversive stimulus is contingent upon the undesirable response having occurred. One form of behavior therapy simply requires the patient to *not* make the undesirable response, thus avoiding the aversive condition. This is passive-avoidance training. A second procedure requires that the undesirable response not be made (as with passive avoidance), but in addition encourages an appropriate substitute response. This is called active-avoidance training. This latter procedure is enhanced when the substitute response is rewarded, creating a counterconditioning circumstance.

22.10   Some people, believing cigarette smoking to be an undesirable response, have tried to eliminate the smoking response from their behavioral repertoires by gradually cutting back—smoking fewer cigarettes in successive time periods (such as per day or per week). What basic principle of instrumental conditioning is being applied in such situations? What other principle indicates that such a procedure may prove fruitless?

The gradual cutting back is comparable to shaping, the reinforcing of closer and closer approximations of a desired behavior. With many short-term goals and appropriate reinforcements, this procedure may work. However, the partial-reinforcement effect would predict that as the frequency of smoking per "smoking situation" diminishes, each actual smoking response will make the smoking behavior more and more resistant to extinction. After reaching some low point (but not zero), the frequency of smoking can be expected to increase again.

22.11   The director of the Boy's Home calls a meeting to inform the residents that a "chit" system is being instituted. What type of behavior therapy is probably going to be used? How does this differ from a demerit system?

"Chit" systems are generally token economies. Appropriate responses are rewarded with "chits," or tokens, that can be traded in later for privileges or desired items (such as a night at the movies or a new record). Token economies differ from demerit systems in that appropriate responding rather than inappropriate responding is stressed. In a demerit system the individual accumulates points for *inappropriate* responding. These points, which result in a loss of privileges, must be "worked off." Inappropriate responses made in token economies might mean that some token will be taken away, but there is no "working off."

22.12   Suppose a man says to his daughter, "You can't go swimming until the lawn is cut."   What behavioral principle is being used?

The father is applying what has been called "Grandma's rule," in which a highly desired response is not allowed until a less desired (but appropriate or necessary) response has been made.   This format, also known as the "Premack principle," uses a desirable response as the reinforcer in reward training.

22.13   Why might the situation in Problem 22.12 also be called privation training, but not punishment training?

The "if-then" format in Problem 22.12 mandates that if the correct response (lawn-cutting) is *not* made, a positive reinforcer (in the form of swimming) will be withheld.   The withholding of a positive reinforcer is not considered to be punishment in the same sense that the administration of an aversive stimulus would be.

22.14   If Erik constantly interrupts conversations, how could omission training be used to modify his behavior?

Assuming that in the past these interruptions have produced some sort of reinforcement for Erik (for example, gaining desired attention), omission training would require that the interruptions be ignored.   Thus, when the undesirable response was made, positive reinforcement would not be given and extinction should take place.   (*Note:* Reinforcing Erik's participation in the conversation at appropriate times would help promote appropriate or desired responses.)

22.15   How might biofeedback training be used to try to alleviate the symptoms of high blood pressure?

Because the body does not provide ample or easily accessible cues to when blood pressure is raised or lowered, mechanical devices need to be employed.   In a biofeedback procedure the blood pressure is monitored and transformed into signals (either visual or auditory) that the subject can easily perceive.   The patient would be instructed to "lower the tone" (or light or whatever feedback signal the device produced).   The level of this tone would correspond to the blood-pressure value being recorded at the time.   With practice and with the change in tone (or possibly other stimuli) serving as reinforcement, patients can learn to reduce blood-pressure levels.   The mechanical devices allow monitoring of behaviors that are not otherwise readily observed.

22.16   How might the solution to Problem 22.15 serve to point out the problem of "generalizability"?

Daily living typically does not involve either a laboratory setting or being attached to mechanical feedback devices.   Research has shown that patients who accomplish marked improvement in the laboratory may not be able to transfer their gains into the environment outside the training circumstance.   Comparable kinds of findings have been obtained for other behavior-therapy techniques, with success in the clinical setting not necessarily generalizing to nonclinical circumstances.

22.17   Describe how modeling might be used as part of the therapy program employed to help a patient overcome a fear of dogs.

Modeling refers to learning through observation.   In this situation part of the therapy program might consist of films, videotapes, or actual sessions showing someone making appropriate coping responses with dogs.   This could include approaching the dog, playing with it, or petting it.   The principle of this type of therapy is that the patient will learn by observing successful responses and incorporate similar responses into his or her behavior pattern.

22.18 Recall Erik the interruptor (Problem 22.14). How might vicarious extinction be used to help modify his undesirable behavior?

If it were possible, arrangements might be made for Erik to observe someone else interrupting unsuccessfully. Erik would be able to determine that such behavior does not work and, assuming this was part of the modeling circumstances, also might be able to observe appropriate responses that could then be copied.

22.19 What basic principle underlies programmed instruction using programmed textbooks or teaching machines?

The basic assumption of programmed instruction is that it promotes a high degree of accurate responding using relatively small steps in advancing through the material. This is thought to be highly reinforcing because there is a relatively high level of success and very little failure experienced. Additionally, most programmed textbooks or teaching machines can be used at the learner's particular pace. Thus, the rate of responding would not affect the total amount of reinforcement delivered. (This would probably not be the case in the classroom.)

22.20 How does a branching program differ from a linear program?

Branching programs are designed to "tailor" later parts of the program according to responses given in the initial segments of the program. Thus, if the respondent shows a particular inadequacy, the program may "branch" in that direction so that sufficient practice in that task can be had. By contrast, a linear program advances along the same step-by-step sequence for all users. There are no deviations according to previous performance. Branching programs are more flexible than linear programs, but more difficult to design as well.

22.21 What advantage is ascribed to computer-assisted-instruction (CAI) more than other forms of programmed instruction?

The range of feedback provided to the learner who uses sophisticated computer technology can be much greater than what textbooks or simpler teaching machines have to offer. It should be recognized, however, that such an advantage may be offset by the much greater expense involved.

22.22 Why are simulators favored as a form of teaching certain responses?

Several advantages might be cited. First, using simulators is often much safer than performing the actual task. Second, simulators may be much less expensive to purchase and maintain than the equipment they represent. In addition, simulators generally can be readily programmed to create many different learning situations in a relatively short period of time, while actual conditions may not be so readily obtainable.

22.23 Define biotechnology. Why is this principle sometimes difficult to implement?

Biotechnology is training animals to substitute for people or machines. While biotechnology is often acceptable (using a horse to pull a cart, for example), it is not always easy to implement. For one thing, humans may sometimes be reluctant to trust the results (such as when pigeons are trained to be quality-control inspectors in a pill-manufacturing factory). Furthermore, some of the biotechnological uses of animals result in their deaths (as when pigeons are used to guide missiles or bombs). Although the performance of the animals may be very accurate and perhaps even superior to that of humans, the problem of public reaction may prevent such procedures from being utilized.

Key Terms

Aversive therapy. A classical conditioning procedure in which an aversive UCS is paired with the CS currently producing the undesirable response.

Avoidance training. Contingency management in which an aversive stimulus is withheld if a correct response is made.

Behavior modification. Any of a number of methods used to change response patterns. These methods focus on the use of learning procedures such as classical conditioning, instrumental conditioning, or modeling. Also, another name for behavior therapy.

Behavior technology. The application of learning principles to daily living situations.

Behavior therapy. The application of learning principles to control responding in order to improve a person's well-being.

Biofeedback. The use of a monitoring device to determine the status of physiological processes not otherwise easily observed.

Biotechnology. Training animals to respond in manners that will replace men or machines.

Branching program. A programmed-learning situation in which progress through the learning sequence depends upon the subject's responses and may vary for each subject.

Cessation training. Contingency management in which a positive reinforcement is delivered if an incorrect response is not made.

Computer-assisted instruction (CAI). A procedure involving the use of a computer as a teaching machine, both for presentation of stimuli and recording of responses.

Contingency management. Manipulation of the delivery of reinforcement or aversive stimuli according to the performance of the subject.

Counterconditioning. Response replacement by extinction of the undesirable response and accompanying reinforcement of an acceptable response.

Escape training. Contingency management in which an aversive stimulus is terminated if a correct response is made.

Flooding. In implosive therapy, the creation of conditions that produce maximum anxiety for the subject.

Implosive therapy. A technique involving pairing of the worst possible anxiety-producing stimuli with a nonthreatening situation.

Intervention. The act of interceding or interfering; in behavior therapies, the therapist's role in modifying the client's behaviors.

Linear program. Any programmed learning situation that progresses in the same way for each subject.

Omission training. Contingency management in which a positive reinforcement is not delivered if an incorrect response is made.

Premack principle. The withholding of the opportunity to perform a desired response in order to reinforce the performance of a less desired response; also called "Grandma's rule."

Privation training. Contingency management in which a positive reinforcement is not delivered if a correct response is not made.

Programmed instruction. Individualized instruction using feedback from sources other than a teacher to improve learning efficiency.

Punishment training. Contingency management in which an aversive stimulus is delivered if an incorrect response is made.

Release training. Contingency management in which an aversive stimulus is withheld if an incorrect response is not made.

Reward training.   Contingency management in which a positive reinforcement is delivered if a correct response is made.

Simulator.   Any mechanical device used to imitate actual training conditions.

Systematic desensitization.   A step-by-step classical conditioning procedure in which successively stronger anxiety-producing stimuli (the CS) are paired with relaxation conditions (the UCS).

Teaching machine.   A mechanical or electronic device that presents programmed instruction.

Token economy.   A procedure whereby the client is rewarded with secondary reinforcers for performing appropriate behaviors; the secondary reinforcers can be traded in later for other reinforcements.

Vicarious extinction.   A modeling procedure in which the client observes an inappropriate response that is not reinforced.

Chapter 23

Motor Learning

Motor Learning—the acquisition, storage, and retrieval of precise patterns of bodily movements—is a topic neglected by most learning psychologists. One reason for this is that motor responses are often investigated only as the final step in perceptual-motor tasks, where the emphasis is likely to be on the processing of incoming stimuli (perception) rather than on the subsequent (motor) responses. Furthermore, learning psychologists tend to think of motor responses as a proper subject of study for investigations in other disciplines, especially medicine and physical education. Nonetheless, these responses can be profitably studied from the perspective of learning, and some of the most important findings about how we learn to make them are discussed in this chapter.

23.1 BASES FOR MOTOR LEARNING STUDY

This section reviews some of the basic principles of learning that are especially important in the study of motor responses.

Learning vs. Performance

As indicated in the first chapter of this outline, the performance of a response is not necessarily an indication that learning has taken place. Experimental procedures, motivation conditions, the particular equipment being used, and many other variables may produce performance effects that mask the actual level of learning.

EXAMPLE 1. The pacing of a task may hide the underlying learning that is taking place. If the subjects are expected to make a particular sequence of motor movements (such as arranging a sequence of blocks into a designated pattern), the level of success in performance will vary considerably as the time allowed for responding is varied. When all subjects are allowed to work at their own pace, the results may be either comparable or very different. However, the fact that performance levels have varied cannot be taken to indicate that learning levels have changed.

Types of Tasks

In general, a motor learning task can be classified as one of two basic types. *Discrete motor tasks* involve periods of responding that are separated by obvious periods of nonresponding. *Continuous motor tasks* are those in which responding progresses in a relatively uninterrupted succession of movements.

EXAMPLE 2. Experiments in motor learning employ both discrete and continuous tasks. In a study where subjects are periodically asked to adjust a lever to make it correspond to a pictorial stimulus, the motor task is discrete. Each adjustment is evaluated before another response is made. Tracking—attempting to keep a constantly moving pointer or "blip" on a screen within the limits of a specified target—is a continuous motor task.

Motor Learning Procedures

Studies of motor learning frequently involve line drawing, stimulus matching, fine motor tasks, gross motor tasks, and the assembly or disassembly of interlocking parts. These and other easily controlled and quantified tasks are most often used in laboratory settings. Outside the laboratory, sports equipment, various types of machinery, and simulators may be used in studies of motor learning.

Measures of Performance

Responses in motor learning tasks are usually measured in terms of accuracy and/or time. *Accuracy measures* are records of the number of correct responses or the number of errors made. *Time measures* include reaction time, time on target, or time necessary for task completion.

EXAMPLE 3.   A simple task such as line drawing can be measured in terms of accuracy and/or time.   For instance, accuracy could be determined as the difference between the drawn line and the standard while the time taken to draw the line can also be taken as an indicator of how well the motor response has been learned.

23.2   CHARACTERISTICS OF MOTOR LEARNING

It has been suggested that motor learning tasks have four general characteristics—the linking of perceptual and motor aspects, the chaining of responses, organization of responses, and feedback.

Perceptual-Motor Linking

As pointed out earlier, motor learning often is viewed as the final step in a perceptual-motor task, in which the information provided by incoming stimuli is related to certain movement sequences.   This has been called *perceptual-motor linking*.

Response Chains

Many motor behaviors consist of a sequence of movements in which each response is at least partially dependent upon the responses that have appeared before or those yet to come.   These *response chains* may in turn be linked into even more general sequences of prolonged motor behavior.

EXAMPLE 4.   Consider the motor behavior of starting a car.   It involves a series of motor responses including inserting the key into the ignition, depressing the accelerator, turning the key, and finally putting the car into gear.   This sequence involves a series of individual motor responses formed into chains that are in turn bonded together to produce the overall result.

Organization of Responses

Example 4 can be used to illustrate the *organization of responses*, the third characteristic of motor learning.   If the person tries to put the car into gear before turning the ignition key, the sequence will be thwarted.   The lever might be placed in the "drive" position, but the car will not start and the end result of moving will not be achieved.   This situation demonstrates that the response chains must have an overall pattern of organization to be successful.

Feedback

Feedback (described later as *knowledge of results*) may be either extrinsic (that is, from outside sources) or intrinsic (internally generated).   Because of feedback, the subject is able to determine what result his or her movement sequence has had, evaluate this result, and if necessary make any appropriate adjustments or alterations to the response sequence.

23.3   PHASES OF MOTOR LEARNING

A suggestion by Paul Fitts, a leading investigator of motor learning, deserves consideration here.   Fitts believed that motor learning progressed in three phases: a cognitive stage, an associative stage, and finally an autonomous stage.

Cognitive Stage

Fitts believed the initial stage of motor learning consists of developing and using a cognitive understanding of what is required in order to carry out a response sequence.

EXAMPLE 5.   A person learning to play pinball can be used to illustrate the importance of the cognitive stage in motor learning.   To use the "flippers" effectively, the player must know where the control buttons are, how they are manipulated, and what results can be expected from varying the pressure exerted on them.   All such cognitive material, even though it may later be modified with experience, must be acquired before appropriate motor responding is possible.

Associative Stage

The second phase of motor learning is called the *associative stage,* during which the person links the stimuli (perceptual aspect) to the responses (motor behavior).

EXAMPLE 6.   Refer again to the pinball player in Example 5.   The knowledge gained in the cognitive stage could now be applied to the acquisition of the appropriate responses.   The player develops a recognition of which stimulus patterns should be followed by which types of responses, and attempts to make them when appropriate.

Autonomous Stage

After sufficient practice, the cumulative experiences lead to the final phase of motor learning, called the *autonomous stage,* where response patterns follow automatically after the stimulus configuration is perceived.   Responses are made on a relatively involuntary level, and they are successful and seemingly impervious to interference.

EXAMPLE 7.   Someone may ask the pinball player this question: "How do you know just when to flip?"   The player responds, "I don't know, I just do it."   Such an answer indicates that the autonomous phase has been reached.   Conscious effort is no longer required.

In general, research suggests that progression through these phases will be slow if the complexity of the task is great.   However, even extremely sophisticated motor behaviors (such as movements required in gymnastics or diving) can reach the autonomous stage if adequate cognitive and associative practice has taken place.

23.4   PERSONAL VARIABLES AFFECTING MOTOR LEARNING

The characteristics of an individual can be roughly divided into two categories—the physical and psychological.   Both types of individual variables can affect motor learning.

Physical Variables

Motor learning can be limited by the physical structure of the person.   Any physical variable may influence performance, including the acuity of the senses, the body type or structure, and factors such as dexterity, durability, or speed of reaction.

Psychological Variables

The list of variables in this section could be as long as the number of topics considered in the study of behavior.   In general, it should be recognized that factors such as developmental history, previous learning, motivation, emotion, social influences, and intelligence all may play a part in the motor learning sequence that develops.

EXAMPLE 8.   The overlap between physical and psychological variables and the effect these may have upon motor behavior can be illustrated by a task as simple as reproducing a drawing of a cube.   At least one student had a terrible time understanding three-dimensional research graphs because he was unable to reproduce a drawing such as the one in Fig. 23-1a.   Inevitably, his drawings would come out looking like Fig. 23-1b or c, and he would be unable to complete his assignment. Poor coordination, poor cognition, or many other factors may have produced such responses. (It should be noted that this instance illustrates how poor motor learning may also affect other learning tasks.)

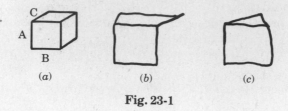

Fig. 23-1

23.5 PRACTICE AND MOTOR LEARNING

Practice, the repeated performance of a motor task leading to the acquisition and storage of a movement sequence, has been judged to be a very important variable. This section explores some of the important findings about practice.

Practice and Success

One important point is simply that practicing wrong or partially wrong responses may lead to learning inappropriate movement sequences. This is particularly true for the responses that are only partially incorrect, because they may be reinforced occasionally and thus become very resistant to extinction (see the discussion of the partial-reinforcement effect in Chapter 7).

EXAMPLE 9. Suppose a bowler gets strikes or spares quite frequently even though she releases the ball from her right hand while her right foot is forward. (This is incorrect form.) Such a response sequence would be very resistant to extinction, even though changing it would in the long run lead to better performance.

Distribution of Practice

There has been extensive study of the effect of distribution of practice on motor learning. Research results generally indicate that spacing of practice trials will yield better performance during acquisition than will massed practice trials. Some research also supports a similar interpretation for measured retention tasks, although other studies indicate performance on retention tests sometimes shows no significant differences between spaced and massed practice groups.

Reminiscence. The improvement of performance following a rest period after a massed practice has been called *reminiscence.* One interpretation of reminiscence implies that this improvement is the result of dissipation of muscle fatigue. However, other studies have shown that comparable results can be obtained even when totally different muscle groups are used. Apparently, reminiscence may be a relatively general phenomenon, perhaps involving some change in the central nervous system.

EXAMPLE 10. In a rotary pursuit task, subjects attempt to keep the tip of a stylus on a target which is spinning on a turntable. In one such task, subjects were initially trained using the preferred hand. After a fixed number of trials, half the subjects continued the task while the other half rested. The second group returned to the task after a ten-minute rest. However, both groups were further divided so that half continued with the preferred hand while half switched to the nonpreferred hand. Comparison of the performance of the continuous-task, nonpreferred-hand group with that of the rested, nonpreferred-hand group showed evidence of reminiscence for the rested group. This obviously could not be the result of dissipation of muscle fatigue because a new muscle group was involved in the second task.

Mental Practice

Another learning variable that has been investigated, particularly as it relates to sports performance, is called *mental practice*. In this case the subject attempts to develop a mental image of how responses should be performed. In general, research evidence indicates that mental practice is better than no practice at all, but not as beneficial as actual physical practice of the responses themselves.

EXAMPLE 11. Mental practice has been suggested as an adjunct to physical practice. Mental practice may be used when physical practice is impossible; for instance, when traveling in a car or plane, the person may rehearse mentally the movements that will be used for a dance step, sports movement, or other types of movement sequences.

Knowledge of Results

Probably the most widely studied aspect of practice has been the area called *knowledge of results* (*KR*), the feedback received during and after performance of the motor behavior. While the information received as feedback is generally used to define KR, most psychologists also believe that KR serves as reinforcement for the response performance.

EXAMPLE 12. A simple example of the reinforcement interpretation of KR is provided by someone scoring a bull's-eye in archery. Not only is the movement sequence seen to be successful, but the person also receives the maximum number of points for one attempt. Furthermore, the term "bull's-eye" itself has positive (reinforcing) connotations.

   Extrinsic vs. intrinsic KR. Knowledge of results may come from extrinsic sources (outside the person) or from feedback from within the person (intrinsic sources).

   Quantitative vs. qualitative KR. Knowledge of results may be presented in terms of some sort of objective measurement (quantitative) or as some subjective evaluation (qualitative).

EXAMPLE 13. Machinery can be used to measure amount of error (in centimeters, for example) in a line drawing task. If this information is then provided to the subject, quantitative, extrinsic KR has been given. However, if before the measurement of error is announced the subject judges the response to have been "pretty close," intrinsic, subjective KR has been demonstrated.

Delaying or Withholding KR

When some time period passes between the completion of a response and the accessibility of KR, *delay of KR* has taken place. When no accessibility to KR is possible, *withholding KR* has occurred.

Interestingly, the effects produced by delaying KR and withholding KR appear to be the same for lower organisms, but not for humans. Poorer performance can be expected for either condition when lower organisms are used as subjects, while humans show poorer performance only when KR is withheld. Moreover, even this result is subject to a practice effect: When a highly practiced response is being studied, it appears that intrinsic feedback can be sufficient to maintain a high level of responding.

Post-KR Delay

One additional variable, *post-KR delay*, appears to affect acquisition of motor responses. This period of time following the accessibility of KR until the next trial begins seemingly allows for evaluation and adjustment to take place in preparation for making the next response. It should be noted that determination of sufficient time for post-KR delay will depend upon the particular task. Also, adding any more than the minimal time necessary will not increase performance appreciably.

23.6   RETENTION OF MOTOR LEARNING

As with other types of learning, retention in motor learning can be studied as either short-term or long-term memory.   In keeping with the general results found, short-term loss is most likely to occur for responses that have been practiced very little and have not been reinforced much.   The responses most likely to be retained are those that have had many reinforcements and been practiced frequently.   Additionally, those best retained seem to be unlikely to suffer loss because of interference with the trace from other tasks, and typically require continuous rather than discrete responses.

EXAMPLE 14.   Swimming is an excellent example of a movement behavior that is retained very well over long periods of time.   It seems to fit all the criteria stated above: generally it is highly practiced, it is reinforced frequently during acquisition and storage, and it is a continuous type of response that is unlikely to be interfered with.

23.7   THEORIES OF MOTOR LEARNING

Four theories of motor learning have gained considerable favor.   To a certain extent, these theories overlap.

Habit Theory

Perhaps the oldest and simplest theory of motor learning is called *habit theory*.   This is basically an associative theory that stresses internal (perhaps physiological) changes in the performer as a result of reinforced performance.

Closed-Loop Feedback

The most important aspect of the *closed-loop feedback theory* of motor learning is that the performer makes comparisons between what has been done and what is expected, evaluating the level of success of responding.   If errors are noted, correction and adjustment of performance can be made.   (*Note:* This theory is directly comparable to the feedback theory presented in Chapter 16; see Fig. 16-1.)

Motor Program Theory

Although similar in some respects to the closed-loop feedback theory, the *motor program theory* proposes that substantial sequences of movement behavior may "run off" once the stimulus starts the responding.   The sequence is thought to progress as if programmed in the brain and requires little or no feedback to be completed.   (It is suspected that occasional feedback may bring about alterations in the program, however.)   It should be noted that research studies designed to compare this theory with feedback theory tend to support the closed-loop feedback theory rather than the motor program theory.

EXAMPLE 15.   One experiment that compared closed-loop and motor program theories used groups receiving feedback that was removed either early or late in the training of the movement behavior.   The prediction of closed-loop feedback theory was supported by the finding that removal of feedback *at any time* produced a decrease in performance success.   (If a program were well-established, late removal of feedback should have had little or no effect upon performance.)

Recall-Schema Theory

The *recall-schema theory* proposes that a person learns a general concept of a motor response (or movement behavior) that can be applied to many different specific situations.   Such a theory helps account for the enormous assortment of movement patterns that are shown in actual performances.

EXAMPLE 16. The spontaneity of many motor responses shown by participants in athletic contests may provide some support for recall-schema theory. It *is* possible to conceive of the performance as the result of habits developed from many hours of practice, but the creativity or ingenuity of some sequences seems to substantiate the proposition that the recall is of a general principle that is applied uniquely to the given circumstances. Thus, the "incredible" move of a soccer player is not a function of practicing that special sequence, but rather is generated at that moment (although it is based upon the recall of a schema).

Solved Problems

23.1 Explain why using a pair of scissors to cut a coupon from a newspaper is a motor learning task. Then indicate why the accuracy with which this is done by a left-handed person may illustrate the learning-performance distinction.

Motor learning tasks often are called perceptual-motor tasks to indicate the necessary relationship between the incoming stimuli (for example, the perception of the position of the coupon, hand, or scissors) and the precise sequence of bodily movements (motor responses) required to accomplish the task. If the scissors in this example are typical, they are designed for use with the right hand. The performance of the left-handed person may therefore not reveal the motor skills the person actually has learned. Most likely, the performance would be considerably better if the appropriate equipment were available.

23.2 Consider again the situation described in Problem 23.1. Explain why the cutting of each side of the coupon might be considered to be a discrete response, while at the same time the actual movement of the scissors along the side could be called a continuous motor movement.

By definition, a discrete response is one where periods of responding are separated by periods of nonresponding. It is likely that there would be a pause as each corner of the coupon was reached, making the cutting of each side discrete from the cutting of the others. Continuous responding refers to instances where the bodily movements progress in a relatively unbroken sequence. Thus, cutting action from one corner to the next probably would follow such a pattern.

23.3 What types of learning tasks are typically used to study motor learning?

A tremendous variety of tasks are used to study motor learning. A cutting task (as in Problems 23.1 and 23.2) is only one of many that might be used. Trying to draw a line of a certain length while blindfolded, attempting to strike a golfball, learning a particular dance step, attempting to track a target using a rotary pursuit apparatus, playing a musical instrument, driving a car, and digging a ditch are all tasks that might be employed, suggesting the range of motor activities that are studied.

23.4 Of the tasks listed in the solution to Problem 23.3, which would most likely be used for experimental study?

While any of the tasks could be studied, the line drawing (discrete response) or tracking task (continuous response) would be the most likely to be used for experimental study. In general, simpler tasks such as these are less likely to be affected by extraneous variables. Investigation of such simple tasks may lead to an understanding of more complex tasks (such as driving), which are not so easily studied in the laboratory.

23.5   Describe the typical measurements of performance used when studying motor learning.

Two general classes of response measurement are used when studying motor learning—those based upon accuracy of performance and those involving some time measurement.   Accuracy measurements may be number of correct responses or number of errors.   Time measurements could be reaction time, time to complete a task, or time on target.

23.6   Analyze the act of serving a tennis ball according to the general characteristics of motor skills.

There are four general characteristics of motor skills: perceptual-motor linkage, chaining of responses, organization of responses, and feedback.   In serving a tennis ball, perceptual-motor linkage would involve the recognition of the stimuli present (angle to be served, wind, tiredness) and the coordination of movements to make the appropriate actions.   The act actually requires a series or chain of movements (the toss, the turn, the arm sequence, the follow-through) and these must be organized (for example, their timing and force must be correctly judged).   Finally, there will be almost continuous feedback allowing adjustments of the response sequence even while it is being performed.   (For example, if the ball was tossed too high, the remainder of the sequence may be delayed a split second.)

23.7   Use the classifications proposed by Fitts to distinguish the three phases that would be involved in learning how to serve a tennis ball.

Fitts proposed a three-phase sequence of motor learning.   In the first the person must develop and use a cognitive understanding of what is required.   In this case, phrases such as "toss before turn" or "strike the ball at top of the swing" would be acquired and stored by the learner.

In the second stage, the required responses become associated with the perceptual cues.   These cues indicate when responding is appropriate.   Generally, the more complex the task to be learned, the greater the length of time required for the cognitive phase and the longer the period before this associative stage can be undertaken successfully.

Finally, the third stage occurs when there has been sufficient practice for the response to become relatively automatic.   Called the autonomous phase by Fitts, the responses seem to become more and more successful and less and less subject to interference from extraneous stimuli.   At this point, the act of serving the tennis ball would be influenced by cognitive considerations only when special adjustments (such as compensating for the wind) are desired.

23.8   Dwight is a "scratch" golfer, averaging around par each season.   In a two-week period, he has the opportunity to play eight times.   His scores for the first seven rounds are par or better, yet in the eighth round he finishes nineteen strokes above par.   Cite some of the physical factors that might have led to Dwight's exceptionally poor eighth round.

The possible solutions to this problem are innumerable.   Physical factors such as stamina or flexibility, psychomotor factors such as dexterity or reaction time, or sensory factors such as vision, kinesthesis, or balance may have affected Dwight's performance.

23.9   What psychological factors might have contributed to Dwight's poor round (Problem 23.8)?

Perceptual disruption, particular cognitive attributes for that day, motivation level (such as "staleness"), emotions, and many other factors also could have contributed to the particularly poor performance.

23.10   What is the hidden error in the statement, "Practice makes perfect"?

A motor response that is practiced will be learned.   The difficulty is that practicing a less-than-perfect response will mean that it rather than the correct one will be learned.   (*Note:* This is especially true if the imperfect response works some of the time, establishing partial-reinforcement conditions that make the response very resistant to extinction.)   Thus, the mere fact that someone practices does not mean that the "perfect" response will be learned.

23.11   What effect does the spacing of practice appear to have upon the acquisition and retention of motor responses?

The solution to this problem depends upon when the measurement of performance occurs.   If the response measure is taken during the acquisition period, the distribution of practice appears to yield better performance.   On the other hand, measurement of performance after some retention interval often shows that groups trained under spaced or massed conditions perform at about the same level.   This latter result is sometimes attributed to the phenomenon of reminiscence, the increase in the performance level observed after a rest period that has followed massed practice.   Despite this, most theorists favor the interpretation that motor skill learning will progress more easily with spaced practice rather than massed practice.

23.12   How does reminiscence (see Problem 23.11) differ from spontaneous recovery?

While reminiscence seems to be very similar to spontaneous recovery in many situations, there is research evidence that indicates that the increase in response strength noted for spontaneous recovery is measured for the *same* response that was extinguished (that is, the same muscle groups). Reminiscence, by contrast, can be found in transfer responses such as switching from one hand and arm to the other.

23.13   Suppose a teacher's task is to instruct inexperienced students in the proper use of hand-held calculators.   Design an experiment that would allow you to determine what effect mental practice and/or physical practice would have upon the students' success in making the appropriate hand and finger manipulations.   What results might be expected?

To thoroughly investigate the problem presented, four groups would be needed.   One, the control group, would have no practice before being tested for proficiency in making calculations.   The second would have physical practice only.   The third would have mental practice only before being tested.   Finally, the fourth would have some combination of both physical and mental practice before testing.   (*Note:* There could be many different varieties of this fourth group.)

If the motor responses necessary for using a hand calculator are comparable to other motor behaviors, it can be expected that the second and fourth groups would do quite well and approximately the same.   The third group (mental practice only) would not do as well as groups two and four, but would be superior to the control group.

23.14   What are the two general properties of knowledge of results (KR) that appear to be important for motor learning?

The first property is stated in the name of the principle—the respondent gains some information (knowledge) regarding the correctness of the behavior (result).   This often is called feedback.   The second property is generally inferred: it is believed the knowledge obtained serves as reinforcement (or lack of it) for the response made.

23.15   Suppose the task requires the subject to learn to make free throws with a basketball while blindfolded.   Describe the kinds of feedback that might be given and the results that could be expected.

One kind of feedback situation would be to give no feedback at all, leaving the respondent only whatever intrinsic feedback might occur (such as the sound of the ball).   A second type would be qualitative ("better . . . worse").   A third type would be quantitative ("about a foot short . . . two feet to the right").   Finally, quantitative and qualitative feedback could be combined.   It would be expected, based on previous research studies, that the third and fourth groups would do better than the others, while the second group should do better than the control group.

23.16 If knowledge of results is delayed or withheld during the acquisition of a motor response, what effect upon performance can be expected? Will the same result be found if the response has been highly practiced?

    In general, when animals are used as subjects, either delay or withholding of KR will lead to poorer performance of the response during acquisition. For humans, delay seems to have little or no effect upon performance, while withholding KR produces poor performance. This latter result is much less likely to be found when the response is very well practiced, however. Indeed, some psychologists believe that the self-reinforcement accompanying responses that have had extensive training will be sufficient to sustain their performance even though feedback is withheld entirely.

23.17 What is a post-KR pause? What effect does it appear to have upon acquisition of the motor response?

    A post-KR pause refers to an interval of time following KR until the next trial begins. The length of this delay period appears to affect acquisition of a motor response: it must be long enough for evaluation of the KR and for anticipation of the adjustments necessary for the next response. Once the post-KR pause is long enough for that to occur, adding additional time to the interval does not appear to have any substantial effect upon acquisition.

23.18 Describe the type of situation most likely to produce short-term forgetting of a motor response.

    The responses least likely to be retained will be those that are discrete, little practiced, and for which there have been few reinforcements given.

23.19 What type of motor response is most likely to be retained in long-term memory?

    The type of response most likely to be retained in long-term memory is the continuous sequence of motor movements that is highly practiced, has been reinforced many times, and is relatively impervious to interference. Frequently cited examples of this type of response are swimming and bicycling.

23.20 Describe the performance of a well-trained pianist according to habit theory, closed-loop theory, and motor program theory.

    The habit theory of motor learning proposes that appropriate motor responses become a reliable part of the behavior repertoire as a result of reinforced practice trials. Often, attempts are made to account for habit physiologically.

    Closed-loop theory emphasizes the concept of feedback. Performance of one series of movements is analyzed, with error recognition and error correction an important part of improved playing.

    The concept of a motor program proposes that the stimulus situation itself initiates a sequence that will run off without the necessity of feedback. This is a more automatic interpretation of motor behavior, rather like a sophisticated habit theory. (*Note:* The bulk of research evidence seems to support feedback theory as the best explanation of motor learning.)

23.21 Why is the recall-schema theory of motor learning thought to be comparable to the verbal concept explanation of speech patterns?

    The recall-schema theory suggests for motor learning the same type of explanation the verbal concept hypothesis does for speech patterns. Prevailing schemata (concepts) are thought to represent general patterns for behavior from which a tremendous variety of situation-specific response groupings may be generated. Such hypotheses are used to try to account for the tremendous creativity of motor sequences or verbal chains that are actually displayed by humans.

Key Terms

Continuous motor tasks.   In motor learning, a task in which bodily movements progress in a relatively unbroken sequence.

Discrete motor tasks.   In motor learning, a task in which periods of responding are separated by periods of nonresponding.

Feedback.   Comparable to knowledge of results; may be intrinsic or extrinsic.

Knowledge of results (KR).   The understanding of the consequences of a response or response pattern; this may modify subsequent responding.

Mental practice.   Use of cognitive imagery to rehearse how movement sequences would be performed if actual movement behavior occurred.

Motor learning.   The acquisition, storage, and retrieval of precise patterns of bodily movement.

Motor program.   The concept proposing that a stimulus will initiate a motor-response chain that will complete itself without the need for feedback.

Post-KR delay.   The interval of time following knowledge of results until the next trial begins.

Practice.   In motor learning, repeated performance leading to acquisition and storage of a movement sequence.

Recall schema.   In motor learning, the concept proposing that general patterns for movement are retained and serve as the source for situation-specific responses.

Reminiscence.   The improvement in performance following a rest period in which there is not any practice or rehearsal.

Response chains.   In motor learning, a sequence of movements in which each is at least partially dependent upon those preceding and/or those yet to occur.

Index

Catalog

If you are interested in a list of SCHAUM'S
OUTLINE SERIES send your name
and address, requesting your free catalog, to:

SCHAUM'S OUTLINE SERIES, Dept. C
McGRAW-HILL BOOK COMPANY
1221 Avenue of Americas
New York, N.Y. 10020